Jumping to Java™

by Dan Parks Sydow

IDG Books Worldwide, Inc.
An International Data Group Company

Foster City, CA ♦ Chicago, IL ♦ Indianapolis, IN ♦ Dallas, TX

Jumping to Java™

Published by
IDG Books Worldwide, Inc.
An International Data Group Company
919 E. Hillsdale Blvd.
Suite 400
Foster City, CA 94404

Library of Congress Catalog Card No.: 96-78273

ISBN: 1-7645-4007-6

Printed in the United States of America

10 9 8 7 6 5 4 3 2 1

1B/QV/RR/ZW/FC

Distributed in the United States by IDG Books Worldwide, Inc.

Distributed by Macmillan Canada for Canada; by Contemporanea de Ediciones for Venezuela; by Distribuidora Cuspide for Argentina; by CITEC for Brazil; by Ediciones ZETA S.C.R. Ltda. for Peru; by Editorial Limusa SA for Mexico; by Transworld Publishers Limited in the United Kingdom and Europe; by Academic Bookshop for Egypt; by Levant Distributors S.A.R.L. for Lebanon; by Al Jassim for Saudi Arabia; by Simron Pty. Ltd. for South Africa; by Pustak Mahal for India; by The Computer Bookshop for India; by Toppan Company Ltd. for Japan; by Addison Wesley Publishing Company for Korea; by Longman Singapore Publishers Ltd. for Singapore, Malaysia, Thailand, and Indonesia; by Unalis Corporation for Taiwan; by WS Computer Publishing Company, Inc. for the Philippines; by WoodsLane Pty. Ltd. for Australia; by WoodsLane Enterprises Ltd. for New Zealand. Authorized Sales Agent: Anthony Rudkin Associates for the Middle East and North Africa.

For general information on IDG Books Worldwide's books in the U.S., please call our Consumer Customer Service department at 800-762-2974. For reseller information, including discounts and premium sales, please call our Reseller Customer Service department at 800-434-3422.

For information on where to purchase IDG Books Worldwide's books outside the U.S., please contact our International Sales department at 415-655-3172 or fax 415-655-3295.

For information on foreign language translations, please contact our Foreign & Subsidiary Rights department at 415-655-3021 or fax 415-655-3281.

For sales inquiries and special prices for bulk quantities, please contact our Sales department at 415-655-3200 or write to the address above.

For information on using IDG Books Worldwide's books in the classroom or for ordering examination copies, please contact our Educational Sales department at 800-434-2086 or fax 817-251-8174.

For authorization to photocopy items for corporate, personal, or educational use, please contact Copyright Clearance Center, 222 Rosewood Drive, Danvers, MA 01923, or fax 508-750-4470.

About the Author

Dan Parks Sydow is a former software engineer and author of numerous books, including *Mac Programming for Dummies, 2nd Edition*; *Foundations of Mac Programming*; and *Internet for Macs for Dummies Quick Reference*. He specializes in Java, HTML, C and C++ programming. He lives in Milwaukee, Wisconsin.

ABOUT IDG BOOKS WORLDWIDE

Welcome to the world of IDG Books Worldwide.

IDG Books Worldwide, Inc., is a subsidiary of International Data Group, the world's largest publisher of computer-related information and the leading global provider of information services on information technology. IDG was founded more than 25 years ago and now employs more than 8,500 people worldwide. IDG publishes more than 275 computer publications in over 75 countries (see listing below). More than 60 million people read one or more IDG publications each month.

Launched in 1990, IDG Books Worldwide is today the #1 publisher of best-selling computer books in the United States. We are proud to have received eight awards from the Computer Press Association in recognition of editorial excellence and three from *Computer Currents*' First Annual Readers' Choice Awards. Our best-selling *...For Dummies*® series has more than 30 million copies in print with translations in 30 languages. IDG Books Worldwide, through a joint venture with IDG's Hi-Tech Beijing, became the first U.S. publisher to publish a computer book in the People's Republic of China. In record time, IDG Books Worldwide has become the first choice for millions of readers around the world who want to learn how to better manage their businesses.

Our mission is simple: Every one of our books is designed to bring extra value and skill-building instructions to the reader. Our books are written by experts who understand and care about our readers. The knowledge base of our editorial staff comes from years of experience in publishing, education, and journalism — experience we use to produce books for the '90s. In short, we care about books, so we attract the best people. We devote special attention to details such as audience, interior design, use of icons, and illustrations. And because we use an efficient process of authoring, editing, and desktop publishing our books electronically, we can spend more time ensuring superior content and spend less time on the technicalities of making books.

You can count on our commitment to deliver high-quality books at competitive prices on topics you want to read about. At IDG Books Worldwide, we continue in the IDG tradition of delivering quality for more than 25 years. You'll find no better book on a subject than one from IDG Books Worldwide.

John Kilcullen
President and CEO
IDG Books Worldwide, Inc.

Eighth Annual Computer Press Awards 1992

Ninth Annual Computer Press Awards 1993

Tenth Annual Computer Press Awards 1994

Eleventh Annual Computer Press Awards 1995

IDG Books Worldwide, Inc., is a subsidiary of International Data Group, the world's largest publisher of computer-related information and the leading global provider of information services on information technology. International Data Group publishes over 275 computer publications in over 75 countries. Sixty million people read one or more International Data Group publications each month. International Data Group's publications include: **ARGENTINA:** Buyer's Guide, Computerworld Argentina, PC World Argentina; **AUSTRALIA:** Australian Macworld, Australian PC World, Australian Reseller News, Computerworld, IT Casebook, Network World, Publish, Webmaster; **AUSTRIA:** Computerwelt Osterreich, Networks Austria, PC Tip Austria; **BANGLADESH:** PC World Bangladesh; **BELARUS:** PC World Belarus; **BELGIUM:** Data News; **BRAZIL:** Annuário de Informática, Computerworld, Connections, Macworld, PC Player, PC World, Publish, Reseller News, Supergamepower; **BULGARIA:** Computerworld Bulgaria, Network World Bulgaria, PC & MacWorld Bulgaria; **CANADA:** CIO Canada, Client/Server World, ComputerWorld Canada, InfoWorld Canada, NetworkWorld Canada, WebWorld; **CHILE:** Computerworld Chile, PC World Chile; **COLOMBIA:** Computerworld Colombia, PC World Colombia; **COSTA RICA:** PC World Centro America; **THE CZECH AND SLOVAK REPUBLICS:** Computerworld Czechoslovakia, Macworld Czech Republic, PC World Czechoslovakia; **DENMARK:** Communications World Danmark, Computerworld Danmark, Macworld Danmark, PC World Danmark, Techworld Denmark; **DOMINICAN REPUBLIC:** PC World Republica Dominicana; **ECUADOR:** PC World Ecuador; **EGYPT:** Computerworld Middle East, PC World Middle East; **EL SALVADOR:** PC World Centro America; **FINLAND:** MikroPC, Tietoverkko, Tietoviikko; **FRANCE:** Distributique, Hebdo, Info PC, Le Monde Informatique, Macworld, Reseaux & Telecoms, WebMaster France; **GERMANY:** Computer Partner, Computerwoche, Computerwoche Extra, Computerwoche FOCUS, Global Online, Macwelt, PC Welt; **GREECE:** Amiga Computing, GamePro Greece, Multimedia World; **GUATEMALA:** PC World Centro America; **HONDURAS:** PC World Centro America; **HONG KONG:** Computerworld Hong Kong, PC World Hong Kong, Publish in Asia; **HUNGARY:** ABCD CD-ROM, Computerworld Szamitastechnika, Internetto online Magazine, PC World Hungary, PC-X Magazin Hungary; **ICELAND:** Tolvuheimur PC World Island; **INDIA:** Information Communications World, Information Systems Computerworld, PC World India, Publish in Asia; **INDONESIA:** InfoKomputer PC World, Komputek Computerworld, Publish in Asia; **IRELAND:** ComputerScope, PC Live!; **ISRAEL:** Macworld Israel, People & Computers/Computerworld; **ITALY:** Computerworld Italia, Macworld Italia, Networking Italia, PC World Italia; **JAPAN:** DTP World, Macworld Japan, Nikkei Personal Computing, OS/2 World Japan, SunWorld Japan, Windows NT World, Windows World Japan; **KENYA:** PC World East African; **KOREA:** Hi-Tech Information, Macworld Korea, PC World Korea; **MACEDONIA:** PC World Macedonia; **MALAYSIA:** Computerworld Malaysia, PC World Malaysia, Publish in Asia; **MALTA:** PC World Malta; **MEXICO:** Computerworld Mexico, PC World Mexico; **MYANMAR:** PC World Myanmar; **NETHERLANDS:** Computer! Totaal, LAN Internetworking Magazine, LAN World Buyers Guide, Macworld Netherlands, Net, WebWereld; **NEW ZEALAND:** Absolute Beginners Guide and Plain & Simple Series, Computer Buyer, Computer Industry Directory, Computerworld New Zealand, MTB, Network World, PC World New Zealand; **NICARAGUA:** PC World Centro America; **NORWAY:** Computerworld Norge, CW Rapport, Datamagasinet, Financial Rapport, Kursguide Norge, Macworld Norge, Multimediaworld Norge, PC World Ekspress Norge, PC World Nettverk, PC World Norge, PC World ProduktGuide Norge; **PAKISTAN:** Computerworld Pakistan; **PANAMA:** PC World Panama; **PEOPLE'S REPUBLIC OF CHINA:** China Computer Users, China Computerworld, China InfoWorld, China Telecom World Weekly, Computer & Communication, Electronic Design China, Electronics Today, Electronics Weekly, Game Software, PC World China, Popular Computer Week, Software Weekly, Software World, Telecom World; **PERU:** Computerworld Peru, PC World Profesional Peru, PC World SoHo Peru; **PHILIPPINES:** Click!, Computerworld Philippines, PC World Philippines, Publish in Asia; **POLAND:** Computerworld Poland, Computerworld Special Report Poland, Cyber, Macworld Poland, Networld Poland, PC World Komputer; **PORTUGAL:** Cerebro/PC World, Computerworld/Correio Informático, Dealer World Portugal, Mac*In/PC*In Portugal, Multimedia World; **PUERTO RICO:** PC World Puerto Rico; **ROMANIA:** Computerworld Romania, PC World Romania, Telecom Romania; **RUSSIA:** Computerworld Russia, Mir PK, Publish, Seti; **SINGAPORE:** Computerworld Singapore, PC World Singapore, Publish in Asia; **SLOVENIA:** Monitor; **SOUTH AFRICA:** Computing SA, Network World SA, Software World SA; **SPAIN:** Communicaciones World España, Computerworld España, Dealer World España, Macworld España, PC World España; **SRI LANKA:** Infolink PC World; **SWEDEN:** CAP&Design, Computer Sweden, Corporate Computing Sweden, Internetworld Sweden, it.branschen, Macworld Sweden, MaxiData Sweden, MikroDatorn, Nätverk & Kommunikation, PC World Sweden, PCaktiv, Windows World Sweden; **SWITZERLAND:** Computerworld Schweiz, Macworld Schweiz, PCtip; **TAIWAN:** Computerworld Taiwan, Macworld Taiwan, NEW ViSiON/Publish, PC World Taiwan, Windows World Taiwan; **THAILAND:** Publish in Asia, Thai Computerworld; **TURKEY:** Computerworld Turkiye, Macworld Turkiye, Network World Turkiye, PC World Turkiye; **UKRAINE:** Computerworld Kiev, Multimedia World Ukraine, PC World Ukraine; **UNITED KINGDOM:** Acorn User UK, Amiga Action UK, Amiga Computing UK, Apple Talk UK, Computing, Macworld, Parents and Computers UK, PC Advisor, PC Home, PSX Pro, The WEB; **UNITED STATES:** Cable in the Classroom, CIO Magazine, Computerworld, DOS World, Federal Computer Week, GamePro Magazine, InfoWorld, I-Way, Macworld, Network World, PC Games, PC World, Publish, Video Event, THE WEB Magazine, and WebMaster; online webzines: JavaWorld, NetscapeWorld, and SunWorld Online; **URUGUAY:** InfoWorld Uruguay; **VENEZUELA:** Computerworld Venezuela, PC World Venezuela; and **VIETNAM:** PC World Vietnam. 10/1/96

To my wife, Nadine.

Credits

Senior Vice President and Group Publisher
Brenda McLaughlin

Acquisitions Director
Walt Bruce

Acquisitions Editor
Nancy Dunn

Marketing Manager
Jill Reinemann

Managing Editor
Terry Somerson

Development Editor
Ron Hull

Copy Editors
Michael D. Welch
Katharine Dvorak

Technical Editor
Peter Ferrante

Editorial Assistant
Sharon Eames

Production Director
Andrew Walker

Production Associate
Christopher Pimentel

Supervisor of Page Layout
Craig A. Harrison

Project Coordinator
Katy German

Production Staff
Mario F. Amador
Laura Carpenter
Tom Debolski
Stephen Noetzel
Andreas F. Schueller
Elsie Yim

Quality Control Specialist
Mick Arellano

Proofreader
Carrie O'Neill

Indexer
Steve Rath

Cover Design
Lew Design

Preface

Welcome to *Jumping to Java!* This book gets C and C++ programmers up and running, using the new Java programming language in no time at all. By reading this book, you'll move from the platform-based world of monolithic applications to the online world of applets—those small, cross-platform programs that any Internet surfer can view and interact with using a Web browser.

The C and C++ programming languages form the foundation of Java. In fact, as you read this book, you'll recognize much of the terminology and source code: The languages are that similar. What you *don't* recognize from your programming background will be explained in detail.

If you know some C or C++ and have written programs (even very simple ones), this book is for you. Many programming books are aimed at only one of two camps—Windows or Macintosh. Because the development of programs for these two systems normally requires a knowledge of different sets of library routines, that approach makes sense. Java, however, is different. Once you learn Java and write a Java source code file, you can compile that same file on computers running Windows 95 as well as Macintosh computers. And the applet that results from this compilation? It too can run, without modification, on either type of machine.

Jumping to Java provides detailed discussions, plenty of figures, slow walk-throughs of source code listings, and short, straight-to-the-point examples that will soon have you writing your own applets. If you have a Web page, you can integrate your own applets onto that page. If you haven't yet established a presence on the Web, don't worry. This book's CD-ROM includes applet runner software that helps you test out applets without actually making them a part of a Web page.

To get the most out of this book, you'll need an understanding of either the C or C++ language. While you don't need to know advanced programming techniques, you should be familiar with the basics of one or the other of these languages.

To write your source code, all you need is a text editor. To compile that source code, you need a Java compiler. This book's CD-ROM includes such a compiler as a part of Sun Microsystems' Java Development Kit. The CD-ROM includes two versions of this programming kit—one for users of Windows 95, the other for Macintosh users. Refer to the end of this book for more information. Optionally, you can use a different Java development package; several are available from your usual source of software and programming development tools.

As for a computer system, you should have either a PC running Windows 95 or a Macintosh or Power Macintosh. A total of 8MB of RAM on your machine and a few free megabytes of hard drive space are the only other requirements—except, of course, a CD-ROM drive so that you can read the included CD-ROM.

That's all you need to get started with *Jumping to Java*. Let's go!

Acknowledgments

Thanks to Ron Hull, development editor at IDG Books Worldwide, for comments, questions, and constructive criticism, and to Michael D. Welch, who brought his keen editor's eye to the manuscript, with help from Katharine Dvorak. Thanks too for another helpful technical edit from Peter Ferrante. Thanks also to Carole McClendon, Waterside Productions, for making this book happen.

Contents at a Glance

Table of Contents

CHAPTER 1

Applets, Java Bytecode, and Java Applications

If you're a programmer with a background in either C or C++, you have an advantage in reading this book—it's written primarily for you. With all of the hype about the World Wide Web, you most likely know something about Java, too. You probably know, for example, that *Java* is a programming language developed by Sun Microsystems, and that *Java applets* are basically small applications that result from compiling Java source code files. Building on your knowledge of C or C++ and the Internet, this book launches you into the exciting new world of Java programming.

As an experienced programmer, you may be tempted to skip this fundamental chapter and jump right into the thick of Java programming. But first consider what this chapter offers. In this chapter you get useful background knowledge on important Java- and Web-related terminology. You'll learn how applets work with the World Wide Web and get a sense of how they're changing the world of computing. In addition, you get a brief introduction to Java applications. Finally, you'll see what makes both Java applets and Java applications platform-independent: Java bytecode. So, check out this chapter for an overview of Java basics.

Java Applets

Java applets are applications—usually small in size and singular in purpose—written in the Java programming language. Applets differ from applications written in other programming languages in one chief respect: an applet isn't a stand-alone program. An applet is meant to be embedded into a World Wide Web page—much as a graphics file is. In order to execute, an applet requires the help of special *interpreter* software. The interpreter must be built into browsers that display applet-powered Web pages. (The Java interpreter is covered in more detail later in this chapter.)

APPLETS AND THE WORLD WIDE WEB

The origin of applets is closely tied to the evolution of the World Wide Web. As the Internet continues to grow, applets are likely to play an increasingly greater role.

The text-based capabilities of the Internet have long been popular among programmers, who, as a rule, are used to working with complex text. In recent years, new graphical elements of the Internet have caught the interest of nonprogrammers and have drawn them to the Net, too. The graphics-oriented World Wide Web has greatly contributed to the explosive growth of the Internet. You can only imagine how much more popular the Web will become as sound and video, animation, and true user-interaction become commonplace features of Web pages. Java applets are making all of this possible.

WEB BROWSERS AND HTML

The popularity of the Web has accelerated rapidly because Web browsers pack a lot of power. Here's an overview of how Web browsers work. A *Webmaster*—the person who manages a Web site—usually creates a site by uploading a set of text, graphics, and sound files to a home directory on a server. Visitors to the Web site access those files using a Web browser, which locates and reads the files. Hypertext Markup Language (HTML) enables Web browsers to read and execute the files.

Hypertext Markup Language is the Web's programming language. A single HTML file specifies the layout and formatting of each Web page. Each HTML file consists of numerous *tags* (or commands) that incorporate the text, graphics, icons, sounds, and hypertext links into the Web page. For example, an HTML file uses the `<img>` tag to display a graphic image. Each tag can have a number of different *attributes* (parameters). For example, one attribute of the `<img>` tag indicates which graphics file holds the image, another attribute specifies where the image appears on the page, and so forth.

Figure 1-1 depicts the process of displaying a simple Web page using files from a home directory on an Internet server. The home directory on this server holds two files: an HTML text file that contains the page layout information for the Web page and a GIF file that holds a single graphics image. Figure 1-1 illustrates how users who visit a Web site use a Web browser (Netscape Navigator in this example) to access the files on an Internet server.

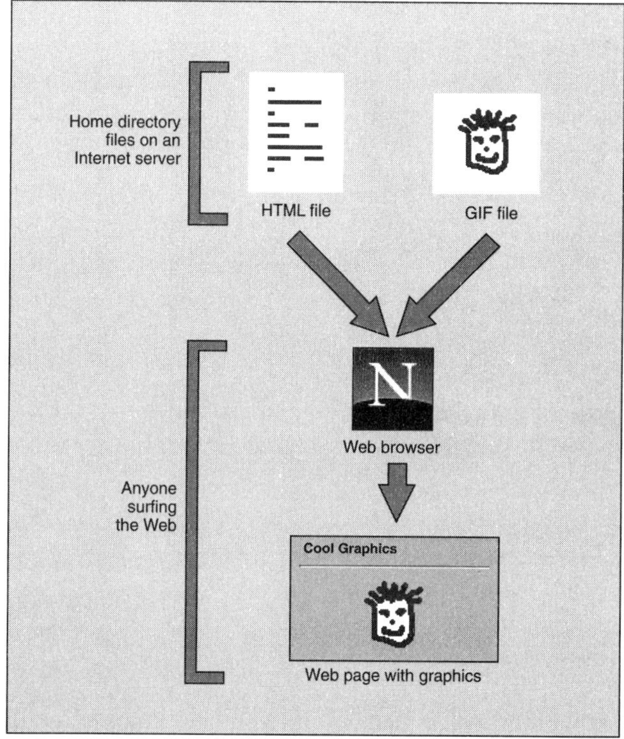

Figure 1-1
A Web browser displays a Web page by accessing files on an Internet server.

HOW APPLETS FIT IN

At this point, you may be wondering how Java applets fit into the picture. Figure 1-2 shows how an applet, like a graphics file, resides on the Internet server that holds a Web page's data. If you compare Figure 1-2 with

Figure 1-1, you can see that the way users encounter an applet is very similar to the way they view graphics files on the Web.

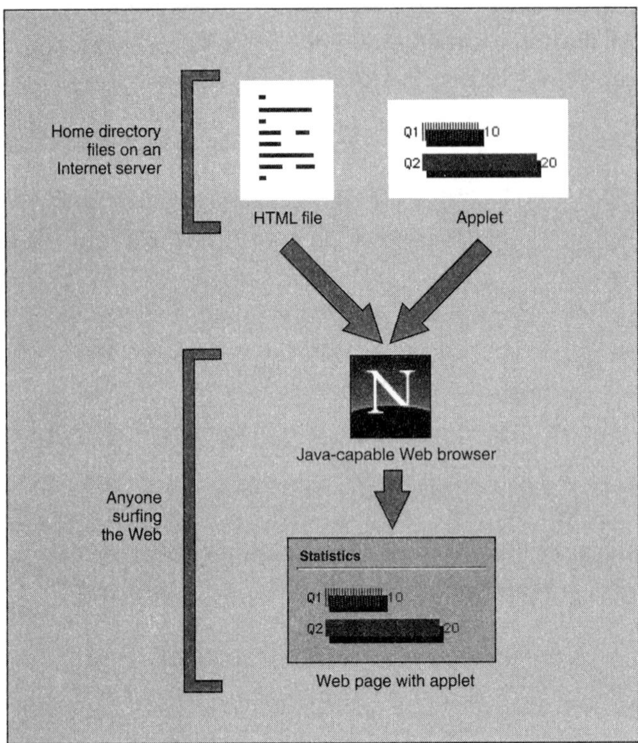

Figure 1-2
A Web browser displays a Web page that contains an applet.

Although most Web browsers can display graphics images in either GIF or JPEG format, many browsers do *not* yet have the capability to recognize applets. A Web browser that *does* recognize applets is said to be *Java-compatible* (or *Java-enabled*). Netscape Navigator version 2.0 or higher and Sun's HotJava are two examples of Java-compatible browsers. As Java gains popularity, the number of Web browsers that are Java-compatible will undoubtedly increase.

DYNAMIC WEB PAGES

In Figure 1-2, the applet appears to be a simple bar chart. If this chart were merely a static image, then you wouldn't need an applet to display it. A GIF image would suffice, and the graphics file would be easier to create. Assume that the bar chart in Figure 1-2 does more than merely display a fixed image. Suppose you could click on the chart to display the bars vertically, rather than horizontally. Alternatively, suppose you could click on the chart to open a new window that displays an enlarged version of the chart. Or suppose instead that you could scroll through quarterly sales figures for the last five years, displaying the statistics two quarters at a time. In all of these cases, the applet is *dynamic* because it actually does something. Java applets are hot because they enable Web page designers to create dynamic pages. Instead of offering static pages at which you can only look, Java applets bring tremendous interaction potential to the World Wide Web.

Figure 1-3 shows a real-world example of an applet that adds interactivity to a Web page. This screen shot comes from Netscape Navigator running in Windows 3.1. The tic-tac-toe board on this Web page is more than a simple graphic. It's a game you can actually play. Try doing *that* without a Java applet!

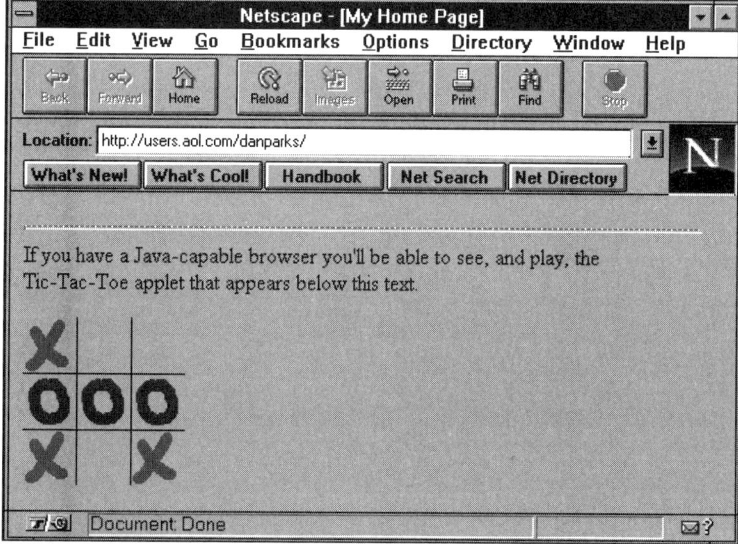

Figure 1-3
Users can interact with Web pages that have applets like the Tic-Tac-Toe applet.

The Tic-Tac-Toe applet is not just a hypothetical example simply dreamt up for this book. It's a real applet developed by Sun Microsystems. You can find the applet on the CD-ROM that comes with this book.

PLATFORM-INDEPENDENCE

Java applets are *platform-independent*. What this means is that, if you have a Java-compatible Web browser, you'll be able to see and interact with all applets that appear on Web pages—regardless of the type of machine you use. For example, if you use the Windows 95 version of Netscape Navigator 2.0 and a friend uses the Macintosh version, you'll both be able to interact with the same applet on a Web page. Figure 1-4 shows portions of a Web page in both the Windows and Mac versions of Netscape Navigator. The text looks a little different, but, as you can see, the applet appears identical on both platforms: it doesn't matter what type of machine you use to surf the Web. What makes platform-independence possible is the Java interpreter—more on that subject later in this chapter.

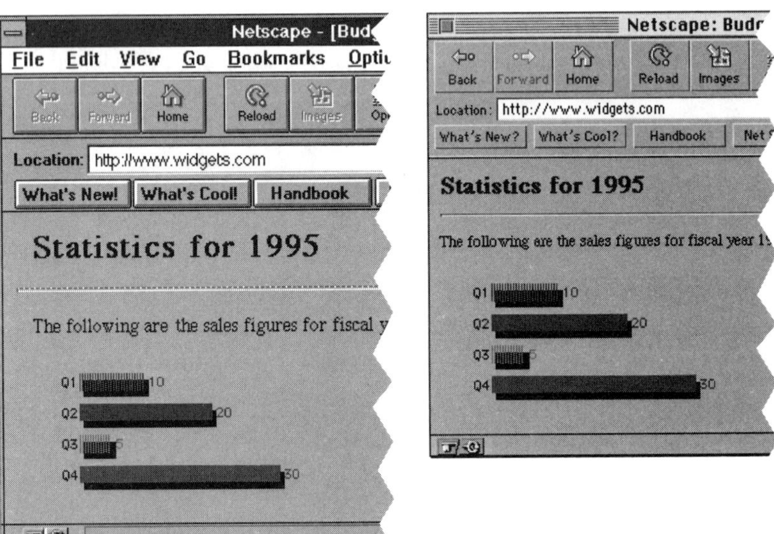

Figure 1-4
A single version of an applet can run on many different types of computers.

No doubt you've surfed the Web plenty of times and have already experienced platform-independent Web pages. Long before Java applets arrived, you could view Web pages with different browsers on various computer systems. It's a good thing, too, because it means home directories for Web sites don't need to waste storage space with separate files for every type of Web browser and computer system out there. A single HTML text file is all they need (as well as a single graphics file for each image). Java applets are an important breakthrough because they can do much more than simple text or graphics files. As a programmer, you know that cross-platform applications have been popular in theory but elusive in practice—until now.

Java Bytecode and Java Interpreters

When you compile Java source code to create an applet or application, the resulting executable, as you already know, can run on a great variety of machines—regardless of the platform used for development. This happens because the Java compiler generates a *bytecode* file, which looks the same no matter what kind of computer you use. See Figure 1-5.

How is it that the instructions in a single binary file can be meaningful to processors that normally recognize instructions from very different instruction sets? If you think this sounds too good to be true or feel that there must be some catch to this, your skepticism is justified. A bytecode file *can't* simply run on any computer. The computer that attempts to execute the bytecode file must have a Java bytecode *interpreter* on it. The interpreter makes Java applets look and perform identically no matter what platform they appear on.

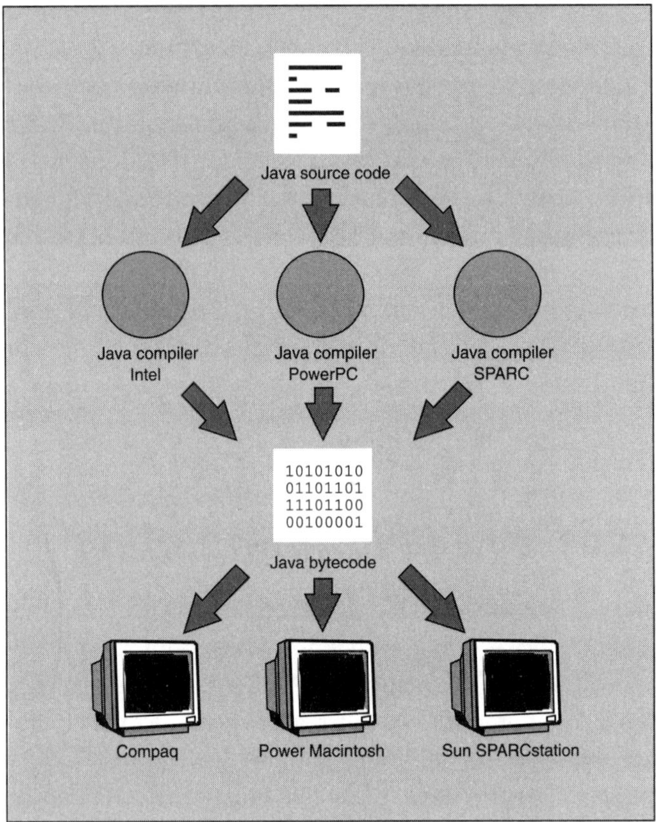

Figure 1-5

When you compile a Java source code file using different compilers, you end up with an identical bytecode (binary) file that can run on different machines.

A Java bytecode interpreter is specific to the machine it runs on. For example, the Java interpreter used on a Power Macintosh knows how to interpret a bytecode file, so it runs properly on a computer driven by a PowerPC chip. A different Java interpreter, such as the one used on computers running Windows 95, knows how to interpret the same bytecode file, so it executes on a computer with an Intel microprocessor. Figure 1-6 illustrates this distinction.

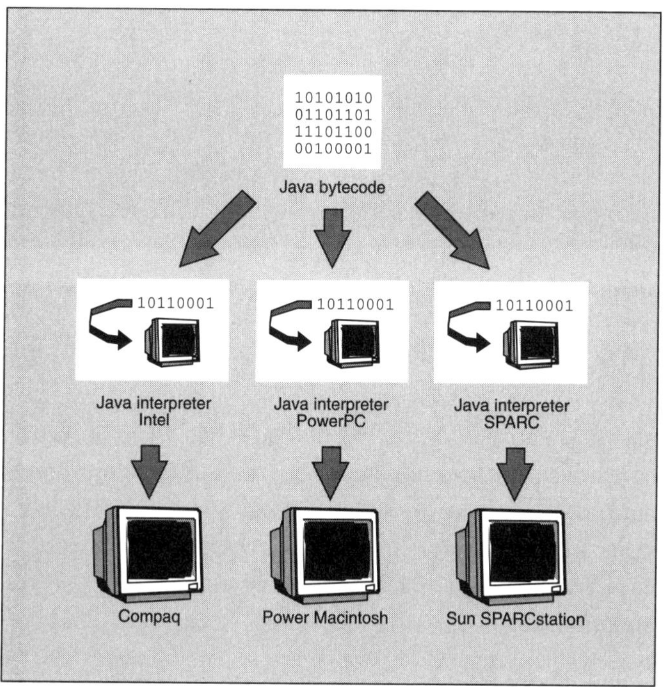

Figure 1-6
Different machines can run the same bytecode, but they require different versions of the Java interpreter.

A Java bytecode interpreter goes by several names: ***Java interpreter***, ***Java runtime***, or ***Java virtual machine***. Regardless of the name it's given, any computer that is to run Java bytecode *must* have one. All Java-compatible Web browsers have Java bytecode interpreters built into them. A Java-compatible browser actually downloads the bytecode that makes up an applet. The bytecode is retained in memory while needed, then purged. For example, versions 2.0 and higher of Netscape Navigator for Windows have a built-in Java interpreter. When a Windows user running Netscape Navigator is browsing the Web and encounters a Web page that includes an applet, the browser is able to access the page properly, download the applet bytecode, and execute that code. After the user finishes running the applet, the bytecode is purged from memory.

Java Applications

You can use Java to create full-scale applications as well as applets. Like a Java applet, a Java application is platform-independent. After you write your Java source code and compile it, you end up with a single executable file that you can run on all of the popular computer systems on the market.

A Java application also resembles an applet in that it requires a Java interpreter to execute it. To execute Java applets, that interpreter is generally a built-in part of a Java-compatible Web browser. For Java applications, the interpreter is itself a stand-alone software application. Java code can run on any machine—provided that the machine has a Java interpreter. You run a Java application through the interpreter in different ways on different systems. For example, if you're running Windows 95, you can run a Java application from the command line by typing `java` followed by the name of the Java application. For a Java application named `Flyer`, you would type the following:

```
C:\> java Flyer
```

At the time of this writing, the Java application interpreter is available for computers running Windows 95, Windows NT, and Solaris 2.3 or higher. Each version of the interpreter is distributed as a part of the Java Development Kit (JDK), which is included on this book's CD-ROM.

Although the bulk of this book deals with Java applets, in Chapter 14 you'll find all the information you need to jump into creating Java applications.

The Java Revolution

Now you know basic but important Java- and Web-related terminology and background information. In the next chapter you can get your feet wet by creating your first Java applet. Later we'll cover Java programming in greater detail. As you can see, Java applets and applications have tremendous potential to affect the World Wide Web with enhanced interactivity—the transformation has already begun. By coupling your C or C++ experience with Java programming, you too can join the Java revolution.

CHAPTER

2 Creating Your First Java Applet: Introduction to the Java Development Environment

This chapter walks you through the process of creating a Java source code file, compiling it, and then testing the resulting applet. This chapter does *not* teach you the Java programming language. Chapter 3 introduces you to the Java language itself. There, you get a line-by-line explanation of the source code listing for the sample applet used in the present chapter. For now, take comfort in knowing that you can create a functional applet like the one in this chapter with just a few lines of code.

Integrated Development Environments and the Java Development Kit

Certain compilers are *integrated development environments*, or IDEs. They're *integrated* in the sense that each combines into a single interface a text editor for source code editing, a compiler for compiling the source code, a debugger for tracking down errors, and a linker for creating executables.

When you first began programming in C or C++, you had to select which compiler to use. If you program on a Windows machine, you might have used Symantec C++ for Windows or Borland C++. If you're a Mac programmer, you probably worked with Symantec C++ for Macintosh or Metrowerks CodeWarrior.

When you program in Java, you must also choose a compiler. Several compilers support Java programming. In fact, some of the previously mentioned C/C++ compilers have recently been upgraded to support programming in the Java language.

The examples in this book, however, use Sun Microsystems' own development environment, called the *Java Development Kit*, or *JDK*. The JDK is not an integrated development environment. It does not include a text editor and doesn't support debugging. What it *does* include is a Java compiler and an applet-runner—a small program that enables you to test your compiled applets without having to place them on a Web page and without having to connect to the Internet.

As of this writing, Sun Microsystems has released three versions of the Java Development Kit: one for programmers who work on machines running Windows 95 or Windows NT, one for programmers running Solaris 2.x, and a third for programmers using Macintosh System 7.5. All three versions of the development kit appear on this book's CD-ROM. Sun plans to make more versions of the JDK available. When they do, you'll find them posted for downloading at the following address:

```
http://www.javasoft.com/
```

As we walk through the development of your first Java applet, we'll use the JDK included on this book's CD-ROM. Even if you've already purchased a third-party IDE that supports Java programming, you should still read this chapter in its entirety. Many compiler vendors base their Java upgrade (or add-on, or tool, or some other similar phrase) on the Java Development Kit. In fact, some include the entire JDK as a part of their IDE. So it won't hurt to become familiar with the components of the JDK. Additionally, using the JDK is a simple, straightforward process—perfect for the development of a simple, straightforward applet.

The Source Code Listing for the Sample Applet

Each version of the Java Development Kit comes with almost two dozen applets, complete with source code files. You can find all of these applets in the example applets folder on the accompanying CD-ROM. Although we could use one of Sun's examples for our sample applet, we won't. Instead, we'll start from scratch so you can work though the entire applet development cycle.

Because this chapter focuses on Java programming tools—not on the Java programming language itself—we'll study the development of a very *simple* applet rather than a complex one. By looking at a simple applet, you can focus on how to create a Java applet rather than on the syntax of the Java programming language. The techniques you learn here apply to *all* applets—both simple and complex.

The entire source code listing for the applet—aptly named MyFirstApplet—is as follows:

```
import java.awt.*;
import java.applet.*;

public class MyFirstApplet extends Applet {

    public void paint(Graphics g) {
        g.drawString("This applet simply draws text", 10, 20);
    }
}
```

Java source code is platform-independent. Consequently, you should use this listing exactly as it appears here—regardless of the system you use for programming.

Figure 2-1 shows what the applet looks like on a Web page. As you can see, the applet merely displays the sentence "This applet simply draws text."

Now that you've seen the source code, it's time to type it in and compile it. In short, it's time to create your first applet. If you're working on a machine running Windows 95, read the next section. If you're developing on a Macintosh, skip ahead to the section on Creating the Sample Applet Using a Macintosh.

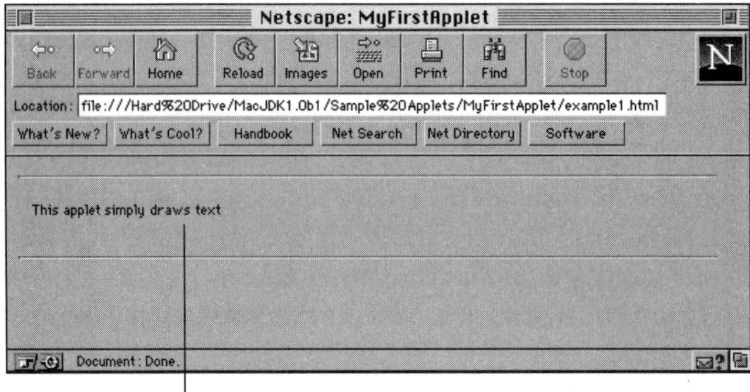

Figure 2-1
Here is what the sample Java applet looks like on a Web page.

Creating the Sample Applet Using Windows 95

If you program using Windows 95, you can develop the applet with the Windows 95 JDK that's included on this book's CD-ROM.

Using the Sun JDK for Windows 95

You should find the Windows 95 version of the JDK on the CD-ROM in a folder named java. If you find the JDK in a different folder—or if you've renamed the root folder yourself—you should change the name of the folder to `java` so you can more easily follow along with this walk-through of the applet development process.

Within the java folder, you should find several other folders and some files. For our purposes, the most important folders are the bin folder and the demo folder. The bin folder holds the executables of the tools you use when you develop an applet. The tool named *javac* is the Java compiler, which you use to compile your Java source code. The tool named *appletviewer* is what you use to test an applet after it has been compiled. The Applet Viewer enables you to test an applet without a Web browser or a connection to the Web. Figure 2-2 shows javac and appletviewer in the bin folder.

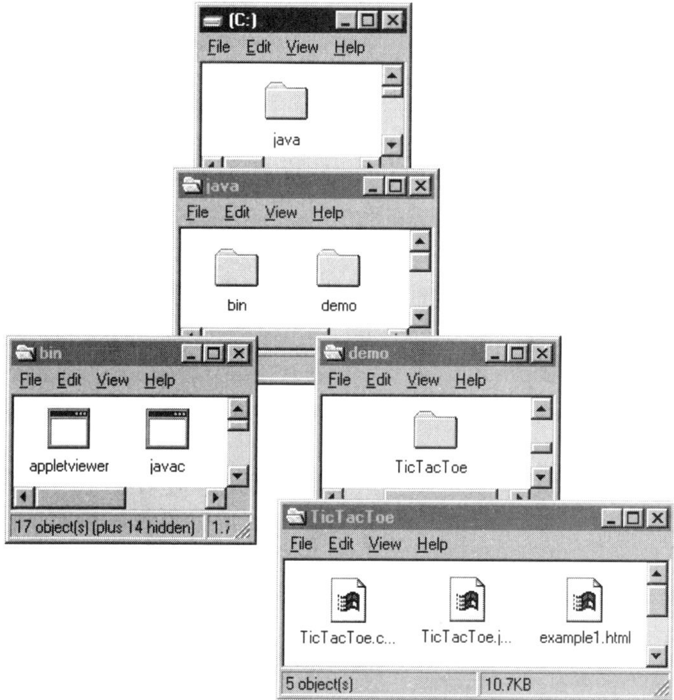

Figure 2-2
Here you can see the structure of the Windows 95 Java Development Kit and some of the files for the Tic-Tac-Toe applet.

The demo folder contains several additional folders that hold example applets. In each folder you'll find a file that holds the Java source code (the file with the `.java` extension). You'll also find one or more files with a `.class` extension. When you compile a Java source code file, you end up with a separate `.class` file for each *class* defined in the source code file. (You'll learn more about Java classes in Chapters 3, 4, 5, and 8.) The applet itself is located in the `.class` file that bears the name of the applet. For example, the Tic-Tac-Toe applet is located in the file named `TicTacToe.class`.

A third type of file in each demo folder is a text file with the extension `.html`. You can use the HTML file in each folder along with the Applet Viewer program or your Java-compatible Web browser to test the applet in that folder.

Figure 2-2 shows all three kinds of files—`.java`, `.class`, and HTML—in a folder named TicTacToe. Note that the bottom of the TicTacToe window indicates that five objects exist in the folder. The two additional files in the TicTacToe folder are the graphics and sound files that the Tic-Tac-Toe applet requires. You can learn more about including graphics in your applets in Chapter 9.

WRITING THE JAVA SOURCE CODE

Now that you know the structure of the Windows JDK and where to find its example applets, you can start your own Java applet. First, create a new folder to hold the files you'll build for your new applet. In this walkthrough, we'll call this new folder `MyFirstApplet` and place it in the existing demo folder.

As with C or C++ source code, you create Java source code in a text file. Because the JDK doesn't come with its own text editor, you'll need to use your own editor. You can use either a text editor or a word processor to edit your Java code. So everyone can follow along, we'll use the text editor available at the DOS prompt. In Windows 95, you can enter a DOS command at any time by clicking on the Start button, choosing the Programs menu, and then clicking on the MS-DOS Prompt item. When you do so, the window shown in Figure 2-3 appears.

To use the DOS editor, first move to the MyFirstApplet directory. Then type `edit` followed by the name of the new text file. A Java source code file always has the same name as the applet itself followed by the `.java` extension. Figure 2-4 shows what you should type if you have created the MyFirstApplet folder in the demo folder.

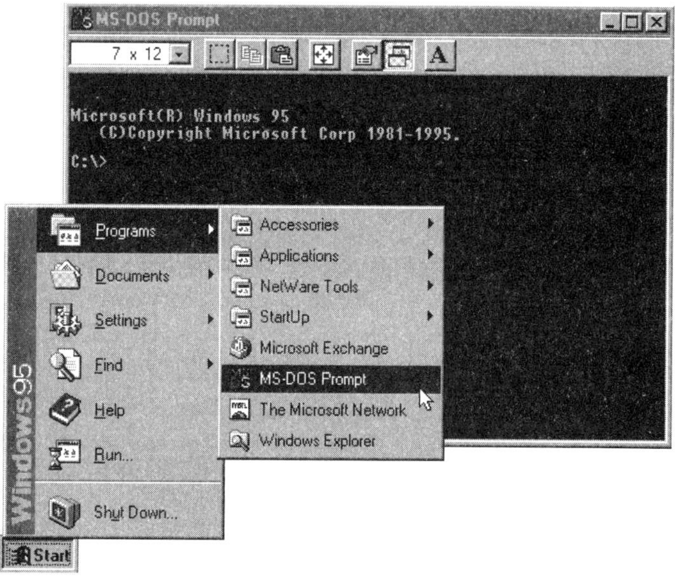

Figure 2-3
Choose Start and then Programs and then the MS-DOS Prompt to go to DOS.

Figure 2-4
Use the DOS editor to create a new, empty Java source code file.

Now, in the blank text file, type in the following code:

```
import java.awt.*;
import java.applet.*;
```

```
public class MyFirstApplet extends Applet {

    public void paint(Graphics g) {
        g.drawString("This applet simply draws text", 10, 20);
    }
}
```

If you're using the DOS editor, your editor window should look similar to the one shown in Figure 2-5.

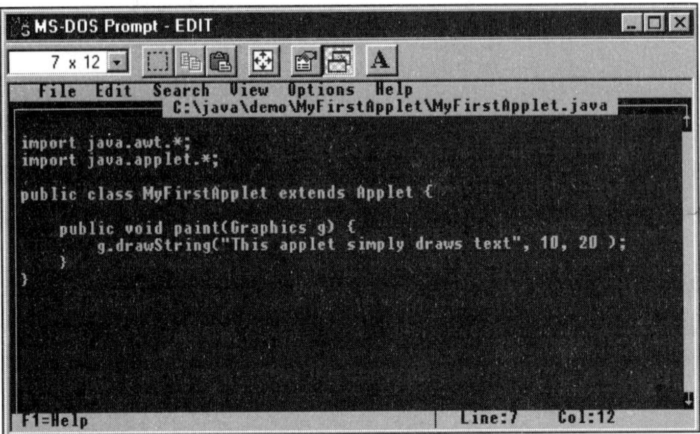

Figure 2-5
Your source code for MyFirstApplet.java should look like this.

If you're using a different editor or word processor, create a new document and save it as `MyFirstApplet.java`. If you're using a word processor (such as Microsoft Word), be sure to save the file using the application's text-only option. That's important because the Java compiler only compiles source code found in text files.

Finally, save the file and quit the text editor or word processor. Now you're ready to compile the source code.

COMPILING THE JAVA SOURCE CODE

To compile your Java source code file use the Java compiler that comes with the JDK. If you're not at the DOS prompt, go there now. From the directory that holds the source code file, type `javac` (the name of the Java compiler), followed by the name of the source code file—in this example, `MyFirstApplet.java`. Figure 2-6 shows what the screen should look like.

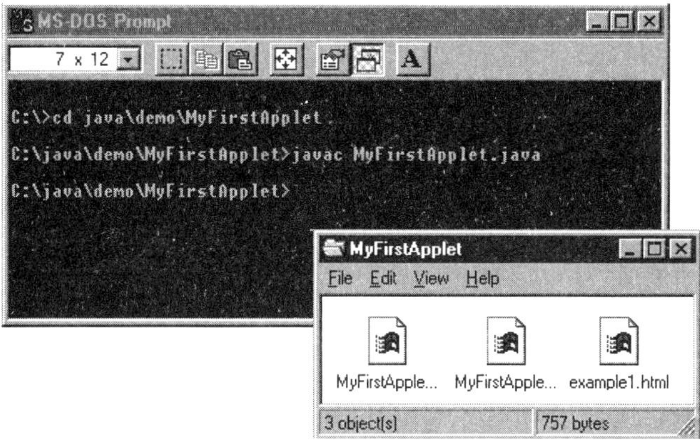

Figure 2-6
At the DOS prompt, compile the MyFirstApplet.java source code file.

After a few moments, the javac program finishes compiling. You'll know compilation is complete when the DOS prompt reappears. As shown in Figure 2-6, your MyFirstApplet folder should now have two MyFirstApplet files in it—the `MyFirstApplet.java` source code file and the `MyFirstApplet.class` file, which contains the applet.

Figure 2-6 shows a third file in the MyFirstApplet folder—the `example1.html` text file, which you can use to test to the new applet. We'll create the HTML file a little later.

If the compilation failed, you'll see an error message in the DOS window. If that happens, look over the code in your `MyFirstApplet.java` source code file and verify that it matches the code in Figure 2-5 exactly. If it does match, you might want to try using a couple of commands that eliminate compile-time errors. Move to the C: drive and then, from the DOS prompt, type the following:

```
C:\>set homedrive=c:
```

Press Enter and then, at the next DOS prompt, type the following:

```
C:\>set homepath=\
```

After you have entered the two commands, try running the Java compiler again. The compilation should be successful.

TESTING THE JAVA APPLET

After you have successfully compiled the MyFirstApplet.java source code file, you'll have a MyFirstApplet.class file in your MyFirstApplet folder. This new file is the bytecode that represents the MyFirstApplet applet. In this section you'll learn a couple of ways to quickly and easily test this new applet.

CREATING THE HTML TEST FILE

To test an applet you need to create a simple HTML file that includes the <applet> tag, which is used to place applets in HTML files. (Don't worry if the <applet> tag is new to you; it's also relatively new to HTML. The tag is explained in detail later in this chapter.) Like the Java source code file, this file can be created using any text editor or word processor that can save the file in text-only format. You can give the file any name you'd like; example1.html and index.html are two common names people use for this file.

If you are using the DOS editor, you'll want to move to the MyFirstApplet directory and then open a new window:

```
C:\>cd java\demo\MyFirstApplet
C:\java\demo\MyFirstApplet>edit example1.html
```

In your new, blank window, type the following:

```
<title>MyFirstApplet</title>
<hr>
<applet code="MyFirstApplet.class" width=200 height=40>
</applet>
<hr>
```

If you use the DOS editor, Figure 2-7 shows what your editor window should look like.

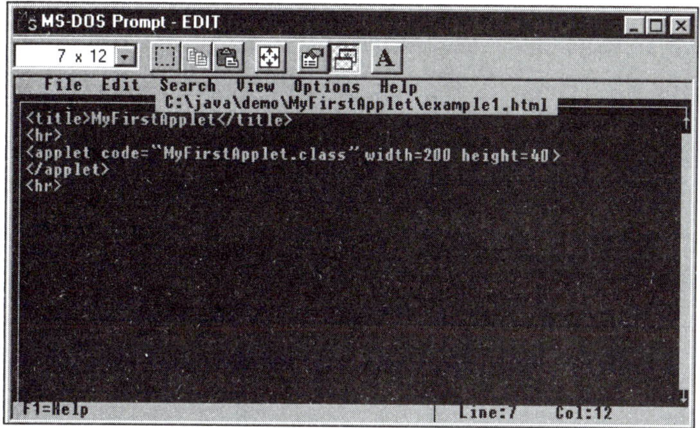

Figure 2-7

If you use the DOS editor to create example1.html, the window should look like this.

USING APPLET VIEWER TO TEST AN APPLET

Applet Viewer is a small application that enables you to run an HTML file without a Web browser. Because Applet Viewer is a Java-compatible application, it can execute your applet's bytecode.

You can run Applet Viewer from the DOS prompt by first moving into the folder that holds your applet. Then, type `appletviewer example1.html`, which is the name of the Applet Viewer executable file followed by the name of the HTML file that holds the reference to your applet. Figure 2-8 shows how the window should appear.

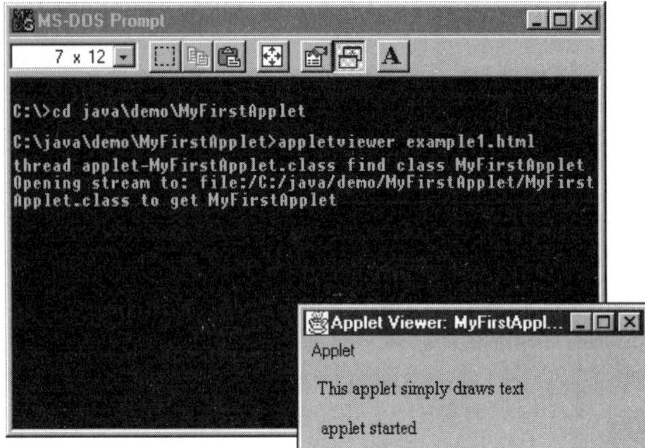

Figure 2-8
Applet Viewer in action—running your first applet!

You can use Applet Viewer to run any of the applets in the demo folder. Figure 2-9 shows what you should type to run the Tic-Tac-Toe applet.

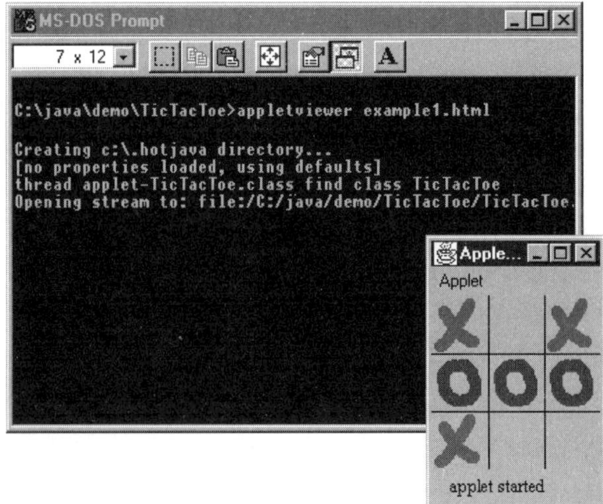

Figure 2-9
You can run any applet using Applet Viewer.

USING YOUR JAVA-COMPATIBLE WEB BROWSER TO TEST AN APPLET

The Applet Viewer program is handy, but if you have a Java-compatible Web browser, your browser can do the same job. First, start up your browser.

You don't need to be connected to the Internet to run your applet. The browser's Java interpreter, not the Internet, can execute your bytecode.

With your browser running, choose the menu command that opens a local file—a file on your computer's hard drive. In Netscape Navigator, use the Open File option from the File menu. (Other Web browsers have similar commands.) Move to the MyFirstApplet folder and choose the HTML file—for example, the file we've named `example1.html`. When you do that, your browser loads the HTML file and the applet referenced in that HTML file (MyFirstApplet). You can now be confident that once you load the applet to the Web server that holds your Web page files, your applet can be viewed by anyone surfing the Net with a Java-compatible Web browser.

If the applet ran in Applet Viewer, but doesn't appear in the browser window, then there's a problem with your HTML file. Look over your HTML file for errors. If you're new to HTML, see Appendix A for more information on this language.

Creating the Sample Applet Using a Macintosh

If you program on a Macintosh and you have any version of System 7.5, you can develop your first applet using the Macintosh JDK that's included on this book's CD-ROM.

USING THE SUN JDK FOR MACINTOSH

The Macintosh version of Sun's Java Development Kit is located in a folder named MacJDK1.0b1. If you find the JDK in a different folder—or if you've renamed the folder yourself—you should change the name of the folder to MacJDK1.0b1 so you can more easily follow along with this walk-through of the applet development process.

When you open the MacJDK1.0b1 folder, you should find a few other folders and several files. Of the files, the ones named Java Compiler and Applet Viewer are the most important for your purposes. You use Java Compiler to compile your Java source code and use Applet Viewer to test compiled applets—without a Web browser and without connecting to the Web. Figure 2-10 shows these two programs in the top window, along with a folder named Sample Applets (with the Tic-Tac-Toe applet folder open).

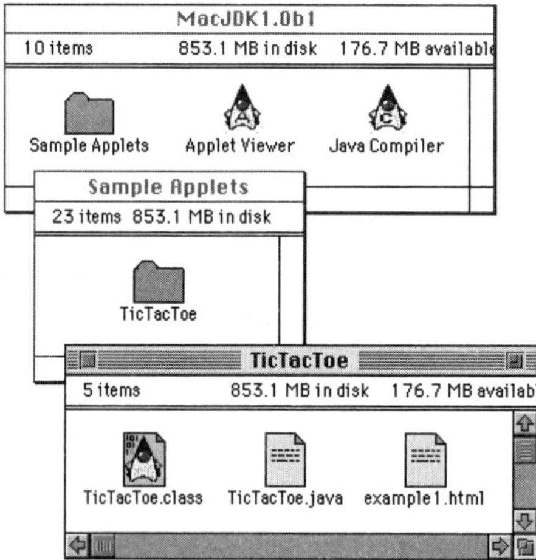

Figure 2-10

Here you can see the structure of the Macintosh Java Development Kit and some of the files for the Tic-Tac-Toe applet.

The Sample Applets folder holds several more folders—each containing an example applet. In each folder you'll find a file with a `.java` extension. These files hold the Java source code for the applets. You'll also find one or more files with a `.class` extension. When you compile a Java source code file, you end up with a separate `.class` file for each *class* defined in the source code file. (You'll learn more about Java classes in Chapters 3, 4, and 5.) The applet itself is located in the `.class` file that bears the name of the applet. For example, the Tic-Tac-Toe applet is located in the file named `TicTacToe.class`.

A third type of file in each example folder is a text file with the extension `.html`. You can use the HTML file in each folder along with the Applet Viewer program or your Java-compatible Web browser to test the applet in that folder.

Figure 2-10 shows all three files in a folder entitled TicTacToe in the Sample Applets folder—the `.class`, `.java`, and HTML files. The information at the top of the TicTacToe window, however, indicates that five files exist in the folder. The two items in the TicTacToe folder that you can't see are folders that hold the graphics and sound files that the Tic-Tac-Toe applet uses. You can learn more about including graphics and sounds in your applets in Chapters 8 and 9 respectively.

WRITING THE JAVA SOURCE CODE FILE

Now that you're familiar with the structure of the Macintosh JDK, you can begin your own Java applet. First, create a new folder to hold the files you'll build for your new applet. In this walk-through we'll name this new folder `MyFirstApplet` and place it in the existing Sample Applets folder.

You store Java source code in a text file, as with C or C++ source code. Because the JDK doesn't come with a text editor, you'll need to use an editor of your own. You can use any text editor or a word processor to write and edit your Java code. If you do use a word processor, be sure to save the code as a plain text file rather than as a file with formatting. For example, if you use Microsoft Word, save the file using the Text Only option.

Regardless of the editor or word processor you use, open a new, empty file and type in the following code:

```
import java.awt.*;
import java.applet.*;

public class MyFirstApplet extends Applet {

    public void paint(Graphics g) {
        g.drawString("This applet simply draws text", 10, 20);
    }
}
```

If you use a text editor such as SimpleText, your editor window should look similar to the one shown in Figure 2-11.

MyFirstApplet.java

```
import java.awt.*;
import java.applet.*;

public class MyFirstApplet extends Applet {

    public void paint(Graphics g) {
        g.drawString("This applet simply draws text", 10, 20);
    }
}
```

Figure 2-11
The source code file for MyFirstApplet.java looks like this in the SimpleText editor.

Before quitting the editor, save the file as `MyFirstApplet.java`. A Java source code file always has the same name as its corresponding applet followed by the `.java` extension.

Compiling the Java source code

To compile your Java source code use the Java compiler program that comes with the JDK. The JDK takes full advantage of the drag-and-drop capabilities of a Macintosh running System 7.5. To compile a source code file, click once on the file and drag the file to the Java compiler icon. When the icon's name changes from black text to white—as shown in the top window in Figure 2-12—release the mouse button.

When you drop a file with a `.java` extension on the Java compiler icon, the compiler launches and compiles the file. Figure 2-13 shows the window you see as the `MyFirstApplet.java` file is compiled.

In environments other than the Mac OS, this Sun compiler is named *javac*. When you come across references to javac, you should recognize this as essentially the same thing as the Java compiler.

The compiler window indicates that the compiler is idle when compilation is complete. As shown in Figure 2-14, your MyFirstApplet folder should now have two MyFirstApplet files in it: the source code file (`MyFirstApplet.java`) and the applet (`MyFirstApplet.class`).

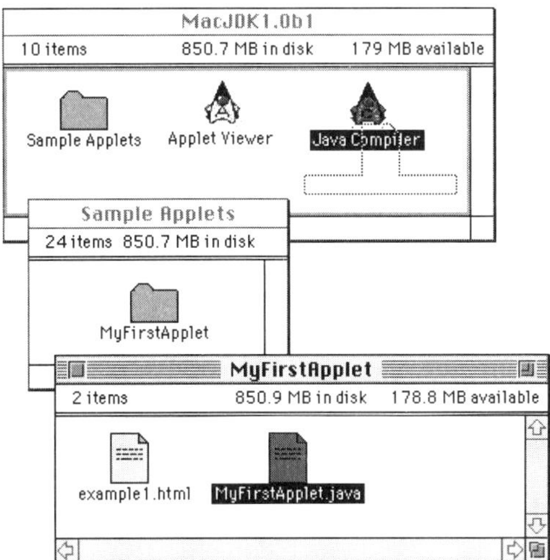

Figure 2-12
Compile the MyFirstApplet.java source code file by dragging its icon onto the Java compiler icon.

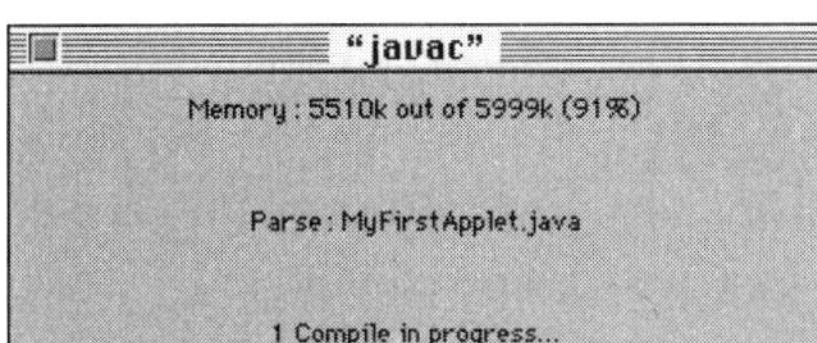

Figure 2-13
The Java compiler window while the MyFirstApplet.java source code file is being compiled.

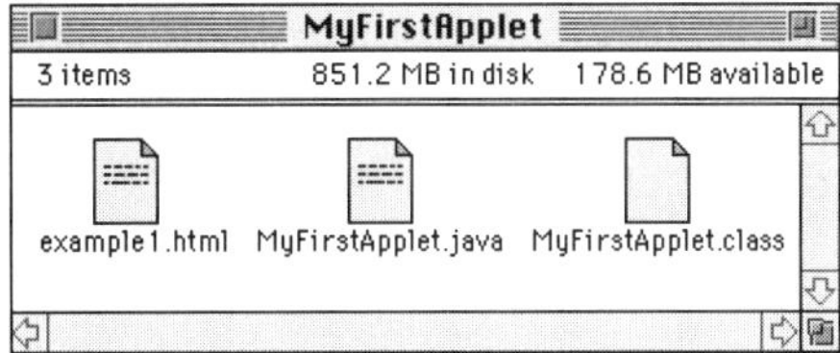

Figure 2-14
When compilation is complete, a .class file appears in the MyFirstApplet folder.

If the compilation isn't successful, you'll see an error message in a separate window. If that happens, look over the code in your `MyFirstApplet.java` source code file and verify that it is identical to the sample code shown earlier in Figure 2-11.

Figure 2-14 shows a third file in the MyFirstApplet folder—the `example1.html` text file. You use this file, which we'll create in a moment, to test to the new applet.

TESTING THE JAVA APPLET

After you compile the `MyFirstApplet.java` source code file, you'll have a `MyFirstApplet.class` file in your MyFirstApplet folder. This new file is the bytecode that represents the MyFirstApplet applet. In this section, you'll learn two different ways you can test this new applet.

CREATING THE HTML TEST FILE

To test an applet you need to create a simple HTML file that includes the `<applet>` tag, which is used to place applets in HTML files. (If the `<applet>` tag is new to you, don't be alarmed; it's also relatively new to HTML. The tag is explained in detail later in this chapter.) Like the Java source code file, the HTML file can be created using any application that is capable of saving a file in text-only format. In a new, empty window, type the following:

```
<title>MyFirstApplet</title>
<hr>
<applet code="MyFirstApplet.class" width=200 height=40>
</applet>
<hr>
```

Now save the file. Although you can choose any name you like for the HTML file, people usually name the file either `example1.html` or `index.html`.

USING APPLET VIEWER TO TEST AN APPLET

Applet Viewer is a small application that enables you to run an HTML file without a Web browser. Applet Viewer can do this because it is capable of executing Java bytecode.

To run an applet using Applet Viewer, you simply click on the HTML file and, with the mouse held down, drag the file onto the Applet Viewer icon and release the mouse button. If you drag the `example1.html` file from the MyFirstApplet folder and drop it on the Applet Viewer icon, you should see the window shown in Figure 2-15.

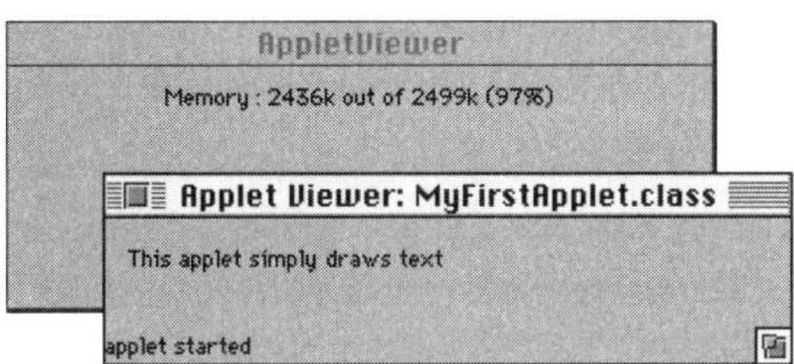

Figure 2-15
Use the Applet Viewer to run the MyFirstApplet applet.

You can use Applet Viewer to run any of the applets in the Sample Applets folder. Just drag the HTML file to the Applet Viewer, and the corresponding applet executes.

Using your Java-compatible Web browser to test an applet

Instead of Applet Viewer, you can use a Java-compatible browser to test an applet. You don't need to be connected to the Internet to do this. Simply launch your browser and use the menu command that enables you to open an HTML file directly from your hard disk. In Netscape Navigator, select the Open File option from the File menu. (Other Web browsers have similar commands.) Move to the MyFirstApplet folder and choose the HTML file—for example, `example1.html`. When you do that, your browser loads the HTML file and the applet referenced in that HTML file (for example, MyFirstApplet). You can be confident that when you load the applet to the Web server that holds your Web page files, your applet can be viewed by anyone on the Internet who has a Java-compatible Web browser.

If the applet ran in Applet Viewer, but doesn't appear in the browser window, then it is likely you have a problem with your HTML file. Check your HTML file for errors. If you're new to HTML, see Appendix A for more information about HTML.

Including Your Applet on a Web Page

After you create an applet, you usually embed it in a Web page by including the <applet> tag in the HTML file for the Web page. In this section, you'll learn how to do that. You can use what you learn here to embed the MyFirstApplet applet in a Web page.

If you don't know HTML, see Appendix A—it's a very short Hypertext Markup Language (HTML) "survival guide" that provides you with just enough HTML syntax to get you started.

THE <APPLET> TAG

When a Java-compatible Web browser encounters a Web page that includes the <applet> tag, the browser downloads the applet's bytecode and executes it. For each applet, you need both a start tag (<applet>) and an end tag (</applet>). The following listing, which includes the <applet> tag, shows the HTML file for a complete, though very simple, Web page:

```
<html>
<head>
<title>MyFirstApplet</title>
</head>
<body>
<hr>
<applet code="MyFirstApplet.class" width=200 height=40>
</applet>
<hr>
</body>
</html>
```

Figure 2-16 shows the Web page that would be displayed using the preceding HTML listing. The placement of the applet on the page is dependent on the location of the <applet> tag in the HTML file. As you might expect, the MyFirstApplet applet appears between the two horizontal rule dividers created by the two <hr> tags.

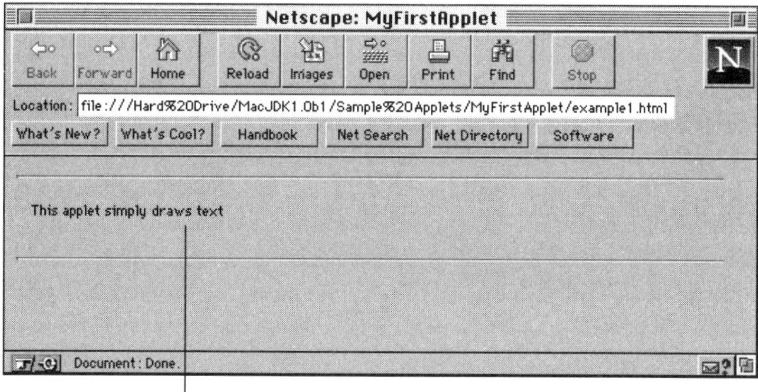

Figure 2-16
The `<applet>` *tag displays the applet on a Web page.*

MANDATORY <APPLET> ATTRIBUTES

The `<applet>` tag has three required *attributes*, or parameters. The `code` attribute gives the name of the applet to be displayed. As you know, when you compile Java source, you end up with a file that has the `.class` extension. (This file holds the applet itself.) The `code` attribute requires the file's *complete* name. Consequently, in our example we set code equal to `MyFirstApplet.class`.

When you define the `code` attribute, you must place quotation marks around the applet's filename.

The other two mandatory `<applet>` attributes specify the size of the applet. The size is the amount of Web-page real estate that the applet occupies. The values of the `width` and `height` attributes are expressed in pixels. Figure 2-17 shows the size and placement of the MyFirstApplet applet with the following tag:

```
<applet code="MyFirstApplet.class" width=200 height=40>
```

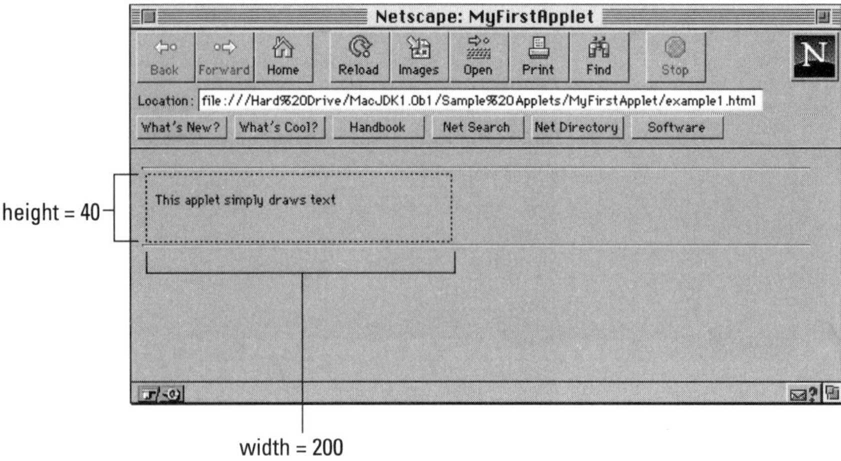

Figure 2-17
Here is MyFirstApplet with a width of 200 pixels and a height of 40 pixels.

To see the effect of changing the `width` and `height` attributes, contrast Figure 2-17 with Figure 2-18. The Web page in Figure 2-18 was created using the following `<applet>` tag:

```
<applet code="MyFirstApplet.class" width=100 height=80>
```

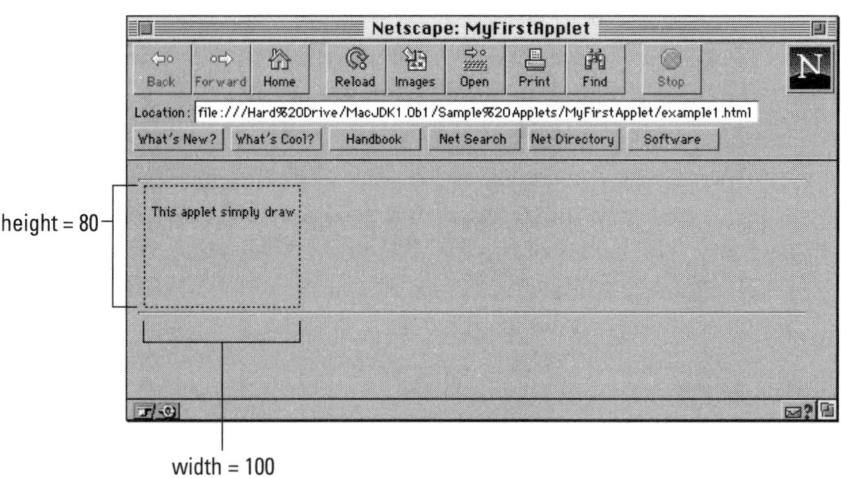

Figure 2-18
Here is MyFirstApplet with a width of 100 pixels and a height of 80 pixels.

Optional <APPLET> Attributes

In addition to using the three mandatory attributes (`class`, `width`, and `height`), you can use a number of optional attributes with the `<applet>` tag.

The `<applet>` attributes explained in this section are the most common, but there are others. Refer to a recent book on HTML for more information.

The align Attribute

Because neither the `<applet>` nor the `</applet>` tag adds a line break to your Web page, you can have text in your HTML file appear on the same line as the applet. You can use the `<applet> align` attribute to specify the vertical starting point for the text. By default, an applet appears flush-left on a Web page. Unless you add a line break after the `</applet>` end-tag (by using a tag such as `<br>`, `<hr>`, and so forth), the next text in your HTML file will begin to the right of the applet rather than below it. The following listing tells the Web browser to start the text aligned horizontally with the top of the applet:

```
<hr>
<applet code="MyFirstApplet.class" width=200 height=40 align=top>
</applet>
This text appears next to the applet
<hr>
```

Figure 2-19 shows the effect of aligning text to the top, middle, and bottom of an applet.

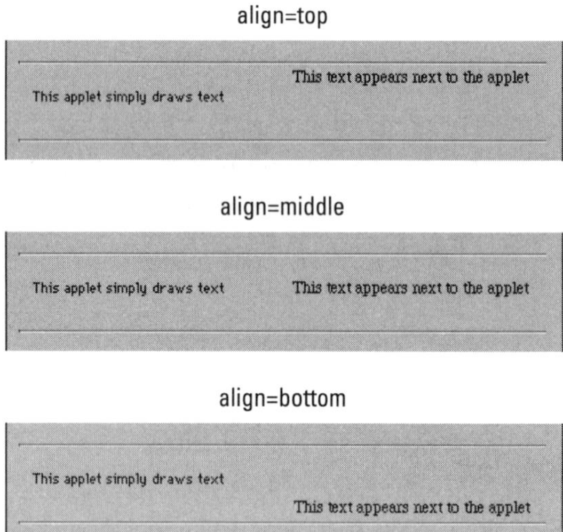

Figure 2-19
Here is MyFirstApplet with additional text displayed using three different values for the align attribute.

THE CODEBASE ATTRIBUTE

To make an applet available to your Web page, you simply upload the applet (in other words, the `.class` file) to your home page directory on the Internet server that holds the Web site's files. By default, the `code` attribute indicates that the `.class` file is in the same directory as the HTML file that references it. If you want to store applets in different directories, you can use the `codebase` attribute to tell Web browsers where to look. Here's an example:

```
<applet code="MyFirstApplet.class" codebase="applets" width=200
    height=40>
</applet>
```

Java-compatible Web browsers can tell from the preceding listing that the `MyFirstApplet.class` file is located in a subdirectory named applets. When you name a directory in the `codebase` attribute, that directory is always a subdirectory of the HTML file's directory.

If you *don't* have your own Web page but you *do* have an America Online account, you can create your own Web page in a matter of minutes. AOL supplies all account-holders with free space on its Internet server; you can use this private space to store your HTML file and any other Web files you use, such as graphic files and applets. See Appendix B (if you're a Windows user) or Appendix C (if you're a Macintosh user) for more information on how to create your own Web page.

BROWSERS THAT ARE NOT JAVA-COMPATIBLE

Anyone with a Java-compatible browser who encounters your applet-powered Web page will be able to view your applet. However, people using browsers that don't have a built-in Java interpreter will not be able to view the `<applet>` tag. When those people view your Web page, they simply see the page as if it contained no applets. To notify those people that your page does in fact hold an applet, you can add some informative text between the `<applet>` start-tag and the `</applet>` end-tag. Here is an example of how you might do that:

```
<applet code="MyFirstApplet.class" width=200 height=40>
Your Web browser doesn't recognize Java applets. Try revisiting
this page with a "Java-aware" browser to see its applet!
</applet>
```

As you can see on the left side of Figure 2-20, a Java-compatible browser ignores the text embedded between the `<applet>` and `</applet>` tags. The right-hand side of Figure 2-20 shows what you would see using a Web browser that is not Java-compatible.

Viewed from a Java-capable browser

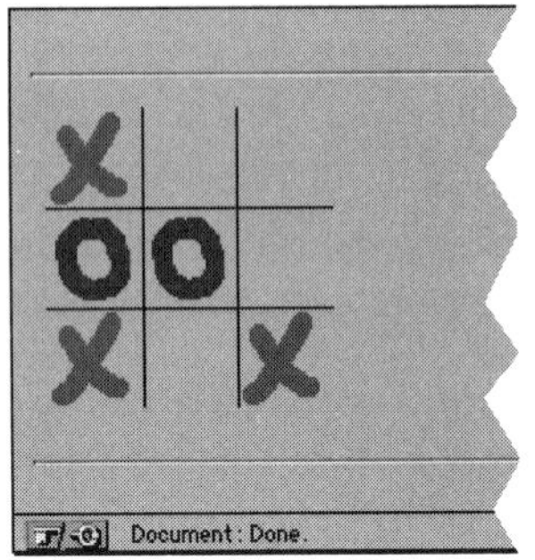

Viewed from a browser that doesn't include a Java interpreter

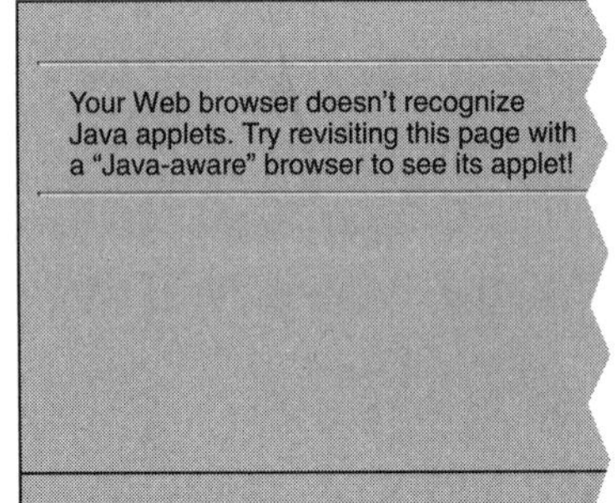

Figure 2-20

Here is what the same Web page looks like when viewed using a Java-compatible browser (left) and a browser that is not compatible with Java (right).

What You've Learned

You're only two chapters into the book, and already you've written, compiled, and tested a Java applet. Not only that, you've also got it on your Web page. Of course, you'll want to create applets that do much more than write a line of text. The remainder of this book can help you achieve this goal.

CHAPTER 3

Introduction to the Java Language

This chapter introduces you to the Java language itself. Not only will you get an overview of the language's basic characteristics and structure, but you'll also learn how the few lines of source code you saw in Chapter 2 (the source code for MyFirstApplet) create a fully functional applet.

While Java can be used to create both applets and applications, it is applets that launched this new language into prominence. Because of this, the focus of this book—and especially this chapter—is on the Java language as it's used to develop applets.

Characteristics of the Java Language

Now that you know what source code written in the Java language *produces*, what about the Java language itself? You've probably heard a few buzzwords used by developers to describe the features that make Java so interesting. In its "Java Short Summary" paper posted on its Web site, Sun Microsystems, the company that created Java, has this to say about its language: "Java is a simple, object-oriented, distributed, interpreted, robust, secure, architecture-neutral, portable, high-performance, multithreaded, and dynamic language." Sun's claims regarding its new language aren't surprising—new technologies are usually accompanied by great fanfare. What *is* surprising is that the words and phrases you see used in conjunction with the word "Java" aren't just hype. Many of the buzzwords really do accurately describe this exciting new language. Here we take a quick look at why some of these buzzwords do describe Java accurately.

SIMPLE

The designers of Java wanted their new language to have similarities to the most commonly used languages of the day—C and C++. They felt that would flatten the learning curve for programmers who would want to shift to this language of the World Wide Web. But while Java is similar to C and C++, it is actually much simpler. Memory management—probably the most bug-inducing area of programming—has been greatly simplified by Java's elimination of pointers. Phrases such as "dangling pointers" and "memory leaks" are not a part of Java terminology. Chapters 4 and 5 point out many of the differences between Java and the C and C++ languages.

OBJECT-ORIENTED

An object-oriented language forces programmers to focus not only on data but also on how data should be manipulated. A language that encourages a programmer to concentrate chiefly on keeping track of data probably isn't object-oriented. The C language, with its emphasis on structures and the `struct` data type, isn't object-oriented. The C++ language, which encourages a programmer to combine data and the functions that act on that data into a single class, *is* object-oriented. The chief advantage of an object-oriented language is said to be its "code reusability." Java is an object-oriented language. Sun Microsystems has fostered code reusability by developing a huge set of reusable Java classes—and by making these classes freely available to Java programmers. Much of the Java code you use in the development of your own applets will be code written by Sun engineers!

DISTRIBUTED

Java is the language of the Web because it fully supports applications that were developed to execute over a network—specifically, distributed applications. In fact, any time your Java-compatible Web browser encounters a Web page that holds an applet, your browser actually downloads the applet's code to your own computer in order to execute that applet.

INTERPRETED

You've already seen that Java is an interpreted language. For an applet to execute on a computer, that computer must have an interpreter that can process the applet's Java bytecode. Such interpreters are a part of Java-compatible Web browsers.

SECURE

Programs designed to run on a network should be written in a secure language. Because the code that makes up an applet is downloaded to a user's machine, safeguards should be built into the applet's language—safeguards that prevent an applet from doing damage to files on a user's machine. Java has such defenses.

ARCHITECTURE-NEUTRAL

Being an interpreted language makes it easy for Java to be *architecture-neutral*. As long as an interpreter exists for a given machine (or, more specifically, for a given operating system), that machine can run a Java applet.

PORTABLE

When you develop a Java applet, you develop only one version of that applet. You don't use different Java compilers to create different versions of an applet, each capable of running on only one type of machine. That means Java is a *portable* language. One way such portability is ensured is by avoiding operating-system-dependent code.

MULTITHREADED

When connected to the Internet, the ideal situation is one in which multiple tasks can be performed simultaneously. For example, you don't want a long file download session to prevent your computer from performing some other task—such as displaying an animation or video clip. A multithreaded language such as Java allows this to happen. Multiple threads of execution handle different tasks at the same time. Java isn't the only multithreaded language; both C and C++ allow for concurrent task handling. However, Java has much better built-in support for threads. As such, Java frees the programmer from much of the planning that normally accompanies the addition of multithreading to an application.

Using Sun's Java Language Code

When you program in C or C++, you often rely on code written by others. Programming in Java is no different. In C and C++, this code is contained in a compiled format in libraries. In Java, this prewritten code is also held in a compiled format. In Java, though, such a collection of code is referred to as a *package*.

C/C++ LIBRARIES AND HEADER FILES

Your C or C++ programs most likely include calls to functions that you didn't write—functions whose code was supplied in precompiled libraries. The `printf()` and `scanf()` functions are two examples. When you write a C or C++ program that calls either of these functions, you also make use of an ANSI C library that holds the code the comprises these routines.

The name of the library or libraries that hold compiled ANSI C code varies from development environment to development environment. Exactly how such a library is associated with your program is also a factor dependent on the programming environment you use; development environments that group a program's related files in a project file require that you add a library to this project. In all cases, however, it is the linker that binds this library code to your compiled source code to create an executable program. Figure 3-1 illustrates the C linker in action.

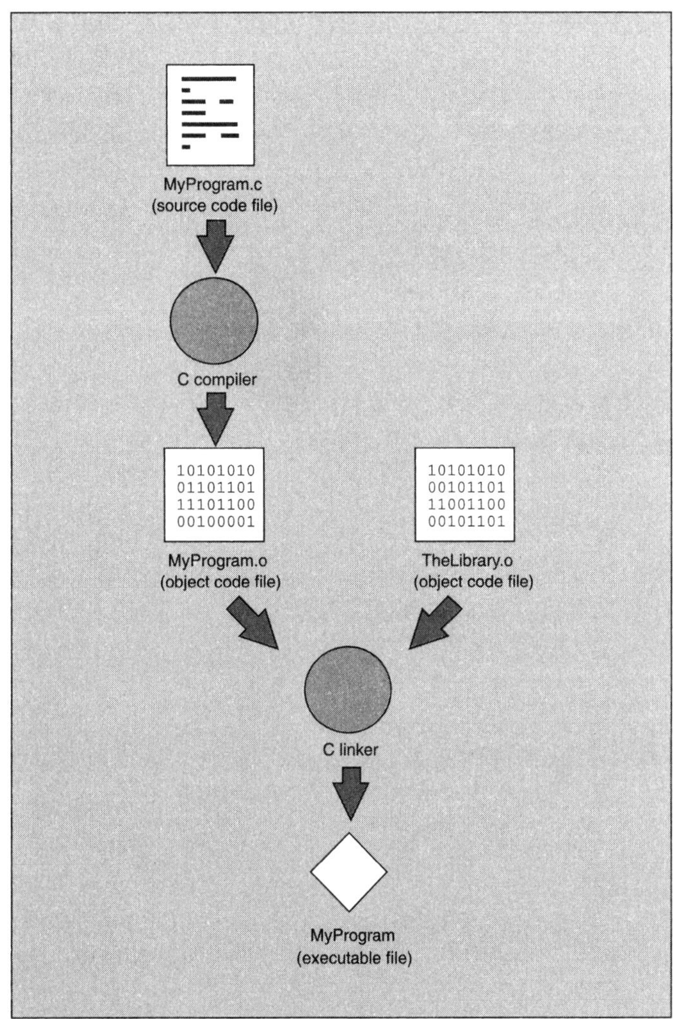

Figure 3-1

The C linker binds compiled source code and library code to generate an executable file.

You may be wondering how a library becomes object code in the first place. As shown in Figure 3-2, a library starts as source code that is then compiled. This compiled code is the library that is distributed with your development environment.

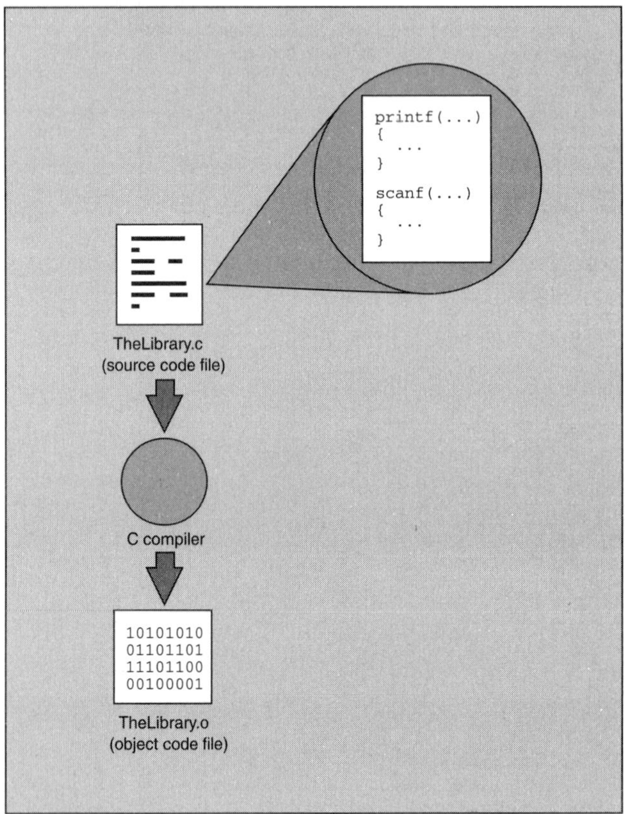

Figure 3-2
A C library is the result of compiling C source code.

In the C/C++ program development cycle, as you know, the compiler never sees the source code for library functions; after compiling your source code, your program's object code is linked with library object code. This means that the compiler never sees the source code that makes up library functions. So how does the compiler know if the syntax you've used for a call to, say, `printf()` is correct? It compares your use of the function call with the declaration, or prototype, of the function. And where does the compiler find this prototype? In the appropriate header file that you've included near the top of your source code listing. For `printf()`, the prototype is found in the `stdio.h` header file supplied with your development environment. You add the contents of this file to your own source code using the `#include` directive:

```
#include <stdio.h>
```

As Figure 3-3 illustrates, when your source code file uses an `#include` directive, the compiler actually compiles a second file along with your source code file.

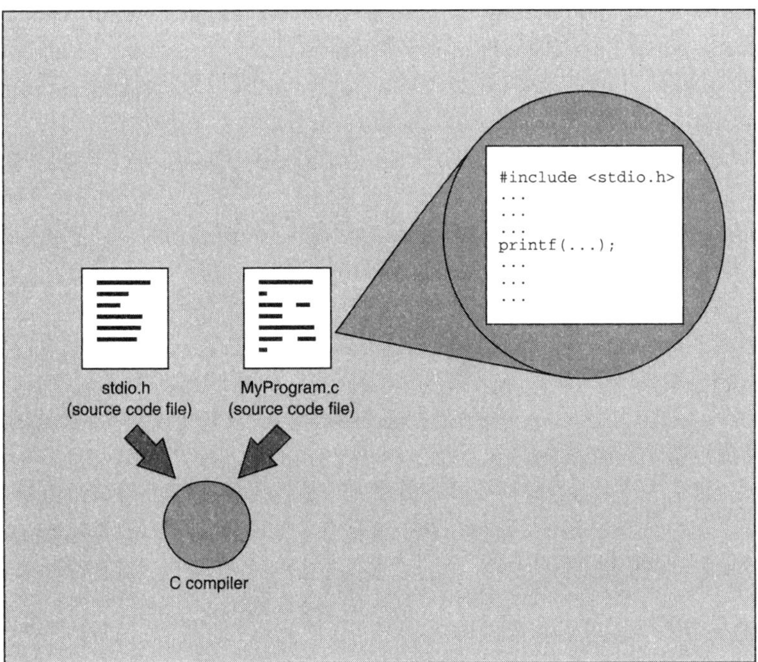

Figure 3-3
Including a header file in a C source code file causes the C compiler to compile more than one file.

JAVA PACKAGES AND CLASSES

With the preceding refresher on C/C++ libraries out of the way, let's turn our attention to the way Java works with compiled libraries. In Java, a *package* is analogous to a C or C++ library. In fact, in some Java reference material you'll see the words *package* and *library* used interchangeably.

Unlike a C library, which holds the object code of compiled functions, a Java package holds the object code of compiled classes. If you're a C++ programmer, further explanation is probably unnecessary. If you're a C programmer, for now you should accept the sweeping generalization that a class is similar to a function. The vagueness of that notion will disappear when you read Chapter 4.

Besides holding class object code, a Java package can hold other packages. The Java Development Kit (JDK) comes with a single file that is a package—a package simply named `java`. This one package, however, holds six other packages. Figure 3-4 names each.

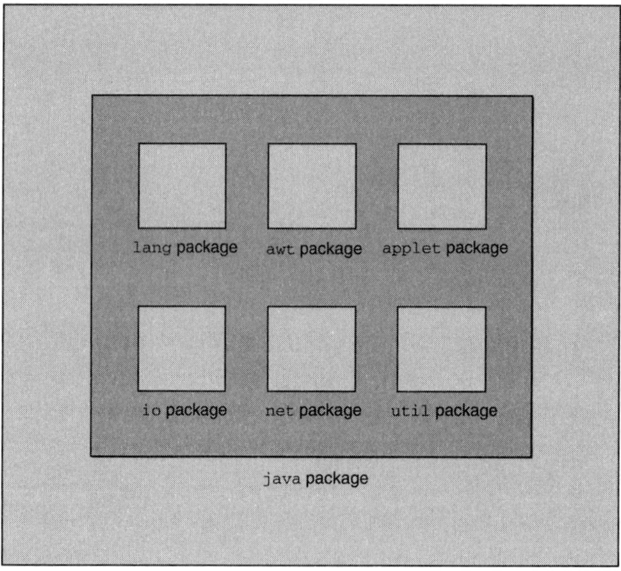

Figure 3-4
The purpose of the java package is to contain other Java packages.

When referencing a package, you need to state the package's hierarchy. This is done by placing a period between package names. For instance, the `lang` package, which is in the `java` package, is referred to as `java.lang`.

A package is the Java way of grouping together several logically related classes. For instance, the classes in the `java.io` package all have something to do with, quite obviously, input and output. Table 3-1 provides a short overview of the purpose of each of the six packages found in the `java` package. You'll learn more about these classes throughout this book.

Table 3-1
Java's Six Packages

Java Package	*Purpose*
`java.lang`	Holds the essential Java classes—classes that define the Java language.
`java.io`	Holds the classes used when working with data input and output.
`java.awt`	Holds the classes used to give your applets a graphical user interface. AWT stands for Abstract Windowing Toolkit.
`java.applet`	Holds the classes necessary to create an applet.
`java.net`	Holds the classes used for communicating with a network.
`java.util`	Holds utility classes.

A package holds the compiled code for several classes. To reference a single class in a package, you specify both the package hierarchy and the class—again separated by periods. For instance, the `java.awt` package contains a class named `Font`. To refer to the `Font` class, you need to use the syntax `java.awt.Font`.

Components of the Sample Applet

The MyFirstApplet source code listing is very short and very simple. Yet it very adequately demonstrates the basic components, or elements, that you'll find in the listings of most applets: import statements used to make Java classes available to the applet, a main class that is the applet itself, and a method that carries out the tasks of the applet. In the MyFirstApplet listing, the `import` statements make the `java.awt` and `java.applet` packages available to the applet; the main class is named `MyFirstApplet`, and the method defined in the main class is named `paint()`:

```
import java.awt.*;
import java.applet.*;

public class MyFirstApplet extends Applet {

    public void paint(Graphics g) {
        g.drawString("This applet simply draws text", 10, 20);
    }
}
```

The primary difference between MyFirstApplet and your own applet will be that your applet will consist of more than one method—your applet will hopefully do more than write a single line of text to the user's browser window.

IMPORT STATEMENTS

In Java programming, an `import` statement is somewhat analogous to a C/C++ `#include` directive. The MyFirstApplet listing includes two `import` statements:

```
import java.awt.*;
import java.applet.*;
```

An `import` statement can be written such that it refers to either a single class from a package or to all of the classes from a package. Ending a package name with an asterisk tells the Java compiler that the `import` statement applies to the entire package. Here the following `import` statement refers to all of the classes from the `java.awt` package:

```
import java.awt.*;
```

If you'll be referencing a single class from a package and you know the name of that class, you can use the `import` statement to selectively refer to just that class. In this snippet only the `Graphics` class from the `java.awt` package is being referenced:

```
import java.awt.Graphics;
```

At this early stage of your Java studies, you won't be familiar with the names of the classes in the various Java packages. Consequently, you'd do best simply to play it safe and import entire packages. Don't worry about a huge increase in the memory footprint of your applet. Contrary to what's implied by its name, the `import` statement doesn't actually bring in, or merge, the code from a package with your applet. Instead, it simply allows an applet to use an abbreviated name when calling a class defined in a package. You'll see an example of this a few pages ahead in a discussion of how the `Applet` class from the `java.applet` package is used.

THE JAVA.AWT PACKAGE

The first `import` statement in MyFirstApplet allows this applet to reference all of the many classes found in the `java.awt` package. As with all packages that begin with the word `java`, the code in the `java.awt` package is written by Sun and supplied as a part of the Java Development Kit. The `java.awt` package is an important one: it holds the code that makes it easy for you to include graphics, and a graphical interface, in your own applets. You'll find more details of the `java.awt` package throughout this book.

THE JAVA.APPLET PACKAGE

The second `import` statement in MyFirstApplet allows the applet to reference classes found in the `java.applet` package. For an applet, this package is a necessary one. Among other things, it provides the code that allows an applet to operate within a browser.

THE MAIN CLASS

Every applet relies on the code that is in a class named `Applet`. The code for the `Applet` class is found in the `java.applet` package. Each applet you develop must create a main class that is a subclass of this `Applet` class. If you're a C programmer, you'll read in Chapter 4 that a *subclass* is a class that *inherits* all of the code of an existing class. In Java, you use the `extends` keyword to designate a class as a subclass. The `extends` keyword is particularly descriptive in that a subclass not only obtains all the functionality of another class but also *extends* the functionality of that class.

The definition of an applet's main class always follows the same format—the format shown here:

```
public class AppletName extends Applet {

    // body of the AppletName class
}
```

An applet definition must begin with the Java keyword `public`. When your applet appears on your Web page, and is subsequently encountered by someone surfing the Web, it will be the fact that the applet is public that makes the applet accessible to the Java interpreter in the surfer's Java-capable Web browser.

After the keyword `public` comes another Java keyword: `class`. As in C++, this keyword tells the compiler that the name that follows is the name of a new class. The name of this main class *must* be the same as the name of the applet, and because Java is case-sensitive, the case of the names must match as well. To make that perfectly clear, the name of the main class in this general example is `AppletName`. In our specific example, this means that the main class in the `MyFirstApplet.java` source code file must be named `MyFirstApplet`.

After the name of the class comes the already-mentioned `extends` keyword. Following the `extends` keyword is the name of the class on which this new class is going to be based: the `Applet` class. Because the `Applet` class is a part of the `java.applet` package, and because the `java.applet` package has been imported using the `import` statement, the compiler will recognize `Applet` as an existing class.

You could achieve the same effect by not importing the `java.applet` package and instead specifying the full name of the `Applet` class in the definition, like this:

```
public class AppletName extends java.applet.Applet {

    // body of the AppletName class
}
```

So why not just write the class this way? Because you'll want to get in the habit of importing Java packages and then referencing classes by their class names. You'll be using existing Java classes for the functionality they provide. As long as a class does what you want it to do, you really aren't too concerned with which package the class comes from. When your sophisticated applet uses a dozen, or dozens, of Java classes, leaving off the package names will serve to make your Java source code more readable.

As mentioned earlier, the `import` statement allows for the abbreviated naming of classes. All classes in all of the various Sun `java` packages are always available to your applet—even without the use of `import` statements. But if your applet doesn't import a package, any classes your applet references from that package will have to be references by the complete package name (such as `java.applet.Applet`) rather than by the class name alone (such as `Applet`).

METHODS

Up until now, we have glossed over the body of the sample applet. In between the opening and closing braces of the main `applet` class lies all of an applet's code. The main `applet` class serves as a sort of wrapper that holds the Java source code for the applet. Because this code varies with each applet, we've used a Java one-line comment (denoted by two forward slashes, as in C++) between the braces for simplicity:

```
public class AppletName extends Applet {

    // body of the AppletName class
}
```

Now, let's make a couple of changes. First, we'll replace the generic AppletName with the name of a real applet—the MyFirstApplet applet to which you're growing accustomed:

```
public class MyFirstApplet extends Applet {

    // body of the AppletName class
}
```

Next, we'll replace the Java comment with the body of MyFirstApplet:

```
public class MyFirstApplet extends Applet {

    public void paint(Graphics g) {
        g.drawString("This applet simply draws text", 10, 20);
    }
}
```

As a C or C++ programmer, you're undoubtedly familiar with the concept of functions. Java, however, uses no functions. Instead, it uses *methods*. If you program in C, consider a method similar to a function. If you program in C++, consider a method *identical* to a class member function. Some object-oriented languages (Smalltalk being one example) refer to class member functions as methods. Some C++ programmers use this terminology as well. Chapters 4 and 5 fully describe methods.

The body of an applet's main class consists of one or more methods—usually many more than one. In the case of MyFirstApplet, the body consists of a single method—a method named `paint()`.

UNIQUE VERSUS COMMON METHODS

The names of some of the methods defined in your applet may be unique to the applet. That is, some methods will serve a function very specific to your applet. For instance, if you were the author of the previously mentioned Tic-Tac-Toe applet, you'd write a method with a name such as `bestMove()`. The purpose of this method would be to determine where the computer should place an O in response to the placement of a user's X. It should be quite plain to see that very few other applets, if any, will need a `bestMove()` method.

Besides methods unique to your own applet's needs, your applet will include methods that perform actions common to most or all other applets. Consider this scenario: A surfer of the Web (who of course is using a Java-capable browser) comes to a Web page that holds the Tic-Tac-Toe applet. As the user's browser loads the Web page, the Tic-Tac-Toe board gets drawn to the page. Later, if the user drags the browser window off-screen, then back on, the applet again has to redraw the board. A similar case occurs for the MyFirstApplet applet. It initially draws a line of text to the Web page. If the window of the user's browser needs updating, this line of text is redrawn. In both applets you'll find a method named `paint()` that takes care of the drawing, or painting, of the applet's graphics to a Web page.

INHERITANCE OF METHODS

The key benefit of creating a subclass is *inheritance*. A subclass inherits all of the methods of the class on which it is based. The subclass can then call any of the inherited methods, just as if they were defined in the subclass itself. Inheritance is a powerful feature of object-oriented languages such as C++ and Java—and as such it is a topic thoroughly covered in the next couple of chapters.

If you haven't already guessed it, the `paint()` method is one of many methods that are inherited by a subclass of the `Applet` class. The class named `MyFirstApplet` is a subclass of the `Applet` class, so the `MyFirstApplet` class automatically has access to a method named `paint()`. Figure 3-5 shows that all of the methods available to the `Applet` class are also available to a class that extends the `Applet` class.

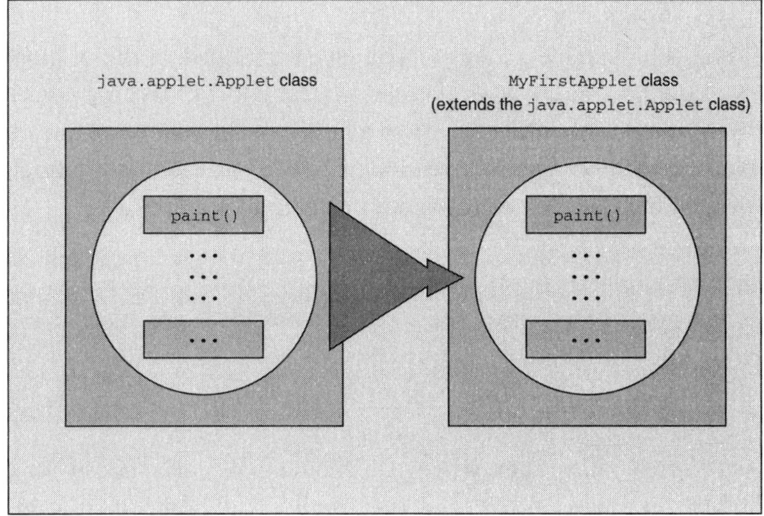

Figure 3-5

A class that extends another class gains access to all of the methods from the extended class.

OVERRIDING INHERITED METHODS

As just stated, a subclass can use an inherited method as if it were its own method. There's no need to define the method because it is defined in the class that is being extended. Yet the `MyFirstApplet` subclass *does* in fact redefine the `paint()` method as follows:

```
public void paint(Graphics g) {
    g.drawString("This applet simply draws text", 10, 20);
}
```

When a subclass chooses to redefine an inherited method, then it is said that the subclass is *overriding* the inherited method. The original version of the method then typically goes unused (we say "typically" because while an applet generally uses the version of the method that it defines, it is possible for the applet still to invoke the original version of the method).

Recall that the `Applet` class is one class in the `java.applet` package of classes. As a consequence, the `Applet` class can also be referred to as the `java.applet.Applet` class. As you've just seen, we'll simply be referring to this class as the `Applet` class.

When you override a method, you give up the use of the original inherited method and have to go through the effort of writing your own version of the method. These facts certainly beg the following question: If an inherited method is to be overridden, why even use that method in the first place? That question is answered in the next section.

CALLING METHODS

In the case of MyFirstApplet, it seems to make as much sense to simply write a new method, perhaps named `redrawText()`, as it does to override the `paint()` method. The reason you shouldn't do this can be found in the explanation of how a method is invoked.

As Figure 3-6 illustrates, when you create a class and then write a method that is a part of that class, that method can be invoked from a second method that is in the class. In C that's somewhat like a program that defines a `FunctionA()` and a `FunctionB()`, where `FunctionB()` makes a call to `FunctionA()`, as follows:

```
void FunctionA( void )
{
    ...
    ...
}

void FunctionB( void )
{
    FunctionA();
    ...
}
```

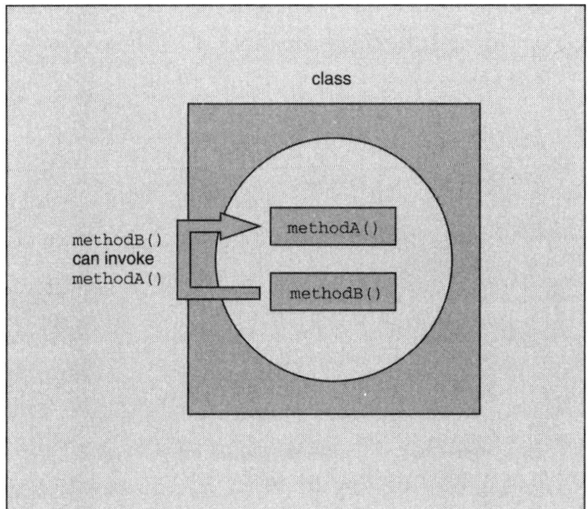

Figure 3-6
In Java, one method from a class can invoke another method from that same class.

Because a Java method is comparable to a C++ member function, the idea of a method invoking another method is the same as a situation in C++ where one class member function invokes another member function from the same class.

In Java, there's another way—a very common way—to invoke a method. The Java interpreter that is built into a Java-capable Web browser can itself make a call to an applet's method. The previous section described exactly such a scenario: a Java-capable browser that has a window that is currently displaying a Web page with an applet. When this window is moved off-screen, then back on, the applet is redrawn. What's happening here is that the Java interpreter in the Web browser is invoking the applet's `paint()` method.

When an applet needs updating, the interpreter *always* attempts to call the applet's `paint()` method. If you choose to implement your own drawing method—one with a name other than `paint()`—the interpreter will be unable to properly update your applet. This should make perfect sense to you: there's no way for the interpreter, which was written long before your applet was written, to know where your applet's update code is if you chose to place it in a routine other than `paint()`.

A little earlier you read about the object-oriented concepts of inheritance of methods and overriding inherited methods. On those pages you learned that when a class is defined to be a subclass of another class, the subclass inherits the methods of the *base* class—the class on which the subclass is based. You also learned that an inherited method can be overridden. That is, a method can be rewritten, or redefined. The applet repainting example we've been using provides a good example of the point of overriding a method. When a Java interpreter needs to update an applet, it always looks to a method named `paint()`. So a `paint()` method *must* be defined. To satisfy this requirement, the `Applet` class (the `java.applet.Applet` class) has such a method. Here's how the `Applet` class defines the `paint()` method:

```
public void paint(Graphics g) {

}
```

That's right. The `paint()` method that your applet inherits from the `Applet` class is an empty method. No single updating feature is guaranteed to be common to all applets, so there's no point in including any code in the `Applet` version of the `paint()` method: it's assumed each applet will override this method.

By including an empty `paint()` method in the `Applet` class—a class that your applet must subclass—the Java language ensures that your applet won't freeze in response to the interpreter's attempt to update it. Consider what would happen if, in the preliminary stages of your applet's development, you didn't include a `paint()` method, and then compiled and tested the applet. If you tested the applet by using your Java-capable browser to open an HTML file that included the applet, then moved the browser window off-screen and back on to force an update, what would happen? As shown in Figure 3-7, the interpreter first looks to your applet's code to see if a `paint()` method is defined. Failing to find one explicitly defined by your main class, the interpreter uses the `paint()` method inherited from the `Applet` class. While this empty `paint()` method doesn't do any drawing, the execution of the method does satisfy the Java interpreter.

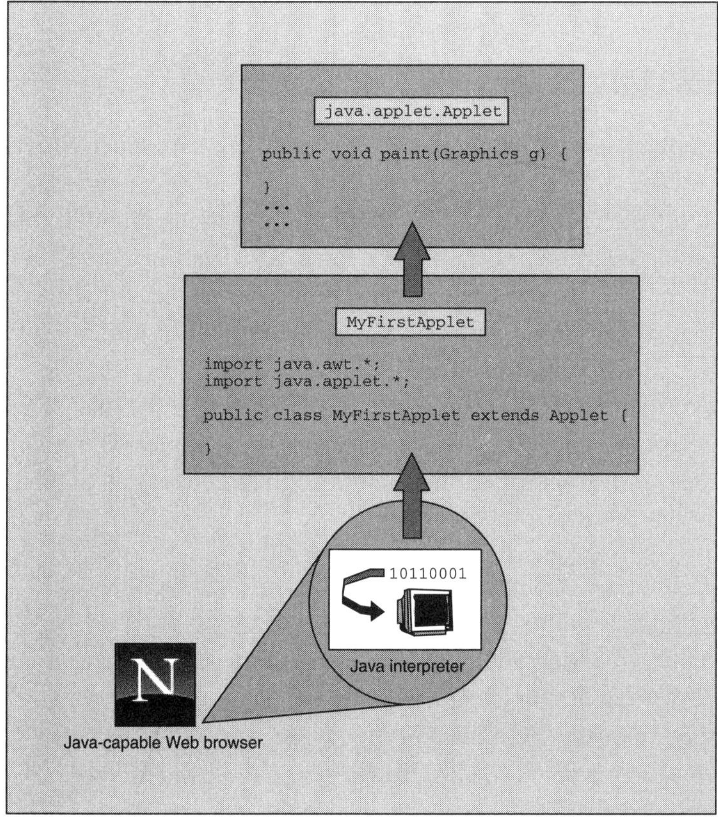

Figure 3-7

If an applet doesn't override the inherited paint() method, a Java interpreter uses the paint() method from the base class.

Incorporating Graphics into the Sample Applet

MyFirstApplet merely writes a single line of text to the browser that displays the applet. So it might not seem that much can be said about Java graphics when we discuss this example applet. In fact, MyFirstApplet *does* demonstrate several elements of Java graphics—as you'll see in this section.

The Graphics class

To add graphics to your applet you'll rely on the Java Abstract Window Toolkit (AWT). The AWT is a set of graphical user interface classes contained in the `java.awt` package. The numerous methods found in these classes enable you to work with color, fonts, text, buttons, scroll bars, dialog boxes, and a host of other graphical components—all without regard for the type of system on which you're programming or for the types of systems on which your applet eventually appears.

The `java.awt.Graphics` class is one of the classes in the AWT. The `Graphics` class provides a means for supplying your applet with a device-independent interface. Your applet will recognize references to this class if you use the following `import` statement:

```
import java.awt.Graphics;
```

It's more likely that you'll give your applet the capability to reference all of the AWT classes by using the following, more general, `import` statement—the same statement used in the MyFirstApplet applet:

```
import java.awt.*;
```

GRAPHICS OBJECTS AND THE WEB BROWSER

Any time your applet draws, it draws to an object of the `Graphics` class type. If you're a C++ programmer, you know that a class serves as a template, or pattern, for creating objects. If you're a C programmer, this concept will make more sense when you read all about classes and objects in Chapter 4.

When a Java-capable browser encounters a Web page that holds an applet, the browser automatically creates a `Graphics` object for the applet. This object serves as a sort of palette to which applet drawing is directed. When the Web page needs updating, the browser passes the `Graphics` object to the applet's `paint()` method. That explains why the `paint()` method is always defined with a single argument:

```
public void paint(Graphics g) {
    // draw the applet here
}
```

USING A METHOD FROM THE GRAPHICS CLASS

The `Graphics` class consists of a few dozen methods. You've already worked with one of these—the `drawString()` method. This method draws a single line of text to an object of the `Graphics` class type. Because it's possible to create an applet that uses more than one `Graphics` object, you need to tell `drawString()` which object it will be drawing to. To use any of the `Graphics` methods, you first name the `Graphics` object, then follow that name with a period and the name of the method:

```
g.drawString("This applet simply draws text", 10, 20);
```

As you saw with the `paint()` method, Java methods, like C functions and C++ member functions, can have arguments. The `drawString()` method has three. The first is the string of text to draw, while the second and third specify the string's starting location within the `Graphics` object. Chapter 9 has more to say about the coordinate system used to establish where strings, shapes, and images are drawn. For now, we'll just mention that the above call to drawString() uses the second and third argument values to specify that the string starts 10 pixels in from the left of the Graphics object and 20 pixels down from the top of the object.

Throughout this book you'll see plenty of examples of the use of the paint() and drawString() methods. Many applets will *define* a paint() method—a method inherited by the applet's main class from the java.awt.Applet class and overridden by the applet's main class. And many of these paint() methods will *invoke* the drawString() method—a method of the Graphics class, accessible to all Graphics objects—including the Graphics object passed to the paint() method by the browser. For example, the sample applet explained in this chapter includes a paint() method that invokes the drawString() method. Here's a last look at the paint() method defined in MyFirstApplet:

```
public void paint(Graphics g) {
    g.drawString("This applet simply draws text", 10, 20);
}
```

What You've Learned

Java has become very popular very quickly due to a number of the language's features. Java is all of the following:

- Java is simple: Think of it as a stripped down version of C++.
- Java is an object-oriented language: So it passes on the benefits of any object language—a tight relationship between data and the functions that operate on that data, and code reusability.
- Java is distributed: It supports networked applications.
- Java is interpreted: An applet's code can be executed on any operating system that has a Java interpreter resident on it.
- Java is secure: Safeguards are built into the language so that an applet's code cannot damage data on a user's computer.
- Java is architecture-neutral: One source code file generates one applet file that can execute on several types of machines.

- Java is portable: It contains no operating-system-dependent code.
- Finally, Java is multithreaded: An applet can perform more than one task at one time.

The source code for Java applets contains many similarities. A Java source code file begins by importing one or more packages—libraries of classes that can be used to handle many of the tasks an applet needs to perform. The code that makes up any applet exists in its own class. Within this class are any number of instance variables that hold data that are of use to the applet. This class also holds any number of methods, or functions, that perform whatever it is the applet was designed to do.

CHAPTER 4

OOP Basics for C Programmers

Java is an object-oriented programming (OOP) language. This chapter introduces object-oriented programming techniques in general terms, with comparisons to analogous C concepts where applicable. Here you'll also find discussions of OOP principles that are specific to Java.

C programmers often know very little about object-oriented programming. If you've dabbled in C++ programming but don't feel completely at ease with it, you probably don't feel comfortable with OOP either. If either of these descriptions fits you, then you'll want to pay careful attention to the concepts presented in this chapter. After reading this chapter, you'll be up to speed on OOP in general and Java in particular. That means you can skip Chapter 5—it's written for programmers familiar with C++. If you are already well-versed in C++, you can skim the present chapter or jump right into Chapter 5.

Review of C's Struct Keyword

As a C programmer, you should be familiar with the practice of storing data in structures: You use the C `struct` keyword for that purpose. The Java language replaces the `struct` keyword with `class`—a keyword that enables the creation of data types similar to those created using the `struct` keyword. Java classes, however, are a little more complex and far more powerful than C structures. If you're completely comfortable with the use of the `struct` keyword, you're ready to take a look at the Java `class` keyword. If you haven't used the `struct` keyword in a while, read this section to get a refresher on its use. When you get your first exposure to the Java `class` keyword, you'll appreciate having a full understanding of the simpler C structure.

KNOWING WHEN TO USE THE STRUCT KEYWORD

If your C program must store information about several similar items, you'll want to keep this information in records using the `struct` keyword. The traditional example is that of a program designed to keep track of employee information. Without the use of the `struct` keyword, you would have to declare separate variables for each item that the C program must keep track of—items such as the name and salary of an employee.

Rather than use this disjointed approach of declaring separate variables that have no apparent relationship, C enables you to define a single `struct` that itself consists of several items. This one `struct` can be defined to hold both name and salary data for an employee. The true advantage of the `struct` keyword is found in the capability of your program to declare any number of structure variables—all based on the one `struct` definition. Figure 4-1 provides a general look at how the `struct` keyword enables you to better organize a program's data.

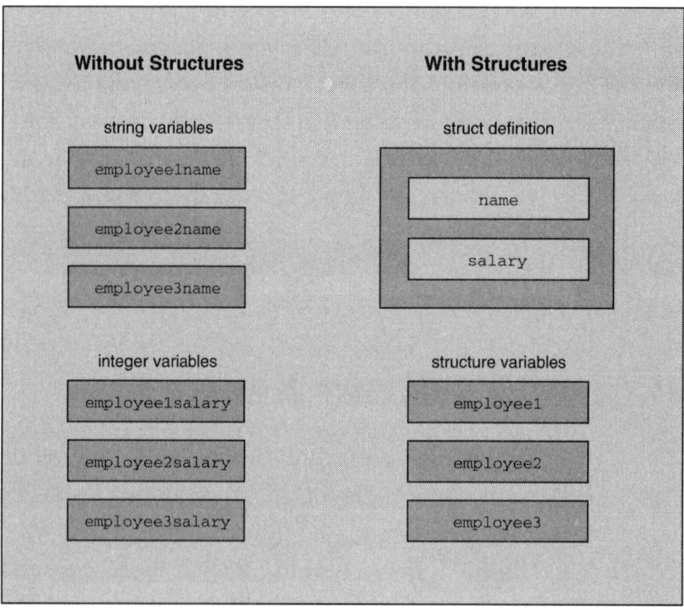

Figure 4-1

A C program that uses structures can better organize related data.

The abundance of variables in a C program without structures can be alleviated somewhat by using arrays. For example, each element in a single array can hold an employee name. The problem remains, however, of having no obvious correlation between related data. The program would still need separate arrays for each data item category—an array of strings to keep track of all of the names and an array of integers to keep track of all of the salaries. In the structure example, a single array could be defined to hold any number of employee structures.

Defining a structure

Rather than continue with the mundane employee example, in this section we'll consider a computer game, written in C, that has any number of aliens that will be attacking the player-controlled hero. We'll call it "Plutoskeet" for two of the four alien types who will lurk in its deep-C depths. As new aliens appear on the screen, they will each be given two attributes, or traits. In this simple game, each alien will have an attribute that relates to its strength. The strength attribute is represented by a number from 1 through 10. Each alien will also have a second attribute—the number of lives it has. This characteristic of the alien will also be represented by a value in the range of 1 through 10. On the following pages you'll see how to define and work with a `struct` that is modeled on this game.

A structure is used to package together any number of *members*. Each member is declared just as any C variable is declared. The following is an example of a structure that could be used to hold information about a single alien in the Plutoskeet game:

```
struct Alien {
    int      strength;
    int      lives;
};
```

A *structure template* defines one particular structure. As just shown, a template consists of six key elements, in the following order:

- The C keyword `struct`
- The structure template's *name*, or *tag*

- An opening brace
- Any number of structure members
- A closing brace
- A semicolon

Figure 4-2 shows one way of picturing the `Alien` structure.

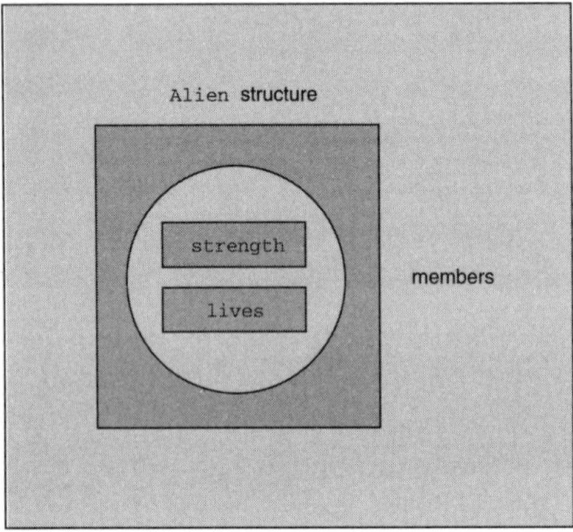

Figure 4-2
A C structure consists of members.

CREATING A STRUCTURE

A structure template defines the format of a structure, but it doesn't actually create any structures that can be used to store program data. To do that, you need to declare one or more variables of the new structure type. The following snippet defines a `struct` named `Alien`, then declares three variables—each of the `Alien` structure type:

```
struct Alien {
     int       strength;
     int       lives;
};

Alien martianAlien;
Alien superAlien;
Alien weakAlien;
```

Because these three declarations all use the `Alien` structure as their data type, each of the three structure variables will consist of a `strength` member and a `lives` member. Figure 4-3 carries on with the idea of equating a structure definition with a template by showing how the `Alien` structure can be used as a sort of pattern from which three `Alien` structure variables have been created.

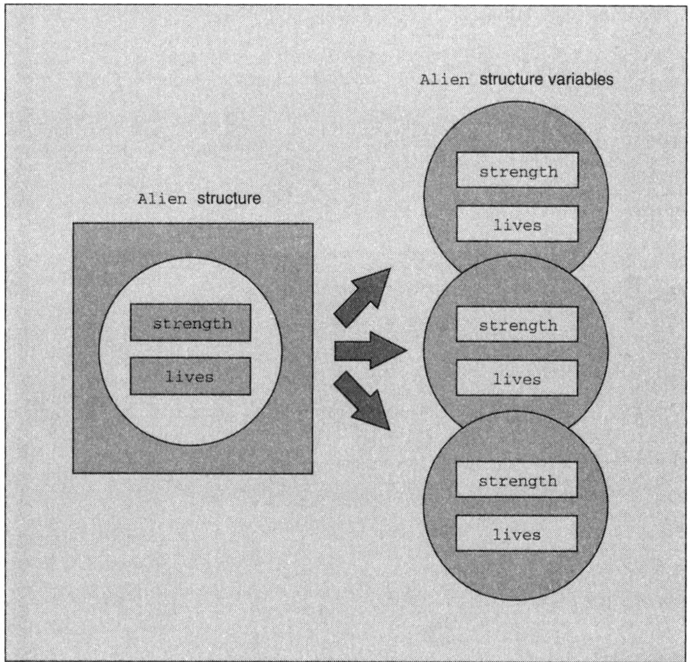

Figure 4-3
A struct is used as a template from which any number of structures are created.

ASSIGNING VALUES TO STRUCTURE MEMBERS

Each member of a variable based on a `struct` has its own value. You assign any one member a value by using the structure member operator (a period) between the structure variable name and the member name. The following snippet assigns a value of 3 to the `lives` member of an `Alien` structure variable named `martianAlien`. For reference, the `Alien` structure template is repeated here. Figure 4-4 shows how this snippet assigns a value to only the second member of the `Alien` structure variable.

```
struct Alien {
    int       strength;
    int       lives;
};

Alien  martianAlien;

martianAlien.lives = 3;
```

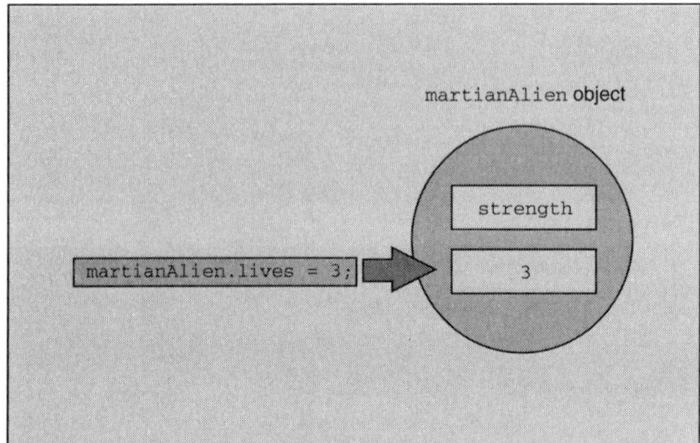

Figure 4-4
Each C structure member has a value.

USING STRUCTURE MEMBERS

Because a structure member acts as a variable, your C program is free to use the member as it would use any variable of that same type. For instance, because the `lives` member of the `Alien` structure is an `int`, it can be used in any operation that requires an integer. In this next snippet the `lives` member of an `Alien` structure named `martianAlien` is first assigned a value of 3 and then, later in the program, incremented by 2:

```
struct Alien {
    int       strength;
    int       lives;
```

```
};

Alien martianAlien;

martianAlien.lives = 3;
...
...
martianAlien.lives += 2;
```

USING FUNCTIONS TO ACCESS STRUCTURE MEMBERS

If your C program declares only one structure variable, assignment to the structure variable members is straightforward:

```
Alien martianAlien;

martianAlien.strength = 8;
martianAlien.lives = 3;
```

If your program declares several structure variable of the same type, it makes more sense to write one function that can be used to handle member assignments for each structure variable:

```
void EnterAlienInfo( Alien *theStruct, int theStrength, int theLives
    )
{
    theStruct->strength = theStrength;
    theStruct->lives = theLives;
}
```

The `EnterAlienInfo()` function has three arguments. The first is a pointer to the `Alien` structure variable. A pointer to the structure (rather than the structure itself) is passed to the function so that any changes made to the structure by the function are retained after `EnterAlienInfo()` ends. As shown in this routine, to access a member of a structure referenced by a pointer, use the membership access operator—a hyphen followed by a greater-than sign (`->`). The second and third arguments are the values that are to be assigned to the structure referenced in the first argument.

The following snippet declares two `Alien` structure variables, then uses the `EnterAlienInfo()` function to assign values to the members of both structure variables:

```
Alien  martianAlien;
Alien  plutonian;

EnterAlienInfo( &martianAlien, 5, 3 );
EnterAlienInfo( &plutonian, 9, 2 );
```

Introduction to Java's Class Keyword

The Java language doesn't have a `struct` keyword. Instead, you organize data in your Java applets using the more powerful Java `class` keyword.

Knowing when to use the class keyword

In the example of the C program that keeps track of employee information, you saw how a program that uses the `struct` keyword can provide better organization of data than a program that foregoes structures. As you'll see in this section, the Java classes provide still more organizational power than the C structures.

In the example of the computer game, you saw that it's wise to define functions that operate on the members of a structure. You write one function to avoid having to repeat the same block of code throughout your source code. The purpose of the Java `class` is to take the usefulness of this member/function relationship one step further. Where a structure consists of *data* only , a class consists of *data and functions* that operate on the data.

Defining a class

Like a C structure, a Java `class` is used to group together any number of data items. In a structure, one data item is referred to as simply a *member* of the structure. In a `class`, a data item is referred to as an *instance vari-*

able. Again, like the structure, an individual data item in a `class` is treated as a variable; each instance variable can be of any Java data type. As you'll see in the chapter that discusses the Java language (Chapter 7), many of the Java primitive data types are common to those defined in C. Some examples are the `short`, `int`, `long`, and `float`. The following Java `class` template is an example of a `class` that could be used to hold the same alien information used in this chapter's C `struct` examples:

```
class Alien {

    int       strength;
    int       lives;

    void      enterAlienInfo(int theStrength, int theLives) {
        strength = theStrength;
        lives = theLives;
    }
}
```

In this example you can see that two primary elements differentiate the `Alien class` template and the `Alien struct` template. The first is that, in a class, the keyword `class` is used in place of the keyword `struct`. The second difference is that, in a class, both data and functions are defined. In Java, functions are referred to as *methods*.

A class template defines one particular class. The following list, along with Figure 4-5, summarizes the elements of a class:

- The Java keyword `class`
- The class template's *name*
- An opening brace
- One or more class instance variables
- One or more methods
- A closing brace

Java naming conventions dictate that a `class` name begin with an uppercase character (as in the `Alien class`), while instance variables and methods begin with a lowercase character (as in `strength` and `enterAlienInfo()`).

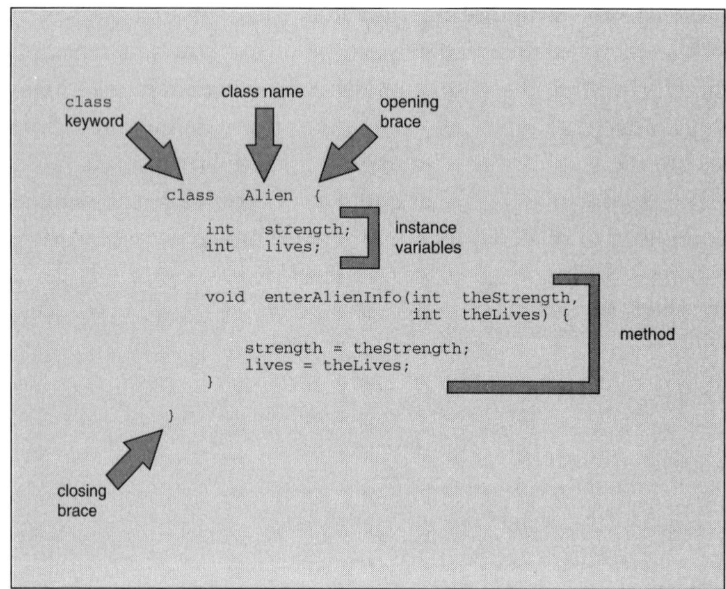

Figure 4-5
These are the elements that make up a class definition.

Figure 4-6 shows a `class` using a model similar to the one used earlier in this chapter for visualizing a `struct`.

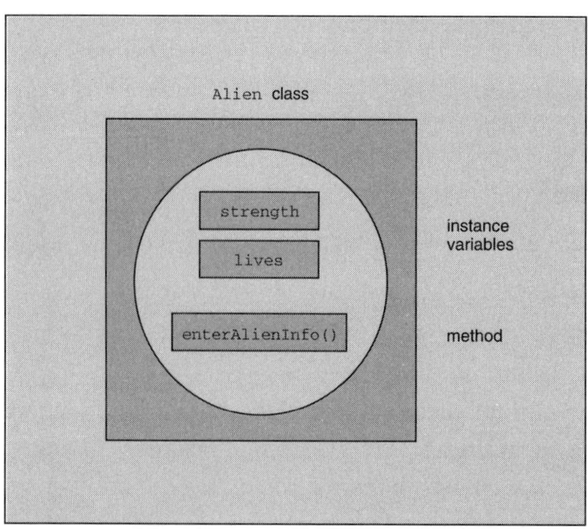

Figure 4-6
A Java class consists of instance variables and methods.

Comparison of C Structures and Java Classes

In the C version of the Plutoskeet computer game example, we defined an `Alien` structure template with two members. This structure then relied on the application-defined function `EnterAlienInfo()` to assign values to its members. You've just seen that to achieve the same results in Java, you would define a `class` template that consists of both instance variables and methods.

A Java `class` instance variable is analogous to a C `struct` data member. A Java `class` method serves a similar purpose as a C function that operates on data members of a C `struct`. However, because nothing specifically ties a C function to a particular C `struct` (as a method *is* bound to a particular `class`), the comparison of a C function to a Java `class` method is a weak one.

Just as a C `struct` can have as few or as many data members as is necessary to define the data for the `struct`, so too can a Java `class` have any number of instance variables to define the data for the `class`. And just as a C program can define as many functions as necessary to operate on the data members of a `struct`, so too can a Java `class` define any number of methods.

Figure 4-7 shows that the primary difference between a `class` and a structure is that in the `class`, the functions "belong" to the `class`. In the structure, no direct correlation exists between the structure and the functions that the structure uses. We'll have a lot more to say about instance variables, methods, and the exact syntax of a `class` definition in Chapter 7. In Chapter 7, we'll examine why it's beneficial to bind functions and data into one entity—the way a `class` definition does.

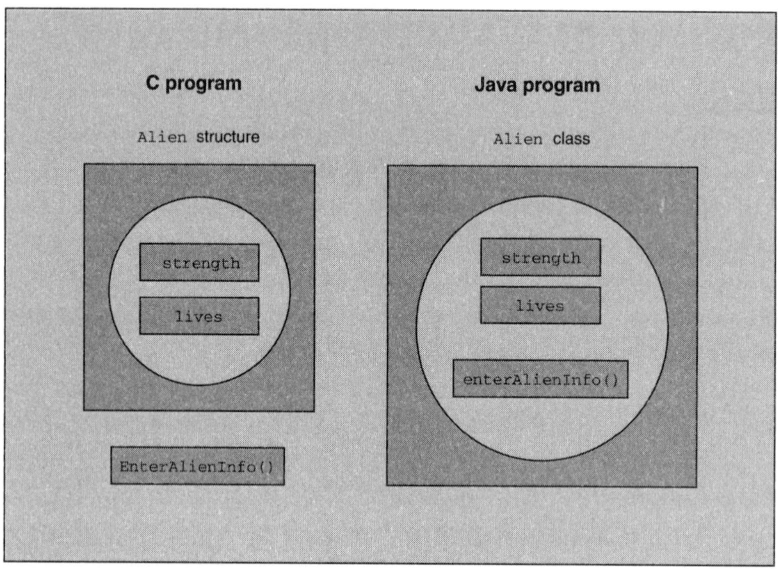

Figure 4-7
A C struct consists of data; a Java class consists of both data and functions.

Java Objects

In C, a `struct` definition is followed by the declaration of one or more structure variables. In Java, a `class` definition is followed by the declaration of one or more class variables. A `class` variable is said to hold one *object* (or one *instance*) of a class. The terms *object* and *instance* can be used interchangeably. A `class` is used to "stamp out" objects, just as a structure is used to "stamp out" structure variables. Figure 4-8 illustrates a single `class` definition being used as the basis for the creation of three objects.

Because a `class` variable consists of both data and functions, it is capable of *representing* much more than a typical variable. A `class` variable can be thought of as a *model* of something. In our example, an `Alien` object models, of course, an alien.

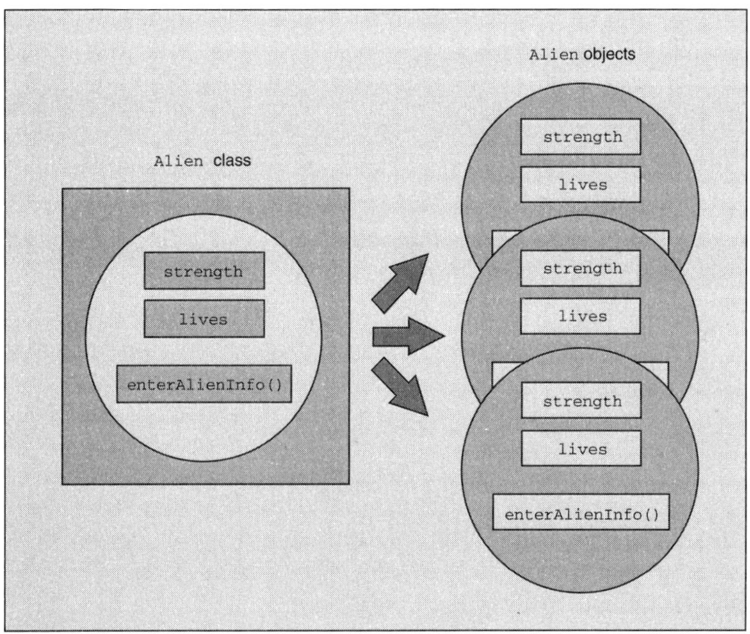

Figure 4-8
A Java class is used as a template from which any number of objects can be generated.

An instance of a `class` is called an *object* because, like a real-world object, it has both attributes and behaviors. *Attributes* describe characteristics of what is being modeled; *behaviors* describe what this thing being modeled is capable of doing. An object's instance variables are used to define the attributes of that object, while an object's methods define that object's behavior. Relating this explanation to the `Alien` `class`, you can see that an `Alien` object's attributes are its strength and its number of lives. In this simple example an `Alien` object's behavior is its capability to take on different strengths and change the number of lives it has.

CREATING AN OBJECT

In C, a `struct` definition alone doesn't allocate any memory. To do that, you create a structure. Declaring a variable of a `struct` type takes care of that. After the following code snippet executes, memory is allocated for one `Alien` structure:

```
struct Alien {
    int       strength;
    int       lives;
};

Alien  martianAlien;
```

In Java, the process begins the same way—you define a `class`, and then you declare a variable of that `class` type as follows:

```
class Alien {

    int       strength;
    int       lives;

    void      enterAlienInfo(int theStrength, int theLives) {
        strength = theStrength;
        lives = theLives;
    }
}

Alien plutonian;
```

At this point the process diverges from C. Here, Java is a little more complex—though not terribly. In Java, the declaration of a `class` variable *doesn't* allocate any memory. Instead, memory is allocated dynamically—at some point during the execution of the applet. A `class` variable can eventually hold an object, but at the time of its declaration it *doesn't*. To create an object, you use the Java `new` keyword:

```
Alien plutonian;              // declare a variable of type Alien

plutonian = new Alien();      // create an Alien object
```

As you can see in this snippet, the `new` keyword is followed by a `class` type, which in turn is followed by a pair of parentheses. The `class` type followed by parentheses might give the impression that a function is being called. In fact, that is exactly the case.

CONSTRUCTOR METHODS

A constructor is a special kind of method that is used to implement initialization code. Each time an object of a `class` is created, a constructor method is invoked. Use of the `new` keyword automatically triggers the execution of a constructor method. Every `class` has at least one constructor method.

DEFAULT CONSTRUCTORS

Every time you define a `class`, Java defines a constructor for that `class`–you don't have to include a constructor as a part of your `class` definition. So, while the `Alien class` doesn't explicitly list a constructor method, implicitly one is defined. Here's the constructor method that Java defines for the `Alien class`:

```
Alien() {

}
```

Figure 4-9 emphasizes the idea that while the listing of the `Alien class` shows no `Alien()` method, such a method is a part of the `Alien class`.

Remember that Java naming conventions dictate that method names begin with a lowercase character. Constructors are an exception to this convention. Because a constructor *must* have the same name as a `class` (which always begins with an uppercase character), a constructor begins with an uppercase character.

As you can see from the preceding listing, the body of the `Alien()` method is empty, so this constructor doesn't do anything. As you'll see just ahead, though, this situation can be remedied easily. When you define a `class`, Java enables you to define your own constructor for that `class`. While the default constructor that Java has defined for you has no parameters and performs no action, your own constructor can have parameters and will perform some initialization task.

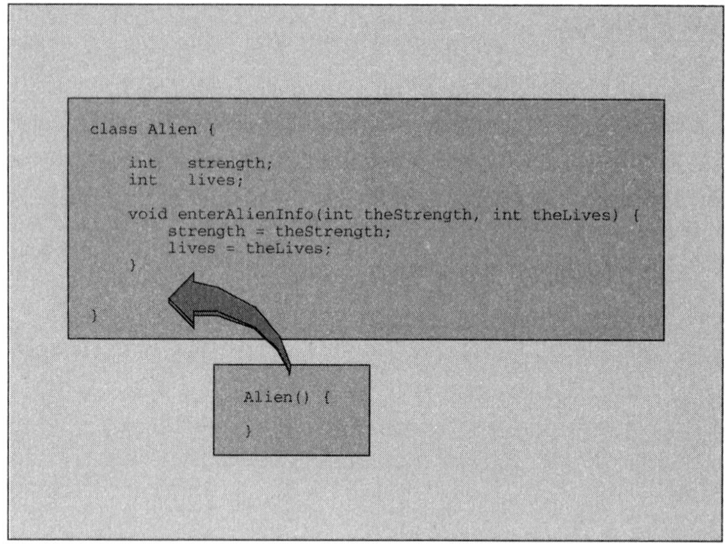

Figure 4-9
Every class has an implied constructor method, defined by Java.

CHARACTERISTICS OF CONSTRUCTOR METHODS

A constructor method always has the traits shown in the following list. A constructor:

- Has the same name as the `class` it belongs to
- Has no return type
- Can have any number of parameters, including none

The earlier definition of the `Alien()` method shows that this constructor follows the points in the preceding list: It has the same name as the `class` (`Alien`), has no return type associated with it, and has no parameters.

CONSTRUCTORS AND THE NEW OPERATOR

With a knowledge of constructors, more light shines on what is going on when you use the `new` keyword. Here's another look at `new`:

```
Alien  plutonian;             // declare a variable of type Alien

plutonian = new Alien();      // create an Alien object
```

This code should now make more sense to you. The `new` operator creates a new object. Here the object is of the `Alien class`. The `new` operator then invokes the object's constructor. Here the `Alien` object's constructor has no parameters.

AN EXAMPLE OF A CONSTRUCTOR

A constructor's purpose is to handle any initialization tasks that are warranted for new objects of a particular `class` type. For the `Alien class` it might be a good idea to provide each of the two instance variables of a new `Alien` object with some initial value. If somewhere in the applet we create an `Alien` object and inadvertently fail to call `EnterAlienInfo()`, at least the object will have attributes of *some* kind. Here's how such a constructor would appear:

```
Alien() {
     strength = 1;
     lives = 1;
}
```

Earlier you saw that when you define a `class`, a constructor is implicitly defined for you. It is this constructor that executes when a new object is created—*if* you haven't defined your own `class` constructor. If you do define your own constructor, it is your constructor that now automatically gets invoked.

The following snippet shows a version of the `Alien class` that includes our new constructor. The snippet also shows that this constructor method is the one that gets invoked when the new `Alien` object is created.

```
class  Alien {

     int      strength;
     int      lives;
```

```
    void enterAlienInfo(int theStrength, int theLives) {
        strength = theStrength;
        lives = theLives;
    }

    Alien() {
        strength = 1;
        lives = 1;
    }
}

Alien plutonian;

plutonian = new Alien();  // this line executes our constructor
```

METHOD OVERLOADING

Method overloading is a feature of Java that enables a `class` to define any number of methods that each share the same name. While your first thought may be that this supposed feature would do nothing but add confusion to a source code listing, closer examination reveals that it can be of great use.

First, how is it that one `class` can contain two or more identically named methods without generating a compile-time error? The answer is that as long as any one or more of the following characteristics differ, the Java compiler can tell the methods apart:

- Number of arguments
- Argument types
- Argument ordering

As an example, consider the following methods—each with the name `addToList()`. For brevity, we've only provided the method declaration; assume that each method has the task of adding an argument or arguments to a list and, perhaps, returning a Boolean value that tells if the list is now full or not. Because something about each method differs from each of the other methods, a `class` could define all four methods.

```
void addToList( int itemToAdd )
void addToList( float itemToAdd )
boolean addToList( float item1, int item2 )
boolean addToList( int item1, float item2 )
```

While method overloading works for any methods, it is a particularly useful tool where constructors are involved. The first version of the `Alien` constructor sets each of the two instance variables to 1 in a new object. This second version of the `Alien` constructor enables you to specify the values to which these two instance variables should be initialized:

```
Alien( int initialStrength, int initialLives ) {
    strength = initialStrength;
    lives = initialLives;
}
```

The first version of the `Alien` constructor has no arguments, while this new version has two. This difference is enough to satisfy the Java compiler.

We'll end the discussion of constructors with yet another version of the `Alien class`. Also included in this next snippet is a call to each of the two versions of the `Alien` constructor. After the following code executes, two new `Alien` objects will exist. The object named ***plutonian*** will have a `strength` value of 1 and a `lives` value of 1, while the object named ***drakonian*** will have a `strength` value of 7 and a `lives` value of 4.

```
class  Alien {

    int       strength;
    int       lives;

    void enterAlienInfo(int theStrength, int theLives) {
        strength = theStrength;
        lives = theLives;
    }

    Alien() {
        strength = 1;
        lives = 1;
    }

    Alien( int initialStrength, int initialLives ) {
        strength = initialStrength;
        lives = initialLives;
    }
}

Alien  plutonian;
Alien  drakonian;
```

```
plutonian = new Alien();
drakonian = new Alien( 7, 4 );
```

The remaining examples in this chapter will use an `Alien class` that doesn't define any constructors. Again, brevity wins out. Now that you know all about constructors, there's no need to add the extra code to each version of the `Alien class` that we develop.

INSTANCE VARIABLES

For C structure variables you saw that assigning a value to a structure member was accomplished using the structure member operator (.). The following example is one with which you're familiar; it uses a structure variable of type `Alien`:

```
struct Alien {
    int      strength;
    int      lives;
};

Alien  martianAlien;

martianAlien.lives = 3;
```

Java uses a similar approach in assigning a value to a `class` instance variable. To make such an assignment to an object's instance variable you first name the object, then follow the object name with a dot (.). Finally, name the instance variable that is to be altered:

```
plutonian.lives = 3;
```

Both C and Java use a dot, or period, in field assignments. In C, the dot is considered an operator—it's the structure member operator. In Java, this field accessor isn't considered an operator. Instead, it's called *dot notation*, or simply *dot*.

Now, a look at the previous line of Java code in the context of a more comprehensive snippet:

```
class Alien {

    int       strength;
    int       lives;

    void      enterAlienInfo(int theStrength, int theLives) {
        strength = theStrength;
        lives = theLives;
    }
}

Alien  plutonian;

plutonian = new Alien();

plutonian.lives = 3;
```

Once given a value, a Java instance variable can be used with other Java variables and Java operators—just as C structure members can be. For example, the `lives` instance variable of the plutonian `Alien` object could be used in a Java statement such as this one:

```
int totalLives;

// totalLives accumulates some value

totalLives += plutonian.lives;
```

In the preceding snippet it is assumed the total lives of all aliens present in a game are stored in an integer variable named `totalLives`. To add the lives of the plutonian alien to this total, the value of the `lives` instance variable is simply added to the value of the `totalLives` variable.

As an aside, the use of the Java += operator in the preceding snippet provides you with a hint as to the type of operators you'll be using in Java. When you read about the fundamentals of the Java language in Chapter 6, you're knowledge of the C language will make you feel right at home.

METHODS

Using dot notation with an object and one of its instance variable is one of two ways of assigning a value to an instance variable. A more indirect way of accomplishing the same task is to perform the assignment from within a method. Assigning a value to an instance variable through a method involves some extra work on your part, but it's effort well spent. Relying on only methods to access instance variables enables a `class` to better hide, or encapsulate, its data.

Object-oriented languages often refer to data hiding, or encapsulation. The purpose of creating an object is to *encapsulate* a set of attributes and behaviors into a single entity. In doing so, the object's attributes—its data—get hidden from "the rest of the world." Keeping an object's data private is advisable: It keeps the object self-contained and prevents accidental modification of the data by other code in the applet. You'll read more about data hiding in Chapter 7.

SETTING THE VALUE OF AN INSTANCE VARIABLE

The `enterAlienInfo()` method from the `Alien class` assigns a value to both the `strength` and `lives` instance variables:

```
void enterAlienInfo(int theStrength, int theLives) {
    strength = theStrength;
    lives = theLives;
}
```

In the preceding method you can see that the two assignments are made with no mention of the object that is to be acted upon. No object is passed to the method, and no object name or dot notation is used in conjunction with the instance variable names. This method definition, which is a part of the `Alien class`, refers to `Alien class` instance variables but does not refer to any particular `Alien` object. Recall that a `class` definition itself is not an object; it is analogous to a data type. From a data type, any number of variables are declared. Each `class` variable, or object, is allocated its own storage for its own set of instance variables. And each object will be capable of invoking the `enterAlienInfo()` method to act on its own set of instance variables.

INVOKING A METHOD

For an object to call a method, the dot is used. To the left of the dot is the object's name; to the right is the name of the method to invoke. While the object and dot parts of the method invocation are new to C programmers, the syntax of invoking a method isn't; it's identical to that used to call a C function. Following the object name and dot is the method name. The method name is followed by parentheses, between which are any arguments required by the method. The following line of code invokes the `enterAlienInfo()` method from an `Alien` object named `plutonian`. Assume that prior to this line of code an `Alien` variable was declared and an object created:

```
plutonian.enterAlienInfo( 3, 5 );
```

The result of executing the preceding code is that the `strength` instance variable of the `plutonian` object will have a value of 3, while the `lives` instance variable of this same object will have a value of 5.

OBJECTS, METHODS, AND INSTANCE VARIABLES

Understanding how method invocation and instance variable assignments relate to objects is an important part of understanding object-oriented programming. As such, this topic warrants further study.

From one `class` definition any number of objects can be created. Figure 4-10 illustrates this concept by showing that two `Alien` objects are created by the following snippet:

```
Alien  plutonian;
Alien  drakonian;

plutonian = new Alien();
drakonian = new Alien();
```

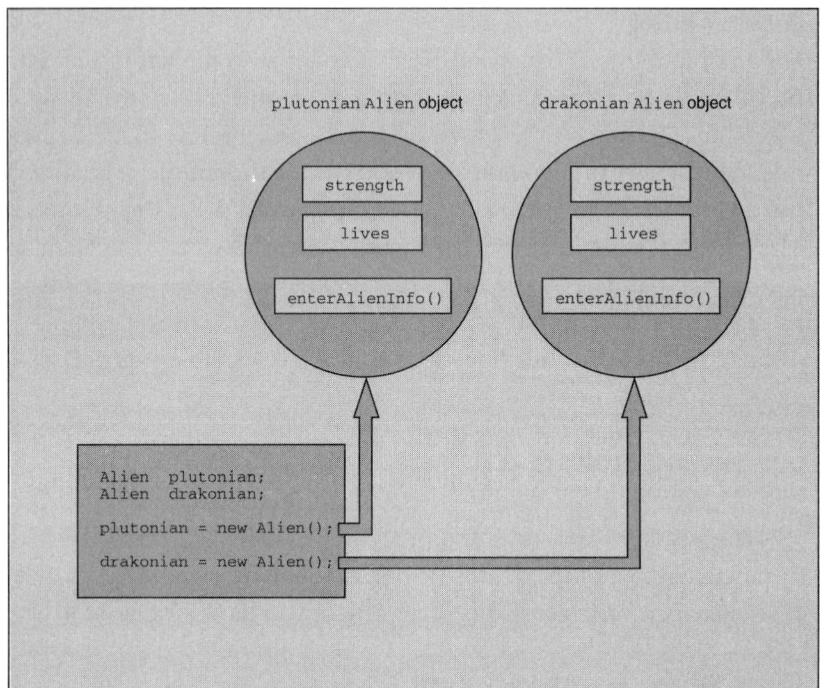

Figure 4-10
One class, such as the Alien class, is used to create any number of objects.

When a method call is made, the object upon which the method is to act *must* be included. Doing so tells the method which instance variables should be affected. For example, the `enterAlienInfo()` method can be used by any `Alien` object. The `enterAlienInfo()` method makes assignments to the appropriate pair of instance variables because the object to be affected is named along with the call to the method. Here the `enterAlienInfo()` method is being used to assign values to the instance variables in the two previously created `Alien` objects. Figure 4-11 illustrates the effect of this code on the two objects.

```
plutonian.enterAlienInfo( 3, 5 );
drakonian.enterAlienInfo( 7, 1 );
```

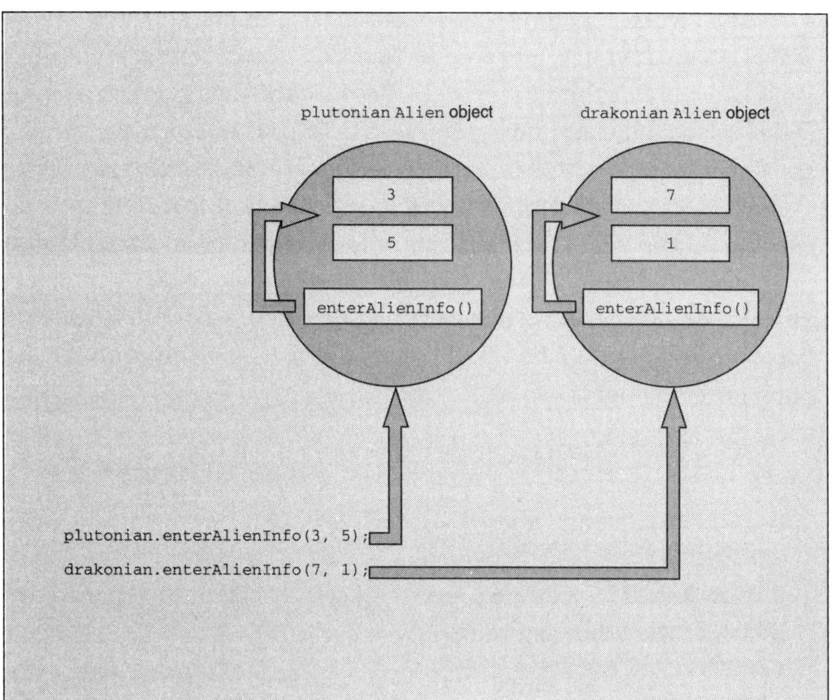

Figure 4-11
Each object can use the same method to assign values to its own instance variables.

GETTING THE VALUE OF AN INSTANCE VARIABLE

Knowing that a method can be used to set the value of an instance variable should have led you to guess that a method can also be used to get the value of the same variable. The one method that you've seen, `enterAlienInfo()`, has a return type of `void`. Methods, like C functions, can have a return type other than `void`. Consider the following method:

```
int getStrength() {
    return strength;
}
```

You already know that the `int` is a valid Java data type, so it's no surprise that a Java method can return a value of type `int`. You now know that a method, to return a value, uses a `return` statement in the exact same way that a C function can.

You invoke a method that returns a value in the same way that you invoke a method that sets a value: Name an object to the left of the dot and name the method to the right. Because the method returns a value, you'll place the entire invocation to the right of an equal sign. To the left of the equal sign will be the variable that is to be assigned the returned value. Again, the similarities to calling a C function that returns a value should be apparent. The following snippet provides an example of using a method that returns a value. Here you should assume an `Alien` object named `plutonian` has been declared and created. Also assume that the object's instance variables have been assigned values prior to the execution of this snippet:

```
int currentStrength;

currentStrength = plutonian.getStrength();
```

Now take a look at the preceding method call in the context of some Java code. The following snippet:

- Defines a new version of the `Alien class`
- Creates an object of this `class` type
- Assigns a value to the object's two instance variables
- Invokes the object's `getStrength()` method to get the value of the `strength` instance variable and assign that value to a variable unrelated to the object

The result of executing the following snippet will be that variable `currentStrength` has a value of 4—the value previously assigned to the `strength` instance variable.

```
class Alien {

    int      strength;
    int      lives;

    void enterAlienInfo(int theStrength, int theLives) {
        strength = theStrength;
        lives = theLives;
    }
```

```
    int getStrength() {
        return strength;
    }
}

Alien plutonian;
int   currentStrength;

plutonian = new Alien();

plutonian.enterAlienInfo( 4, 9 );
currentStrength = plutonian.getStrength();
```

ACCESSOR METHODS

At this point you're comfortable with using methods to access an instance variable both to set it to a new value and to get its current value. Most object-oriented programs call such routines *accessor methods*: Their sole purpose is to *access* an instance variable. While we chose to write the `enterAlienInfo()` method so it set the values of two instance variables, the preferred way of writing accessor methods is to have each method either set the value or get the value of just a single instance variable: one simple method—one straightforward, clearly defined task. While we didn't follow that sound practice for the `enterAlienInfo()` method, we did for the `getStrength()` method:

```
int getStrength() {
    return strength;
}
```

Now that you know about accessor functions, it's a good time to rewrite the `Alien class` so that it matches our guidelines. This latest version of the `class` now has both a "set" and "get" accessor method for each of its two instance variables:

```
class Alien {

    int       strength;
    int       lives;

    void setStrength( int theStrength ) {
        strength = theStrength;
    }
```

```
    int getStrength() {
        return strength;
    }

    void setLives( int theLives ) {
        lives = theLives;
    }

    int getLives() {
        return lives;
    }
}
```

This next snippet provides an example of the use of two of the four `Alien` accessor methods.

```
Alien  plutonian;
int currentStrength;

plutonian = new Alien();

plutonian.setStrength( 4 );

// later, when the applet needs the current value of
// the plutonian object's strength instance variable:

currentStrength = plutonian.getStrength();
```

DESTROYING AN OBJECT

So far in this chapter you've learned how objects are created. You've also learned something about how objects are stored in memory. Here you'll get a little more information about objects in memory. This information will be a set up for how objects get destroyed, or deallocated.

MEMORY ALLOCATION AND POINTERS

In C, memory allocation is often performed using the ANSI C function `malloc()`. When passed a number of bytes, `malloc()` finds a free memory block of this requested size, reserves it, and returns a pointer to the start of the reserved block. In Java, the `new` keyword is somewhat analogous to the C `malloc()` function. Like `malloc()`, the keyword `new` allocates a block of memory. Unlike `malloc()`, new *doesn't* return a pointer. And while the object variable that is involved in the allocation performed by `new` is a reference to a block of memory, you'll treat the object as a nonpointer variable. You've seen this already. Here the dot is used to access an instance variable of an object, much as the member access operator is used in C to access a `struct` member:

```
Alien  plutonian;

plutonian = new Alien();

plutonian.strength = 3;
```

In C, you allocate a pointer to a structure using the `*` operator. To then dereference the pointer and access a structure variable member, you use the `->` operator. Java has no similar pointer allocation and dereferencing. In fact, Java has no pointers at all!

If you've ever been tripped up by pointers in your C programming endeavors, the preceding sentence alone might make you partial to Java. While a Java applet works with memory, all of the details of memory references are hidden from you, the programmer. In Java, there are no pointers to allocate, delete, or leave dangling!

GARBAGE COLLECTION

In C, a program that is finished with a block of memory allocated by a call to `malloc()` can return the block to the pool of free memory by calling another ANSI C function—`free()`. Java, however, has no function analogous to `free()`. That turns out to be exceedingly good news for you. Once you create a new object, you don't ever have to worry about the memory it occupies. Keeping track of objects in memory is the job of the Java interpreter: At any point in the execution of your applet it knows what objects exist, where they are in memory, and when your applet is finished with them.

Recall that it is the Java interpreter software that is responsible for interpreting applet bytecode such that it can run on the host computer.

In Java, *garbage collection* is the term for freeing up the memory that is occupied by an object that is no longer of use to an applet. Once again, the fact that Java doesn't use pointers makes your programming life much easier. When you write C source code, memory deallocation and the resulting possibility of leaving dangling pointers behind is always present. When you write Java source code, you'll never have to worry about when to release an object's memory and what the effects of an object's destruction are. Garbage collection only destroys an object if the Java interpreter finds that none of your applet's other objects or variables refer to the object in question.

Inheritance

Your Java applets won't be constrained to a single `class`; you can write as many classes as make sense for your applet. Some of these classes that you write will be completely unrelated. Others—ones that are meant to model similar things—will be related. Here you'll see how Java makes it easy to write a new `class` based on an existing one, and how such a new class *inherits* the instance variables and methods of the class upon which it is based. Before discussing the details of this *inheritance*, though, we'll take a look at determining how you should organize your applet's data into classes.

Examining What an Applet Models

Object-oriented programs model things, with each object being an instance of one thing. These "things" can be as varied as stamps in a collection, vehicles on a dealer's lot, records of employee information, or, of course, aliens in a computer game.

Categories

Upon examination of what an object models, it might be apparent that the one thing that was to be kept track of can actually be better represented by a few (or several) categories. An item's attributes are usually what determine this. Recall that attributes are the individual pieces of information that define an object: what it looks like, what information it holds, and so forth.

Vehicles are a good example of something that can be divided into categories. For an object-oriented program (or in our case, an applet) that maintains information about vehicles, it might make more sense to think in terms of the two vehicle categories of *automobiles* and *trucks* rather than simply to group everything together as *vehicles*. While the two categories share many attributes (each has objects that will have an engine, a color, a gas gauge, and so forth), some attributes just won't be common to both (such as number of axles for an object in the truck category).

ALIEN APPLET CATEGORIES

Enough about cars and trucks—what about aliens? A superficial look at the Plutoskeet space game applet might leave us with the impression that a single `Alien class` would suffice quite nicely. From that one `class` the applet can generate any number of aliens that can descend upon the user's Web browser window. But if the game is to reach another level of sophistication, it will certainly have different *types* of aliens.

Figure 4-12 provides an example of how the objects in the Plutoskeet game applet might be best placed into categories. Because we're dealing with the hypothetical, we have the luxury of laying out the scenario however we want. Let's say we settle on a game that will have four categories of aliens, each with the attributes listed beneath them in the figure. While each category has some common attributes (a strength factor and the number of lives an alien posses), some attributes aren't common to each (zallians can change their level of visibility, while skeetians can vary the speed at which they move about the browser window). Even the two categories that have identical attributes (the plutonians and the drakonians) might have differences. For example, one might have a maximum strength factor of 5, the other 10.

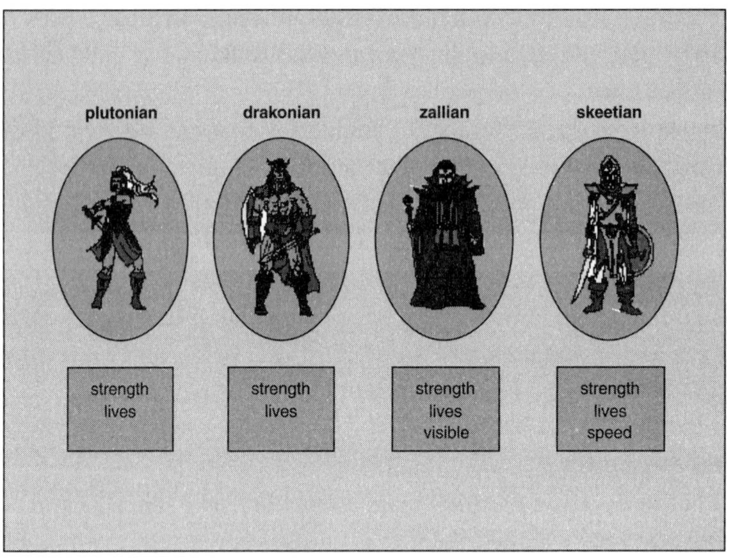

Figure 4-12
The four types of aliens, and their attributes, used in the remaining chapter examples.

POSSIBLE SOLUTIONS TO THE PROBLEM OF ORGANIZING CLASSES

Knowing what you now do about Java, object-oriented programming, and classes, you may have a couple of thoughts on how classes can be used to create objects that fall into multiple categories. This section anticipates those ideas and explains why the title of this section should read "Possible (But Not the Best) Solutions." Also explained is why you'll want to wait until you learn all about the topic of *subclasses* before jumping into Java programming.

A CLASS FOR ALL PURPOSES

Because a `class` can consist of any number of instance variables and any number of methods, one way to handle the creation of a variety of similar, but different, objects is to create one large `class` that "covers all bases." Such a `class` for the Plutoskeet alien game is shown in Figure 4-13. This figure assumes the game will make use of the four alien types described back in Figure 4-12. To keep the figure size manageable, the `class` doesn't specifically name the eight accessor methods (a "get" and a "set" for each instance variable) that would be included in the `class`.

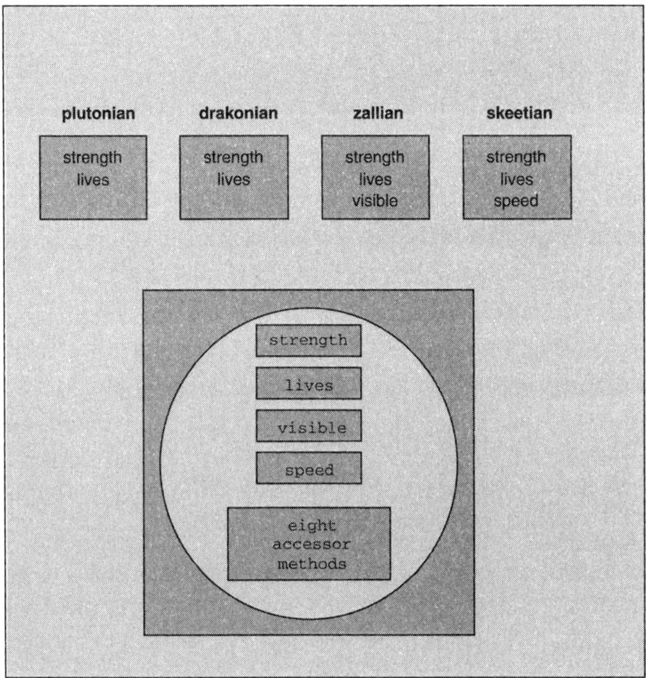

Figure 4-13
A single class could be used to define any number of aliens.

The approach of using a single `class`, such as the one pictured in Figure 4-13, carries at least a couple of drawbacks. For each `Alien` object, at least one instance variable doesn't apply. For example, a plutonian object has no need for either the visible or speed instance variables. In addition, at least two—and up to four—accessor methods don't apply to any one `Alien` object. A zallian object, for example, has no need for the `setSpeed()` and `getSpeed()` accessor methods.

Even though any one object contains instance variables and methods that it doesn't need, the Java compiler compiles the following code without complaint. This next snippet compiles without error—even though the speed instance variable is meaningless for the plutonian object:

```
Alien plutonian;

plutonian = new Alien();

plutonian.setSpeed( 50 );
```

A `class` is meant to definitively group together the attributes and behavior of something being modeled. Each object instantiated from that `class` is then meant to be a container of sorts—an object that holds only certain specific data and carries out certain specific functions. While defining a "do-all" `class` will work, it defeats the purpose of object-oriented programming in general and Java programming in specific.

A SELF-CONTAINED CLASS FOR EACH CATEGORY

If the notion of creating a single `class` to define various types of objects isn't an adequate one, neither is the opposite extreme—defining a separate, self-contained `class` for each object type. Because we've defined four types of aliens for our Plutoskeet game, four separate classes could be defined. Or, because two of the aliens have identical attributes (the plutonian and drakonian aliens both have the same `strength` and `lives` instance variables and, it's assumed, the same accessor methods to work with these variables), possibly three self-contained classes could be defined. Figure 4-14 illustrates how three classes might be defined to represent the four different alien types.

Figure 4-14 shows that the problem with this latest solution is a repetition of effort, and that's contradictory to the spirit of object-oriented programming. Object-oriented languages such as Java stress *code reusability*. This idea applies to the reuse of code both within a single applet and among several applets. Here we're concerned with the first scenario; that is, code you write at one point in an applet should be usable at some other point in the same applet. You'll see how to do that next.

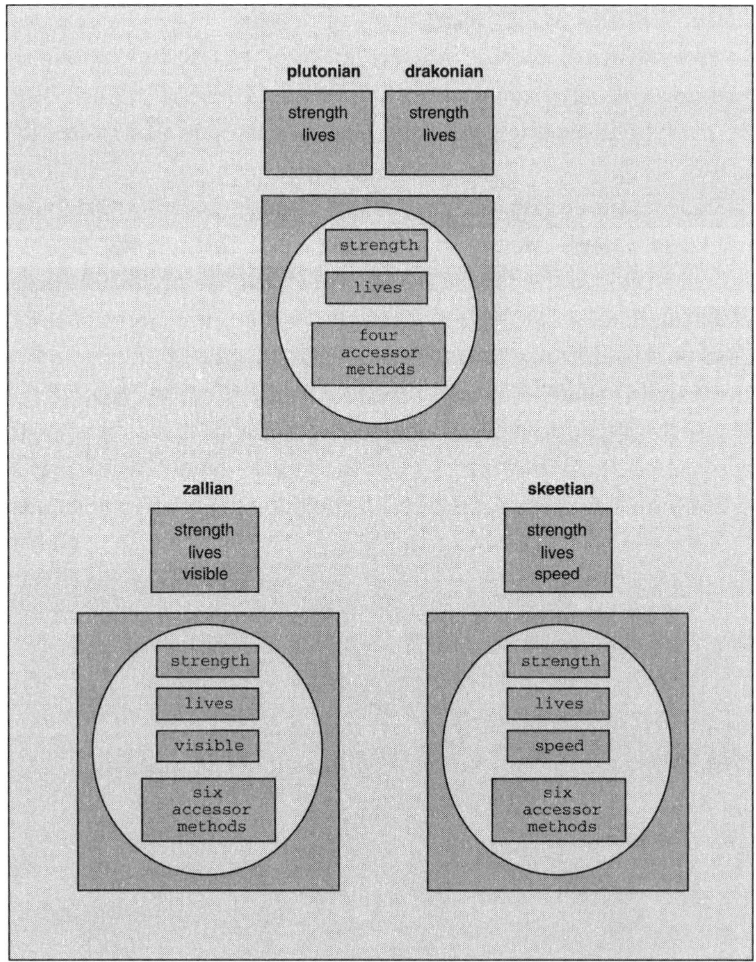

Figure 4-14

The four alien types could be represented by three classes.

SUBCLASSES

If your applet is to model something that can be described by more than one category of related things, it should use *subclasses*. Subclasses enable you to write new classes that take advantage of the code that defines an existing `class`.

SUPERCLASSES, SUBCLASSES, AND INHERITANCE

In Java you can write a single *superclass*—a `class` that holds code that is to be common to any number of other classes. These additional other classes are subclasses. Each subclass *inherits* the code that makes up the superclass.

Consider a superclass that consists of a single instance variable named `variable1` and a single method named `method1()`. You can see such a superclass in the upper left of Figure 4-15. Beneath the superclass in this same figure is a single object of this `class` type. To the upper right of the figure is a subclass. Like its superclass, this subclass happens to define a single instance variable (named `variable2`) and a single method (named `method2()`). But if you look at an object created from this subclass—the object pictured at the bottom right of the figure—you can see that it consists of the combined contents of both the superclass and the subclass.

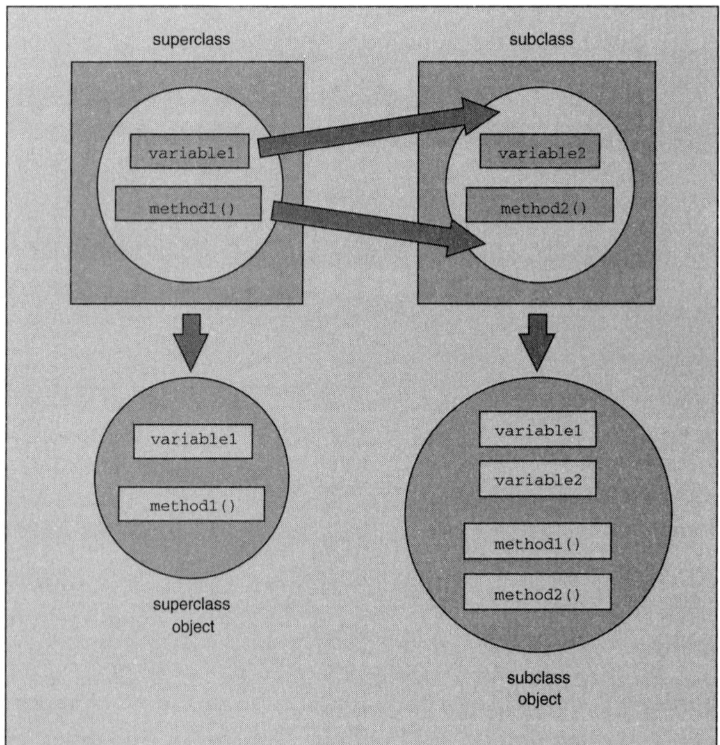

Figure 4-15
A subclass inherits the variables and methods from its superclass.

It's important to note that the subclass pictured in Figure 4-15 doesn't actually define the `variable1` instance variable or the `method1()` method. Instead, as demonstrated by the two arrows moving from the superclass to the subclass, the subclass inherits them.

SUBCLASSES AND THE ALIEN CLASS

Back in Figure 4-14 we show how three classes could be defined to describe four types of aliens. Here we will again use three classes to model the same four alien types. This time, however, we'll make one of those classes a superclass and the other two classes subclasses.

Choosing the content of the superclass is straightforward. Because anything that is defined in a superclass automatically becomes a part of any of its subclasses, the `Alien` superclass should be used to model only the attributes and behaviors that are common to all alien types. We've already established that those attributes can be represented by `strength` and `lives` instance variables, and the behaviors can be defined using four accessor methods. Such a superclass is shown at the far left of Figure 4-16.

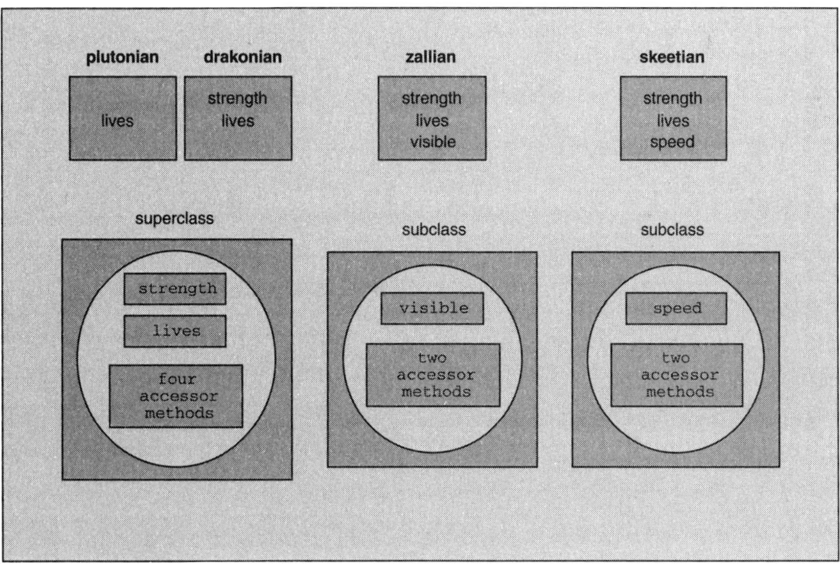

Figure 4-16

A superclass defines the attributes and behaviors common to its subclasses.

The contents of the superclass should look familiar: They're the same instance variables and accessor methods that appeared in the last version of the `Alien class` example. Later in this chapter you'll see the Java code used to define the `Alien` superclass and the two subclasses.

Determining what to include in the two necessary subclasses is also a straightforward process. Whatever attributes and behaviors that are particular to an alien type should be represented by instance variables and methods in a subclass. The two subclasses are shown to the right of the superclass in Figure 4-16.

To see if using subclasses makes our `Alien class` definitions more succinct, compare the three classes in Figure 4-16 with those pictured back in Figure 4-14. While our new system has indeed reused existing code (the code that makes up the superclass), the objects created by both of the `class` definitions shown in Figure 4-14 and Figure 4-16 will be the same. Figure 4-17 shows what these objects look like.

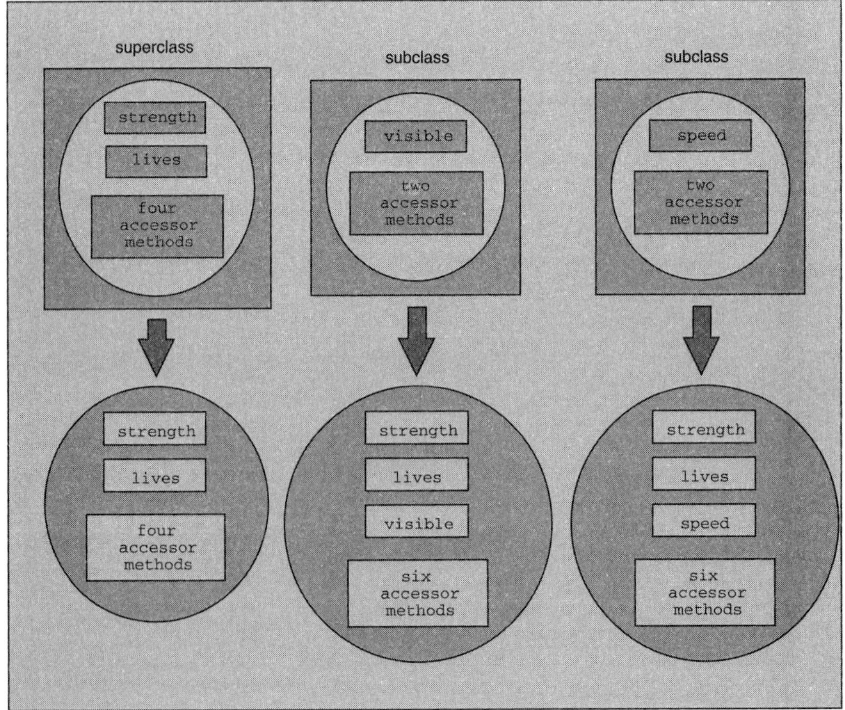

Figure 4-17

Using a superclass and subclasses, each object holds the desired variables and methods.

Classes versus objects: a reminder

As we discuss classes, superclasses, subclasses, objects, and aliens, keep in mind that from any one `class` any number of objects can be created. We've mentioned the four alien types and the three classes used to model these types so often that it might be easy to slip and think that the three classes can only create four objects. Figure 4-18 serves to remind you that from these three classes any number of objects of the four alien types can be created.

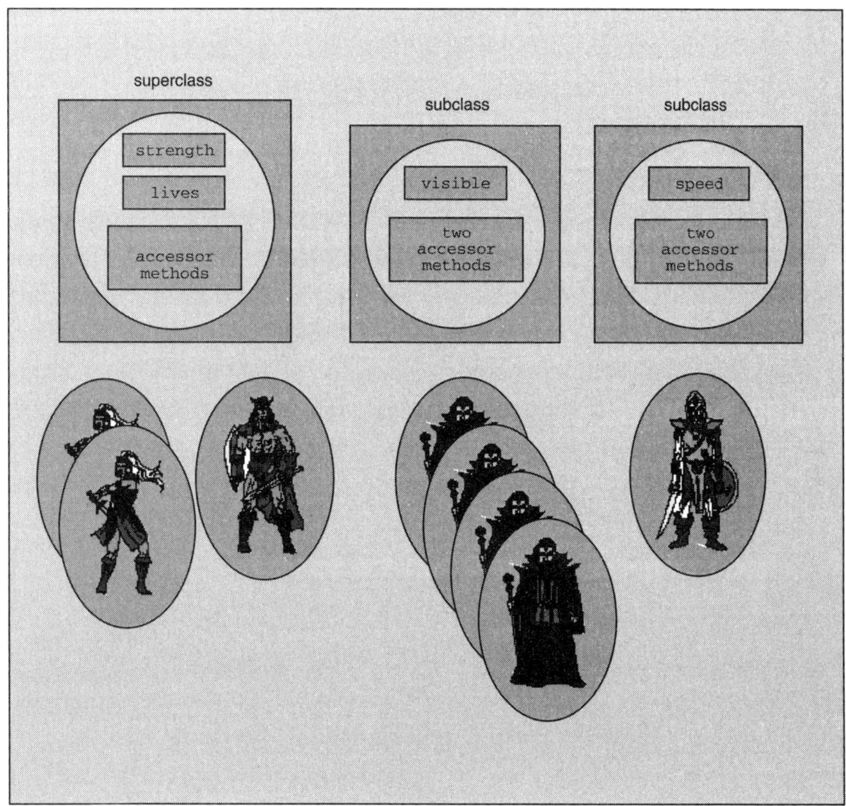

Figure 4-18

A superclass and each of its subclasses can generate any number of objects.

EXTENDING A CLASS

In Java, you create a subclass by defining a `class` that is an extension of an existing `class`. This is done using the `extend` keyword. Here's an example:

```
class FastAlien extends Alien {

    int       speed;

    void setSpeed( int theSpeed ) {
        speed = theSpeed;
    }

    int getSpeed() {
        return speed;
    }
}
```

The `FastAlien class` extends the `Alien class`. That's simply another way of saying that the `FastAlien class` is a subclass of the `Alien class`.

When a `FastAlien` object is created, it has three instance variables: the one defined by the `FastAlien class` and the two inherited from the `Alien` superclass. The `FastAlien` object is capable of calling any of six methods: the two defined in the `FastAlien class` and the four inherited from the `Alien` superclass. Here's another look at the `Alien class`, which remains unchanged from its last version:

```
class Alien {

    int       strength;
    int       lives;

    void setStrength( int theStrength ) {
        strength = theStrength;
    }

    int getStrength() {
        return strength;
    }

    void setLives( int theLives ) {
        lives = theLives;
    }
```

```
        int getLives() {
            return lives;
        }
    }
```

No code or keywords need to be added to a class definition to make it a superclass. When a second class uses the first class name along with the extend keyword (the way the FastAlien class uses the Alien class), the first class is said to be a superclass of the subclass.

Creating an object from a subclass definition is the same as creating an object from a "normal" class definition. The syntax for invoking a method is also the same. In the following snippet two objects are created: one based on the Alien class, the other based on the FastAlien class. The code then assigns values to both of the instance variables that are a part of the Alien object and to the three instance variables that are a part of the FastAlien object.

```
Alien         plutonian;
FastAlien     skeetian;

plutonian = new Alien();
skeetian = new FastAlien();

plutonian.setStrength( 1 );
plutonian.setLives( 2 );

skeetian.setStrength( 3 );
skeetian.setLives( 4 );
skeetian.setSpeed( 5 );
```

In the preceding snippet the plutonian object could *not* invoke the setSpeed() method. While an object created from a subclass inherits the instance variables and methods of its superclass, an object created from a superclass doesn't know about any of the instance variables or methods defined in any of its subclasses. While its name doesn't reflect the fact, a subclass is thus more powerful than the superclass that it extends.

A SECOND EXAMPLE OF A SUBCLASS

To create a subclass you follow the Java class keyword with the name of the new subclass. After that comes the Java extend keyword followed by the name of the class that is to be extended. Knowing that, you should be able to write your own `Alien` subclass named `VisibleAlien`. Here's one version, followed by code that creates two objects of this new subclass type and gives values to the instance variables of each object:

```
class VisibleAlien extends Alien {

    int  visible;

    void setVisible( int theVisibility ) {
        visible = theVisibility;
    }

    int getVisible() {
        return visible;
    }
}

VisibleAlien  zallian1;
VisibleAlien  zallian2;

zallian1 = new VisibleAlien();
zallian2 = new VisibleAlien();

zallian1.setStrength( 4 );
zallian1.setLives( 2 );
zallian1.setVisible( 1 );

zallian2.setStrength( 6 );
zallian2.setLives( 2 );
zallian2.setVisible( 0 );
```

Overriding methods

A subclass inherits all of the methods defined in its superclass. As you've witnessed, this means that a subclass object can invoke any of these inherited methods as if they were defined directly in the subclass. Gaining the use of these prewritten methods is one of the biggest advantages of implementing a subclass. At times, however, the functionality of an inherited method doesn't meet the needs of a particular subclass. In such cases, the subclass can redefine the unsatisfactory inherited method and use this new version in its place. In effect, the subclass *overrides* the inherited method.

WHEN TO OVERRIDE A METHOD

When a superclass method comes close to—but doesn't exactly match—the functionality a subclass is looking for, the subclass should override that method.

Consider the following scenario. Aliens in our Plutoskeet space game all have the ability to move. So the `Alien` superclass should define a `move()` method that handles this task. This method could be written such that an alien moves a specified distance across the user's browser window.

Next, assume that the `move()` method is adequate for three of the four alien types: the two types of aliens based on the `Alien` superclass and the one type of alien based on the `FastAlien` subclass. For objects based on the `VisibleAlien` subclass, however, `move()` doesn't suffice. To an alien of this type, movement doesn't mean gliding along across a window. Instead, movement involves remaining at a fixed location and rotating. For such an alien, the `move()` method inherited from the `Alien class` obviously won't work. The subclass that is to create alien objects that rotate should override the inherited `move()` method and rewrite it to match its needs.

While our focus up to this point has been on accessor methods, it should now be quite apparent that a `class` doesn't have to (and usually doesn't) consist of only accessor methods.

HOW TO OVERRIDE A METHOD

Carrying on with our latest plot, here's a look at the `move()` method that is to be defined in the `Alien` superclass—the method that will work for three of the four alien types:

```
void move( int horiz, int vert ) {
    // move alien
}
```

For simplicity we've left out the specifics of how the `move()` method implements movement of an alien. For now, suffice it to say that the alien is a graphic image, and movement is accomplished by altering the image's pixel coordinates. You'll read about graphics in Chapter 8 and animation in Chapter 9.

While the body of the `move()` method isn't shown, it's a safe guess that the method will use the two parameters to determine the new position at which the alien should be redrawn—perhaps by adding the `horiz` and `vert` values to the current coordinates of the image.

For the fourth type of alien a different `move()` method must be defined. Because objects created from the `VisibleAlien class` need special handling, this is the `class` that should override `move()` and redefine the method:

```
void move( int rotate ) {
    // rotate alien
}
```

Again we've opted to omit the body of the method. What's important here isn't the specifics of how this method is implemented but rather that the method can be rewritten. For the curious, assume that the single parameter to this version of `move()` indicates the number of pixels the image should be rotated. Figure 4-19 further demonstrates how method overriding works.

In the code snippet near the bottom left of Figure 4-19 an object of the `FastAlien class` is created and then moved. Because the object is of the `FastAlien class`, the Java runtime looks to this `class` to execute the `move()` method. Finding no such method in this `class`, the runtime looks to the superclass—the `Alien class`. There it encounters, and executes, the `move()` method.

The code snippet near the bottom right of Figure 4-19 shows an object of the `VisibleAlien class` being created. After that, the object is moved. Again, the Java runtime looks to the object's `class` to see if a `move()` method is defined. Here the new version of `move()`—the version that overrides the one in the `Alien` superclass—is found. The runtime executes this version of `move()`. Satisfied that the call to `move()` has been handled, the runtime doesn't look to the superclass.

OVERRIDING VERSUS DEFINING A NEW METHOD

In addition to inheriting methods from its superclass, a subclass can define any of its own methods. Consequently, you may be wondering if it wouldn't make more sense for the `VisibleAlien class` to implement the rotation of an object by defining a new method—a `rotate()` method—rather than by overriding the inherited `move()` method. When it comes time to rotate a `VisibleAlien` object, this new method could then be invoked:

```
zallian.rotate( 35 );
```

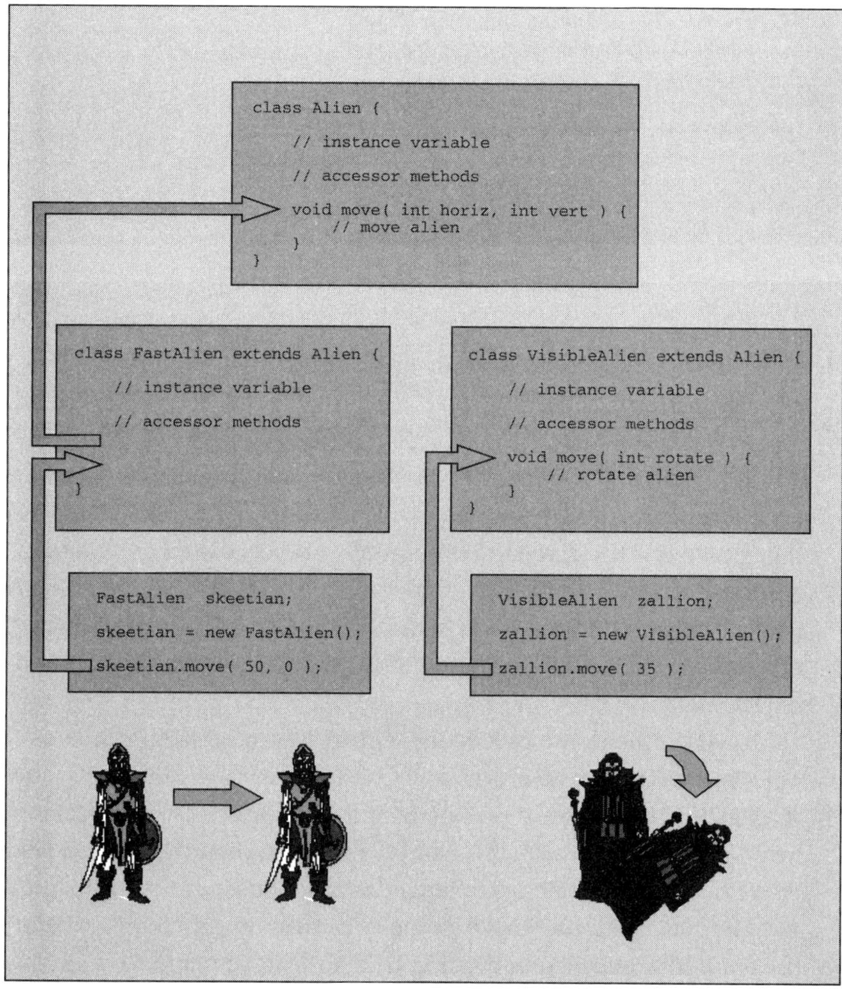

Figure 4-19

A subclass that overrides a superclass method generates objects that use the subclass-defined method rather than the superclass-defined method.

While this technique is a viable option, it might not be the best route to take. Consider this Java snippet:

```
Alien          plutonian;
VisibleAlien   zallian;
Alien          theAlien;
int            totalAliens;
```

```
plutonian = new Alien();
zallian = new VisibleAlien();

// other code here

if ( totalAliens > 10 )
    theAlien = plutonian;
else
    theAlien = zallian;

// other code here

theAlien.move( 100, 20 );
```

The preceding snippet begins by declaring three aliens, but then goes on to create only two alien objects. The third variable, `theAlien`, is used by the applet as a reference to different alien objects; the conditions of the applet affect the object this variable references. As shown in the preceding snippet, the current value of the `totalAliens` variable determines whether `theAlien` will reference the `Alien` object or the `VisibleAlien` object.

The last line in the preceding snippet has most significance. Here, the object's `move()` method is invoked. Consider the case of `theAlien` currently referencing the `VisibleAlien` object. If the `VisibleAlien class` has implemented movement through a `rotate()` method, then the desired results *won't* be obtained. Failing to find an overridden `move()` method in the `VisibleAlien class`, the Java runtime executes the superclass version of the method. So instead of rotating (the only movement of which this type of object is supposed to be capable), the object moves across the screen.

The lesson to be learned from this discussion is as follows. If a superclass method will be used by a variety of subclass objects, then a subclass that expects *different* behavior from a superclass method should override that method. In an earlier example the `VisibleAlien` subclass did just that when it overrode the `move()` method to implement object rotation. In this latest example, this principle wasn't followed. The result was an object that behaved in an unexpected manner.

What You've Learned

In this chapter you received a refresher on how a C program organizes data into structures. That background led you to see how a Java applet organizes data in a similar way—through the use of classes. The Java class is more powerful than the C structure, however, because it encapsulates, or groups together, data and the methods, or functions, that operate, or work with, that data.

As a C structure is used to "stamp out" any number of structure variables, a Java class is used as a template to create any number of objects, or instances of the class. Each object has its own set of instance variables so that its data is separate from the data of all other objects. Each object uses the methods defined in the class from which the object was defined.

An important concept when working with Java classes and objects is the idea of inheritance. In Java, you can define a single, general class that defines the data and methods that will be of use to any number of more specific classes. Each specific class can then inherit these instance variables and methods. Additionally, each specific class can define its own instance variables and methods that are particular to its unique needs.

CHAPTER

5

OOP Basics for C++ Programmers

Java is a very pure object-oriented language. While some languages are basically object-oriented, they do accommodate code that is not object-oriented. C++ is such a language. Your C++ program may be largely object-based, for example, but it can include stand-alone functions that aren't a part of any class. Java, on the other hand, doesn't allow for such non-OOP elements.

If you're a C++ programmer who feels comfortable with the principles of object-oriented programming, read this chapter to see the similarities between object-oriented programming using Java and object-oriented programming using C++. If you've programmed in C++ but aren't too comfortable with the language, make sure you've gotten up to speed by reading Chapter 4 before delving into this chapter.

Review of the C++ Class Keyword

As a C++ programmer, you're familiar with encapsulating related data and functions into a class, and then creating instances, or objects, of that class. As a Java programmer, you'll be doing the same. If you're completely comfortable with the use of the C++ class, then you're ready to look at classes as Java uses them. If you haven't used the C++ `class` keyword in a while, read this section to get a refresher on its use. When you take a look at Java classes later in this chapter, you'll appreciate having this full understanding of classes in C++ for reference.

KNOWING WHEN TO USE THE CLASS KEYWORD

To store related information in a single record in C, you use a structure. In C++, you use a class. When programming in C, you define the functions that will work on the data that is held in the fields of structure variables. When programming in C++, you also define functions that work on data—the data held in the fields, or members, of classes. In C++, you also define functions to work on the class data. In C++, however, you list these functions as a part of the class that also defines the data on which these functions operate. The binding of functions to data is the chief difference between C++ and C. It is also the primary advantage of C++ over C.

One common example showing how related data can be organized into records is that of a program that keeps track of employee information. Without the use of a class, your C program would declare a structure to hold the employee data and at least one function to work with that data. You could then declare structure variables, each holding the data of a single structure. This scenario is shown on the left of Figure 5-1.

In C++, you'd achieve the same results using a single class. The class definition would include the function that was defined as a separate entity in the C version of the program. Your C++ program would then create instances, or objects, of the class type. Each object would hold its own set of data (the way a C structure variable does). Additionally, each object would be aware of, and capable of making use of, the function defined as a part of the class from which the object was *instantiated*. This scenario is shown on the right of Figure 5-1.

Because Java is an object-oriented language like C++, your Java applets will share the C++ advantage of encapsulating data and functions into a single entity—the class.

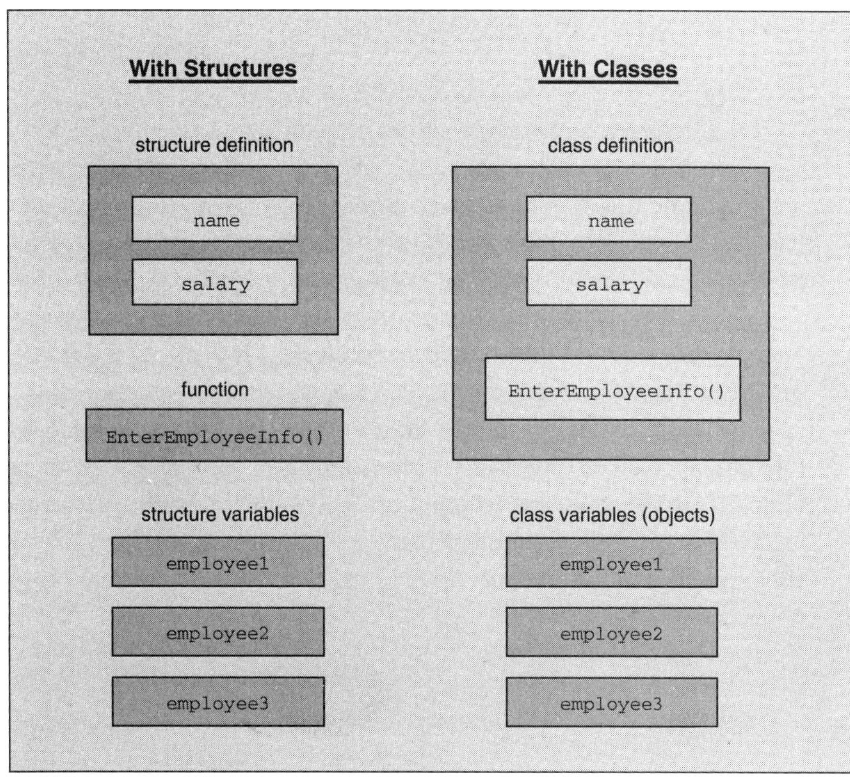

Figure 5-1
A C++ program that uses classes can better organize related data.

DEFINING A C++ CLASS

The employee example has been around for a long while. Instead of relying on an example that's a bit tired, the remainder of this chapter (and on into other chapters) uses a more interesting example. In this chapter we'll develop a class for an applet that serves as a simple game. We'll assume the applet (written in Java, of course) has any number of aliens that will be attacking the player-controlled hero. As in Chapter 4, we'll call the game "Plutoskeet" for two of its four alien fiends. As new aliens appear on the screen, they will each be given two attributes, or traits. In this simple game, each alien will have a strength attribute represented by a number from 1 through 10. Each alien will also have a second attribute—the number of lives it has. This characteristic of the alien will also be represented by a value in the range of 1 through 10.

On the following pages you'll see how to define and work with a C++ class that is modeled on the Plutoskeet game. A little later in this chapter we'll redefine this C++ class using Java. There, as the similarities between Java and C++ unfold, you'll see how your thorough knowledge of C++ pays off.

A C++ class is used to package together any number of *data members* and any number of *member functions*. Each member is declared the same way any C++ variable is declared. Each function is either listed as a function prototype or is defined later in the source code listing. If the function appears as only a prototype, then the function is later formally defined outside of the class definition. The following snippet shows an example of a class that could be used to hold information about a single alien in our Plutoskeet game:

```
class Alien {
    private:
        int  strength;
        int  lives;

    public:
        void EnterAlienInfo( int theStrength, int theLives );
};
```

A C++ class definition defines one particular class. As just shown, a class definition consists of nine key elements, in the following order:

- The C keyword `class`
- The class definition's *name*, or *tag*
- An opening brace
- A keyword that describes the level of access to data members
- Any number of data members
- A keyword that describes the level of access to member functions
- Any number of member functions
- A semicolon
- A closing brace

Figure 5-2 shows one way of picturing the `Alien` class.

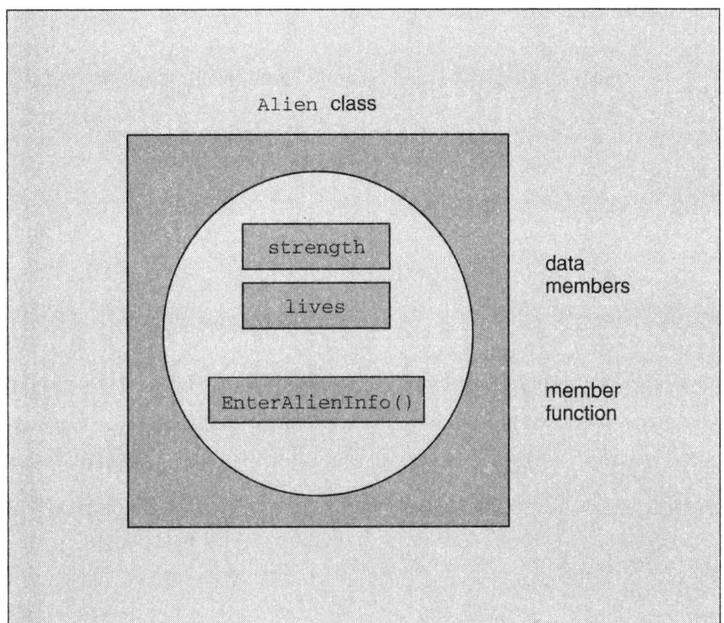

Figure 5-2
A C++ class consists of data members and member functions.

The `private`, `public`, and `protected` keywords found in C++ are also found in Java. As in C++, in Java a `private` data member is accessible only by functions defined as part of the data member's class. Chapter 8 has more to say about the use of these access-limiting keywords in Java.

DEFINING A MEMBER FUNCTION

If a C++ class lists a member function as a prototype, then that function must be defined somewhere outside of the class. The class name followed by the :: operator associates a function with a class. For the `Alien` class, which lists a member function named `EnterAlienInfo()`, the function definition might look like this one:

```
void Alien::EnterAlienInfo( int theStrength, int theLives )
{
    strength = theStrength;
    lives = theLives;
}
```

The `EnterAlienInfo()` function has the simple task of setting the values of the two data members to the values of the parameters `theStrength` and `theLives`.

In C++, a class can list a function prototype and then define that function externally—as just shown—or it can define the function within the class itself. This next version of the `Alien` class uses the second technique.

```
class Alien {
    private:
        int  strength;
        int  lives;

    public:
        void EnterAlienInfo( int theStrength, int theLives ) {
            strength = theStrength;
            lives = theLives;
        }
};
```

Creating an Object

A C++ class defines the format of a class, but it doesn't actually create any objects that can be used to store program data. To do that, you need to create one or more objects of the class type. To create an object, begin by declaring a variable of the class type. Typically, you'll declare a pointer and then use the C++ new operator to allocate memory for a single instance, or object, of a class type. The following snippet declares three variables of the `Alien` class type and then creates three Alien objects:

```
Alien *martianAlien;
Alien *superAlien;
Alien *weakAlien;

martianAlien = new Alien;
superAlien = new Alien;
weakAlien = new Alien;
```

Because the preceding three declarations all use the `Alien` class as their data type, each of the three variables consists of a `strength` data member and a `lives` data member. Figure 5-3 equates the idea of a class definition with a template by showing how the `Alien` class can be used as a sort of pattern from which three `Alien` objects have been created.

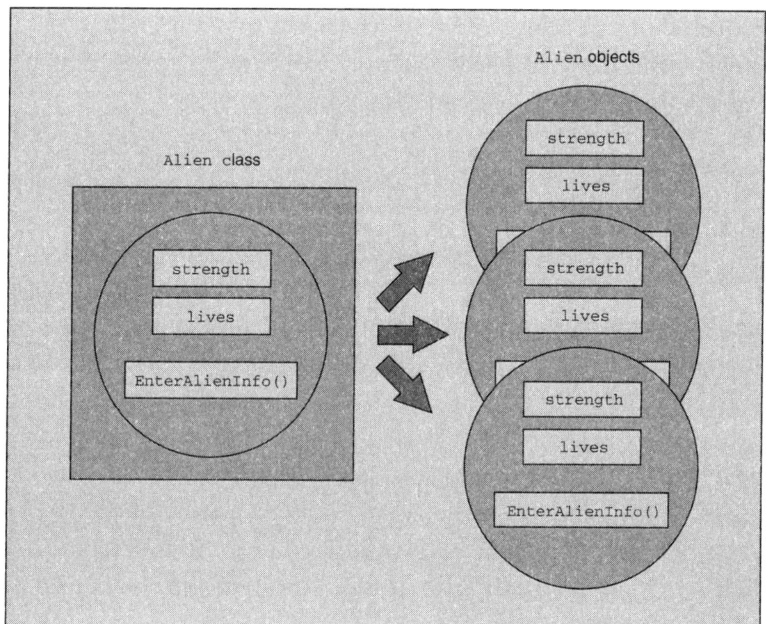

Figure 5-3
A C++ class is used as a template from which any number of objects are created.

Introduction to Java's Class Keyword

The Java language, like C++, relies on classes to define how data is organized and manipulated.

KNOWING WHEN TO USE THE CLASS KEYWORD

A class in Java has the same advantage as a class in C++—it encapsulates data. Related data are grouped together and hidden from the rest of an applet's code.

In Java, classes are so important that an applet itself is a class. You've already seen that the source code listing for an applet contains no `main()` function and no function definitions unrelated to a class. Chapter 8 expands on this topic. In particular, you'll see how an applet runs without having a `main()` function as its starting point.

DEFINING A JAVA CLASS

Like a C++ class, a Java class is used to group together any number of data items, along with the functions used to operate on that data. In a C++ class, one data item is referred to as a *data member* of the class. In a Java class, a data item is referred to as an *instance variable*. Again, like the C++ class, an individual data item in a class is treated as a variable; each instance variable can be of any Java data type. As you'll see in the chapter that discusses the Java language data (Chapter 7), many of the Java primitive data types are common to those defined in C and C++. Some examples are `short`, `int`, `long`, and `float`. Figure 5-4 points out the key components of a Java class definition.

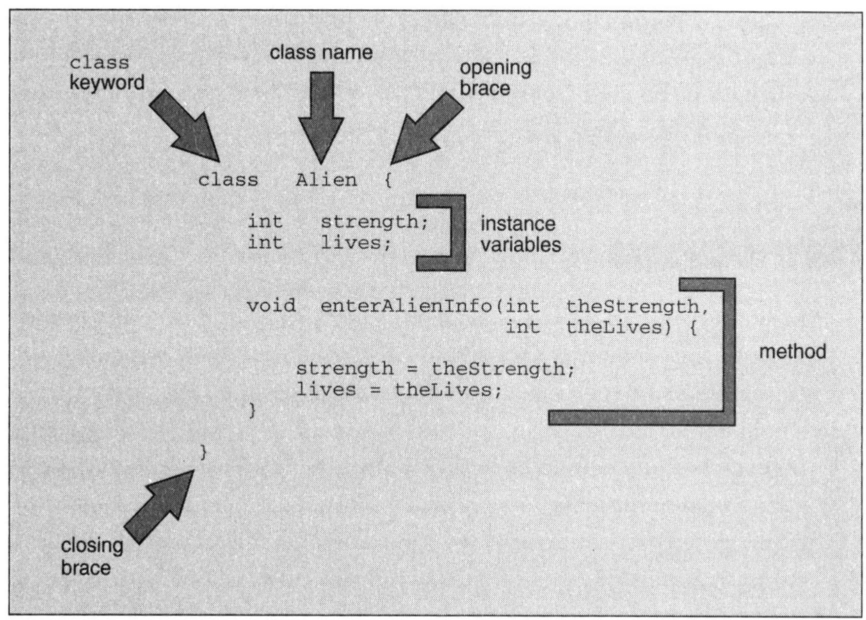

Figure 5-4
These are the components that make up a class definition.

Java naming conventions dictate that a class name begin with an uppercase character (as in the `Alien` class), while instance variables and methods begin with a lowercase character (as in `strength` and `enterAlienInfo()`).

Comparison of C++ Classes and Java Classes

In Figure 5-4 you can see that with the exception of the lack of the `private` and `public` keywords and the final semicolon, the Java definition of the `Alien` class is the same as this chapter's C++ version. In Chapter 8 you'll see that a Java class can, and usually does, make use of these same access specifier keywords.

In C++, a class can either provide a list of member functions, with the actual function definitions appearing elsewhere in the code, or it can define the member functions directly within the class definition. In Java, only this latter method is used. A Java class *always* defines all of its methods within the class definition.

Java Objects

As in C++, in Java a class definition is used to "stamp out" any number of objects. Any one object represents a single instance of whatever it is the class models. Specifically, an object of a class named `Employee` represents a single employee. An object of the `Alien` class represents a single alien. The object's instance variables describe the attributes, or characteristics, of what is being modeled. The object's methods define the behavior of what is being modeled. For our `Alien` class, an `Alien` object's attributes are its strength and its number of lives, while the object's behavior is its capability of taking on different strength and lives values.

CREATING AN OBJECT

Objects are created in Java in a manner similar to, but not identical to, objects created in C++. First, define a class. Then declare a variable of that class type. Finally, use the `new` keyword to allocate memory for an instance of that class:

```
class Alien {

    int       strength;
    int       lives;

    void      enterAlienInfo(int theStrength, int theLives) {
        strength = theStrength;
        lives = theLives;
    }
}

Alien  plutonian;            // declare a variable of type Alien

plutonian = new Alien();     // create an Alien object
```

In C++, `new` returns a pointer to the newly created object. As you can see in the preceding Java listing, the value returned by `new` isn't considered a pointer: Java has no pointer or dereference operators.

In C++, `new` is followed by the name of the class from which a newly created object should be based. In Java, the `new` keyword is also followed by a class type. However, this class type is in turn followed by a pair of parentheses. The class type followed by parentheses looks suspiciously like a function call. As it turns out, that's exactly what it is. As it does in C++, in Java the use of the `new` keyword automatically invokes a class *constructor* method.

CONSTRUCTOR METHODS

Every class has at least one constructor method—a method that is invoked each time an instance of a class is created.

DEFAULT CONSTRUCTORS

Every time you define a class, Java defines a default, empty constructor for that class. For the `Alien` class, that constructor looks like this:

```
Alien() {

}
```

Java does this as a courtesy to you. The use of `new` always triggers the execution of a constructor method. If Java didn't define a constructor for a class, and you didn't either, an error would result.

Earlier we noted that Java naming conventions dictate that method names begin with a lowercase character. Constructors are an exception to this convention. Because a constructor *must* have the same name as a class (which always begins with an uppercase character), a constructor begins with an uppercase character.

As in C++, when you define a class in Java, you can define your own constructor for that class. Again like C++, a Java constructor can have any number of parameters.

CHARACTERISTICS OF CONSTRUCTOR METHODS

A Java constructor method always has the same traits as a C++ constructor function. A Java constructor has the following properties:

- Uses the same name as the class to which it belongs
- Has no return type
- Can have any number of parameters, including none

One variance from C++ is that a Java method that has no parameters does *not* use the `void` keyword in its parameter list.

AN EXAMPLE OF A CONSTRUCTOR

A Java class constructor is typically used for the same purpose as a C++ class constructor—to handle initialization tasks for new objects of the class type. As an example, consider that we might want to provide initial values for the two instance variables associated with an `Alien` object. Here's how that constructor would appear:

```
Alien() {
     strength = 1;
     lives = 1;
}
```

If a class defines no constructor, Java defines an empty constructor for that class and uses it each time an object is created using `new`. If a class does define a constructor, then that constructor is the one that gets used in place of the empty one that Java created.

The following snippet shows a version of the `Alien` class that includes the previously defined constructor method. The code also shows the creation of a new `Alien` object that uses this same constructor.

```
class  Alien {

     int       strength;
     int       lives;

     void enterAlienInfo(int theStrength, int theLives) {
          strength = theStrength;
     lives = theLives;
     }
```

```
    Alien() {
        strength = 1;
        lives = 1;
    }
}

Alien  plutonian;

plutonian = new Alien();  // this line executes our constructor
```

METHOD OVERLOADING

Method overloading is a feature of Java that enables a class to define any number of methods that each share the same name. Method overloading in Java is the same as it is in C++: two methods may have identical names, provided that one or more of the following characteristics of the methods differ:

- Number of arguments
- Argument types
- Argument ordering

While method overloading works for any method, this tool is particularly useful where constructors are involved. The following listing defines yet another version of the `Alien` class. Here, the class has two constructors. The first constructor initializes the value of an object's instance variables to 1. The second constructor initializes the instance variables to values passed to it. The listing ends by creating two new `Alien` objects, each of which uses a different constructor. After the following code executes, two new `Alien` objects will exist. The object named `plutonian` will have a `strength` value of 1 and a `lives` value of 1, while the object named `drakonian` will have a `strength` value of 5 and a `lives` value of 2.

```
class  Alien {

    int       strength;
    int       lives;

    void enterAlienInfo(int theStrength, int theLives) {
        strength = theStrength;
```

```
            lives = theLives;
        }

        Alien() {
            strength = 1;
            lives = 1;
        }

        Alien( int initialStrength, int initialLives ) {
            strength = initialStrength;
            lives = initialLives;
        }
    }

    Alien plutonian;
    Alien drakonian;

    plutonian = new Alien();
    drakonian = new Alien( 5, 2 );
```

For brevity's sake, the remaining examples in this chapter use an `Alien` class that *doesn't* define any constructors.

INSTANCE VARIABLES

For a C++ object, a data member can be accessed in one of two ways. If the object is being referenced using a variable, the direct selection, or dot, operator (.) can be used:

```
Alien martianAlien;   // C++ variable example

martianAlien.lives = 3;
```

If the C++ object is instead being referenced by a pointer, the indirect operator (->) is used:

```
Alien *martianAlien; // C++ pointer example

martianAlien = new Alien;

martianAlien->lives = 3;
```

Java doesn't use pointers, so in Java only the first of the two C++ techniques works for accessing object instance variables:

```
Alien plutonian;              // Java example

plutonian = new Alien();

plutonian.lives = 3;
```

Both C++ and Java use a dot, or period, in field assignments. In C++, the dot is considered an operator; it's the direct selection operator, or dot operator. In Java, this field accessor isn't considered an operator. Instead, it's called *dot notation*, or simply *dot*.

ACCESSOR METHODS

Object-oriented languages often refer to data hiding, or encapsulation. The purpose of creating an object is to *encapsulate* a set of attributes and behaviors into a single entity. In doing so, the object's attributes—its data—get hidden from "the rest of the world." Keeping the object self-contained prevents accidental modification of the data by other code in the applet.

Enabling the use of dot notation to access an object's instance variable works, but it gives any code access to the data of an object. That defeats the usefulness of encapsulation. In Java, as in C++, encapsulation is promoted through the use of accessor methods. Instead of enabling object data to be accessed using dot notation, a class can be defined such that only class methods are allowed the privilege of working with an object's data.

INVOKING A METHOD

For a Java object to call a method, the dot is used. To the dot's left is the object's name; to the dot's right is the name of the method to invoke. This syntax is similar to that used by C++ programmers when working with an object referenced by a variable rather than by a pointer.

The Alien class has a method named `enterAlienInfo()`. Here, an `Alien` object named `plutonian` calls this method in order to set the values of its `strength` and `lives` instance variables:

```
Alien  plutonian;

plutonian = new Alien();

plutonian.enterAlienInfo( 8, 2 );
```

Each object has its own set of instance variables. When a method call is made, the object upon which the method is to act must be included. That tells the method which instance variables should be affected. For example, the `enterAlienInfo()` method can be used by any `Alien` object. `enterAlienInfo()` makes assignments to the appropriate pair of instance variables because the object to be affected is named along with the call to the method. In this next snippet two objects make calls to the `enterAlienInfo()` method:

```
Alien  plutonian;
Alien  drakonian;

plutonian = new Alien();
drakonian = new Alien();

plutonian.enterAlienInfo( 8, 2 );
drakonian.enterAlienInfo( 5, 3 );
```

SETTING THE VALUE OF AN INSTANCE VARIABLE

Earlier you saw that the dot can be used to assign a value to both the `strength` and the `lives` instance variables of an `Alien` object:

```
plutonian.strength = 8;
plutonian.lives = 2;
```

And in a preceding snippet, you saw the `enterAlienInfo()` method from the `Alien` class being used to carry out the same task. Using an accessor method—a method whose sole purpose is to access an instance variable—such as `enterAlienInfo()` to indirectly set an instance variable value is the preferred means of making such an assignment.

When any changes to an object's data can be made only through an accessor method (rather than through the use of the dot), it becomes less likely that code will inadvertently change this data. Most object-oriented programs call a routine that sets or returns the value of a field of an object an *accessor method*: Its sole purpose is to *access* an instance variable. While `enterAlienInfo()` can be considered an accessor method, the preferred way of writing accessor methods is to have each method either set the value or get the value of just a single instance variable. Your applet may not need to change the value of each instance variable at the same time. Here's a pair of accessor methods that could be put in place of the one `enterAlienInfo()` method:

```
void setStrength( int theStrength ) {
    strength = theStrength;
}

void setLives( int theLives ) {
    lives = theLives;
}
```

GETTING THE VALUE OF AN INSTANCE VARIABLE

The methods we've developed for the `Alien` class each have a return type of `void`. Java class methods, like C++ class member functions, can have a return type other than `void`. An accessor method that returns the value of an instance variable is a good example. The following methods could be added to the `Alien` class so that an object of the `Alien` class type would have a means of examining the values of its two instance variables:

```
int getStrength() {
    return strength;
}

int getLives() {
    return lives;
}
```

You've seen the Java `int` data type in the past, so it should be apparent that a method can return a value of this type. For a Java method to return a value, a `return` statement is used—just as in C++.

To invoke a method that returns a value, again use the dot: Name an object to the left of the dot and name the method to the right. Because the method returns a value, you'll place the call to the right of an equal sign. To the left of the equal sign will be the variable that is to be assigned the returned value. In this next snippet, an `Alien` object sets its `strength` instance variable using its `setStrength()` method and then obtains the value of that same instance variable using its `getStrength()` method:

```
Alien  plutonian;
int currentStrength;

plutonian = new Alien();
plutonian.setStrength( 9 );

currentStrength = plutonian.getStrength();
```

Here's how the `Alien` class looks with accessor methods in place of the `enterAlienInfo()` method:

```
class Alien {

     int       strength;
     int       lives;

     void setStrength( int theStrength ) {
          strength = theStrength;
     }

     int getStrength() {
          return strength;
     }

     void setLives( int theLives ) {
          lives = theLives;
     }

     int getLives() {
          return lives;
     }
}
```

DESTROYING AN OBJECT

In C++, you create an object using the `new` operator and dispose of an object using the `delete` operator. In Java, you also use `new` to create an object. To dispose of a Java object, however, you need do nothing: Garbage collection takes care of object destruction.

The Java runtime knows what objects have been created and which variables reference these objects. The runtime can therefore determine when an object has no references to it. When it does make this determination, it goes ahead and frees the memory occupied by the object.

Recall that the Java runtime, or Java interpreter, is the software responsible for interpreting applet bytecode such that it can run on the host computer.

Inheritance

Object-oriented programs—whether written in C++ or Java—model things. When more than one item is to be modeled, and a relationship exists between these things, your Java applet will use subclasses and inheritance—just as you've done in C++ programs.

An item's attributes are usually what determine this behavior. Recall that attributes are the individual pieces of information that define an object: what it looks like, what information it holds, and so forth.

CHOOSING CATEGORIES

The Plutoskeet alien example that we've developed in this chapter could use a single class from which all alien objects are generated. However, if the game is to display different types of aliens, each with different attributes, it makes more sense to categorize the types of aliens and define a class for each. Then any number of alien objects can be created from each class type.

Assuming our applet will be capable of displaying aliens of any of four types, Figure 5-5 provides an example of how the objects in the game applet might be best placed into categories. In this figure, the attributes of each alien type are listed beneath the alien. Note that some attributes are common to each alien type, while others aren't.

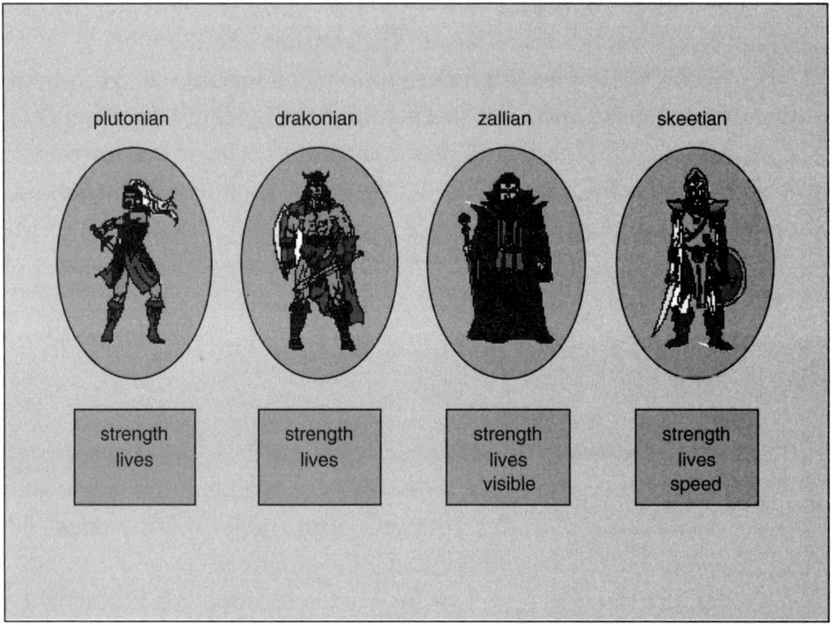

Figure 5-5
The four types of aliens, and their attributes, used in the remaining chapter examples.

SUBCLASSES

As they do in C++, subclasses enable you to write new classes that take advantage of the code that defines an existing class.

SUPERCLASSES, SUBCLASSES, AND INHERITANCE

In Java you can write a single *superclass*—a class that holds code that is to be common to any number of other classes. These additional other classes are *subclasses*. Each subclass *inherits* the code that makes up the superclass. In C++, multiple inheritance can be used: A class can inherit the code of more than one superclass. In Java, only single inheritance is allowed. Figure 5-6 illustrates.

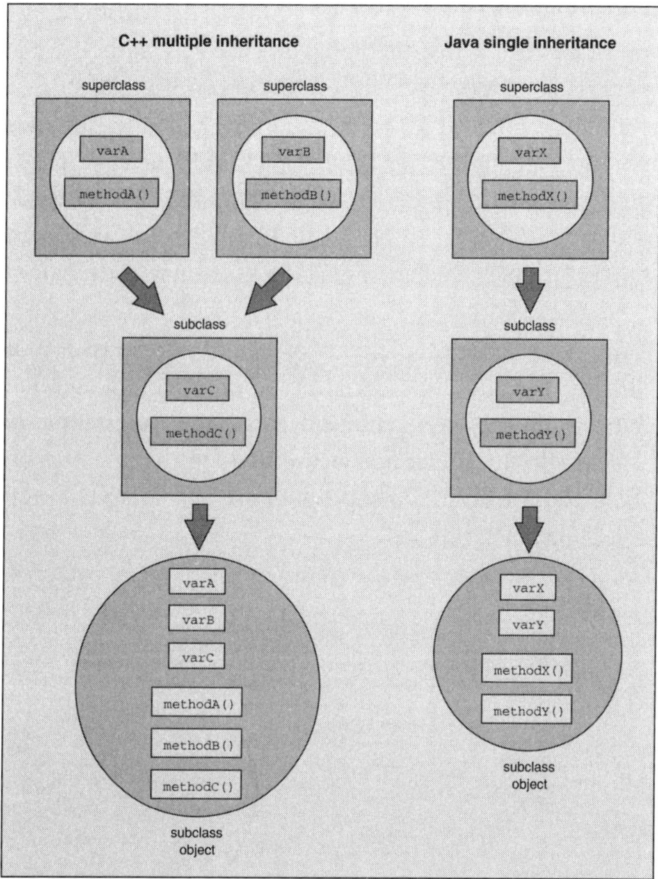

Figure 5-6
C++ allows multiple inheritance; Java does not.

Multiple inheritance is a useful feature of C++, but it can also add needless complexity to a program. Java eliminates this source of confusion by allowing only one superclass for any subclass. Java's designers didn't want to completely dismiss the advantages of multiple inheritance, however. In Chapter 8, you'll see how the concept of *interfaces* enables one class to implement code from several other classes.

SUPERCLASSES, SUBCLASSES, AND THE ALIEN CLASS

From your background in the object-oriented C++ language, you know that defining what goes in a superclass is a straightforward process. All you do is determine the attributes and behaviors that are common to all classes that will be derived from the one superclass. In Java, the attributes are the instance variables of a class while the behaviors are the methods of a class.

If the `Alien` class is to serve as a superclass in our Plutoskeet game applet, then it should consist of `strength` and `lives` instance variables—the attributes common to all alien types shown back in Figure 5-5. The `Alien` superclass should also include accessor methods so that objects based on the `Alien` class or any of its (yet to be defined) subclasses can work with these two instance variables. Such a superclass is shown at the far left of Figure 4-16.

As in C++, the determination of the contents of a subclass is a direct process: Any attributes unique to a certain type of object should be made instance variables in the subclass definition. Any behaviors unique to this same type of object should be defined as methods in the subclass definition. For the alien example, the two subclasses are shown to the right of the superclass in Figure 5-7.

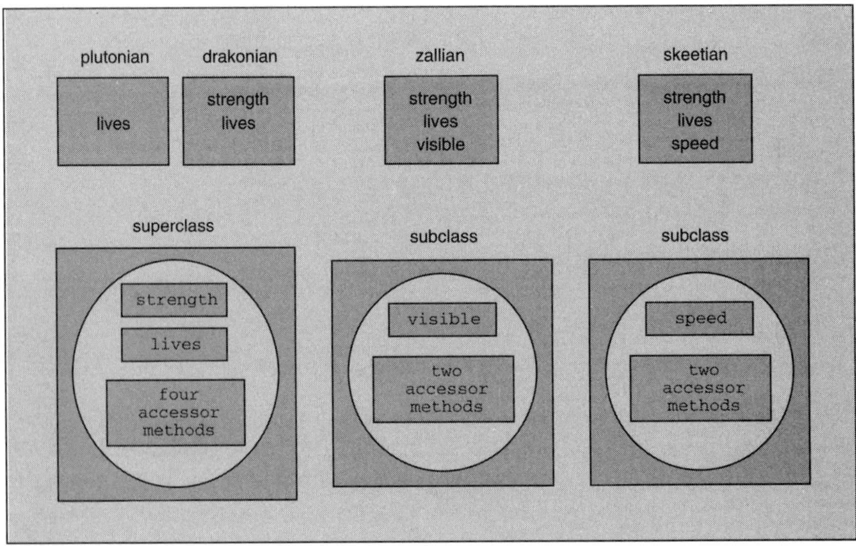

Figure 5-7

A superclass defines the attributes and behaviors common to its subclasses.

Figure 5-8 shows the superclass and subclasses that could be defined to support the four types of aliens pictured back in Figure 5-5.

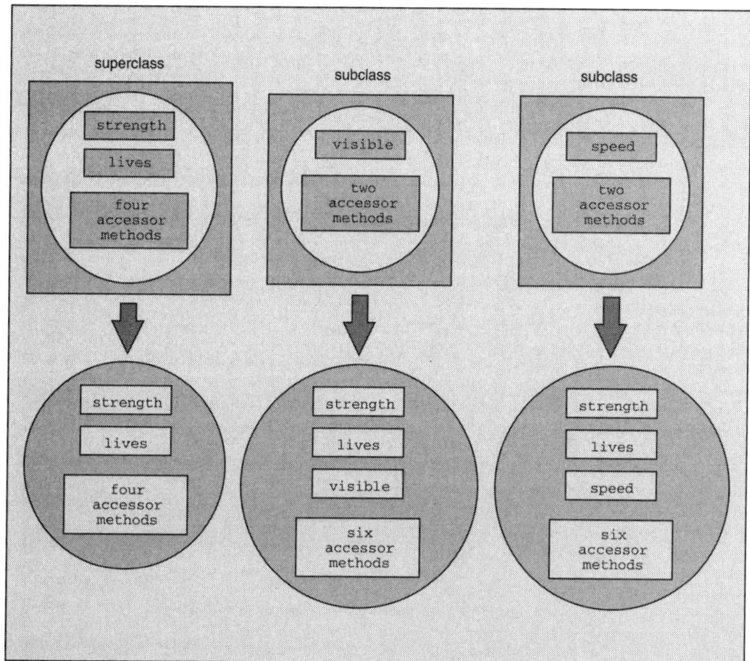

Figure 5-8
Using a superclass and subclasses, each object holds the desired variables and methods.

EXTENDING A CLASS

In C++, you specify that a class be a derived class by including all of the following in the first line of the derived class definition: the `class` keyword, the derived class name, a colon, an access specifier (such as the keyword `public`), and the base class name. The definition for a C++ class named `FastAlien` that is to be derived from a base class named `Alien` would look like this:

```
class FastAlien : public Alien {               // C++ derived class
    // data members and member functions
};
```

To create the same subclass definition in Java, you replace the colon and `public` keyword with the `extends` keyword, like this:

```
class FastAlien extends Alien {                // Java subclass
    // instance variables and methods
}
```

Assuming we want objects of the `FastAlien` class to have three instance variables (`strength`, `lives`, and `speed`) and six methods (a `set` and `get` method for each instance variable), the `FastAlien` subclass definition would look like this:

```
class FastAlien extends Alien {

    int  speed;

    void setSpeed( int theSpeed ) {
        speed = theSpeed;
    }

    int getSpeed() {
        return speed;
    }
}
```

As with C++-derived classes, think of a Java subclass as including all of the elements of its superclass, along with the elements unique to the subclass. Here's another look at the `Alien` class—which is now a superclass to the `FastAlien` subclass:

```
class Alien {

    int  strength;
    int  lives;

    void setStrength( int theStrength ) {
        strength = theStrength;
    }

    int getStrength() {
        return strength;
    }
```

```
    void setLives( int theLives ) {
        lives = theLives;
    }

    int getLives() {
        return lives;
    }
}
```

As is the case for a C++ base class, the definition of a Java superclass requires no special code or keywords. A Java class becomes a superclass when a different class extends it.

Creating an object from a subclass definition is done just as it is for creating an object of any other class type. The following snippet creates an object of the `Alien` class type and an object of the `FastAlien` class type. The snippet also assigns values to the instance variables of each of the two objects.

```
Alien          theAlien;
FastAlien      theFastAlien;

theAlien= new Alien();
theFastAlien= new FastAlien();

theAlien.setStrength( 6 );
theAlien.setLives( 5 );

theFastAlien.setStrength( 3 );
theFastAlien.setLives( 1 );
theFastAlien.setSpeed( 8 );
```

What You've Learned

This chapter provided you with a refresher on how a C++ program organizes data and functions in classes. A Java applet uses this same style of organization, so your C++ background is a great help in understanding the Java class. In Java, as in C++, a class encapsulates, or groups together, data and the methods, or functions, that operate, or work with, that data.

Just as a C++ class definition is used to "stamp out" any number of objects, so too is a Java class definition used as a template to create any number of objects, or instances, of the class. Each object has its own set of instance variables so that its data are separate from the data of all other objects. Each object uses the methods defined in the class from which the object was defined.

An important concept when working with Java classes and objects is the idea of inheritance—a topic you're familiar with from your C++ programming. In Java, as in C++, you can define a single, general class that defines the data and methods that will be of use to any number of more specific classes. Each specific class can then inherit these instance variables and methods. Additionally, each specific class can define its own instance variables and methods that are particular to its unique needs. Unlike C++, Java does not allow for multiple inheritance. That is, one class cannot have more than one superclass; a subclass can only directly inherit the properties of one other class.

CHAPTER

6 Java Operators and Data Types

Applets, like programs written in any language, work with data. In Java, each of the many data types fall into one of two categories: primitive or reference. In this chapter, you'll see many familiar types listed among the primitive data types: the `short`, `int`, and `float`, to name a few. The same can be said of the reference types, of which the array is included. You'll see, though, that these data types do have some differences from similarly-named C types: Type sizes, ranges, and how assignments are made are a few of these differences.

After seeing the different ways in which Java enables you to represent data, you'll want to see the different ways in which Java enables you to process data. In this chapter, you'll examine the numerous Java operators, including arithmetic, comparative, logical, and bitwise operators. As a programmer with a background in C or C++, you'll quickly feel comfortable with these operators: Many behave similar to, and many behave exactly as, their C and C++ counterparts.

Because this chapter examines the very basics of the Java language, this is the place to briefly describe the basic components of source code: expressions and statements. And because the source code examples are sprinkled with comments, this is as good a place as any to describe the types of comments Java allows. These topics are, in fact, the ones we'll examine next.

Expressions and Statements

In Java, as in C, statements are the basic instructions that make up source code. And, as in C, a Java statement is constructed from expressions.

EXPRESSIONS

The definition of an expression in Java is the same as it is in C. An expression is any combination of operands and operators, and always has a value. Each of the following lines holds one expression:

```
5
71 - 4
total = score + bonus
speed > 10
```

Java uses many of the same operators found in C—as you can see by the use of the -, +, =, and > operators in the preceding code fragment. The Java operators are covered later in this chapter. As a reminder, operands are what an operator acts upon.

The first three expressions in the preceding snippet are examples of *numeric* expressions: Each evaluates to a number. The first expression consists of a single operand, the second is made up of two operands and one operator (the subtraction operator), while the third expression consists of three operands and two operators (the addition operator and the assignment operator).

The last expression is a *Boolean* expression: It evaluates to either `true` or `false`. Unlike in C, in Java these two Boolean values are *not* equal to 1 and 0, respectively. This particular example of a Boolean expression consists of two operands and one operator (the greater than operator).

COMPOUND EXPRESSIONS

Expressions can be combined to form compound expressions. Each individual expression in the compound expression has a value, as does the combination of these individual expressions. Consider this example of a compound expression:

```
(score < 0) || (score > 100)
```

The preceding compound expression tests to ensure that the value of a variable named "score" is in the range of 0 to 100. Each of the two expressions evaluates to either true or false. Between the two expressions is the Java logical OR operator. If either of the individual expressions evaluates to true, the compound expression evaluates to true. If both individual expressions evaluate to false, then the compound expression evaluates to false.

STATEMENTS

An expression on its own is not valid Java code. To make an expression valid, you must end it with a semicolon. As in C, Java offers a variety of statements, as shown in the following snippet:

```
int     score;       // declaration statement
boolean validScore;  // another declaration statement

score = 47;          // assignment statement

if ( (score < 0) || (score > 100) )  // if conditional
    validScore = true;               //       statement
```

The if statement illustrates that a statement can have more than one part. The if conditional statement begins with the keyword if, is followed by a test condition between parentheses, and concludes with the body of the loop. In the preceding example, the body of the if statement consists of a single statement: validScore = true;.

As in C, a statement body can consist of more than a single statement. In such cases the body must be enclosed in braces:

```
if ( (score < 0) || (score > 100) ) {
    validScore = true;
    score += bonus;
}
```

Together, the if keyword, the conditional test, and the body all make up the if statement. While the individual statements within the body end with a semicolon, the line containing the first line of the if statement—

the one holding the conditional test—and the last line of the `if` statement—the closing brace—don't. The `if` statement is called a *structured statement* because it has a structure that is more complex than other statements. As in C, Java-structured statements *don't* end with a semicolon. You'll encounter a more thorough description of the `if` statement, along with the other Java structured statements, in Chapter 7.

Comments

You can add comments to your Java source code using either the C-style multiline delimiters (`/*` and `*/`) or the C++-style single line delimiter (`//`).

To create a comment that extends across a single line, or to block out a section of code, use `/*` to begin the comment and `*/` to end it:

```
/* This applet, named MyFirstApplet, writes
   a single line of text to the user's Web
   browser window  */
```

To create a comment that is only one line in length, or only part of a line in length, use double-slashes:

```
int   testValue;     // this variable is used for testing only
```

Java also supports a third type of comment. Beginning a comment with the `/**` delimiter and ending it with the `*/` delimiter creates a multiline comment, just as the C-style comment delimiters do. However, this type of comment is helpful only if you're using Sun Microsystem's javadoc automatic documentation software tool.

Primitive Data Types

Java defines eight primitive data types: the `byte`, `short`, `int`, `long`, `float`, `double`, `boolean`, and `char`. These data types are referred to as primitive because they are simple types defined in the same way by all implementations of the Java language. For instance, any vendor that develops a Java compiler will define the short to be an integral data type that is 16 bits in size, has an initial default value of 0, and has a range of -32768 to +32767.

Having the basic data types defined to be machine-*dependent* is one portability issue for programs written in C or C++. For instance, some C compilers define a variable of type `int` to be two bytes, while others define such a variable to be four bytes. Machine-dependent basic data types are not an issue with the Java language.

Variables of any of the primitive types are always worked with *by value*. That is, a variable of a primitive type always holds a value rather than a reference to data elsewhere in memory. When a variable of a primitive type is passed to a method, the actual value of the variable is what gets passed.

Besides the primitive types of data, Java defines two *reference* types: objects and arrays. As you'll see later in this chapter, reference types are worked with *by reference* rather than by value.

OVERVIEW OF THE PRIMITIVE DATA TYPES

You're already very familiar with six of the eight Java primitive types—the `short`, `int`, `long`, `float`, `double`, and `char`. These six types are the standard data types defined by C. Depending on the C or C++ development environment you use, you may also be familiar with the remaining two Java primitive types—the `byte` and the `char`. While not a part of the standard C language, many C and C++ integrated development environments define these types for you. If your IDE doesn't, you may have to define the `byte` and `char` types yourself using the C `enum` keyword.

The Java primitive data types have names that are identical to, and uses that are similar to, their C counterparts. As you can see in Table 6-1, however, one difference is that Java strictly defines the size of its versions of these types. Again, this lack of ambiguity in data type size is one factor in making Java a machine-independent language.

Table 6-1
Primitive Data Types

Data Type	Use	Size	Initial Value	Range
byte	integer	8 bits	0	-128 to +127
short	integer	16 bits	0	-32768 to +32767
int	integer	32 bits	0	-2147483648 to +2147483647
long	integer	64 bits	0	-9223372036854775808 to +9223372036854775807
float	floating-point	0.0	32 bits	-3.40282347E+38 to +3.40282347E+38
double	floating-point	0.0	64 bits	-1.7976931348623157E+308 to +1.7976931348623157E+308
boolean	true or false	false	1 bit	N/A
char	Unicode character	\u0000	16 bits	\u0000 to \uFFFF

The Initial Value column in Table 6-1 makes it clear that in Java, uninitialized variables always have a known value. This is in contrast to C, in which the value of an uninitialized variable cannot always be relied upon.

The following sections provide additional details about the individual data types. Included in each section is a discussion about literals—explicit values entered into your code by you or entered into your applet (and read by your code) by the user. Integrals require special attention because they can be assigned to variables of different data types. For instance, here the literal 7 becomes both a `short` and an `int` data type:

```
short theShort = 7;
int   theInt;

theInt = 7;
```

INTEGRAL TYPES

Java defines four integral types of data: `byte`, `short`, `int`, and `long`. Variables of these types always occupy one, two, four, and eight bytes of memory, respectively.

DECLARATIONS AND ASSIGNMENTS

Variables of an integral type are defined just as they are in C. You've already seen examples of declarations of `int` variables. The following snippet demonstrates declarations and assignments using integral types. As in C, variables can optionally be assigned a value on declaration:

```
byte  theByte = 50;
short theShort = -623;
int   theInt;
long  theLong;

theInt = 5;
theLong = 6500000000;
```

Integral variables are always considered signed—no `signed` or `unsigned` keywords exist in Java. Variable declarations using any of these types cannot be prefaced by `signed` or `unsigned`. Similarly, declarations cannot be prefaced by `long` or `short`. Both of the following C declarations are illegal in Java:

```
unsigned int  theInt; // illegal in Java
short int     theInt; // illegal in Java
```

LITERALS

By default, an integral literal that is in the range of an `int` value (-2147483648 to +2147483647) is considered an `int`. The literals -5, 0, 88, or 3432223 are all examples. An integral literal that is outside of the range of an `int` is considered a `long`. Integral literals within the range of an `int` can be forced to occupy the full eight bytes of a `long` by appending either the `l` or `L` character to the literal. Examples include `-2L`, `72l`, and `835L`.

By default, integral literals are in decimal format. The Java technique for specifying that a literal be considered either a hexidecimal or octal value is identical to the C technique. You can specify that a literal is a hexadecimal (base 16) value by prefacing the number with a zero and either the x or X character. For example, decimal 32 can be represented as `0X20` or `0x20`. To specify that a literal is an octal (base 8) value, preface the number with a zero. An example of this is the decimal number 17, which in octal is expressed as `021`.

FLOATING-POINT TYPES

Java provides two floating-point types: `float` and `double`. Variables of these two types always occupy four and eight bytes of memory, respectively.

DECLARATIONS AND ASSIGNMENTS

Like integral variables, variables of a floating-point type are defined just as they are in C. The following snippet declares a variable of each of the two floating-point types. Assignment of a value at declaration is optional, as it is in C. Once a floating-point variable is declared, assign it a value as you would a C floating-point variable:

```
float  theFloat;
double theDouble;

theDouble = 2.05E4;
```

As in C, the exponent of a floating-point literal may be either the e or the E character. Examples include: `-3.2e5`, `4.54E10`, and `0.492e-2`.

LITERALS

By default, a floating-point literal is a `double`—regardless of its value. A floating-point literal can be forced to occupy only four bytes (rather than the eight bytes of a `double`) by appending either the `f` or `F` character to the literal. Examples include `-5.2e3F`, `6.3E-4f`, and `1.44F`.

Forcing a floating-point literal to type `float` is a technique that is not uncommon in Java. Consider the following snippet:

```
float  float1 = 4.9;  // illegal assignment
float  float2;

float2 = 0.875e3;             // illegal assignment
```

Both of these assignment statements result in an error during compilation. Because the variables in the preceding snippet are declared to be type `float`, and floating-point literals are, by default, type `double`, the compiler recognizes an incompatibility in the data types used in the assignment statements. To remedy this incompatibility, make sure to preface a floating-point literal with either an `f` or `F` character when assigning it to a variable of type `float`:

```
float  float1 = 4.9f;          // legal assignment
float  float2;

float2 = 0.875e3F;             // legal assignment
```

THE BOOLEAN TYPE

Java defines a `boolean` data type—a type C and C++ programmers are used to inventing on their own.

DECLARATIONS AND ASSIGNMENTS

C and C++ programmers may be used to defining their own Boolean data type, as in the following:

```
enum boolean { false, true }; // false = 0, true = 1
```

Because the C compiler maps `enum` values to their corresponding integer equivalent (the first `enum` value being 0), `enum` types can always be treated as integers:

```
boolean       allDone;
allDone = 0;  // same as allDone = false;
```

The same can *not* be said for Java `boolean` variables. In Java, `boolean` values are *not* integers and can *not* be used as integers. Instead, only the values `true` and `false` may by assigned to a Java `boolean` variable.

LITERALS

As just mentioned, Java `boolean` variables cannot be assigned the literals 0 and 1, as a C enumerated data type can be. Instead, the Java keywords `true` and `false` are always used.

THE CHAR TYPE

Unlike characters in C, Java characters always occupy two bytes. This is necessary because Java uses the 16-bit Unicode character set. Having two bytes to represent any one character means that the Unicode character set can consist of up to 65,536 different characters, compared to the 256 different characters of the ASCII character set. Having a character set this large enables the inclusion of alphabets of non-English countries. This makes Java an ideal programming language for internationalization—the art of creating programs that can be used by non-English speaking users.

The Unicode set can consist of over 65,000 characters, but it *doesn't.* Not yet, anyway. At this writing the set consists of about 34,000 defined characters. Don't worry about determining which of these thousands of characters you should be familiar with. The Unicode character set is compatible with the ASCII set: The first 256 characters of each set are identical. That means your ASCII chart is still applicable to your Java programming efforts.

The full list of Unicode characters appears in the two volume set, *The Unicode Standard, Worldwide Character Encoding*, Version 1.0, published by Addison-Wesley.

DECLARATIONS AND ASSIGNMENTS

As in C, you declare a variable of type `char` and then assign that variable a value by surrounding a character in single quotes. A value may be given to a `char` variable at declaration or anytime after:

```
char  failGrade = 'F';
char  averageGrade;

averageGrade = 'C';
```

LITERALS

As you've seen, a character literal consists of a character surrounded by single quotes. The Unicode set also supports the standard C character escape sequences, such as `\n` for a new line and `\t` for a tab:

```
char  newLineChar = '\n';
char  tabChar = '\t';
```

It's unlikely that your keyboard supports the thousands of Unicode characters beyond the ASCII characters. If you want to assign a `char` variable a Unicode character from, say, the Japanese language, you can't do so by simply typing in the character and surrounding it by single quotes. To make it possible to easily assign a `char` variable a foreign-language character, the Unicode character set also has its own escape sequence. The form of a Unicode escape is `\uhhhh`, where `hhhh` is four hexadecimal digits. Any of the Unicode characters can be expressed by using this escape sequence. Consider the character `A`, which is ASCII hexadecimal 41 (decimal 65). Because the ASCII characters map directly to Unicode characters, the Unicode character `A` is also hexadecimal 41. In Java, you can assign a `char` variable the `A` literal by either of the following two methods:

```
char   theLetterA = 'A';
char   anotherLetterA = '\u0041';
```

Your applet will easily be capable of displaying to the screen the A character held in variable `anotherLetterA`. That's because no matter which font your applet uses to display text, that font includes the A character. As of this writing, however, few fonts support the full Unicode character set. While you can use the Unicode escape sequence to assign a `char` variable any of the thousands of Unicode characters, displaying that character is another matter. If Java's popularity continues to increase at its current rapid pace, there will no doubt be new fonts soon that do include these characters.

Reference Data Types

Java data types fall into one of two categories: primitive or reference. Earlier in this chapter you saw that a variable that is of one of the primitive types holds a value. For instance, a variable of type `int` holds an integer, such as the number 37. A variable of one of the Java reference types, on the other hand, holds a reference to data. That is, such a variable refers to some other memory location in which the actual data is stored. In Java, arrays and objects of any class are reference types.

As you'll see in upcoming pages, Java strings are actually objects. `String` objects have a few peculiarities, which gives us cause to examine them apart from other types of objects.

JAVA REFERENCE TYPES AND C AND C++ POINTERS

The astute reader will notice that the preceding discussion of reference types seems suspiciously like discussions of C and C++ pointers. After all, when we describe a variable of a reference data type as something that "refers to some other memory location," aren't we really just talking about the same thing a pointer variable holds—an address? In fact, we are. Given that, the assertion that Java doesn't make use of pointers is incorrect. Java does in fact use pointers. A Java programmer, however, doesn't.

C and C++ provide the `&`, `*`, and `->` operators for determining a variable's address and for dereferencing a variable that holds an address. In those languages, the burden is on the programmer to allocate, reference, dereference, and deallocate memory properly. While Java also works with memory addresses, the burden of referencing, dereferencing, and deallocating memory never lies with the programmer. Only allocation (via `new`) is in the hands of the programmer.

Java documentation quite intentionally uses the word "reference" rather than the word "pointer" in an attempt to make a break from the C and C++ way of thinking. When programming in Java, trouble with accessing pointers, dereferencing pointers, explicitly releasing memory and destroying pointers, and dangling pointers will not be a source of headaches—as they were while tracking down bugs and crashes during your history as a C or C++ programmer! In Java, simply use `new` to allocate memory for an object or array and then forget about the object's or array's relationship with memory: Java will handle all memory-related concerns automatically.

In Java, a variable that is a reference to an object is generally thought of as the object itself. As you study Java, you may encounter illustrations similar to either of the ones shown below the code snippet in Figure 6-1. The bottom illustration in this figure is more technically correct than the top illustration: A variable that is an instance of a class doesn't hold the object itself, it holds a reference to the object. However, because as a Java programmer you aren't concerned with the details of memory allocation, addressing, or deallocation, the top illustration suffices just fine.

To summarize, variables of any of the Java primitive types, such as the `char`, `int`, and `float`, are worked with by value, while variables of the reference types—arrays and objects—are worked with by reference. For instance, consider a variable of type `float` that holds the value 3.14.

Passing this variable to a method results in the actual value being passed—the number 3.14. Now, consider a variable that is an object of the `Alien` type. Passing this variable to a method results in the address of the start of the `Alien` data being passed.

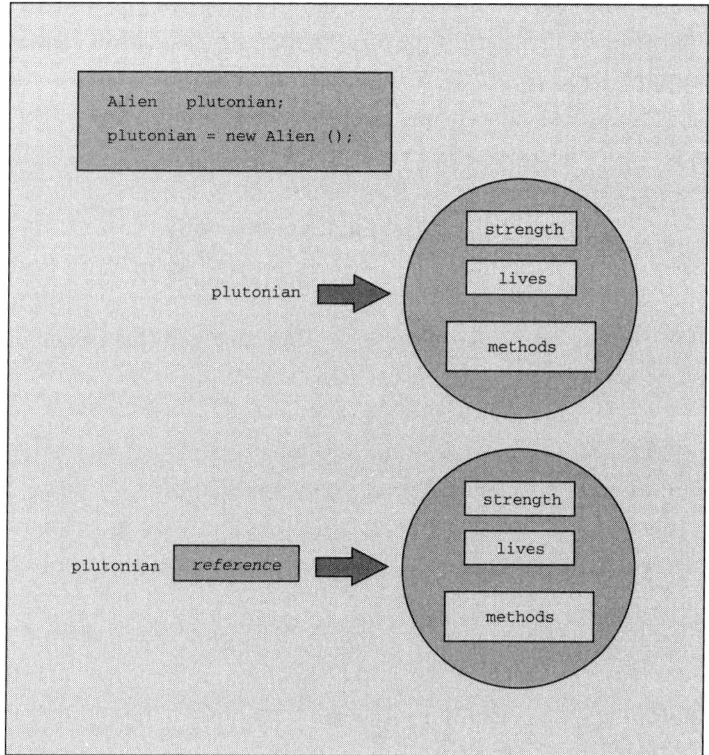

Figure 6-1

This shows two ways of illustrating that an object variable holds a reference to an object.

OBJECTS

Chapters 4 and 5 supply a sound introduction to objects from the standpoint of a C and C++ programmer, respectively. Chapter 8 is also dedicated to objects. In this chapter we'll concentrate on one particular type of object—the string.

STRINGS

Java isn't just a programming language: It's a huge set of classes your applets can use. You use the Java `import` statement to give your applet access to the classes in one or more Java packages. Recall from Chapter 3 that a package holds the compiled code for a number of classes. These classes, often (but not restricted to) Sun Microsystems-written classes, enable you to provide your own applet with a wide variety of functionality. Chapter 8 provides an overview of these classes, and many of the remaining chapters in this book are centered on the classes belonging to certain Java packages. Chapter 8 also discusses how objects of some of these class types can be created and then worked with.

Without repeating the material that makes up Chapter 8, we'll simply mention here that one of these Java classes is the `String` class. An instance of the `String` class is, of course, an object. That means in Java, each and every string is an object.

ARRAYS AND STRINGS

Programmers rely on strings in almost every application they write. Yet standard C and C++ do not offer a data type explicitly designed to hold a string. Instead, these languages rely on the array data type to hold the characters that make up strings.

While an array of characters is a somewhat satisfactory solution, it does have its drawbacks. Foremost is the fact that an array has a clearly defined, finite number of elements. Using an array with a fixed number of elements allows for the possibility of an out-of-bounds error—an error in which a program attempts to assign too many characters to an array. Java circumvents this problem by defining a `String` class from which `String` objects are instantiated.

Because a Java string is an object rather than an array, there exists no null character terminator to the string, as there is in a C string. The details of string termination in Java are unimportant to the programmer, because Java is responsible for verifying that no illegal string access takes place.

As you'll see a little later in this chapter, Java performs a similar bounds check on an array. In Java, unlike C, you won't ever encounter a run-time error related to an illegal array index.

STRING OBJECTS AND STRING LITERALS

To make use of any class (either defined by Java or defined by you), you must first declare a variable of the class type:

```
String   helpString;
```

To allocate memory for a `String` object, use `new`. The `String` class defines several constructors. Among them is a constructor that takes a single parameter: a string literal, enclosed in double quotes, to which the object should be initialized, as follows:

```
helpString = new String("Click on a button for help");
```

Java provides a second means of allocating memory for a string. When you declare a `String` variable, you can assign that variable a string literal. In Java, a string literal is any number of characters enclosed in double quotes. If you do this, Java automatically creates a `String` object, allocates memory for that object, and initializes the object to the string literal used in the assignment:

```
String   helpString = "Click on a button for help";
```

To create a `String` object without using `new`, the assignment doesn't have to take place at the time of declaration. Anytime Java encounters a string literal, it instantiates a `String` object. In this next snippet, Java creates a `String` object when `helpString` is assigned the string literal ***Click on a button for help***.

```
String helpString;

// other code here

helpString = "Click on a button for help";
```

Only objects of the `String` class make use of `new` optional when creating an object. The declaration and assignment of strings is such a common practice in programming that it makes sense for Java to take care of memory allocation for you.

STRINGS AND THE + OPERATOR

For concatenating two strings, Java redefines the + operator. Here are a couple of examples of the string concatenation operator:

```
String helloString = "Hello," + " World!";
String theBeat = "A one" + " and a two" + " and a three";
```

The two `String` objects created from the preceding assignments would have the value *Hello, World!* and *A one and a two and a three*.

Java gives the + operator two very different usages—the capability to add numbers and the capability to concatenate strings. C++ programmers will recognize this as something that appears to be operator overloading. Operator overloading isn't, however, a feature of Java. Your own Java code can't redefine how an operator works.

The two strings used in the prior snippet are somewhat artificial examples in that the strings `helloString` and `theBeat` could be assigned the same literals without the use of the + operator. The following snippets exhibit more practical applications of the string concatenation operator:

```
String      helpString;
String      finalValueStr;
String      buttonColor;
int         finalValue;

buttonColor = "red";
finalValue = 5422;

helpString = "Click on the " + buttonColor + " button for help";
finalValueStr = "Final value was " + finalValue;
```

After the preceding snippet executes, the `helpString` object will have a value of *Click on the red button for help*, while the `finalValueStr` object will have a value of *Final value was 5422*.

In the last line of the preceding snippet, you see that the + operator is capable of concatenating an integer variable and a string. The string concatenation operator is especially powerful in that Java can concatenate non-`String` object operands with `String` object operands. It will do this by making a copy of the contents of any variable of any primitive type that appears as an operand, converting that copy to a `String` object, and then concatenating this temporary object with any other `String` object operands.

STRING METHODS

A string is an object based on the `String` class. Java defines the `String` class to consist of a number of methods that can be used to work with objects of type `String`. As you read in Chapters 4 and 5, you use the dot to invoke a method. To the left of the dot is the object's name, to the right is the name of the method to invoke. Invoking a method of the `String` class to act upon a `String` object follows this same process.

The CD-ROM bundled with this book includes Sun Microsystem's API (application programming interface) documentation for the Java language. In that documentation, you'll find a brief description of each of the dozens of methods that are a part of the `String` class. Chapter 8 of this book provides a hierarchy of the Java classes, as well as a look at how Sun's documentation can best be used.

Determining a string's length The `String` class defines a `length()` method that returns an `int` that holds the length of the string. The length of a `String` object is the number of Unicode characters in the string. Note that because each Unicode character occupies 16 bits, the length of a string is not the same as the number of bytes in the string. The `length()` method can be used on any `String` object:

```
String   introStr = "Welcome to Java!";      // 16 character string
String   byeStr   = "Goodbye";               // 7 character string
String   theString;                          // no string yet
int      strLength;

strLength = introStr.length();       // strLength becomes 16
strLength = byeStr.length();         // strLength becomes 7
```

In the preceding snippet, `strLength` is first assigned a value of 16—the length of the `introStr` string. Next, the same variable is assigned a value of 7—the length of the `byeStr`. Notice that we didn't invoke the length method on the third string—`theString`. Recall that Java doesn't create a `String` object until it encounters a string literal. Because `theString` hasn't been assigned a string literal yet, there is no object upon which to act.

Converting a string to lowercase To convert a string to lowercase, invoke the `String` method `toLowerCase()`. Calling this method creates a copy of the string being acted upon, converts any uppercase characters in this copy to lowercase, and assigns the new, converted string to the `String` variable named to the left of the assignment operator:

```
String    introStr = "Welcome to Java!";
String    lowerStr;

lowerStr = introStr.toLowerCase();
```

After the preceding code executes, the `lowerStr` variable will have a value of *welcome to java!* The `introStr String` object retains the original, unaltered version of the string: *Welcome to Java!* Assigning `lowerStr` this literal string causes Java to create a new `String` object—one referenced by the `lowerStr` variable.

Converting a string to uppercase If you understand how the `toLowerCase()` method works, you also understand how its companion method, `toUpperCase()` operates.

```
String introStr = "Welcome to Java!";
String upperStr;

upperStr = introStr.toUpperCase();
```

After the preceding snippet runs, `upperStr` has a value of *WELCOME TO JAVA!*

COMPARING STRING OBJECTS

As you'll see later in this chapter, Java employs the use of many of the same operators found in C. Among these are the relational operators (<, >, <=, >=) and the equality operators (==, !=). These operators can be used with variables of primitive types as expected: to see if the value of one variable is less than the value of another, and so forth. Objects consist of both data and methods. For this reason, it wouldn't make sense to use the relational operators on two objects: Checking to see if an object is less than another isn't a practical test. However, the other comparative operators, the equality operators, *can* be used in object comparisons.

EQUALITY OPERATORS AND STRINGS

Later in this chapter, you'll encounter detailed descriptions of the two Java equality operators: the equal operator (==) and the not equal operator (!=). These operators are used to make comparisons of variables of the primitive integral data types, such as the `int`:

```
int          score1 = 57;
int          score2 = 59;
boolean      areEqual;

areEqual = (score1 == score2);       // false, scores are not the
    same
```

The two equality operators can also be used to make comparisons of objects, though perhaps not in the manner you might expect. Rather than test to see if the *contents* of two operands are identical, the `==` and `!=` operators can be used to see if two operands *reference* the same object. Consider the following snippet:

```
String    string1 = new String("abc");
String    string2 = new String("abc");
boolean   areEqual;

areEqual = (string1 == string2);
```

While the strings `string1` and `string2` certainly hold identical text, `areEqual` nonetheless ends up with a value of `false`. This is because in Java, strings are objects: The equality test made in the preceding snippet is to see if `string1` and `string2` both refer to the same object. Figure 6-2 clearly shows that the two variables reference different objects. This figure conceptualizes a `String` object by showing the value and length of the string. The dozens of methods defined for a `String` object aren't shown.

When using the equality operators on two `String` objects, you should heed one caveat: Java is clever enough to recognize two identical strings and optimizes the two string literals such that only one object exists. Consider the following snippet:

```
String string1 = "abc";
String string2 = "abc";

areEqual = (string1 == string2);
```

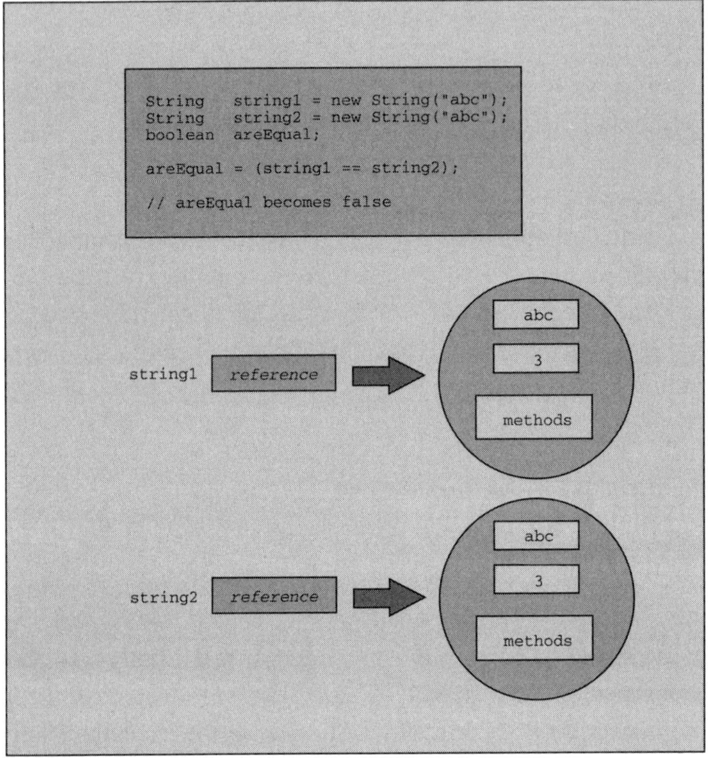
String string1 = new String("abc");
String string2 = new String("abc");
boolean areEqual;
areEqual = (string1 == string2);
// areEqual becomes false
abc
3
string1
reference
methods
abc
3
string2
reference
methods

Figure 6-2
The == operator reports whether two `String` *variables reference the same object—not whether two* `String` *variables each hold identical strings.*

In the preceding code, the content of the two strings is the same as the content of the two strings shown back in Figure 6-2. The equality tests used in the preceding snippet and the snippet shown in Figure 6-2 are also the same. Yet the value `areEqual` takes on in the two snippets differs. In this latest example, Java reports that the two strings are equal; in the Figure 6-2 example, the strings were deemed unequal. In Figure 6-2, the objects were explicitly allocated using `new`. In the preceding code, `new` isn't used. Instead, allocation of the two `String` objects is left to Java.Given its freedom to perform the memory allocation, Java saves memory by allocating a single `String` object that is referenced by both the `string1` and the `string2` variables. Figure 6-3 illustrates.

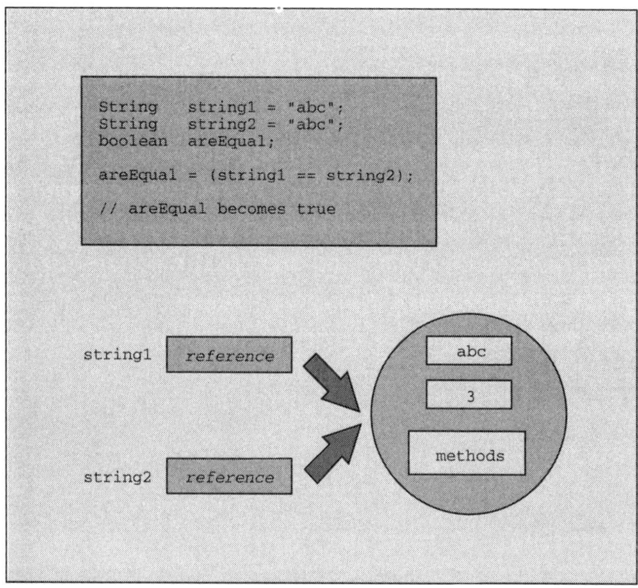
String string1 = "abc";
String string2 = "abc";
boolean areEqual;
areEqual = (string1 == string2);
// areEqual becomes true
string1
reference
string2
reference
abc
3
methods

Figure 6-3

The == operator reports that two String variables are equal if both variables reference the same String object.

THE STRING EQUALS() METHOD AND STRINGS

So how *do* you go about determining if the characters that comprise the strings of two different String objects are identical? By invoking the equals() method—one of the many methods provided by the String class. To make use of the equals() method, invoke it on either String object. This method requires a single argument—the second of the two strings that are to be compared.

```
String      string1 = new String("abc");
String      string2 = new String("abc");
boolean     areEqual;

areEqual = string1.equals(string2);
```

In the preceding example, areEqual is assigned a value of true—the two strings hold the same characters and are of the same length. Figure 6-4 highlights the fact that the equals() method asks if the *characters* of two strings are identical.

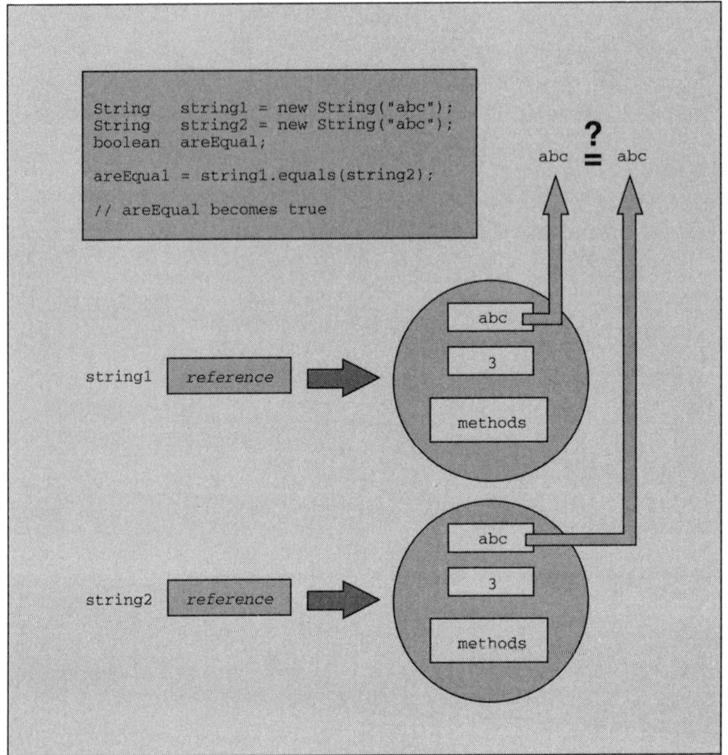
String string1 = new String("abc");
String string2 = new String("abc");
boolean areEqual;
areEqual = string1.equals(string2);
// areEqual becomes true
abc ? = abc
abc
3
methods
string1
reference
abc
3
methods
string2
reference

Figure 6-4
The `equals()` *method of the* `String` *class reports whether two* `String` *objects hold identical strings.*

AN EQUALS() METHOD FOR OBJECTS OF ANY CLASS TYPE

The `equals()` method that is a part of the `String` class is clearly the route to take if your applet is to compare two strings for equality. This method returns a `boolean` value that tells if the characters of each string are identical. The equality operators (`==` and `!=`) return a `boolean` value that contains the less valuable information of whether the strings reference the same object.

For objects of other class types, similar methods should be developed. While you *can* use either of the equality operators (`==` or `!=`) on objects of your own class types, what you'll really want to do is write `equals()` methods instead. As a specific example, we'll again rely on our own `Alien` class—a class introduced in Chapters 4 and 5. To consider two aliens equal, we might compare the strength and lives instance variables of each to see if they have identical values. Given that definition of equality of two `Alien` objects, an `equals()` method added to the `Alien` class would look like this:

```
class Alien {

    int       strength;
    int       lives;

    // other methods here

    boolean equals( Alien compare ) {

        if ( (strength == compare.strength) && (lives ==
    compare.lives))
            return true;
        else
            return false;
    }
}
```

In Java, the `&&` operator works as it does in C: Only if the first expression and the second expression are true does the entire compound expression resolve to a value of true. More on the `&&` operator and the other logical operators will be discussed later in this chapter.

Invoking the preceding version of `equals()` would accomplish what is expected: The dot is used with one `Alien` object, while another `Alien` object is passed as a parameter. In the following snippet, the Boolean variable `aliensEqual` resolves to `false`. Changing the value of the parameter from 3 to 2 in the call to the `setLives()` method for `alien2` would result in `aliensEqual` evaluating to `true`.

```
Alien          alien1;
Alien          alien2;
boolean        aliensEqual;

alien1 = new Alien();
alien2 = new Alien();

alien1.setStrength( 5 );
alien1.setLives( 2 );
alien2.setStrength( 5 );
alien2.setLives( 3 );

aliensEqual = plutonian.equals(drakonian);    // false, lives differ
```

ARRAYS

As it is in C and C++, an array is a data structure used to store any number of items of the same data type. For instance, a Java array can hold a number of `ints` or a number of `floats` or a number of `String` objects or a number of applet-defined objects, such as `Alien` objects. But a *single* array cannot hold a *combination* of these types. Like a C or C++ array, a Java array is created with a set number of elements—placeholders in which values can be added and from which values can later be removed.

THE DUALITY OF ARRAYS

Arrays have a sort of dual nature in C and C++. While generally treated as a data structure holding a number of elements, a C or C++ array can also be treated as the pointer that it really is. For instance, a C or C++ array name can be used as a pointer. Consider the following C snippet:

```
int intArray[5];
int theInt;
int anotherInt;

intArray[3] = 99;
theInt = intArray[3];
anotherInt = *(intArray + 3);
```

The preceding example results in both `theInt` and `anotherInt` taking on a value of 99—the value of the fourth element in the array `intArray`. The first case is straightforward—provided you keep in mind that in a C array element, indices start with 0. That means that the fourth element of the array `intArray` has an index of 3.

In the second case, pointer arithmetic is used. The name of an array serves as a pointer to that array—the starting address of the array. Adding a value to an array name is done to provide an offset into the array. This offset is in terms of array elements—not bytes. Thus, adding 3 to an array name always has the effect of referencing the fourth element in the array—the third element *beyond* the element pointed to by the array name (element 0). This is true *regardless* of the byte size of each array element.

Finally, using the * operator dereferences this pointer and returns the value in the fourth element. In the preceding example, the value of the fourth element of the array is the integer 99.

So far our discussion of arrays has centered on C language arrays in general and the dual nature of these C arrays in particular. The intent is to make you feel comfortable with the idea that a data type can seemingly be two things at once. This is important in dealing with Java arrays because while Java arrays don't behave identically to C arrays, they also have a dual nature.

A Java array is like an object in that it is a reference data type. Passing an array to a method results in a reference to the array (rather than the array itself) being passed. As you're about to see, memory for an array is allocated using `new`—just as it is for an object. Once your applet is finished with an array, garbage collection automatically disposes of it—as is true with an object. Finally, as discussed ahead, an array has a single instance variable associated with it. The length variable holds the length of, or number of elements in, an array.

How does an array, which can be considered an object, differ from other types of objects? An array can't be subclassed. That is, you can't use the extend keyword on an array. When an array is created, no constructor is invoked.

This discussion should aid in your understanding of why some other Java references refer to arrays as objects, while others refer to arrays as a nonobject data type.

CREATING AN ARRAY

To create an array in Java, first declare an array variable. Because the declaration of the array doesn't reserve memory for the array, at this time you *don't* specify the number of elements that the array will hold. Instead, follow the array name with a pair of brackets:

```
int intArray[];
```

Alternately, you can place the brackets after the data type rather than after the variable name:

```
int[] intArray;
```

While perfectly valid in Java, this technique is less legible to C programmers and results in a little extra work should you be required to port your Java code to C or C++.

After the declaration, allocate memory for the array by using `new`. Follow `new` with the data type of the elements of which the array will consist. Follow the data type with a pair of brackets between which should be a number that specifies the number of elements of which the array should consist:

```
intArray = new int[5];        // an array of 5 integers
```

Java offers a second method for creating an array—one that doesn't use new. If you assign values to an array at declaration, then Java knows the number of elements of which the array will consist and hence knows the memory requirements of the array. In that case, Java can go ahead and allocate the array without your explicit use of new:

```
int intArray[] = {1, 3, 6, 9, 12};
```

Except for the omission of the number of array elements between the brackets, the preceding statement looks identical to a C initialization of an array.

The two techniques for creating an array are comparable to those for creating a string. Recall that a String object can be created using new, or it can be created without new if at the time of declaration the string variable is initialized. For both the array and the string, memory can be allocated at initialization because the compiler can determine the size of each from the initialization.

ACCESSING ELEMENTS OF AN ARRAY

Accessing an array element in Java is identical to accessing an array element in C: Name the array, follow the name with the dot, then place the index to the element between brackets.

```
int intArray[] = { 1, 3, 6, 9, 12 };
int theInt;

intArray[0] = 2;       // set the value of the 1st element to 2
theInt = intArray[4];  // assign theInt the value of the 5th
                       // element of the array
```

Java arrays offer one feature not found in C or C++: You can determine the number of elements of an array by checking the array's only instance variable—the length variable. The value of length is set by Java; you don't have to worry about ensuring that its value is correct. In fact, because length is read-only, you can't alter its value. This next snippet provides a look at a typical use for length:

```
int intArray[];
int i;
```

```
intArray = new int[6];     // array with six elements, 0 through 5

for (i = 0; i < intArray.length; i++)
    intArray[i] = i*2;     // set array elements to: 0,2,4,6,8,10
```

USING PRIMITIVE DATA TYPES AND REFERENCE DATA TYPES AS ARRAY ELEMENTS

As you'd expect, a Java array that consists of elements of one of the Java primitive types (such as `int`, `short`, or `float`) holds actual values rather than references. When you assign such an array element the value of a variable, a copy of the variable's value is placed in the array. In the following snippet the first element of an integer array consisting of three elements is assigned the value of variable `theInt`, as Figure 6-5 illustrates.

```
int intArray[];
int theInt = 5;

intArray = new int[3];
intArray[0] = theInt;
```

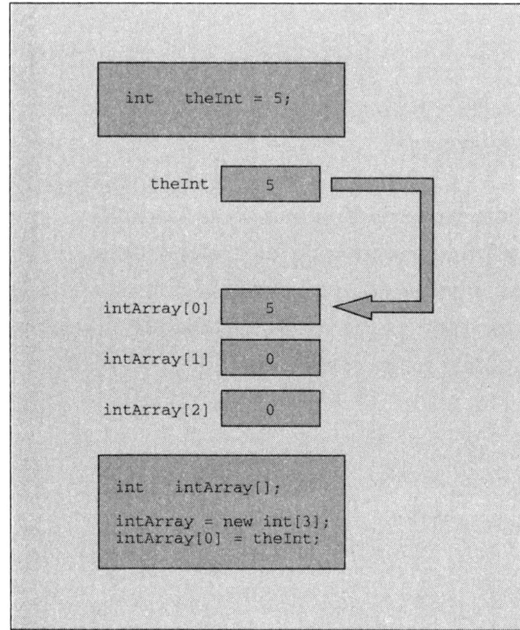

Figure 6-5

An array of elements of a primitive data type holds actual values—not references.

Because the actual number 5 has been stored in the first element of the array, rather than a reference to `theInt`, no association exists between the array element and variable `theInt`. Figure 6-6 illustrates this by showing that a change in the value of `theInt` does not affect the value in the first array element.

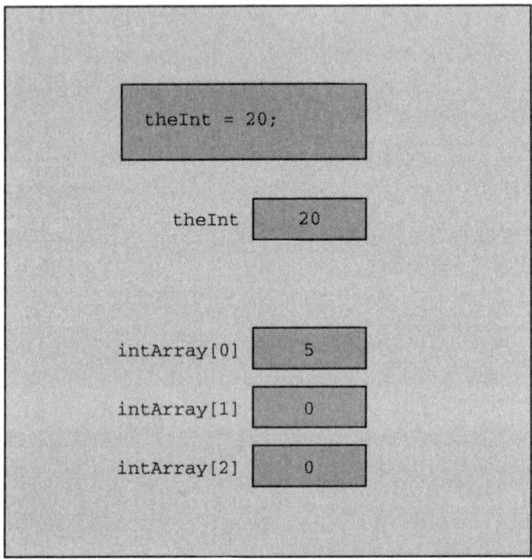

Figure 6-6
Changes to variable values have no effect on the elements in an array consisting of elements of a primitive type.

While the preceding information about arrays and primitive types may seem intuitive, it is helpful groundwork for understanding how arrays work with objects. In Java, an array of an object type consists of references to objects—not of the objects themselves. Consider the following snippet, which uses the familiar `Alien` class:

```
Alien alienArray[];
Alien plutonian;

plutonian = new Alien();
plutonian.setStrength( 5 );
plutonian.setLives( 6 );

alienArray = new Alien[3];
alienArray[0] = plutonian;
```

The preceding snippet declares an array of `Alien` objects and a single `Alien` object. Memory is then allocated for the single object, and that object's two instance variables are assigned values. After that, memory is allocated for the array, which consists of three elements. Finally, the first element of the array is assigned a reference to the object that `plutonian` references. Figure 6-7 shows that the assignment of `plutonian` to `alienArray[0]` results in both referencing the same object. Notice that no copy of the object is made. This differs from the earlier example that used an array of a primitive type. Note that in Figure 6-7 the remaining two elements of the array have reference values of `null`—the default value Java gives to elements of an array of objects.

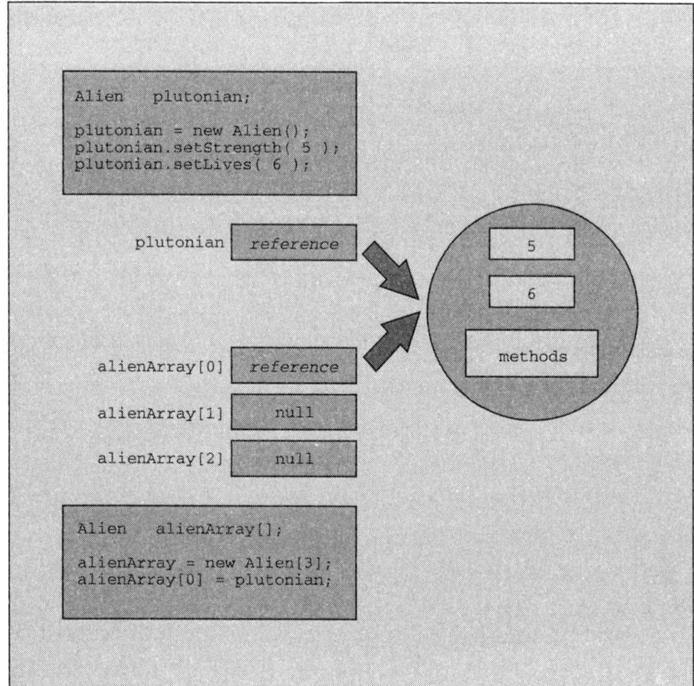

Figure 6-7
An array of elements of an object data type holds references to objects.

Because both the object variable `plutonian` and the first element of the object array, `alienArray`, reference the same object, changes to the object will affect both the variable and the array element. Again, this differs from arrays of a primitive type. Figure 6-8 uses the following snippet to illustrate that the calling of methods of the plutonian object will affect the object referenced by `alienArray[0]`:

```
plutonian.setStrength( 7 );
plutonian.setLives( 8 );
```

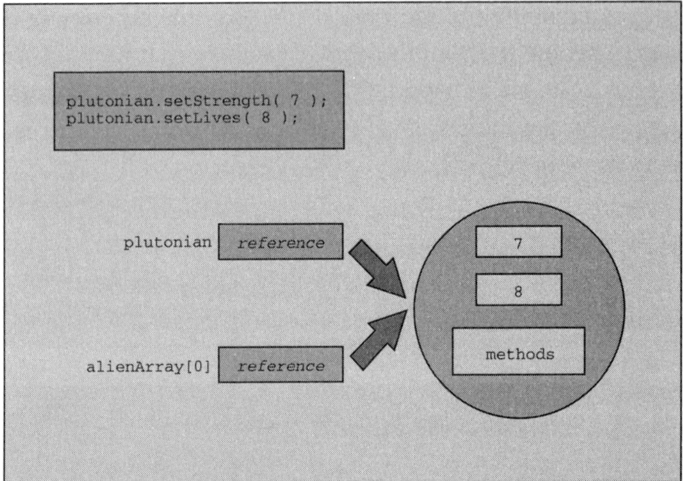

Figure 6-8
Changes to variable values can affect the elements in an array that consists of elements of an object type.

Operators

The Java language includes a wealth of operators—including most of the same operators that are a part of C. This means we can move quickly in our coverage of most of the Java operators.

VARIETIES OF OPERATORS

Java operators include six main varieties: arithmetic, relational, equality, conditional, logical, and bitwise.

ARITHMETIC OPERATORS

All of the basic C arithmetic operators are found in Java. If you're familiar with C or C++, you'll feel right at home in this section. Table 6-2 summarizes the operators that are described in this section. In this table, assume that in each example, variable *x* is of an integral data type, and that at the start of each example this variable has a value of 10.

Table 6-2
Arithmetic Operators

Operator	Operation	Example (x initially 10)	Result (x becomes)
+	Addition	x = x + 5	15
-	Subtraction	x = x - 12	-2
*	Multiplication	x = x * 2	20
/	Division	x = x / 3	3
%	Modulus	x = x % 3	1
+=	Add and assign	x += 6	16
-=	Subtract and assign	x -= 6	4
*=	Multiply and assign	x *= 6	60
/=	Divide and assign	x /= 6	1
%=	Modulus and assign	x %= 6	4
++	Increment	x++	11
--	Decrement	x--	9

FUNDAMENTAL OPERATORS

The basic arithmetic operators used in Java are the same as those used in C: +, -, *, and /, for addition, subtraction, multiplication, and division, respectively. As expected, each operator acts as it does in C.

When an operator is used in an expression consisting of both an integral operand and a floating-point operand, the result is stored as a floating-point—that's true in C as well. One difference with Java is that this result must be explicitly typecast to an integral type if it is to be stored in an integral variable. In C, the following snippet would compile: The intermediate result of 3.4 would be truncated to 3 and then stored in variable `int2`:

```
int   int1 = 3;
int   int2;
float float1 = 0.4f;
```

```
int2 = int1 + float1; // legal code in C/C++, not in Java
```

In Java, the preceding code would result in a compile-time error: You can't assign a floating-point (the result of int1 + float1) to an integer (int2). To carry out this operation, typecast the operation result to match the data type of the operand to the left of the assignment operator. Here, the result of the addition is typecast to an int—the data type of int2:

```
int   int1 = 3;
int   int2;
float float1 = 0.4f;

int2 = (int) (int1 + float1); // legal code in Java
```

The preceding example illustrates that in Java you typecast a value or expression by preceding the value or expression with the data type to which to cast, enclosed in parentheses. Typecasting is discussed in detail in Chapter 7. The preceding example also introduces the float data type—a type covered later in this chapter.

MODULUS OPERATORS

In Java, as in C, the result of integral division that is to be stored in an integral variable is truncated: The remainder is dropped. In this Java snippet int3 is assigned a value of 4:

```
int int1 = 14;
int int2 = 3;
int int3;

int3 = int1 / int2;   // 14/3 = 4 with a remainder of 2
```

To preserve the remainder of integral division, use the modulus, or remainder operator—just as you would in C:

```
int int1 = 14;
int int2 = 3;
int int3;
int int4;

int3 = int1 / int2;   // int3 becomes 4
int4 = int1 % int2;   // int4 becomes 2 (the remainder of 14/3)
```

ASSIGNMENT OPERATORS

You've worked with the assignment operator (=) countless times already, so no explanation of that operators function is necessary. When one of the fundamental operators, or the modulus operator, is used in conjunction with the assignment operator, the result is a new operator—an arithmetic assignment operator. Your C or C++ background may have given you experience with each of these five Java operators: +=, -=, *=, /=, and %=.

The Java arithmetic assignment operators work as they do in C: The operator acts on the operands to its left and right and stores the result in the operand to the left. In the following example, int1 will have a value of 9 after execution:

```
int int1 = 4;
int int2 = 5;

int1 += int2; // same as int1 = int1 + int2;
```

INCREMENT AND DECREMENT OPERATORS

To increment the value of a variable by one, use the Java increment operator (++). To decrement by one, use the decrement operator (--):

```
int theCount = 6;
int theIndex = 15;

theCount++;    // theCount becomes 7
theIndex--;    // theIndex becomes 14
```

As in C, either of these operators can be used in prefix or postfix mode. The mode used affects the time at which the operation takes place. If the operator is used in prefix mode (++theCount), the operation takes place before the expression in which the variable appears takes place. If the operator is used postfix (theCount++), the operation takes place after the expression. The following is a prefix mode example:

```
int theCount = 6;

if ( ++theCount < 7 );        // test fails
```

In the preceding example, the test will fail: theCount is *not* less than 7. That's because prefix mode causes the value of theCount to increment from 6 to 7 *before* the comparison is made. In the following postfix example, the test will pass: theCount *is* less than 7. This is true because postfix mode prevents theCount from being incremented until *after* the comparison is made:

```
int theCount = 6;

if ( theCount++ < 7 );        // test passes
```

The preceding examples previewed the Java relational operators (the less than operator, <) and a Java if conditional. Comparison operators are covered next. The if conditional, which is essentially the same in Java and C, is covered in Chapter 7.

RELATIONAL OPERATORS

In Java, comparisons between two values are made using the same relational, or comparison, operators found in C. While the operators are the same as those used in C, the value returned isn't. In C, the result of a comparison is 0 for false and 1 for true. In Java, a comparison result is of type boolean. As discussed earlier in this chapter, a Java boolean can have a value of either false or true only. Java doesn't equate integer values with false or true. Table 6-3 lists each of the Java relational operators.

Table 6-3
Relational Operators

Operator (expression evaluates to)	Operation	Example (x initially 10)	Result
<	Less than	if (x < 5)	false
>	Greater than	if (x > 5)	true
<=	Less than or equal to	if (x <= 10)	true
>=	Greater than or equal to	if (x >= 10)	true

EQUALITY OPERATORS

The two Java equality operators are similar to the Java relational operators in that each is used to compare two values, and each returns a boolean value that isn't mapped to an integer value. Table 6-4 shows the two equality operators.

Table 6-4
Equality Operators

Operator (expression evaluates to)	Operation	Example (x initially 10)	Result
==	Equal to	if (x == 5)	false
!=	Not equal to	if (x != 5)	true

CONDITIONAL OPERATORS

The Java conditional operator (?:) works as it does in C. The three operands—each itself an expression—the ?: operator works with are arranged in the following format:

```
expression1 ? expression2 : expression3
```

If expression1 evaluates to true, then the entire expression evaluates to expression2. If expression1 instead evaluates to false, then the entire expression instead evaluates to expression3. Here's an example:

```
int x = 5;
int y = 3;
int z;

z = (x > 4) ? y : 2; // z becomes 3
```

In the preceding example, expression1 is (x > 4), expression2 is y, and expression3 is 2. Because expression1 evaluates to true (x, which is 5, is greater than 4), the overall expression evaluates to expression2, which is y.

As it is in C, the conditional operator serves as a shorthand notation for an if-else statement. The preceding example could be written in Java (or in C) as the following:

```
int x = 5;
int y = 3;
int z;

if ( x > 4 )
    z = y;
else
    z = 2;
```

Obvious to you now is the fact that the Java `if-else` branch is identical to the `if-else` used in C and C++.

LOGICAL OPERATORS

Any two expressions that each evaluate to `true` or `false` can be further evaluated using one of the Java logical operators. Table 6-5 lists these operators.

Table 6-5
Logical Operators

Operator (expression evaluates to)	Operation	Example (x initially 10)	Result
&&	Logical AND	if (x > 5 && x < 8)	false
||	Logical OR	if (x > 5 || x < 8)	true
^	Logical XOR	if (x > 5 ^ x < 8)	false
!	Logical NOT	if (!(x ==5))	true

The AND operator (`&&`) will evaluate to `true` if and only if the expressions on both sides of the `&&` evaluate to `true`.

```
int x = 1;
int y = 2;

if (x < y && x != y) // true: left and right expressions both true
if (x < y && x == y) // false: right expression is false
```

The OR operator (`||`) will evaluate to `true` if either of the expressions being operated on by the `||` operator evaluates to `true`.

```
int x = 1;
int y = 2;

if (x < y || x == y) // true: left expression is true
if (x > y || x == y) // false: neither expression is true
```

The XOR operator (^) will evaluate to `true` if only one of the two expressions on which it operates evaluates to `true`. If both expressions are `true` or if both expressions are `false`, XOR evaluates to `false`.

```
int x = 1;
int y = 2;

if (x < y ^ x == y)   // true: left expression is true, right is
    false
if (x < y ^ x != y)   // false: both expressions are true
```

Unlike the other logical operators, the NOT operator (!) works on only one expression. If the expression to the right of the operator is `false`, the result is `true`. If the expression is `true`, the result is `false`.

```
int x = 1;
int y = 2;

if (!(x > y)) // true: expression is false, so result is true
if (!(x < y)) // false: expression is true, so result is false
```

BITWISE OPERATORS

Like C, Java offers bitwise logical operators and shift operators; they're shown in Table 6-6. Each of the bitwise operators performs a bit-by-bit operation on the two expressions on which the operator works. The only exception is the bitwise NOT, or bitwise complement, operator, which acts on only one operator.

Table 6-6

Bitwise Operators

<table>
<tr><th>Operator</th><th>Operation</th><th>Explanation</th></tr>
<tr><td>&</td><td>Bitwise AND</td><td>Bit-by-bit AND-ing of two operands</td></tr>
<tr><td>|</td><td>Bitwise OR</td><td>Bit-by-bit OR-ing of two operands</td></tr>
<tr><td>^</td><td>Bitwise XOR</td><td>Bit-by-bit XOR-ing of two operands</td></tr>
<tr><td>~</td><td>Bitwise NOT</td><td>Bit-by-bit complement of one operand</td></tr>
<tr><td><<</td><td>Left shift</td><td>Shift left operand bits to the left by the number of places given by the right operand</td></tr>
<tr><td>>></td><td>Right shift</td><td>Shift left operand bits to the right by the number of places given by the right operand</td></tr>
<tr><td>>>></td><td>Right shift with zero extension</td><td>Fill in high bits of shifted value with zeros</td></tr>
</table>

Because the bitwise operators act in a manner identical to their C counterparts and because these operators won't surface again in this book, we'll leave a thorough study of these operators to the C or C++ references you already have. Here we'll simply list an example of each, followed by a few notes:

```
int x = 5;     // binary is 101 (with 29 leading 0's)
int y = 6;     // binary is 110 (with 29 leading 0's)
int z;

z = x & y;     // z becomes 4: 101 AND'ed with 110 gives 100
z = x | y;     // z becomes 7: 101 OR'ed with 110 gives 111
z = x ^ y;     // z becomes 3: 101 XOR'ed with 110 gives 011
z = ~x;        // z becomes -6: NOT of 101 is 010 (+ 29 leading 1's)
               // Two's compliment results in value of -6
z = x << 2;    // z becomes 20: 101 shifted 2 bits left gives 10100
z = x >> 2;    // z becomes  1: 101 shifted 2 bits right gives 001
z = x >>> 2;   // z becomes  1: 101 shifted 2 bits right gives 001
```

Recall from C that the bitwise NOT, or bitwise complement, operator (!) works on all of the bits of the operand. A decimal value of 5 may be thought of as 101 in binary. In fact, if the decimal value 5 is held in an `int` variable (which in Java is always four bytes), then the binary representation is actually 101 preceded by 29 1's (for the full 32 bits of the `int` variable). While the leading bits with a value of 0 are inconsequential in some bitwise operations (such as AND, OR, and XOR), these bits are of importance to the NOT operation—as these leading 0's will all become 1's.

In Java, integral types are always signed. When the right shift operator (>>) is applied to an operand, the operation preserves the value of the operand's upper bit—its sign bit. An operand with a value of 1 in its upper bit represents a negative number. Shifting such a value any number of bits to the right would turn this number into a positive value if the upper bit (which was a 1) was shifted to the right and this upper bit was filled in with a 0. The >> operator will instead preserve the sign bit, filling in this upper bit with a value of 1 after the shift has been made.

Java introduces a bitwise operator not found in C—the right shift with zero extension operator (>>>). This operator works as the right shift operator (>>) does in that it shifts the bits of the left operand to the right. However, the >>> operator will fill in any shifted upper bits with a value of 0. Thus the >>> operator does not preserve the sign of the operand.

Finally, it should be noted that each of the operators shown in Table 6-6, with the exception of the bitwise NOT operator, has an assignment operator counterpart. These operators include: &=, |=, ^=, <<=, >>=, and >>>=. Use of these assignment operators is the same as for the arithmetic assignment operators. Thus the following two expressions evaluate identically:

```
z = z & y;
z &= y;
```

PRECEDENCE OF OPERATORS

In expressions that use more than one operator, order of evaluation becomes important. Consider the following snippet:

```
int   z;
z = 8 + 2 * 3;
```

If the preceding code is executed operand-by-operand, it would evaluate to 30 (8 added to 2 is 10, multiplied by 3 is 30). If instead the multiplication operator had a higher *precedence* than the addition operator (that is, if the compiler evaluated the part of the expression that involved the multiplication operator before it evaluated the part of the expression that involved the addition operator), the preceding code would evaluate to 14 (2 multiplied by 3 is 6, added to 8 is 14). In fact, in Java, as in C, the multiplication operator is of a higher precedence than the addition operator—meaning the preceding snippet would evaluate to 14.

Table 6-7 shows the order of precedence for the Java operators. An operator that appears in a row above another operator is of a higher precedence. All operators appearing in the same row are of a precedence equal to one another. Should the compiler encounter an expression that includes two operators of the same precedence, the compiler will work with the first of these operators that it encounters (that is, the leftmost of the two operators).

As in C, order of precedence can be forced by the inclusion of parentheses. In the previous example, a result of 30 could be achieved by writing the expression as follows:

```
z = (8 + 2) * 3;
```

Barring parentheses, order of evaluation is based on Table 6-7.

Table 6-7
Operator Precedence

<table>
<tr><th>Precedence</th><th>Operator</th></tr>
<tr><td>1</td><td>++ -- ~ !</td></tr>
<tr><td>2</td><td>* / %</td></tr>
<tr><td>3</td><td>+ -</td></tr>
<tr><td>4</td><td><< >> >>></td></tr>
<tr><td>5</td><td>< <= > >=</td></tr>
<tr><td>6</td><td>== !=</td></tr>
<tr><td>7</td><td>&</td></tr>
<tr><td>8</td><td>^</td></tr>
<tr><td>9</td><td>|</td></tr>
<tr><td>10</td><td>&&</td></tr>
<tr><td>11</td><td>||</td></tr>
<tr><td>12</td><td>?:</td></tr>
<tr><td>13</td><td>= *= /= %= += -= <<= >>=>>>= &= ^= != </td></tr>
</table>

What You've Learned

An expression is a combination of operands and operators, and always has some value. Statements are what your Java source code is composed of. At its simplest, a statement is nothing more than an expression suffixed with a semicolon. As discussed in Chapter 7, more complex statements, such as branch and loop statements, involve more than a single line of code.

The simplest Java data types are referred to as primitive data types. Included in this category are the `byte`, `short`, `int`, `long`, `float`, `double`, `boolean`, and `char` data types. Each of these has strong similarities to its C type of the same name.

The second category of Java data is the reference type. A Java reference is analogous to a C or C++ pointer: Both are types that hold a reference to something elsewhere in memory rather than an actual value. The important difference between a Java reference and a C and C++ pointer is from the programmer's perspective. As a Java programmer, you'll never have to worry about how Java makes use of, or disposes of, objects in memory.

Java operators are similar to C operators. Arithmetic operators such as +, *, -=, and ++ all work the same in Java as they do in C. One operator new to C and C++ programmers is the >>> operator. This bitwise operator shifts the bits of the left operand to the right, filling in shifted upper bits with 0. C and C++ programmers will want to take note of Table 6-7, as it lists the precedence of the various Java operators—a precedence that differs in some ways from operators in the C and C++ languages.

CHAPTER 7

Java Variables and Flow Control

Now that you know about Java data types and operators, you'll want to know how to store information in variables of these various types and how then to implement flow control using these variables.

In this chapter, you'll read about variables that hold primitive and reference values. You'll also see how to copy values from one variable to another, as well as how to cast, or change, the values of these variables from one data type to another. You'll also learn how to tell Java when to designate that a variable should be deemed a constant—a simple technique, but one that differs greatly from that used in C. Finally, you'll read about flow control—the use of branching, or conditional, and loops to control the flow of execution of your applet.

Variables

In many ways, Java variables are similar to C variables. This fact enabled us to use Java variables in the numerous discussions and examples in previous chapters without providing detailed introductions or explanations. Java and C do, however, have some differences in both the terminology that accompanies the variables and in how some variables are used. Those differences are the focus of this section.

VARIABLE NAMES

In Java, the first character in a variable name must be a letter, an underscore, or the dollar sign. Remaining characters in a variable name can be any combination of these, along with any digit. The following declarations all contain legal Java variable names:

```
int totalScore;
float _TEST;
short $cost;
String string1;
String string25;
short GrandTotal;
short GRANDtotal;
```

Java variable names are case-sensitive, so the last two declarations in the preceding snippet could both appear in the same block of code.

While all of the variable names in the preceding snippet are valid, your own source code should consist of names in the style of the first one: `totalScore`. Java convention is to begin a variable name with a lowercase letter. The remaining characters in the name should be lowercase as well, with the exception of the first character of a new word. Using these guidelines, the following declarations are more suitable to Java source code:

```
int totalScore;
float test;
short dollarCost;
String titleStr;
String nameString;
short grandTotal;
```

INSTANCE VARIABLES AND LOCAL VARIABLES

In Java, all code is a part of a class. As you saw in the simple applet example presented in Chapter 3, an applet itself is a class. The example also demonstrated that the definitions of class methods lie within the body of classes. In Chapter 3, the applet named MyFirstApplet consisted of just one method—the `paint()` method:

```
public class MyFirstApplet extends Applet {

    public void paint(Graphics g) {
        g.drawString("This applet simply draws text", 10, 20);
    }
}
```

Although you wouldn't be able to tell by looking at this example, in Java an applet can consist of more than one class. And, again unlike MyFirstApplet, a class doesn't have to consist of just a single method: It can define any number of methods. Regardless of how many classes and how many methods of which an applet consists, a variable in Java can appear at one of two levels: at the class level or at the method level.

Variables at the class level are *instance variables.* The instance variables of a class define the attributes of an object of that class. As you saw in Chapters 4 and 5, instance variables can be accessed by any method that is a part of the class that defines them.

Variables at the method level are *local variables.* Java local variables are analogous to C or C++ local variables: They're accessible only to code within the method (or function) that defines them.

The following version of the `Alien` class introduces a new method—`switchStrengthLives()`. This method swaps the value of an object's strength instance variable with the same object's lives instance variable. Here you can see that the two instance variables are accessible to the methods of the `Alien` class; `switchStrengthLives()` uses both of them. The one local variable of the example, `temp`, is accessible only to the `switchStrengthLives()` method. Any other methods defined in the `Alien` class cannot employ the use of this variable `temp`.

```
class Alien {

    int       strength;       // instance variable
    int       lives;          // instance variable

    void switchStrengthLives() {

        int   temp;           // local variable

        temp = strength;
        strength = lives;
```

```
            lives = temp;
        }

        // rest of methods here
    }
```

In addition to instance variables and local variables, there's a third type of variable called a *class variable*. A class variable is declared within a class, just as an instance variable is. However, unlike an instance variable, which becomes part of the class template so that each object of the class has its own version of the variable, a single class variable is shared by *all* objects of a class. You'll learn more about class variables in Chapter 8.

COPYING VARIABLES

You use the assignment operator to copy the value of a literal or variable to another variable. Because Java is an object-oriented language, however, a few of its techniques differ from those used in a procedural language such as C.

COPYING PRIMITIVE TYPE VARIABLES

To copy the value of one variable of a primitive type to another variable of that same type, you simply use the assignment operator:

```
float oldValue = 5.25;        // oldValue is 5.25
float newValue;               // newValue is 0.0

newValue = oldValue;          // newValue becomes 5.25
```

COPYING REFERENCE TYPE VARIABLES

In Java, an instance of a class (an object variable) is actually a reference to an object—as described in Chapter 6. Figure 7-1 reminds you that if you create two objects of a class, you have references to two objects. The code listed in the figure declares two `Alien` variables, then uses `new` to allocate memory for the objects. The values of the instance variables of the first object are then established by calling two set functions defined in the `Alien` class. The values of the instance variables of the second object aren't set, but rather are left with their initial values.

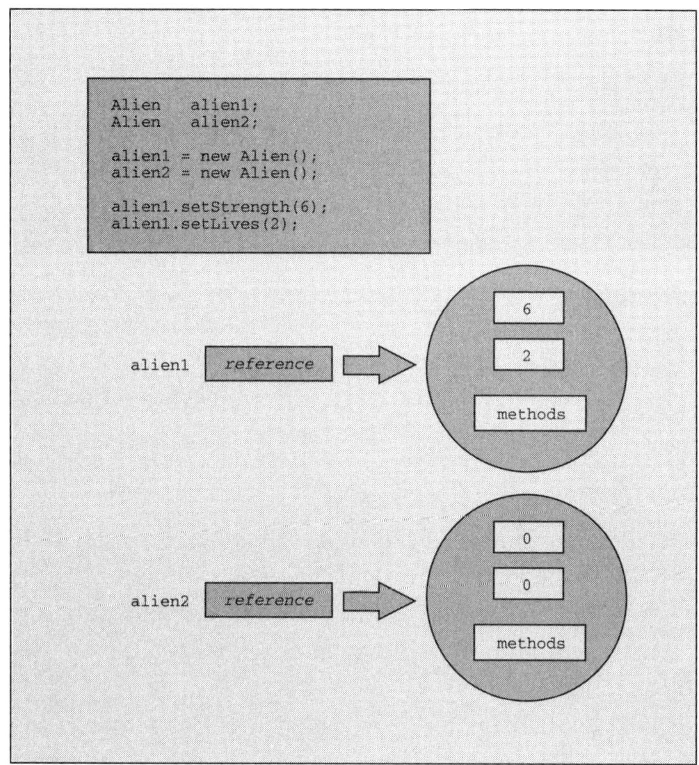

Figure 7-1

Two object variables indicate two references to objects in memory.

Recall that an `int` variable is initialized to 0. This applies to a variable of type `int` as well as an instance variable of type `int`. Table 6.1 in Chapter 6 lists the initial, or default, values given to variables of the various primitive data types.

Now, consider what should take place if we want the second object, the one referenced by `alien2`, to be the same as the first object, the one referenced by `alien1`. In other words, consider the case in which we want the instance variables of the `alien2` object to have the same values as the instance variables of the `alien1` object. With two objects of the same class allocated, there exists the temptation to copy the values of one object to another—as one would do for two variables of a primitive data type:

```
int int1;
int int2;
Alien alien1;
Alien alien2;

int1 = 9;
int2 = int1;  // valid

alien1 = new Alien();
alien2 = new Alien();

alien1.setStrength(6);
alien1.setLives(2);

alien2 = alien1;  // valid, but doesn't yield the hoped-for result
```

The preceding assignment of one object to another is valid. If the intention is to copy the values of instance variables, however, the result won't be as expected. As Figure 7-2 illustrates, the assignment of one object variable to another is an assignment of references, not an assignment of object content.

Two techniques enable you to copy the content of an object to another object. However, only one of the two techniques can be applied to a particular case. If the objects in question are of a Java class (such as the `String` class), there will be a method belonging to that class that copies the contents of objects. If the objects in question belong instead to an applet-defined class (such as the `Alien` class) you'll have to define a method within that class to handle the copying. Chapter 8 describes copying objects of a class defined by Java. In this chapter, we'll look at copying objects that are of an applet-defined class.

For the `Alien` class, a copy method might look like the `copyAll()` method defined here:

```
class Alien {

    int      strength;
    int      lives;

    // other methods here
```

```
    void  copyAll( Alien sourceAlien ) {
        strength = sourceAlien.strength;
        lives = sourceAlien.lives;
    }
}
```

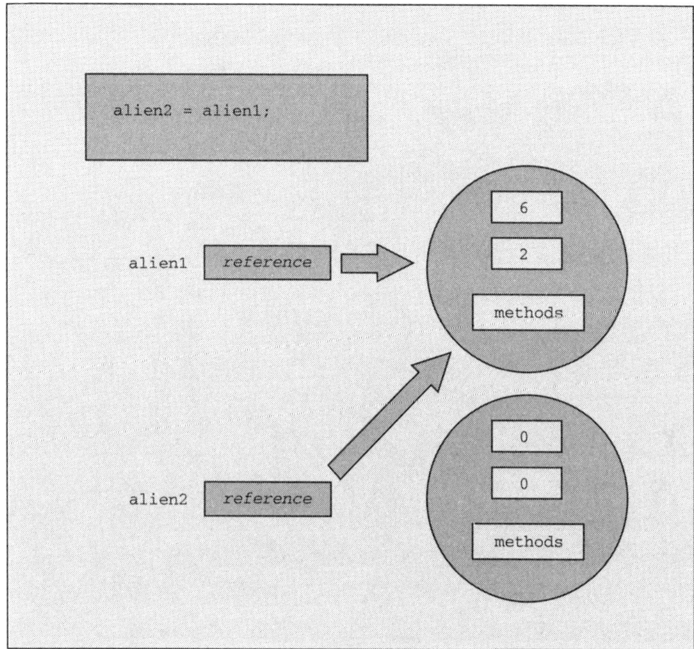

Figure 7-2
Assigning one object variable to another simply changes the reference of one variable.

The `copyAll()` method accepts an `Alien` object as its one parameter. It then copies the values of this passed-in object's instance variables to the object that invokes the `copyAll()` method. If the `alien2` object were to invoke this method in order to take on the values in the `alien1` object, the following code would be used, as illustrated in Figure 7-3.

```
Alien  alien1;
Alien  alien2;

alien1 = new Alien();
alien2 = new Alien();
```

```
alien1.setStrength(6);
alien1.setLives(2);

alien2.copyAll( alien1 );
```

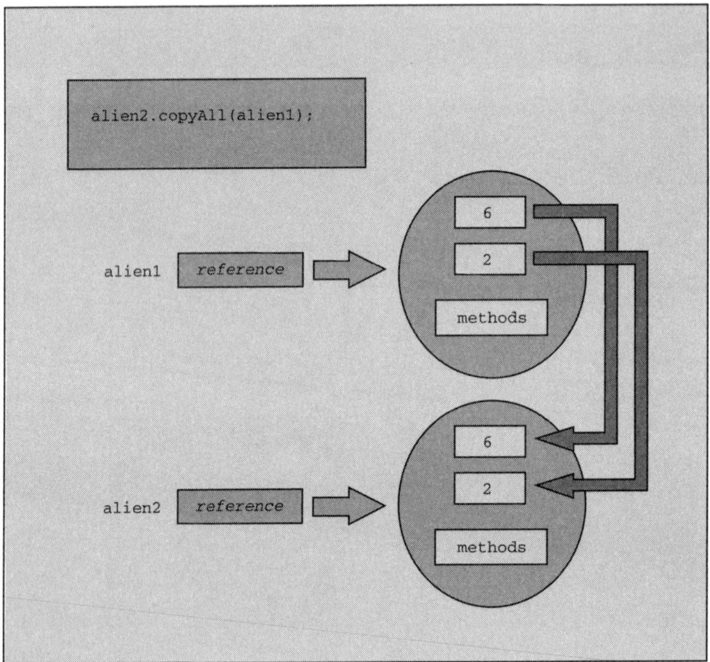

Figure 7-3

To actually copy the values of the instance variables of one object to the instance variables of a second object, invoke a class-defined method.

If you come across a mention of a Java method named `copy()`, skip over that information—it's dated. The `copy()` function was a method that could be used by objects of certain classes. It's no longer a part of the Java language. There is still a method named `clone()` that can, in certain cases, be used to copy the values of the instance variables of one object and assign them to the instance variables of another object. More on `clone()` is found in Chapter 8.

Because the copying of variables of the other reference type—arrays—was covered in Chapter 6, a short recap will suffice here. When assigning an array element that is of a primitive data type, the assignment is straightforward. Simply use the assignment operator (=) to assign the array element the value of a variable of the same primitive type:

```
int intArray[];
int theInt = 5;

intArray = new int[10];
intArray[0] = theInt;
```

When working with an array of objects, recall that each array element holds a reference to an object. An assignment of an object to an array element simply creates another reference to the object. After the following snippet executes, there will be two references to the same object.

```
Alien  alienArray[];
Alien  theAlien;

theAlien = new Alien();
theAlien.setStrength( 9 );
theAlien.setLives( 1 );

alienArray = new Alien[8];
alienArray[3] = theAlien;
```

When this code executes, both `theAlien` and `alienArray[3]` will refer to the same object.

Casting

In Java, some values cannot be assigned to certain types of variables without special effort. That fact often protects you from writing code that won't provide the desired results. For instance, a variable of type `float` can't normally be assigned to a variable of type `char`. While in some cases such an assignment might work (for instance, a `float` value of 65.0 could be considered ASCII 65, or the letter *A*), other cases would not give your applet predictable results. (Just what character *does* 5.3e-14 represent?)

While assigning a value of one type to a variable of a different type isn't the preferred method of making an assignment, sometimes it is a necessity. Your applet may encounter one type of data that needs to be coerced into a variable of a different data type. Java appreciates that such scenarios exist and gives you the freedom to *cast*, or convert, a value from one data type to another.

To cast a value of one type such that it can be assigned to a variable that is expecting a different type, preface the value in question with the data type to cast to, enclosed in parentheses. For instance, to cast a variable of `type` float to an `int`, precede the `float` variable with `(int)`, as shown in the following example:

```
int   theInt;
float theFloat = 5.0;

theInt = (int) theFloat;      // float value is converted to an int
```

A cast first creates a copy of the value that is to be converted, which leaves the original value unaltered. The cast then changes, or converts, the data type of this copied value from the type of the original variable to a new type. In the preceding snippet, variable `theFloat` remains unchanged: It is of type `float` before and after the cast. It is a *copy* of the value of `theFloat` (the number 5.0) that gets converted to an `int`, then assigned to variable `theInt`.

THE TRADEOFF BETWEEN CASTING AND PRECISION

Before an assignment of a value of one data type can be made to a variable of a different data type, Java may require you to perform a cast. Then again, it might not. One reason for the existence of the cast is to help you catch mistakes in logic in your applet. Assignments that involve two different data types may be illogical—such as the `float`-to-`char` example cited earlier.

Casting also exists to alert you to situations where a loss of precision may occur. Loss of precision may occur when a value of one data type size is assigned to a variable of a smaller data type size. For instance, consider a variable of type `long` with a value of 250,000. If this `long` value is assigned to a variable of type `short`, which is capable of holding a value no larger than 32,767, the original value of 250,000 will not be assigned. In some cases (such as this one), the variable assigned will end up with a value not even close to the original number. In other instances (such as some assignments of floating-point values to integral types), the loss of data may be more subtle: Only the loss of a fractional component of the original value may occur.

If a value of one data type is assigned to a variable of a different type and this variable is of a type capable of holding a value at least as large as the value to be assigned, no loss of precision can occur, and no cast is necessary.

```
int   theInt = 5;
float theFloat;

theFloat = theInt;    //valid
```

Regardless of how large a number `theInt` is storing, `theFloat` can take on that value without truncating, or losing, any portion of it. When you assign an `int` variable to a `float` variable, no cast is needed. Java will compile the preceding code without complaint. However, if the situation is reversed and a `float` is to be assigned to an `int`, an error will occur at compilation:

```
int   theInt;
float theFloat = 5.0f;

theInt = theFloat;    // invalid - can't assign float to int
```

Because the `float` type can hold a value larger than the `int` type, Java won't let you make the assignment. To make the preceding code valid, cast the `float` to an `int`, then make the assignment:

```
int   theInt;
float theFloat = 5.0;

theInt = (int) theFloat;     // valid
```

In the preceding example there will be no loss of precision. That's because the initial value assigned to `theFloat` has no fractional part: Floating-point 5.0 will be converted to integer 5. If `theFloat` had been assigned a value of, say, 5.3, there would have been a loss of precision: The cast of `theFloat` to an integer would have resulted in the fractional part of the number being dropped so that floating-point 5.3 would have become integer 5.

CASTING PRIMITIVE TYPE TO PRIMITIVE TYPE

Casting forces the compiler to accept an assignment. However, you won't want to go about indiscriminately casting data of one type to data of another type. For instance, it wouldn't make much sense to cast a primitive type such as a `float` to an object, such as an `Alien` object. An Alien object consists of instance variables, and the cast of the float to such an object wouldn't supply values to these variables. What *is* more common, however, is the casting of a value of a primitive type to a variable of a different primitive type.

Table 7-1 lists primitive data type assignments that involve a possible loss of precision. Any of the assignments in this table require a cast.

Table 7-1

Primitive Data Type Assignments That May Lose Precision

Data Type of rvalue	Cast rvalue if lvalue is One of These Types
byte	no cast necessary
short	byte
int	byte, short
long	byte, short, int
float	byte, short, int, long
double	byte, short, int, long, float
char	byte
boolean	can't cast

As a reminder, lvalue and rvalue are terms that are sometimes used in programming to describe variables in an assignment statement. The variable to the left of the assignment operator is called an lvalue. A variable or constant to the right of the assignment operator is called an rvalue.

To aid you in understanding Table 7-1, consider the following example. Your program has a variable of type `long` that is to used as an lvalue in an assignment statement. That is, it is to receive a value in an assignment statement. The same statement has a variable of type `double` as the rvalue. To see if this assignment necessitates a cast, look for `double` in the first column of the table—the column that lists the data type of the rvalue in an assignment statement. Then look across the `double` row to the second column. If `long`—the data type of the lvalue in the assignment—is one of the data types that appears in this column, a cast is necessary. For this example a cast is needed, as shown in the following code:

```
long   theLong;
double theDouble = 100.2;

theLong = (long) theDouble;   // valid
```

Because a `long` holds only integral values, the cast value will be truncated; variable `theLong` will end up with a value of 100.

CASTING PRIMITIVE TYPES OTHER THAN BOOLEAN

While it's true that in Java the Boolean value can't be explicitly cast to an integral type, and an integral value can't be explicitly cast to a Boolean (see Table 7-1), it is still possible to make such conversions. To determine the integral equivalency of an integer and to assign that value to a `boolean` variable, use the `!=` inequality operator:

```
boolean    theBoolean;
int        theInt = 1;

theBoolean = ( theInt != 0 );
```

In programming, a value of 0 is thought of as equating to a value of `false`, while a value of 1 is associated with a value of `true`. In the preceding snippet, if `theInt` is nonzero the comparison of `theInt` to zero returns a value of `true`. If `theInt` has a value of 0, then the comparison to zero returns a value of `false`. In either case, the result is the same as if `theInt` were cast to type `boolean`.

Using the association of 0 to `false` and 1 to `true`, Java provides a means of converting a `boolean` value to an integral value. By using a `boolean` value as the first expression in a statement that uses the conditional operator, the Boolean can be converted to either a 1 or a 0. Recall the format of a Java statement that uses the conditional operator:

```
expression1 ? expression2 : expression3
```

If `expression1` evaluates to `true`, then the entire expression evaluates to `expression2`. If `expression1` instead evaluates to `false`, then the entire expression instead evaluates to `expression3`. In the following snippet, if `theBoolean` has a value of `true`, `theInt` is assigned `expression2`, or 1. If `theBoolean` has a value of `false`, `theInt` is assigned `expression3`, or 0.

```
boolean  theBoolean = true;
int      theInt;

theInt = theBoolean ? 1:0;
```

CASTING ONE OBJECT TYPE TO ANOTHER OBJECT TYPE

In Java, one object can be cast to another type of object, provided the objects are related through inheritance. If your applet is to cast an object of a subclass to an object of its superclass, then you must explicitly make this cast in a manner similar to that done for primitive types.

Consider the Alien and FastAlien classes discussed in Chapters 4 and 5. Recall that the Alien class has two instance variables, strength and lives. The FastAlien class extends the Alien class. That is, the FastAlien class is a subclass of the Alien class. As such, it inherits the two instance variables of the Alien class. Additionally, the FastAlien class defines a third instance variable—one called speed. Here are the Alien and FastAlien classes, as last defined:

```
class Alien {

    int      strength;
    int      lives;

    void setStrength( int theStrength ) {
        strength = theStrength;
    }

    int getStrength() {
        return strength;
    }

    void setLives( int theLives ) {
        lives = theLives;
    }

    int getLives() {
        return lives;
    }
}
```

```
class FastAlien extends Alien {

    int       speed;

    void setSpeed( int theSpeed ) {
        speed = theSpeed;
    }

    int getSpeed() {
        return speed;
    }
}
```

In the next snippet, two variables are declared—one of each of the preceding class types. An instance of the `FastAlien` class is then created using `new`, and its three instance variables are assigned values.

```
Alien          theAlien;
FastAlien      theFastAlien;

theFastAlien = new FastAlien();

theFastAlien.setStrength( 5 );
theFastAlien.setLives( 6 );
theFastAlien.setSpeed( 7 );
```

Next, the applet could create an instance of the `Alien` class (an `Alien` object) by using `new`. Alternately, the `Alien` variable `theAlien` could be made to reference a `FastAlien` object by casting an existing `FastAlien` object and assigning the result to `theAlien`.

```
theAlien = (Alien) theFastAlien;      // valid cast
```

As in the case of casting a value of a primitive type to a variable of a smaller primitive type, a cast of an object to its superclass type could result in a loss of precision. For an object, this loss of precision is the loss of access to instance variables that are defined by the subclass.

The `FastAlien` class consists of three instance variables (two of which are inherited from the `Alien` superclass), while the `Alien` class consists of only two instance variables. In the preceding cast, the object that results from the cast of the `FastAlien` object will lose the speed instance variable. An object of the `Alien` class holds only two instance variables: `strength` and lives. The cast creates a new Alien object, which by definition has only two instance variables, and assigns this object to theAlien.

After the cast just shown, the strength and lives instance variables of theAlien will have the same values as the strength and lives instance variables of theFastAlien (5 and 6, respectively). The object referenced by theAlien will not have a speed instance variable, so code such as that shown in the following snippet would result in compilation errors:

```
theAlien.speed = 10;          // invalid access
theAlien.setSpeed( 10 );      // invalid access
```

Constant Variables

In C, you create a constant by using either the #define directive or the const keyword. In Java, neither #define nor const exists. But of course, Java does provide a mechanism for creating constants.

Declaring constants

In Java, you define a constant by preceding a variable declaration with the final keyword and then assigning that variable a value at declaration, as shown in the following example:

```
final short   MAX_SCORE = 100;
```

A Java constant doesn't have to appear in uppercase, and it doesn't have to employ underscores between words. However, Java convention, like C convention, encourages this naming style. Following are a few more examples of Java constants:

```
final float   SPEED_OF_LIGHT = 3.0E8f;
final short   DAYS_IN_WEEK = 7;
final char    QUIT_CHAR = 'q';
```

Once declared, a constant cannot be reassigned a new value: Attempting to do so results in a compilation error. Given the purpose of a constant, it makes sense that the value of a Java constant variable cannot be altered.

What might not be as intuitive is the idea that Java uses a variable as a constant. (The oxymoron constant variable does take some getting used to.)

In Java, a constant variable can only be declared at the class level: A constant declaration cannot appear within a method. In other words, a constant must be global to a class and can't be local to a method.

In the following snippet, a class named `Calender` legally declares a constant named `DAYS_IN_WEEK`. The `Calender` class method `daysInMonth`, however, illegally attempts to declare a constant named `MONTHS_IN_YEAR`:

```
class Calender {

    final short     DAYS_IN_WEEK = 7;      // valid

    int daysInMonth( int theMonth ) {

        final short  MONTHS_IN_YEAR = 12;  // invalid !
        ...
    }
}
```

A variable declared at the class level is an instance variable. As you know from Chapters 4 and 5, every object instantiated from a class has its own copy of each instance variable. In Java, a constant is a variable, and a constant is declared at the class level. So does this mean that every object of a class type has its own copy of the constant? Yes! But this doesn't have to be. Because a constant holds no information that is unique to each object, this seems wasteful: A single constant that could be shared by all objects of a class would be more practical. Java in fact enables you to create just such a thing. You'll read about *class variables* in Chapter 8.

USING CONSTANTS

A constant variable can be assigned to a variable, added to a variable, used in a conditional test, and so forth. The following snippet provides several examples:

```
final float   SPEED_OF_LIGHT = 3.0E8f;
final int     DAYS_IN_WEEK = 7;
final char    QUIT_CHAR = 'q';
```

```
float          ufoSpeed;
int            vacationDays;
int            vacationWeeks;
char           theChar;

ufoSpeed = SPEED_OF_LIGHT / 2;

vacationDays = DAYS_IN_WEEK * vacationWeeks;

if ( theChar == QUIT_CHAR )
```

The preceding snippet defines three constants and four variables. The three lines of code that follow the declarations have no relationship to one another; they simply demonstrate a few uses of constants. The first line performs division using a constant; the second line uses a constant in a multiplication operation, and the third line uses a constant in an `if` statement.

Control Statements

Java uses the same control statements found in C: the `if` and `switch` branches, and the `for`, `do`, and `do-while` loops. Some of these statements differ from the C statements of the same type, though.

The most notable way a Java control statement differs from its C counterpart is in the statement's test. Like C, Java defines `if`, `do`, and `do-while` statements. In C, the test section of any of these statement types typically evaluates to a `boolean`, but tests that evaluate to an integer value are also valid. This simple C example uses an `if` statement to illustrate:

```
int theInt = 1;

if ( theInt )
    // do something if theInt is nonzero
```

In Java, the preceding test is illegal and would result in a compile-time error. You can circumvent this problem by always including an explicit comparison test, as follows:

```
int theInt = 1;

if ( theInt > 0 )
    // do something
```

Now the snippet has been converted into valid Java code.

BRANCHING

Like C, Java uses the `if` and the `switch` statements to redirect the flow of control through branching.

IF STATEMENTS

The syntax of the Java `if` conditional is the same as it is in C: first comes the `if` keyword, and then a test that lies between parentheses. The body of the `if` can consist of a single statement, or it can consist of opening and closing braces between which are any number of statements. Optionally, the `if` statement can include the `else` keyword. The following are examples of the `if` and the `if-else` statements:

```
if ( score > 1000 )
    score += bonus;

if ( yearsEmployed <= 3 )
{
    bonus = 500;
    vacationWeeks = 2;
}
else
{
    bonus = 1000;
    vacationWeeks = 3;
}
```

SWITCH STATEMENTS

The syntax of Java `switch` statements is identical to the syntax of C `switch` statements. As in C, the use of the `default` keyword is an optional means of handling all situations not specifically covered by `case` labels. Also as in C, more than one `case` label can share the same code. As a final comparison to the C `switch`, each case section ends with a `break` statement:

```
char          theChar = 'A';
boolean       honors = false;
boolean       pass = false;

switch ( theChar )
{
    case 'A':
        honors = true;
        pass = true;
        break;
    case 'B':
    case 'C':
        pass = true;
        break;
    default:          // 'D' or 'F'
        break;
}
```

The `switch` can use a variable of type `char`, `byte`, `short`, or `int` for its comparison. As in C, a floating-point value (a variable of type `float` or `double`) can't be used. One important distinction between the Java `switch` and the C `switch` is that a variable of type `long` *can't* be used in the Java `switch`. If you must use a `long`, you'll need to cast it to a smaller primitive data type, as done here:

```
long   theLong;

switch ( (int)theLong )
{
    // case labels here
}
```

If your applet is working with values that may be greater than those that can be held by an `int`, it can't run the risk of losing precision. In such a circumstance you can cascade `if-else` statements to achieve the same effect produced by a `switch`:

```
long   theLong;

if ( theLong == FIRST_VERY_BIG_NUM )
    // do something
else if ( theLong == SECOND_VERY_BIG_NUM )
    // do something else
else if ( theLong == THIRD_VERY_BIG_NUM )
    // and so forth
```

In the preceding snippet, only the code under the `if` or under one of the `else-if` statements will execute. When the value of a variable is compared to a number of constants in an `if-else` block (as in the preceding case), only the code under the `if` or `else-if` that produces a match is executed.

LOOPING

For repeating a block of code, Java uses the same three looping statements used in C: `for`, `do`, and `do-while`.

FOR STATEMENTS

The syntax of the Java `for` loop is the same as in C. The first line of the `for` loop consists of three parts: an initialization, a test, and an increment. The body of the loop can be a single statement or multiple statements between a pair of braces. The `for` loop in the following example initializes integer variable `i` to 0, tests the current value of `i` by comparing it to 10, and then increments `i`. The body of the loop is used to assign the next successively higher odd number to the array named `oddArray`. After executing, the elements of `oddArray` will have values of 1, 3, 5, and so forth.

```
int i;
int oddArray[] = new int[10];

for ( i = 0; i < 10; i++ )
    oddArray[i] = (i * 2) + 1;
```

In the preceding snippet, `i` is referred to as the loop's index. In programming, it's common for the index of a loop to exist solely for the purpose of regulating the number of times the loop executes; the index variable isn't used either before or after the loop. The Java language acknowledges this fact and enables you to declare the loop index within the initialization part of the `for` loop. In Java, the preceding `for` loop could also be written as follows:

```
int oddArray[] = new int[10];

for ( int i = 0; i < 10; i++ )
    oddArray[i] = (i * 2) + 1;
```

This feature is not available in C or C++.

WHILE STATEMENTS

The Java `while` statement looks and acts as it does in C: first comes the `while` keyword, followed by a test condition between parentheses, followed by the body of the loop. The following example uses a `while` loop to perform the identical action handled by the example of the `for` loop in the previous section:

```
int i = 0;
int oddArray[] = new int[10];

while ( i < 10 ) {
    oddArray[i] = (i * 2) + 1;
    i++;
}
```

Because the test of the `while` statement doesn't affect the value of the test condition (as is the case in the `for` loop), the test condition must be changed within the body of the loop. If the preceding example *didn't* modify the value of `i`, the result would be a loop that repeated indefinitely—an infinite loop.

As mentioned earlier, make sure that the test condition includes an explicit `boolean` comparison. For instance, in C a `while` loop that counts down from 5 to 0 can be written as:

```
int count = 5;

while ( count-- )
    // do something
```

In Java, the preceding code will fail to compile. Therefore, you should write the Java code as follows:

```
int count = 5;

while ( count-- > 0 )
    // do something
```

The Java equivalent includes the comparison of the decremented count value to 0.

DO-WHILE STATEMENTS

Like the Java `while` statement, the Java `do-while` statement is the same as its C counterpart: first comes the `do` keyword, followed by the body of the loop, followed by a test condition between parentheses. The difference between the `while` loop and the `do-while` loop is this: depending on the test condition, the `while` loop *may* be skipped altogether, whereas the `do-while` loop—with its test *after* the loop body—will *always* execute at least one time. This next snippet uses a `do-while` loop to provide the same results as the examples in both the `for` and `while` loop sections:

```
int i = 0;
int oddArray[] = new int[10];

do {
    oddArray[i] = (i * 2) + 1;
    i++;
} while ( i < 10 );
```

Like the `while` loop, the `do-while` loop body must affect the value of the loop's test condition to avoid an infinite loop. And, like the `if`, `for`, and `while` statements, the test condition must evaluate to a `boolean` value of `true` or `false` rather than an integral value of 1 or 0.

CONTINUE STATEMENTS

Your applet may have occasion to end a particular iteration prematurely. In such a case, you'll rely on the Java `continue` statement. When the `continue` is encountered in a loop body, code following the `continue` in the loop body is skipped, but only for this one iteration.

The following snippet illustrates the use of the `continue` statement. At each iteration, an `if` statement in the body of the loop compares the value of the current array element to 0. If the array element is 0, the loop continues and the array element is assigned a value. Should the `if` statement encounter an array element that has a value other than 0, the continue statement executes, and the assignment to this one array member is not made. In the following example, each array element except `oddArray[5]` will be assigned a value:

```
int i = 0;
int oddArray[] = new int[10];
```

```
oddArray[5] = 99;

while ( i < 10 ) {
    if ( oddArray[i] != 0 ) {
        i++;
        continue;
    }
    oddArray[i] = (i * 2) + 1;
    i++;
}
```

One point worth noting in the preceding example is that the loop index i appears to be incremented twice. In fact, variable i will always be incremented only once at any pass through the loop. The additional increment is necessary because execution of the continue statement causes the increment line below the assignment to oddArray to be skipped.

An Example Applet: A Random Number Generator

It's been awhile since you've seen the listing for a complete applet. We'll remedy that by ending this chapter with a look at a simple applet that makes use of a few of the topics covered in this and the previous chapter. The RandomNum applet generates a random floating-point value between 0.0 and 1.0. It displays the value of the number and also indicates whether the number is less than or greater than the midpoint of the random number generator's range: 0.5. Figure 7-4 shows the applet as it appears in an applet viewer.

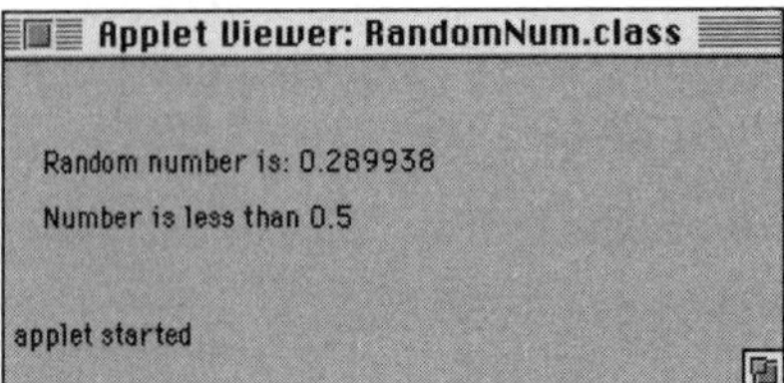

Figure 7-4
The RandomNum applet displays a random number.

SOURCE CODE LISTING

The source code for RandomNum has an overall structure similar to that of the applet you worked with in Chapters 2 and 3—the applet named MyFirstApplet. The following is the complete listing for RandomNum.java:

```
import java.awt.*;
import java.applet.*;

public class RandomNum extends Applet {

    double    theDouble;

    public void paint( Graphics g ) {

         theDouble = Math.random();

        g.drawString("Random number is: " + theDouble, 10, 20 );

        if ( theDouble < 0.5 )
            g.drawString( "Number is less than 0.5", 10, 40 );
        else
            g.drawString( "Number is greater than 0.5", 10, 40 );
    }
}
```

You'll find this file on the CD-ROM that comes with this book.

SOURCE CODE WALK-THROUGH

The source code listing for the RandomNum applet is short and simple. But it still makes use of a wealth of Java topics, as you'll see in the following walk-through of the source code.

IMPORTING PACKAGES

All applets import at least one Java package. Doing so enables your applet to access the Java-defined classes that appear within these packages. Typically, an applet imports the java.awt package and the java.applet package. The java.awt package contains the code that makes it easy for you to include graphics in your own applets, while the java.applet package provides the code that enables an applet to operate within a browser.

EXTENDING THE APPLET CLASS

Every applet extends, or is a subclasses of, the Java-defined class Applet. The Applet class is defined within the java.applet package:

```
public class RandomNum extends Applet {

    // instance variables and methods
}
```

THE JAVA APPLET PAINT() METHOD

From Chapters 4 and 5, you know that a class can define any number of methods. The `RandomNum` class defines just one—the `paint()` method. In Chapter 3, you saw that the `paint()` method is one that is invoked by Java runtime when an applet needs updating. The drawing of text by RandomNum takes place in the `paint()` method. To generate a new random number and have the results written to the applet, you'll force the applet to update itself. You can do this by resizing the applet viewer window or by moving the applet viewer window offscreen and then back onscreen again.

THE DOUBLE DATA TYPE

From earlier in this chapter, you know that a variable declared at the class level is an instance variable. RandomNum defines one such instance variable—`theDouble`. Past chapters used variables of type `int` in most of their examples. Chapter 6 showed you that the Java language defines a variety of data types, including the type of variable `theDouble`—the double type.

THE JAVA MATH CLASS AND ITS RANDOM() METHOD

The assignment of a value to the variable `theDouble` is accomplished by invoking a method called `random()` from an object named `Math`. You'll notice, though, that the RandomNum applet doesn't define a class or variable named `Math`. So where did `Math` come from, and how can you use it in your applets without defining it? The `Math` class is one of the numerous classes Sun defined, documented, and made available for use by your applets. You're already familiar with this concept: Applets are all subclasses of the `Applet` class, and many applets make use of one of the methods inherited from this `Applet` class—the `paint()` method. When invoked, one of the methods defined as a part of the `Math` class—`random()`—generates a random number of type double and returns that value to your applet. Chapter 8 provides more detail about the organization and use of the many classes defined by Sun.

THE APPLET CLASS AND ITS DRAWSTRING() METHOD

After the Sun-defined `random()` method is invoked, the random number is drawn to the browser window. As you saw in Chapter 3, the `drawString()` method handles that task. Recall from Chapter 3 that the `drawString()` method is defined by the `Graphics` class—another of the many Sun classes available for use by your applet. Here in the RandomNum applet, you see an example of the + operator used to concatenate the string "Random number is:" with the value of variable `theDouble`. Because `theDouble` is concatenated to a string, Java knows to convert the number in `theDouble` to its string representation before `drawString()` does its work.

Recall from Chapter 3 that when a Java-capable browser encounters a Web page that holds an applet, the browser automatically creates a `Graphics` object for the applet. Java also automatically passes this graphics object to the `paint()` method when the applet needs updating. As a further aside, recall that the `paint()` method is defined by the `Applet` class—the superclass of each applet class (including, of course, the `RandomNum` class).

THE IF-ELSE STATEMENT AND A COMPARATIVE OPERATOR

The RandomNum applet makes use of an `if-else` statement (described in this chapter) and a comparative operator (described in Chapter 6). The `if` part of the `if-else` statement compares the value of the `double` variable, `theDouble`, to 0.5—a value that represents the midpoint in the range of numbers generated by the `random()` method. The comparison is made using the less than (<) comparative operator.

While the creation of a random number may be of use to your applet, the RandomNum applet itself is of little use. It's a somewhat contrived example used to illustrate a few of the Java language basics described in this chapter and in Chapter 6. After Chapter 8, where you're introduced to the many Sun-defined classes that exist in the Java packages your applets can import, the example applets will become much less forced and much more useful.

CREATING AND RUNNING THE RANDOMNUM APPLET

To create the RandomNum applet, use a text editor, word processor, or your Java environment to create a file called RandomNum.java. Type in the short RandomNum.java Java source code listing that appears in this chapter a few pages back. Then use your Java compiler to compile the code. The result will be a file called RandomNum.class—the RandomNum applet.

You can test the RandomNum applet with the applet viewer that's included on this book's CD-ROM or the applet viewer that came with your Java environment. Regardless of the viewer you use, you'll first create a simple HTML file—one whose contents are nothing more than the following:

```
<applet code="RandomNum.class" width=200 height=100>
</applet>
```

This HTML file, which can have any name you want, is the file in which you'll run your applet viewer. The applet viewer will be looking for the RandomNum.class file (the applet) in the same directory as the HTML file. You make sure these two files are at the same directory level.

If you are using a third party Java integrated development environment and you haven't created an applet yet, refer to the documentation that came with your IDE. If you're using Sun's Java compiler and applet viewer found on this book's CD-ROM, refer to Chapter 2 if you need a walk-through of any of the following: creating a simple HTML file, creating a Java source code file, compiling a Java source code file to create an applet, or testing an applet with the Sun applet viewer.

To generate and display a new random number, resize the applet window, or obscure the applet viewer window, and then bring the window back into view.

What You've Learned

Working with variables in Java is similar to working with variables in C or C++: You declare a variable, assign it a value, and use it in mathematical operations just as you do in these other languages.

In Java, a variable can be an instance variable, a local variable, or a class variable. When an object is created, it receives is own copy of each instance variable that is declared in a class. Each object of a class type doesn't, however, get its own copy of a local variable. A local variable is declared within a method in the class and is of use only in that method; it's not used as storage for data that is of use for the object. A class variable is a variable that is used to hold a single value that is accessible by all objects of a class type. That is, each object doesn't get its own private copy of the variable but instead shares this one variable. Class variables are discussed in further detail in Chapter 8.

In Java, it is sometimes necessary to cast a variable. Casting a variable creates a copy of a variable, then changes that copy's data type. Some operations demand that an operand be of a particular data type. In such a case, a variable of a different type must be cast if it is to be used as the operand.

To designate that a variable be considered a constant, preface the variable's declaration with the Java keyword final. Be aware that in Java the terminology associated with a constant can be somewhat confusing; a constant may be referred to as constant variable, even though once assigned a value, the constant's value cannot vary.

If you're familiar with the control statements defined in the C and C++ languages, you are familiar with the control statements defined in Java. For branching, Java offers `if`, `if-else`, and `switch` statements. Looping is accomplished with the `for`, `do`, and `do-while` statements.

CHAPTER

8 Java Classes

Java isn't just a programming language: It's also a collection of class libraries. These libraries—provided by Sun and referred to as packages in Java—enable you to create applets that have a standard interface no matter what platform on which the applets run. Chapters 6 and 7 describe the Java language. This chapter provides a look at how the Java classes are organized into packages and interfaces. Here you'll also find a summary of the Java classes, or Java Application Programming Interface (API).

Before jumping into a description of the Java classes, this chapter familiarizes you with packages, interfaces, and access modifiers. Together, these topics provide you with a better understanding of classes in general. Equally important, they form the basis for an understanding of many classes that make up the Java API.

Packages

A class is Java's means of grouping related data and functions. A package is Java's way of grouping related classes. A Java package is analogous to a C or C++ library: Each holds code that can be used by any number of applications (or, in our case, applets).

CREATING PACKAGES

Your applet's classes don't have to be explicitly placed into packages. If they are to be added to a package or packages, however, you need to use the Java `package` keyword.

PACKAGE STATEMENTS

The package keyword tells the Java compiler that a particular class is part of a package. Follow the package keyword with the name of the package to which the class should be added. If a source code file includes a package statement, this statement must be the first line of code in the file (though white space and comments may precede it). If the following line appeared at the top of a Java source code file, a package named drawUtilities would be created. Any classes defined in the source code file would become part of this package.

```
package drawUtilites;
```

In Figure 8-1 a package named myStuff is being created. After each of the two .java source code files shown in the figure are compiled, the myStuff package will hold the bytecode (the compiled Java source code) for two classes named ClassA and ClassB.

In Figure 8-1, each class that is to become a part of the myStuff package appears in its own Java source code file, and each source code file uses a package statement. This is a convention—but not a requirement. The same package could be created by using a single source code file that begins with the package statement and then goes on to define all of the classes that are to appear in the package (the ClassA and ClassB classes in this example).

THE PUBLIC KEYWORD

You use the public keyword to make a class accessible to other classes that are not defined in the same package. Up to now you've seen classes defined as follows:

```
class ClassA {
    // instance variables and methods
}
```

If a class is to become a part of a package, you'll want to define the class using the public keyword—like this:

```
public class ClassA {
    // instance variables and methods
}
```

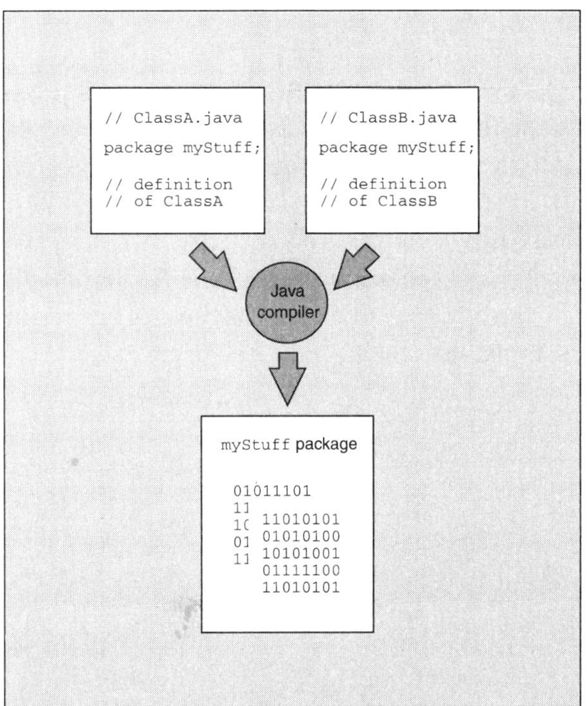

Figure 8-1

The package keyword is used to create a package and add classes to that package.

Making a class public means that any class in any other package can access it. If you don't use the `public` keyword, a class is accessible only to other classes that are defined in the same package. Because the typical purpose of a package is to bundle related classes into a group that externally defined classes can use, it should be obvious that this keyword is one that is used with the definition of classes that are explicitly added to a package.

Besides `public`, other access modifier keywords that are a part of Java are `private` and `protected`. Later in this chapter, you'll see a complete description of all of these keywords.

USING PACKAGES

When you compile a Java source code file, the compiler needs to know which classes used in the file are defined outside the file. You use an `import` statement to give the compiler that information.

IMPORTING EXTERNALLY DEFINED CLASSES

To import the classes of a package into a source code file, use the Java `import` keyword. You've already seen `import` statements—for example, the applet named MyFirstApplet uses them:

```
import java.awt.*;
import java.applet.*;

public class MyFirstApplet extends Applet {

    public void paint(Graphics g) {
        g.drawString("This applet simply draws text", 10, 20);
    }
}
```

The MyFirstApplet example imports packages named `java.awt` and `java.applet`—two packages that are distributed with all Java development environments. For an applet to make use of the `myStuff` package that we've shown in Figure 8.1, the applet's source code file should begin with this `import` statement:

```
import myStuff.*;
```

Ending a package name with a period and an asterisk is a wildcard notation that tells the compiler that it should consider all of the classes defined in the named package usable to the applet. An applet that imports the `myStuff` package could go on to create an object of, say, type `ClassA` by using `new`:

```
ClassA theClassAObject;

theClassAObject = new ClassA();
```

When a Java source code file includes an import statement, compilation of that file results in select code from the package being included in the bytecode file that results from the compilation. Figure 8-2 shows the creation of the same myStuff package shown in Figure 8-1. The figure also shows that the code in this package can be used by an applet if the applet's source code file imports the package. In Figure 8-2 the

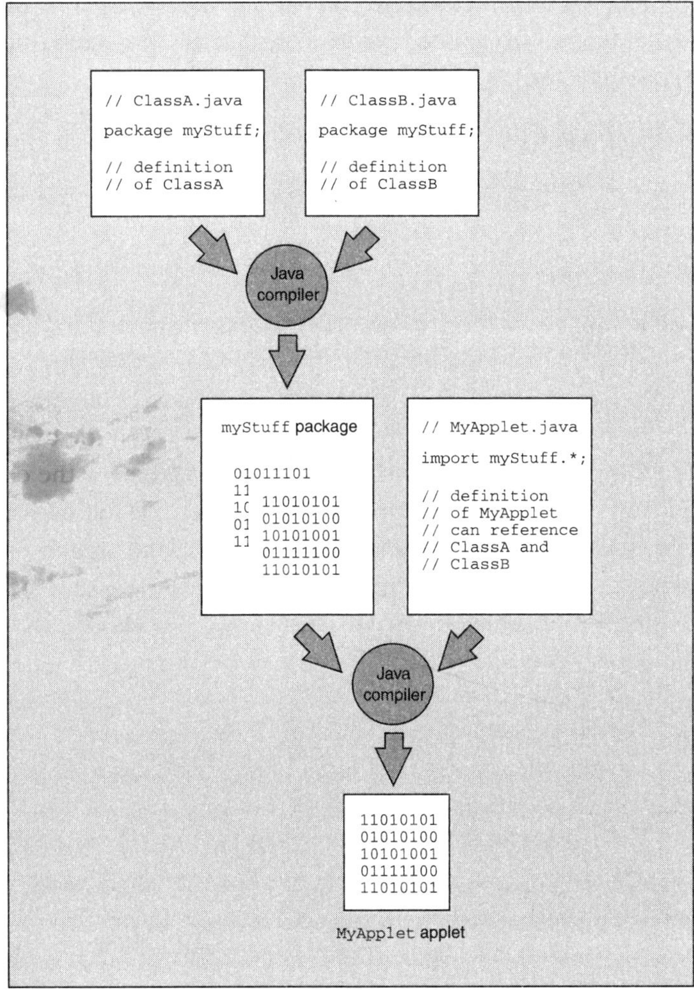

Figure 8-2
An applet gains access to the classes in a package by importing that package.

applet is named MyApplet, and its code appears in the MyApplet.java source code file. When MyApplet.java is compiled, the compiler sees to it that only the package code for the class or classes referenced in MyApplet.java gets included in the resulting applet bytecode file.

USING PACKAGE CLASSES WITHOUT IMPORTING A PACKAGE

An alternative to importing a package is to explicitly name the package with every reference to a class within the package. For instance, if the preceding snippet were to appear in a source code file that didn't import the myStuff package, then it could be rewritten as follows:

```
myStuff.ClassA theClassAObject;

theClassAObject = new ClassA();
```

THE DEFAULT PACKAGE

All compiled Java classes end up in a package—even classes defined in Java source code files that have no package statements. When the compiler encounters a Java source code file without a package statement, the compiler places any classes defined in that file in an unnamed, default package.

The following snippet contains the source code for an applet named AlienGame. Because the file does not include a package statement, compilation of this file results in the AlienGame and Alien classes becoming a part of the default package.

```
// File: AlienGame.java
// This file defines the AlienGame and Alien classes

import java.awt.*;
import java.applet.*;

public class AlienGame extends Applet {

    Alien     theAlien;
```

```
    // methods here
}

class Alien {

    public int        strength;
    public int        lives;

    // methods here
}
```

All of the classes for a small-scale applet typically do appear in a single source code file that doesn't use a `package` statement. Compiling such a file into a nameless package means that the resulting classes can't be imported by other applets that you write. Because the source code is for an entire applet rather than, say, a group of utility classes, taking this approach has no disadvantages.

JAVA API PACKAGES

By now it should be apparent that we've been using packages all along. Each time the import statement has appeared in a snippet, a package has been imported. Specifically, you're familiar with the following two import statements:

```
import java.awt.*;
import java.applet.*;
```

Sun has defined hundreds of Java classes that handle all sorts of programming tasks. These classes have been grouped according to purpose, and each group has been turned into a package. Each of these Sun-created packages has a name that begins with *java*—as in the `java.awt` and `java.applet` packages imported in the preceding snippet. You'll read much more about these Java API packages later in this chapter.

Interfaces: Java's Answer to Multiple Inheritance

In Java, "multiple inheritance" is not allowed. As you know, a class can include the contents of an existing class by extending the existing class. That's called *inheritance*. (Refer to Chapters 4 and 5 for more information about inheritance.) However, a subclass can have only *one* superclass. In other words, Java does not support multiple inheritance. Sometimes, though, it is beneficial for a subclass to inherit the contents of another class. In Java, this can be accomplished by implementing the contents of a Java interface. An *interface* declares a set of methods that define behaviors that can be shared by multiple classes.

MULTIPLE INHERITANCE

In C++, a class can be the base for any number of derived classes. Consider a class named `BaseClassA` that is to be used as the base class from which two classes are derived, while a different, unrelated class named `BaseClassB` is to be used as the base class from which a single class is derived. The C++ code for such a situation would look like this:

```
class BaseClassA {
    // class body
};

class BaseClassB {
    // class body
};

class DerivedClassA1 : public BaseClassA {
    // class body
};

class DerivedClassA2 : public BaseClassA {
    // class body
};
```

Figure 8-3 illustrates the relationship between the classes discussed in the preceding example.

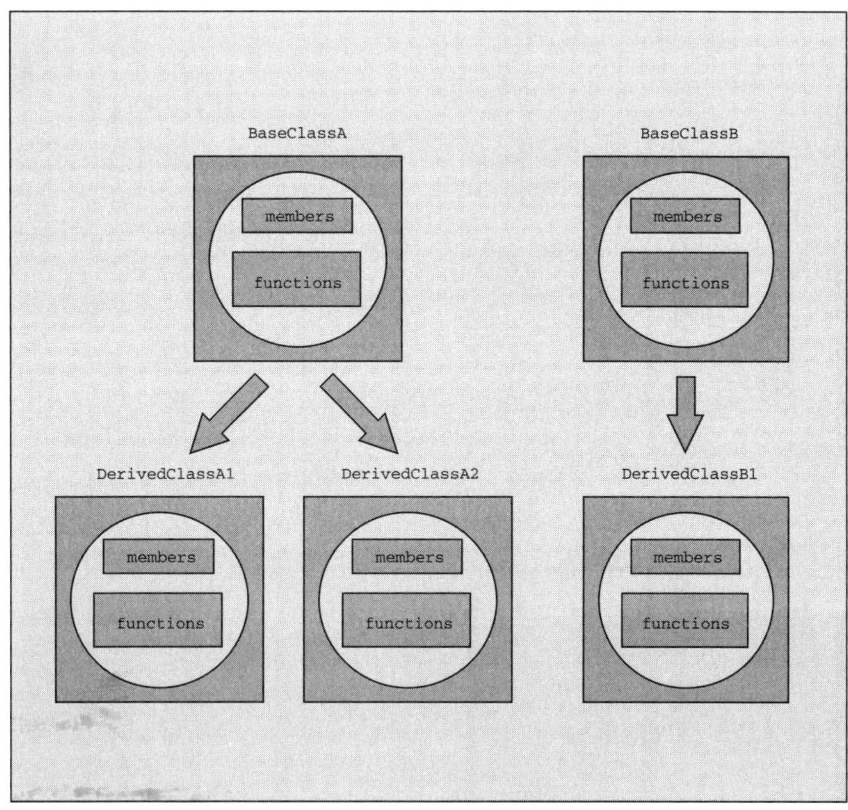

Figure 8-3
In C++, any number of classes can be derived from base classes.

If any of the derived classes illustrated in Figure 8-3 need to inherit the contents of another base class, they can easily do so. If `DerivedClassA2` is to include the contents of both base class `BaseClassA` and another base class, `BaseClassC`, it can do so by naming both classes in its definition. And if `DerivedClassB1` also requires the contents `BaseClassC` (as well as the contents of `BaseClassB`), it too can easily accomplish this. In both cases, multiple inheritance is used:

```
class BaseClassA {
    // class body
};

class BaseClassB {
    // class body
};
```

```
class BaseClassC {
    // class body

};
class DerivedClassA1 : public BaseClassA {
    // class body


};


class DerivedClassA2 : public BaseClassA, public BaseClassC {
    // class body
};

class DerivedClassB1 : public BaseClassB, public BaseClassC {
    // class body
};
```

Figure 8-4 expands upon Figure 8-3 to illustrate the class relationship for the preceding snippet.

USING JAVA INTERFACES

As you learned at the beginning of this section, multiple inheritance is not allowed in Java. A subclass can have only one superclass. Yet in Java it is possible to define unrelated subclasses that inherit the contents of more than one class. To do this, subclasses implement an interface.

The purpose of an interface is to define a set of behaviors that can be made common to any number of classes. An interface *does not* define the specific details of how these behaviors are carried out. That task is left to the classes that make use of the interface. As such, an interface serves as an abstraction. An interface simply functions as a template of what a number of related methods should look like in classes that require this set of methods. For example, if at some point in your applet all of the displayed images are to be darkened, then each object that displays an image should belong to a class that includes a `darken()` method. If the applet performs the darkening by making a single call to `darken()` from within a loop (specifying a different object at each pass through the loop), then all objects will need a `darken()` method with a return type and parameters that are the same.

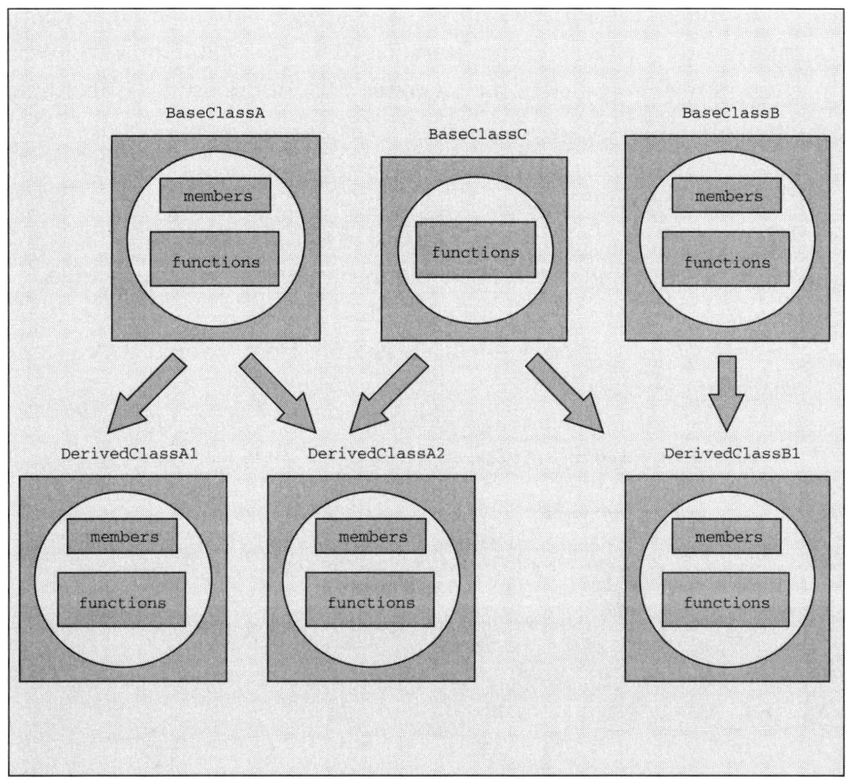

Figure 8-4
In C++, a class can inherit more than one base class.

DEFINING AN INTERFACE

An interface is a declaration of a set of methods. Each method in an interface is nothing more than a prototype of the method. Specifically, a method in an interface does not define any behavior. Consider an interface that establishes a set of methods used to alter images:

```
interface ImageUtilities {
    void darken();
    void lighten();
    void flip( int degrees );
}
```

As the preceding code shows, an interface definition begins with the keyword `interface`. After the keyword comes the name of the interface. Then, between a pair of braces, comes a list of the methods that make up the interface.

USING THE IMPLEMENTS KEYWORD

If our space game applet has a class that defines an alien and a class that defines a space ship, each class might require the behaviors listed in the `ImageUtilities` interface. In this case, these two classes should implement this interface and then define each method from this interface as appropriate for the class:

```
interface ImageUtilities {
    void darken();
    void lighten();
    void flip( int degrees );
}

class Aliens implements ImageUtilities  {

    // instance variables

    void darken() {
        // method body
    }

    void lighten() {
        // method body
    }

    void flip( int degrees ) {
        // method body
    }

    // other methods
}

class SpaceShip implements ImageUtilities  {

    // instance variables

    void darken() {
```

```
        // method body
    }

    void lighten() {
        // method body
    }

    void flip( int degrees ) {
        // method body
    }

    // other methods
}
```

As the preceding snippet shows, a class inherits the contents of an interface by using the keyword `implements` followed by the name of the interface.

COMPARISON OF INTERFACES AND MULTIPLE INHERITANCE

In the preceding example, it may seem that an `ImageUtilities` superclass could have been used rather than the interface of the same name. That, in fact, is a valid point—and a point that demonstrates that an interface is similar to a class. An example that betters shows off the use of an interface is shown here:

```
class FastAlien extends Alien implements ImageUtilities  {

    // class body
}
```

The preceding snippet defines a class named `FastAlien` that is a subclass of the `Alien` class. If the `FastAlien` class wants to inherit the contents of the `Alien` class and it wants to inherit the contents of another, unrelated class, it can't do so. Recall that Java does not allow multiple inheritance—the inheriting of more than one superclass. The work-around is to inherit the contents of the `Alien` class by using the `extends` keyword to make `FastAlien` a subclass of the `Alien` class, and then to use the `implements` keyword to have `FastAlien` inherit the contents of the `ImageUtilities` interface.

A few pages back, Figure 8-4 illustrated a scenario that had two C++ derived classes inheriting functions from more than one base class. Figure 8-5 shows how an interface can be used to achieve similar results in Java.

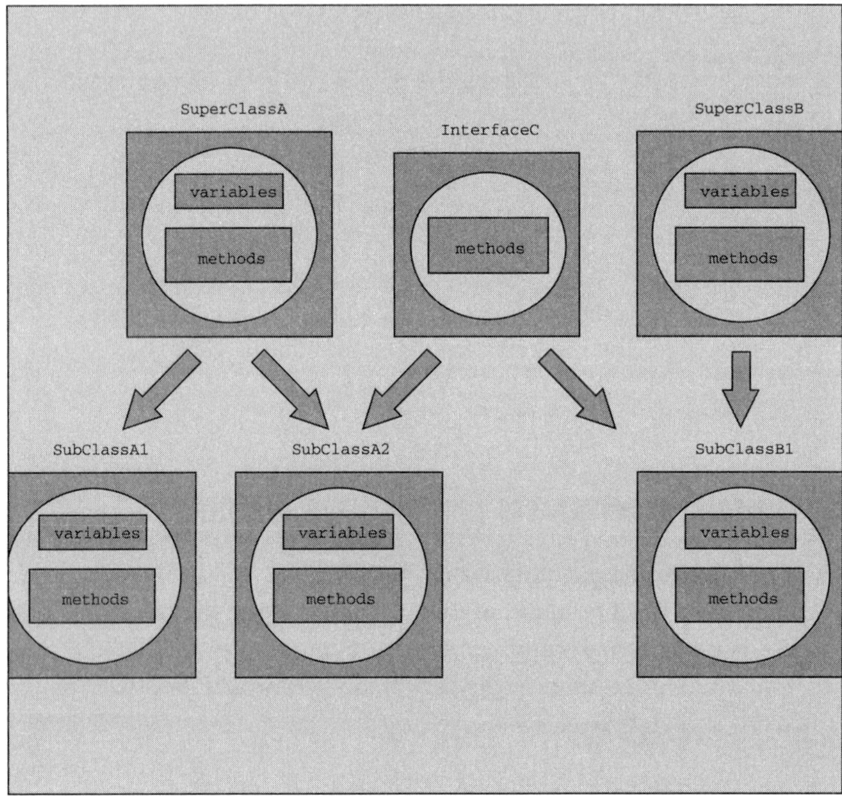

Figure 8-5
In Java, an interface is used to describe the methods that should be in more than one unrelated class.

MULTIPLE SUBCLASSES IN JAVA

The discussions in these interface sections have pointed out that, in Java, multiple inheritance does not exist. Although each subclass can have only one superclass, Java *does* allow a class to inherit from more than one class.

Consider the following snippet, which provides an example of a class that inherits from more than one other class:

```
class Alien {

    int       strength;
    int       lives;

    // methods here
}

class FastAlien extends Alien {

    int       speed;

    // methods here
}

class VisibleAlien extends FastAlien {

    int       visible;

    // methods here
}
```

In the preceding code a class named `FastAlien` extends the `Alien` class, and in turn a class named `VisibleAlien` extends `FastAlien`. Figure 8-6 illustrates the preceding three classes. This same figure also provides a look at what an object of each class type might conceptually look like.

In extending the `FastAlien` class, the `VisibleAlien` class inherits all of the instance variables and all of the methods defined in both the `Alien` class and the `FastAlien` class. This behavior, however, is *not* multiple inheritance. While `VisibleAlien` ends up with the contents of more than one class, it has only one superclass—the `FastAlien` class.

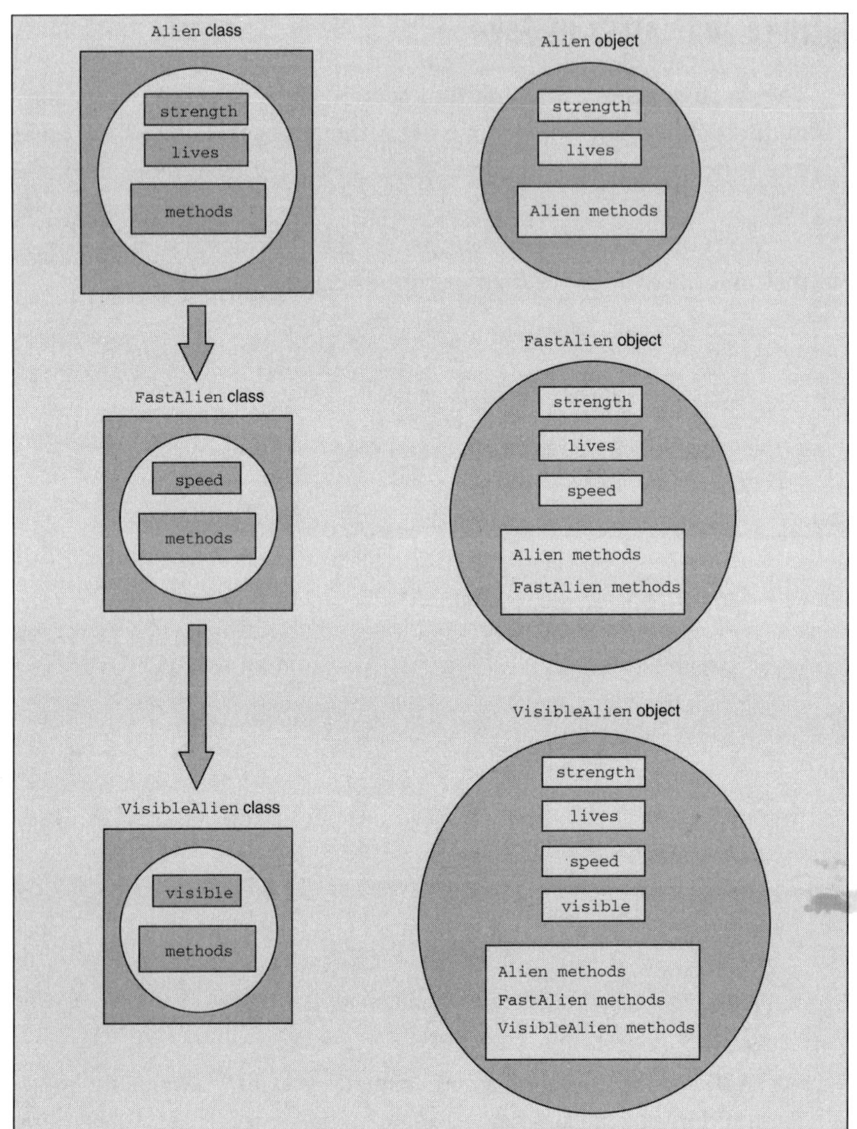

Figure 8-6
In Java, one class can inherit from more than one other class.

Access Modifiers

When you're dealing with object-oriented programming languages, you often hear the terms "data hiding" and "encapsulation." You create an object to *encapsulate* a set of attributes and behaviors into a single entity. In doing so, the object's attributes—its data—are *hidden* from the rest of the world, so to speak. Keeping an object's data private is recommended: It keeps the object self-contained and prevents accidental modification of the data by other code in the applet. In Java, *access modifiers* are used to limit the *visibility* of instance variables. You can also use access modifiers to limit the scope of the methods defined in a class.

ACCESS TO INSTANCE VARIABLES

A method can always access an instance variable defined in the same class as the method. A method can *sometimes* modify an instance variable defined in a different class. A method in a subclass can access an instance variable defined in the superclass. A method can't access an instance variable defined in an unrelated class.

Figure 8-7 provides examples of legal and illegal attempts to access instance variables. The two light gray arrows in the figure point out legal access. Because the `setStrength()` method and the `strength` and `lives` instance variables are defined in the same class, this method can access these variables. The same holds true for the `addWeapon()` method and the `weapons` instance variable; both are defined in the same class (a new class named `Warrior`). The figure's darker gray arrow shows what *can't* be done: One class cannot alter instance variables that belong to a different, unrelated class. Because the `Warrior` class isn't a subclass of the `Alien` class, an attempt by the `Warrior` method `killAlien()` to change the value of the `Alien` instance variable `lives` results in an error when the Java code is compiled.

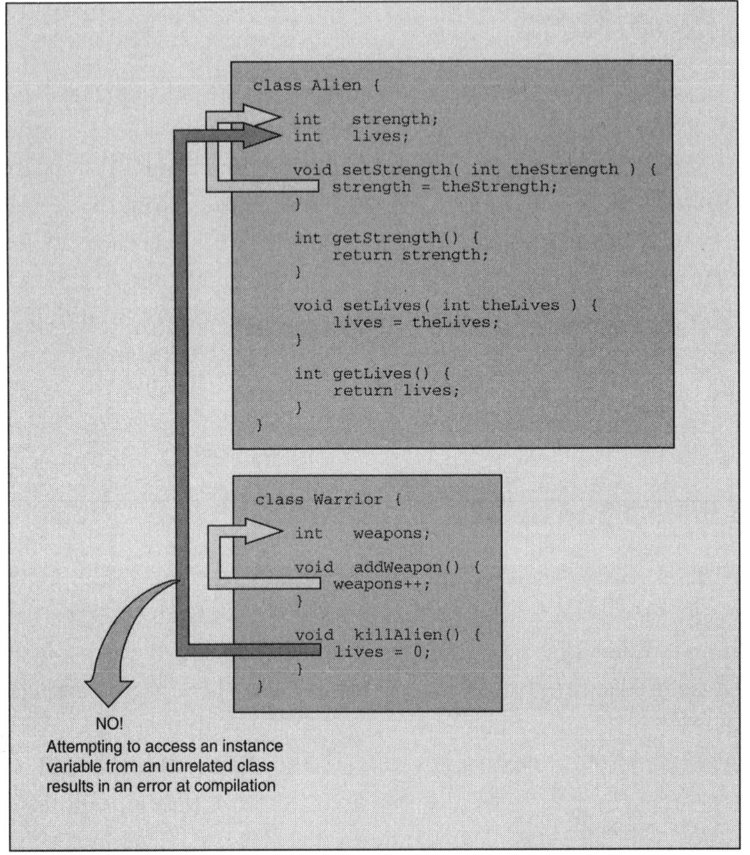

Figure 8-7
A class cannot access an instance variable that is defined in a different, unrelated class.

LIMITING ACCESS TO INSTANCE VARIABLES

You've just read that Java imposes some restrictions on access to an instance variable: It's illegal for a method from one class to access an instance variable of a different, unrelated class. There's another type of access that can be *optionally* enforced. Java includes certain keywords that, when such keywords preface an instance variable declaration, limit the scope of an instance variable. C++ programmers know these keywords as *access modifiers*.

Restricting access to instance variables follows from the notion of data hiding—that is, the concept of encapsulating objects. An object that allows only its own methods to alter its own instance variables is truly self-contained.

When an object hides its data, you (or other programmers working with you) can quickly and clearly see how the instance variables of any one class can be accessed: You need look only at the definition of the methods of that one class.

Java defines three keywords (`public`, `protected`, and `private`) that can be used as access modifiers that limit the level of access to instance variables and to methods.

The three access modifiers, along with the default condition (no modifier), make for four levels of visibility for instance variables in Java. We summarize these levels here and then provide further explanation. A `public` instance variable is accessible everywhere; even classes that exist in other packages can directly access such a variable. A `private` instance variable is accessible only by a method defined in the same class. A `protected` instance variable is accessible by a method defined in the same class and by methods defined in any subclass. An instance variable that is defined with no access modifier is considered to have default visibility and is accessible by classes everywhere within the same package.

PUBLIC INSTANCE VARIABLE

The most liberal access to object data is achieved using the `public` keyword. Making an instance variable public means that any class in any package can access this variable. And it can do so without the use of an accessor method. The following version of the `Alien` class uses the `public` keyword with both of its instance variables:

```
class Alien {

    public int       strength;
    public int       lives;

    void setStrength( int theStrength ) {
        strength = theStrength;
    }
```

```
    int getStrength() {
        return strength;
    }

    void setLives( int theLives ) {
        lives = theLives;
    }

    int getLives() {
        return lives;
    }
}
```

We've stated that an applet can consist of more than one class definition. The applet itself is a class, and any other number of classes can be defined for the applet's use. Assuming our alien game applet is named `AlienGame`, a part of the applet's code might look like this:

```
public class AlienGame extends Applet {

    Alien     theAlien;

    public void init() {
        theAlien = new Alien();
        theAlien.setStrength( 3 );   // legal access
        theAlien.lives = 4;          // legal access
    }

    // rest of methods here
}

class Alien {

    public int       strength;
    public int       lives;

    // methods here
}
```

In the preceding snippet, you can see that the `AlienGame` class defines a method named `init()`. In this method a new object of the `Alien` class is defined. The instance variables of this new object are then assigned values: `strength` is set via the `setStrength()` accessor method defined in the `Alien` class, while `lives` is set directly. Because the `Alien` class instance variables are defined as public, these are both valid means of accessing these variables.

PRIVATE INSTANCE VARIABLES

When an instance variable is defined to be private, only the methods of the class that defines the instance variable may be used to alter that variable. That means that, with private variables, the dot cannot be used for direct access outside of the class. The following snippet provides an example of legal and illegal access to private instance variables:

```
public class AlienGame extends Applet {

    Alien     theAlien;

    public void init() {
        theAlien = new Alien();
        theAlien.setStrength( 3 );   // legal access
        theAlien.lives = 4;          // illegal access!
    }

    // rest of methods here
}

class Alien {

    private int      strength;
    private int      lives;

    // methods here
}
```

As its name implies, the `private` keyword provides the strictest level of access limitation. When an instance variable is defined as private, methods of a subclass cannot directly use the variable. Figure 8-8 shows that if the `FastAlien` subclass of the `Alien` class defines a method, that method cannot directly access instance variables in the `Alien` superclass.

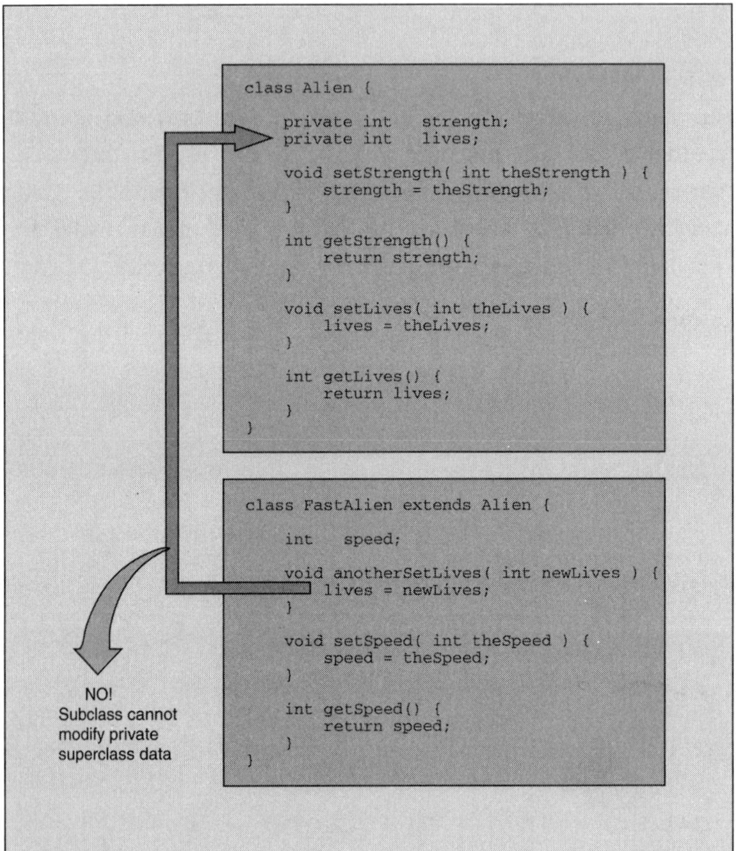

class Alien {
private int strength;
private int lives;
void setStrength(int theStrength) {
strength = theStrength;
}
int getStrength() {
return strength;
}
void setLives(int theLives) {
lives = theLives;
}
int getLives() {
return lives;
}
}
class FastAlien extends Alien {
int speed;
void anotherSetLives(int newLives) {
lives = newLives;
}
void setSpeed(int theSpeed) {
speed = theSpeed;
}
int getSpeed() {
return speed;
}
}
NO!
Subclass cannot modify private superclass data

Figure 8-8

A subclass cannot access an instance variable in its superclass if that variable is defined as private.

A subclass object still inherits the private instance variables of its superclass; it just can't directly access these variables. To access its inherited private variables, such an object needs to invoke an inherited accessor method. If a `FastAlien` object needs to access its copy of the lives instance variable, for example, it will do so using either of the inherited methods `setLives()` or `getLives()`.

PROTECTED INSTANCE VARIABLES

Using the `private` keyword to limit access to instance variables is a precaution that's important to maintaining the integrity of object data. At times, however, you'll want to safeguard object data yet still allow access by subclasses. In other words, you'll want to limit access, but not in the strict manner imposed by `private`. For such cases you can define instance variables to be protected.

The `protected` keyword gives an instance variable a level of access between that provided by the `public` and `private` keywords. As in the case of an instance variable defined to be private, an instance variable defined to be protected disallows access by unrelated classes. Unlike a private variable, however, a protected variable can still be directly accessed by any subclass of the protected variable's class.

If the `FastAlien` class variables shown in Figure 8-8 are changed from private to protected, then the `FastAlien` method `anotherSetLives()` compiles as written. As shown in Figure 8-9, by making the `Alien` instance variable `lives` protected, we've made it possible for subclasses such as `FastAlien` to access it.

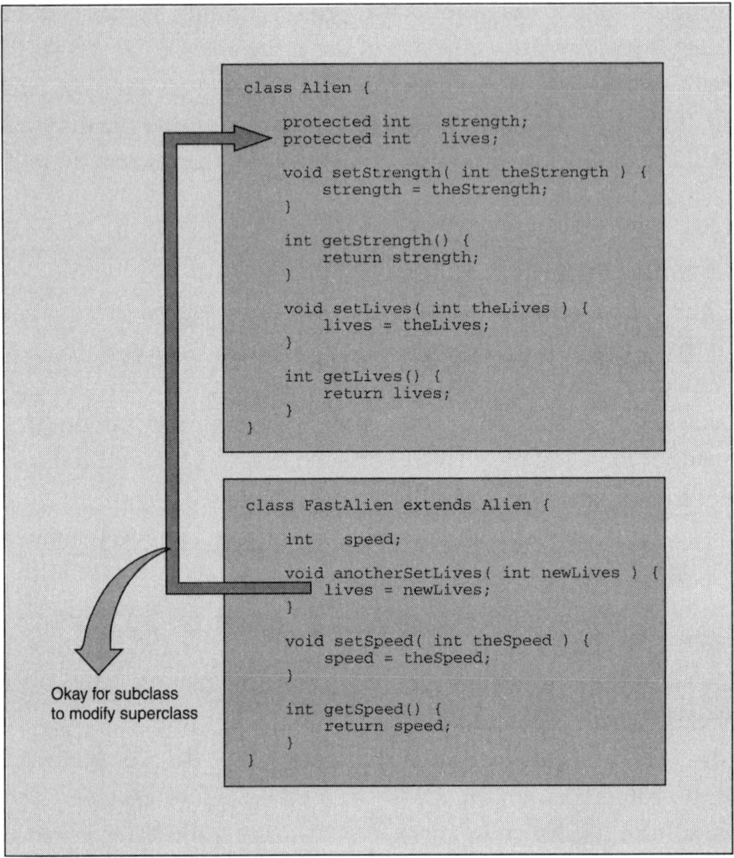

Figure 8-9
A subclass can access a superclass-defined instance variable if that variable is defined as protected.

THE DEFAULT ACCESS LEVEL FOR INSTANCE VARIABLES

If no access modifier keyword appears with the definition of an instance variable, that variable is thought of as having a default level of visibility. This level falls between that of public and protected visibility. Such an instance variable can be accessed from within any class—provided that the class exists in the same package as the class that holds the instance variable. Recall that an instance variable defined to be public can be accessed from within classes that exist in other packages.

LIMITING ACCESS TO AN INSTANCE VARIABLE IN THE SAMPLE APPLET

When we introduced the `Alien` class in Chapters 4 and 5, we said that the values of this class's instance variables range from 1 through 10. If the `Alien` class were to define, say, the `strength` variable as public (or with no access modifier, making it the default level of access), an object could have its `strength` set anywhere in the code:

```
Alien  theAlien;

theAlien = new Alien();

theAlien.strength = 20;
```

Even though the value being assigned to `strength` is out of bounds, the code in the preceding snippet would compile without complaint. That's because the range limitation of 1 to 10 is a limit of our own choosing—not one imposed by the Java language on an `int` variable. To prevent `strength` from being set to an invalid value we could perform a test before each assignment to `strength`. If the applet is one consisting of a lot of code, however, we might need to institute such a test in several places throughout the applet's code.

A better solution to the problem of ensuring that the `strength` variable is always assigned a value within a certain range is to declare this instance variable private. This means that changes to the value of `strength` must always be performed by a method defined in the `Alien` class. With this scenario, the test for a valid assignment to `strength` need only take place in one location in the code—in the `setStrength()` method:

```
void setStrength( int theStrength ) {

    if ( theStrength > 10 )
        strength = 10;              // set to upper limit
    else if ( theStrength < 1 )
        strength = 1;               // set to lower limit
    else
        strength = theStrength;     // set to passed-in value
}
```

If `strength` is defined as private, code such as this won't compile:

```
theAlien.strength = 20;        // illegal access
```

While code such as this will compile:

```
theAlien.setStrength( 20 );   // legal access
```

If the range-checking version of `setStrength()` is used, the preceding line of code not only compiles, but results in assigning `strength` a valid value: `strength` is assigned a value of 10 rather than 20.

LIMITING ACCESS TO METHODS

The same access modifiers that are used for controlling the visibility of instance variables can be used in conjunction with classes and methods. In short, a public method is accessible everywhere (including other packages), a private method is accessible only within the same class, a protected method is accessible to its class and any subclass, and a method with no access modifier is accessible everywhere within the same package.

PUBLIC METHODS

Like an instance variable that is defined as public, a method that is defined to be public is visible to all other classes—including classes that exist in other packages.

PRIVATE METHODS

A method defined as private is accessible only by the class to which the method belongs; even subclasses cannot access such a method. If a method is defined as private, objects cannot invoke the method; only a different method within the class can. In the following snippet, the `checkStrength()` method can be invoked by the `setStrength()` method (because the two methods are a part of the same class), but `checkStrength()` can't be invoked directly by an `Alien` object.

```
class Alien {

    // instance variables here

    private int checkStrength( int theStrength ) {

        if ( theStrength > 10 )
            theStrength = 10;
        else if ( theStrength < 1 )
            theStrength = 1;

        return theStrength;
    }

    void setStrength( int theStrength ) {

        strength = checkStrength( theStrength );    // valid
    }

    // rest of methods here
}

// assume the following is a part of some other class:

Alien  theAlien;
int currentStrength;
int aValue;

theAlien = new Alien();

// set aValue somewhere in code

currentStrength = theAlien.checkStrength( aValue );  // invalid!
```

In the preceding code the object `theAlien` can't access the `current-Strength()` method, even though the method is defined in the `Alien` class.

PROTECTED METHODS

A method that is protected is accessible by both the class in which the method is defined and any subclass of the class in which the method is defined. As expected, this means that a method defined as protected is less visible than a method defined as public and more visible than a method defined as private.

THE DEFAULT ACCESS LEVEL FOR METHODS

A method defined without an access modifier falls into the default level of visibility. Such a method is accessible by any class within the same package as the class that holds the method. Such a method is less visible than a method explicitly defined as public. Recall that a public method is accessible to all classes—even classes that exist in different packages.

MAKING CLASSES PUBLIC USING JAVA ACCESS MODIFIERS

A Java class must always be accessible to all of the classes within the package where it resides. Thus a class cannot be defined as being either `private` or `protected`. Instead, a class can be defined only with the `public` keyword or with no keyword (in which case it has a default visibility).

A class with no access modifier is visible to all other classes within the same package. Examples that define the `Alien` class fall into this category:

```
class Alien {

    // class body here
}
```

If a class is to be made accessible to code outside of the package that holds the class, then the class must be defined using the `public` keyword. Here the `Alien` class is redefined with a public level of visibility:

```
public class Alien {

    // class body here
}
```

The class that represents the applet itself must be public for Java to be capable of invoking it. Recall from Chapter 3 that the MyFirstApplet class was defined using `public`:

```
public class MyFirstApplet extends Applet {

    // class body here

}
```

Failing to declare the main class of an applet as `public` results in an error at compile-time.

CHOOSING THE APPROPRIATE LEVEL OF VISIBILITY

You've seen that, for class data, public access is often too liberal while private access is too restricting. For that reason you'll notice that much of the Java source code you encounter has its class data defined as protected. Methods, on the other hand, are often defined as public. This combination of visibility means that class data can be accessed from anywhere in the applet, but the access must be routed through a method of the class that holds the data.

The remaining examples in this book generally define instance variables as protected and methods as public. Classes defined by the applet could use the default level of visibility (that is, they could be defined without the `public` keyword) but will instead be defined as public. This means that these classes will be available to any other classes in any package. Figure 8-10 illustrates such a setup. As you become comfortable with Java programming, you can decide when it's appropriate to limit access further.

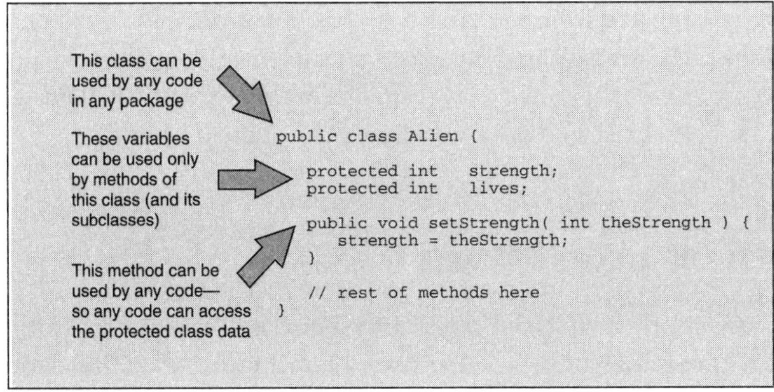
This class can be used by any code in any package
These variables can be used only by methods of this class (and its subclasses)
This method can be used by any code— so any code can access the protected class data
public class Alien {
protected int strength;
protected int lives;
public void setStrength(int theStrength) {
strength = theStrength;
}
// rest of methods here
}

Figure 8-10
Making classes and methods public, and instance variables protected, provides a good access compromise.

Class Variables

In Chapters 4 and 5, you read that a Java class is used as a template from which any number of objects can be created. You've also read that each object stores its own data in its own set of instance variables, and that each object uses its own methods to access its variables:

```
Alien theAlien;

theAlien = new Alien();
theAlien.setLives( 3 );        // call theAlien's setLives() method to
                               // set theAlien's lives variable
```

In Java, there's a second variable type that can be associated with a class. Such a *class variable* doesn't become a part of each object of the class type, as an instance variable does. Instead, only one copy of the class variable exists, regardless of how many objects are created.

When you define a class in Java, you define a number of instance variables to hold data. Each object gets a copy of each instance variable, which allows each object to maintain its own set of data—independent of any other object of the same class. Unlike these instance variables, there is *always* only a single copy of a class variable—no matter how many objects are created from the class type. In other words, each object doesn't maintain a private copy of a class variable. Instead, every object of this class type *shares* this single class variable. In this section you'll see why such variables exist, and how to define and use them.

THE PURPOSE OF A CLASS VARIABLE

Java doesn't provide for global variables, but class variables come pretty close. A class variable has a scope that is global to the class that defines it and to all the objects that are instances of that class. This makes a class variable a good means of sharing some piece of data between different objects of the same class type.

As an example, consider that we'd like to keep track of the total number of aliens present in the applet game as the user plays it. Because this information isn't something that is specific to each `Alien` object, there'd be no need to give each object its own private copy of this information.

That is, there'd be no need to define an instance variable for this data. Instead, the Alien class could define a class variable named totalAliens. Then, no matter how many Alien objects were created, there would still be only one totalAliens variable. Figure 8-11 illustrates.

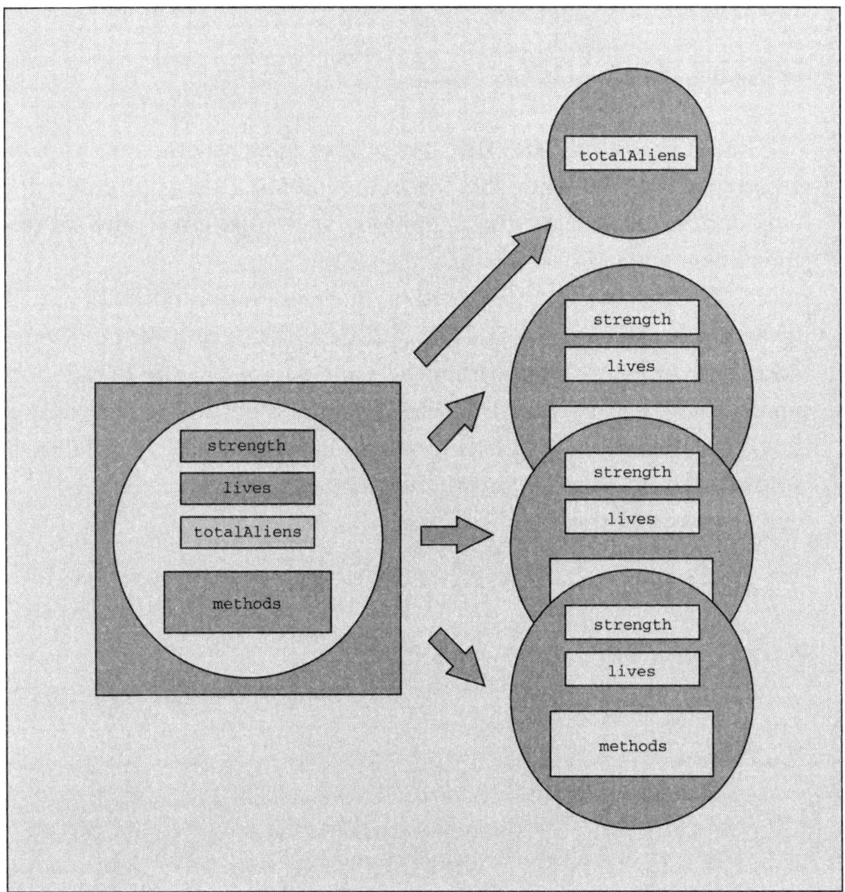

Figure 8-11
A class variable has only one copy; each object of the class type does not have it's own version of this variable.

As a part of the Alien class, the one totalAliens class variable would be accessible by any Alien object. In fact, this class variable would be accessible from anywhere in the applet code that had access to the Alien class. You'll see such an example just ahead.

DEFINING A CLASS VARIABLE

A class variable is declared right along with the instance variables that are a part of a class definition. To specify that a variable be a class variable, begin its declaration with the Java keyword `static`. As with any variable, you can optionally initialize it at the time of declaration:

```
static int totalAliens = 0;
```

Recall from Chapter 6 that Java always initially sets to 0 a variable of an integral type. So while the preceding initialization isn't required, its explicitness does make what's going on very apparent to anyone reading the code.

Note, though, that the preceding declaration doesn't make use of an access modifier, so `totalAliens` will have the default scope of being accessible from any class within the same package as the declaration. To make `totalAliens` accessible to classes defined outside of the package that holds the definition, the variable should be made public. The following snippet does just that. It also shows *where* `totalAliens` would be defined—within the Alien class itself.

```
public class Alien {

    protected int     strength;
    protected int     lives;
    public static int totalAliens = 0;

    // methods here
}
```

By the way, you'll probably recognize the `static` keyword from variable declarations you've made in your C or C++ programs. In those languages, a static variable is one that is local to a function. Unlike other local variables in C or C++ (that "disappear" after the function that declares them finishes its execution), a static variable retains its value between function calls. The commonality between a C or C++ static variable and a Java static variable is that each is initialized only once and each exists for the duration of the program's (or applet's) execution.

USING A CLASS VARIABLE WITHIN ITS CLASS

There's no need to explicitly create an object to get a class variable; simply defining one in a class makes it usable. Note that this is unlike an instance variable, which only exists as a variable when an object is created. Once a class variable is defined in a class, it can be accessed by naming the variable preceded by the class it exists in and a dot. For example, to increment the `totalAliens` class variable defined in the `Aliens` class, do this:

```
Alien.totalAlien++;
```

Yes, using the dot with a class name rather than an object name does take some getting used to—especially for C++ programmers! If you keep in mind that a class variable is just that—a variable that belongs to a class rather than to an object, you'll become comfortable with this syntax.

In the following snippet the `totalAliens` class variable is incremented from within a constructor method of the `Alien` class:

```
public class Alien {

    protected int     strength;
    protected int     lives;
    public static int totalAliens = 0;

    public Alien() {
        Alien.totalAliens++;
    }

    // other methods
}
```

Within the class that defines it (and only within that particular class), the class variable can be referenced without being preceded by the class name and the dot. That's similar to the syntax of an instance variable: you can use an instance variable in a class without preceding the variable name with an object name and the dot. The preceding example does name the class for clarity. The same constructor could have been written as follows:

```
public Alien() {
    totalAliens++;
}
```

With a constructor that increments `totalAliens` now written, each time a new `Alien` object is created, `totalAliens` will be incremented:

```
Alien  theAlien;
Alien  anotherAlien;

theAlien = new Alien();               // totalAliens becomes 1
anotherAlien = new Alien();           // totalAliens becomes 2
```

USING A CLASS VARIABLE OUTSIDE OF ITS CLASS

Like an instance variable, a class variable is not limited to use within its own class. Consider the following code snippet:

```
public class AlienGame extends Applet {

    // instance variables here

    public void paint( Graphics g ) {
        g.drawString( Alien.totalAliens + " aliens.", 10, 20 );
    }

    // other methods here
}

class Alien {

    protected int     strength;
    protected int     lives;
    public static int totalAliens = 0;

    public Alien() {
        totalAliens++;
    }

    // other methods here
}
```

In the preceding version of the Alien class, a constructor increments the class variable totalAliens. As mentioned, within its class a class variable need not be prefaced with the class name and the dot, so that's what we've done here. The totalAliens variable is used a second time in the preceding snippet; it appears in the paint() method of the applet class AlienGame. Here, outside of the Alien class, it's required that the class variable include the class name and the dot. You've seen the paint() method several times, and you know it to be a method inherited by a class that extends the Java-defined class Applet. When the browser window needs updating, paint() is called by the Java runtime. If at the time paint() executes there are, say, four aliens present in the applet, the result will be the following line of text starting near the upper left corner of the applet in the browser window:

```
4 aliens.
```

The previous snippet used totalAliens to output a value to the browser. A class variable can, of course, be used in any way that other variables are used. For example, to see if a new alien should be created, the following code could be used. Here it is assumed that the applet supports a maximum of ten aliens at any given time:

```
if ( Alien.totalAliens < 10 )
    anotherAlien = new Alien();
```

CLASS VARIABLES AND CONSTANTS

In Chapter 7, you learned that the Java keyword final is used to designate that a variable be a constant:

```
final int DAYS_IN_WEEK = 7;
```

In Chapter 7, you also saw constants declared at the class level—right along with other instance variables. Now that you know about class variables, we'll instead define constants as class variables rather than instance variables. This approach is the better of the two, as there's no need to have every object of a class have its own copy of a constant.

In the previous section we used the totalAliens class variable in a comparison with the maximum number of aliens that are allowable in our alien game applet. As in any programming endeavor, it's always best to turn a hard-coded value into a constant so that future changes need take place in only one location—at the definition of the constant. Rather than scatter the number 10 (the value we've chosen as our maximum number of aliens) all about our applet, let's define a constant to be used in its place. And, while not required, let's also use the static keyword to take the efficient step of making that constant a class variable rather than an instance variable:

```
public class Alien {

    protected int     strength;
    protected int     lives;
    public static int totalAliens = 0;
    public static final int MAX_ALIENS = 10;

    public Alien() {
        totalAliens++;
    }

    // other methods
}
```

The following snippet makes use of both of the class variables defined in the Alien class:

```
if ( Alien.totalAliens < Alien.MAX_ALIENS )
    anotherAlien = new Alien();
```

Class Methods

In the preceding section you saw that occasionally it makes sense to define a variable that isn't replicated in each object. Instead, an applet makes only one copy of this *class variable* and makes that copy accessible to any class in the applet—not just to the class in which it is defined. For example, on the preceding pages you saw that the `totalAliens` class variable defined in the `Alien` class was used within both the `Alien` class and the main applet class, the `AppletGame` class. Situations also arise where it makes sense to define a single method that isn't bound to any one object, but instead is accessible throughout an applet. As you may have surmised, such a method is called a *class method*.

THE PURPOSE OF A CLASS METHOD

A class method is often written to act on a class variable. Because a class variable isn't associated with a particular object, you don't need to associate such a method with any particular object.

As an example, consider the `totalAliens` class variable defined earlier in this chapter. When a new `Alien` object is created, this variable is incremented. If this same variable is to be decremented when an alien is killed, we might handle this task by writing a class method. Figure 8-12 illustrates.

As a part of the `Alien` class, the `killAlien()` class method is accessible by any Alien object, as well as by any other class in the applet.

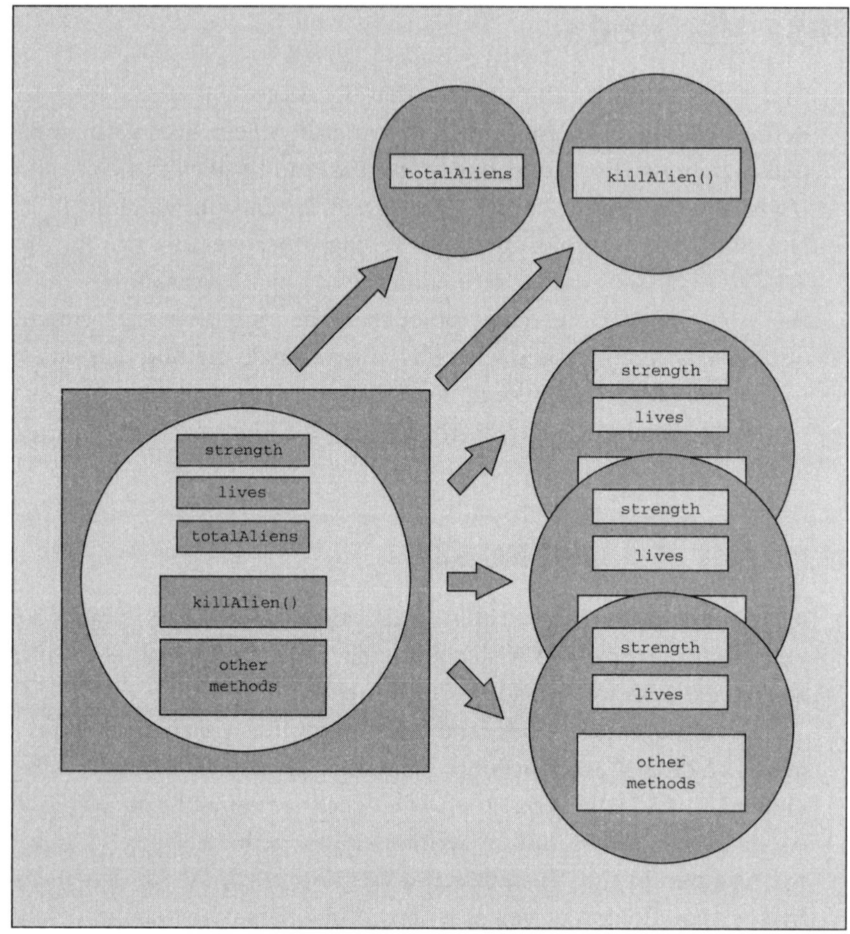

Figure 8-12
Like a class variable, a class method isn't associated with any one object.

DEFINING A CLASS METHOD

A class method is declared in a similar style as a class variable: Precede the method definition with the `static` keyword:

```
static void killAlien() {
    // method body
}
```

To adjust the scope of the method, precede the `static` keyword with a modifier keyword. To make the class method `killAlien()` accessible to classes defined outside of the package that holds the definition, the method should be made public. The following snippet does that. The snippet also shows that the `killAlien()` method is a part of the `Alien` class, and that it affects the `totalAliens` class variable.

```
public class Alien {

    protected int     strength;
    protected int     lives;
    public static int totalAliens = 0;

    public static void killAlien() {
        totalAliens--;
    }

    // other methods here
}
```

USING A CLASS METHOD

As with class variables, there's no need to explicitly create an object in order to make use of a class method. A class method can be accessed at any time by naming the method, preceded by the class in which it exists and a dot. For example, to invoke the `killAlien()` class method defined in the `Alien` class, write this code:

```
Alien.killAlien();
```

As with a class variable, if a class method is used within the class that defines it, the class name and dot notation need not be used.

CLASS METHODS AND UTILITY CLASSES

If your applet has a number of related tasks that it needs to perform, you might consider defining a `static` method to handle each task and then organizing these methods into a single class. If such a utility class doesn't operate on a specific type of object, that class can consist of class methods. Consider math operations as an example. In Java, the primitive data types such as `short`, `int`, and `float` don't exist as objects (refer to Chapter 6 for more information on this topic). Methods that operate on values of these types won't be working with objects, so defining these methods as class methods makes perfect sense. As an example, consider this class, named `Math`:

```
public class Math {

    public final static float PI = 3.141592653f;
    // other useful constants here

    public static int abs( int value ) {
        if ( value < 0 )
            value *= -1;
        return value;
    }

    // other useful methods that work with numbers here
}
```

Our `Math` class defines a constant named `PI` to hold the value of π (pi). Because our applet needs only one version of this constant, it's been defined using the `static` keyword to make it a class variable.

The `Math` class also defines a method named `abs()`. Given an integer value, `abs()` returns the absolute value of the number. This method works with numbers rather than a particular object, so it's been defined as a class method. Let's see how the `abs()` method could be invoked in an applet:

```
int absValue;
int theNumber;

// theNumber assigned a value

absValue = Math.abs( theNumber );
```

To use `abs()`, precede the method name with the class name (`Math`) and a dot—just as you do when using a class variable.

Our `Math` class example is not entirely contrived: The Java API, which is described next, includes just such a class. Of course, the Sun-defined version of this class contains many more class methods than the single one shown in our version of `Math`. Still, the concept is the same, so you might want to spend another moment looking over our example in preparation for the real thing!

Introduction to the Java API

An application programming interface, or API, is the usually large set of functions that accompany an operating system or programming environment. Having these many prewritten functions at your disposal allows you to jump right in and develop sophisticated programs without having to write your own functions to handle many of the commonly performed tasks handled by the API functions.

Windows programmers are familiar with the Windows Application Program Interface that is a part of the Windows operating environment, while Macintosh programmers are knowledgeable of much of the Macintosh Toolbox—the thousands of functions that are a part of that Macintosh operating environment. Regardless of which programming language a programmer uses, he or she becomes aware of the functions in the API of the machine for which he or she programs. The Java language, however, adds a new twist to things.

Java produces machine-independent code, so the Java language itself is machine-independent. You can't directly include calls to functions that are a part of a machine-specific API (such as the Windows API or the Macintosh Toolbox), because the resulting compiled code would no longer be cross-platform. Instead, you'll use Java's own API—the Java Application Programming Interface—to take care of many programming tasks. The Java API is distributed with each Java development environment.

JAVA API PACKAGES

In this chapter's discussion of packages (as well as back in Chapter 3), we mentioned that the classes that comprise the Java API come distributed in a number of packages. Figure 8-13 shows these packages.

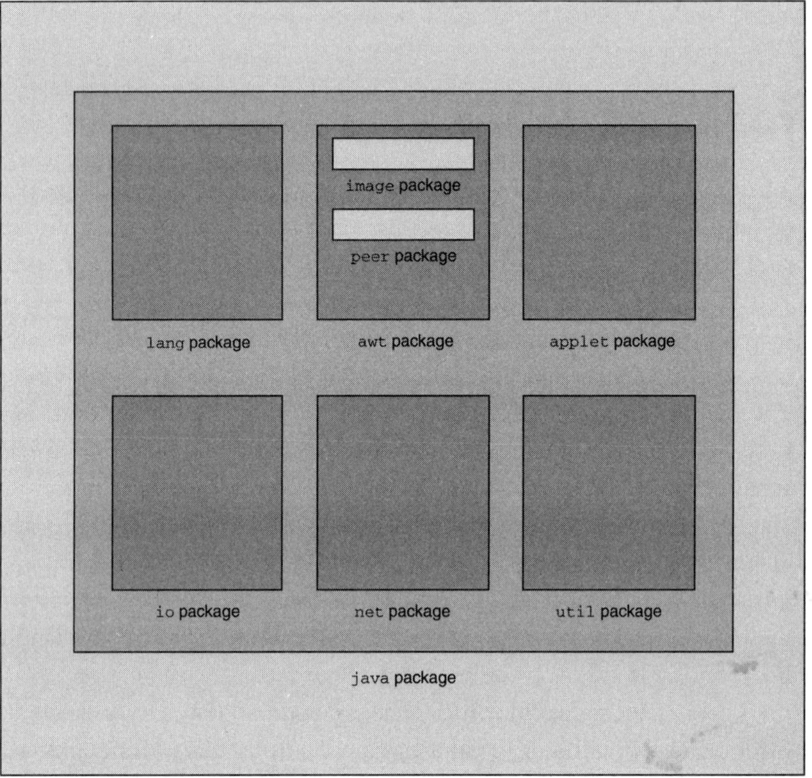

Figure 8-13

The packages that hold the classes that make up Sun's Java application programming interface.

A Java package is used to hold a number of related classes. A Java package can also hold other packages. The classes of the Java API are all a part of a single package named, simply, `java`. Within the `java` package are six other packages. Java package naming conventions dictate that when referring to a package, the entire hierarchy of packages be listed, with a period between package names. Thus the `lang` package is referred to as `java.lang`, while the `awt` package is referred to as `java.awt`.

Each of the six `java` packages holds a number of classes. As shown in Figure 8.13, the `java.awt` package itself also holds two other packages: the `java.awt.image` and the `java.awt.peer` packages. While the Java API could be considered to reside in one package (the `java` package), six packages (each of the six main packages within the `java` package), or eight packages (including the two that are a part of the `java.awt` package), you'll generally hear and read of Java as consisting of six packages.

Together, the Sun-defined classes make up the Java Application Programming Interface, or Java API. A listing of the six `java` packages that make up the Java API, along with a brief description of each, appears in Table 8-1. This book focuses on the six main packages, with particular emphasis on the `java.awt` package.

TABLE 8-1

The Java API Packages

Package	Purpose
`java.applet`	Classes necessary for the implementation of applets
`java.awt`	Classes for graphics and the implementation of a GUI
`java.io`	Classes for handling input and output
`java.lang`	Classes that define the Java language itself
`java.net`	Classes for implementing network capabilities
`java.util`	Classes that define handy utilities

CLASSES AND METHODS OF THE JAVA API

The Java API consists of hundreds of classes and methods. Covering each would be a daunting task worthy of several books. Instead of taking on that chore here, we'll demonstrate that it is sufficient to understand how the Java API is organized, and how to go about finding particular classes and methods that enable you to take care of a particular task required of your applet. Along the way, we'll focus on some of the more commonly used classes in a few of the more commonly used packages.

JAVA.LANG CLASSES

The `java.lang` package consists of the classes that are central to the Java language itself. Figure 8-14 shows several of the classes in this package. Like the remainder of the class hierarchy figures in these sections that discuss the packages of the Java API, Figure 8-14 doesn't show all of the classes that make up this package—as implied by the unlabeled white boxes.

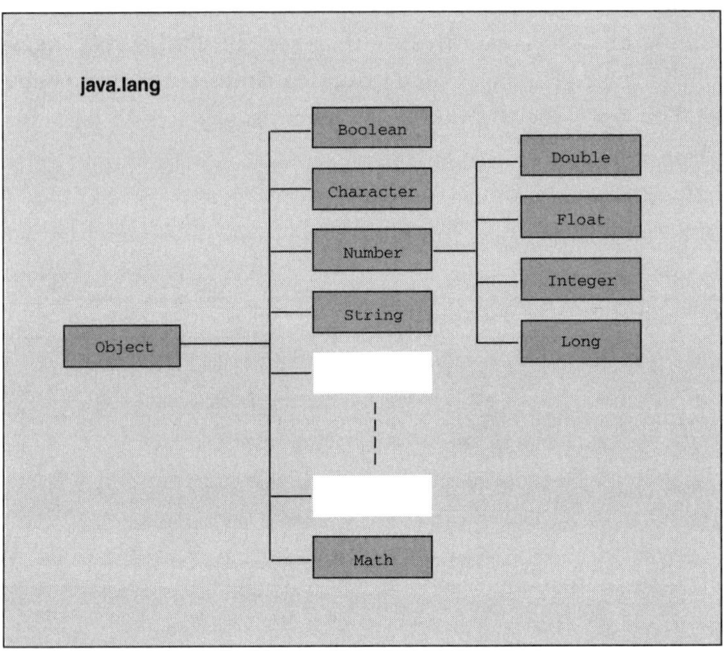

Figure 8-14
A partial class hierarchy of the java.lang package.

Because the `java.lang` package holds classes that are so frequently used, the entire package is implicitly imported into every applet. That is, without your having to state it, the effect of the following statement is always provided to your applet:

```
import java.lang.*;
```

The following sections describe some of the key classes that make up the `java.lang` package.

OBJECT CLASS

At the top of the java.lang hierarchy of classes is the Object class. Figure 8.14 shows that every other class in the java.lang package is a subclass of the Object class. What can't be shown in this figure is that *every* Java class—regardless of the package in which the class resides—is a subclass of the Object class. Because the Java classes are spread about in different packages, that idea might not be immediately intuitive. Recall that a package is simply a means of organizing classes. The Java packages don't create any boundaries in the Java class hierarchy. So a class in one package may be extended from a class in a different package. Figure 8-15 illustrates this by combining the java.lang package from Figure 8-14 with the java.awt package—a package discussed ahead.

The Object class consists of a number of methods, many of which are overridden by subclasses. For example, consider the Object method toString(). The purpose of this method is to return a string representation of an object. In the java.awt package is a class named Point. As expected, the Point class is used to create objects that each represent a single point. As a subclass of Object, the Point class inherits the toString() method. The Point class overrides this method (implements its own version of it) so that when invoked, the method produces a string that accurately describes the point defined by the Point object. Here's an example:

```
Point  thePoint;

thePoint = new Point( 50, 80 );

theString = thePoint.toString();
g.drawString("thePoint as a string = " + theString, 10, 20 );
```

As shown in this snippet, the pixel coordinates of the point can be specified when creating a new Point object. To obtain a string representation of this point, the toString() method is invoked from the Point object. When this string is drawn to the applet, the result is as follows:

```
thePoint as a string = java.awt.Point[x=50,y=80]
```

In the above output, java.awt.Point[x-50,y=80] is the value of theString. It was the toString() method, inherited from the Object class and overridden, that gave theString its value.

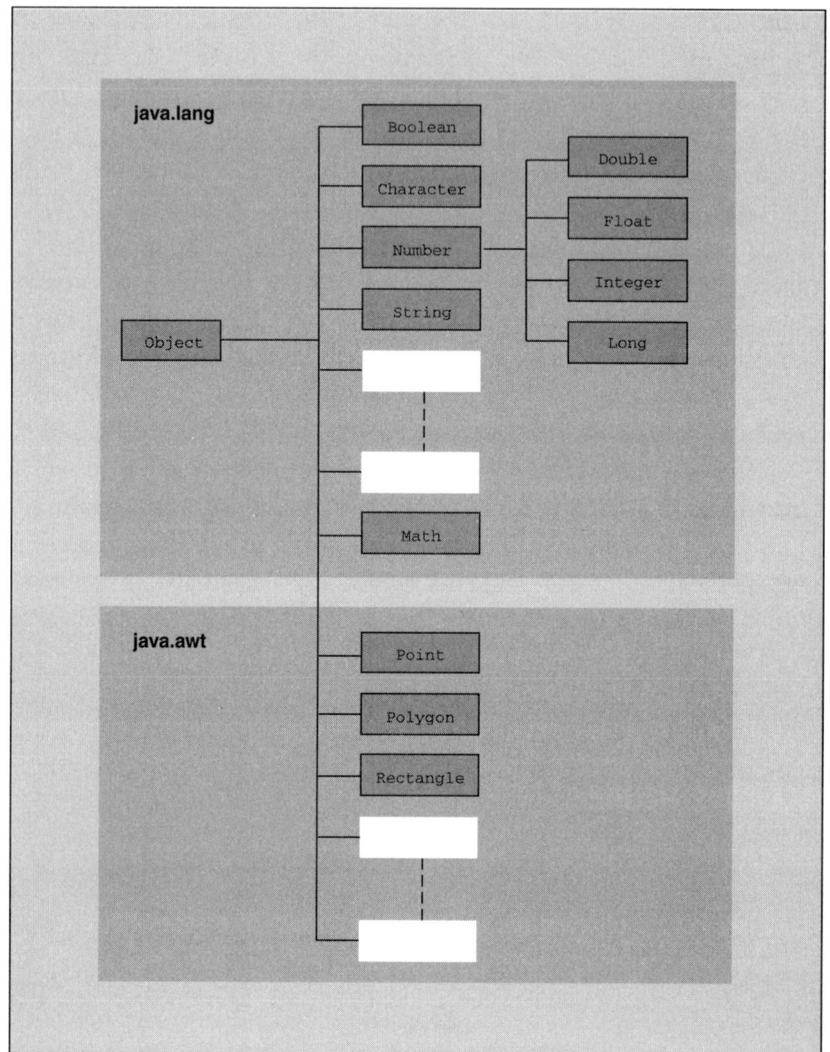

Figure 8-15

A package is an organizational tool only; classes within different packages are not prevented from having dependencies on each other.

Recall that the java.awt package, to which the Point class belongs, defines graphics-related classes. This important package is described in general later in this chapter. The java.awt package is important enough that it's given its own rather lengthy chapter—Chapter 12.

NUMBER CLASS

The Number class exists to provide *wrapper classes* for the primitive data types. Recall from Chapter 6 that the primitive types aren't objects; they are simply values. Occasionally your applet may want to implement a value of a primitive type as an object. To do that, you'll declare a variable of one of the class types extended from the Number class. Here an Integer object is declared, memory is allocated for the object, and the object is given an initial value:

```
Integer intObject = new Integer( 500 );
```

The Number class and the classes extended from it define several methods that can be used to examine or alter the values these types of object hold. While your applet will normally find it sufficient to work with numbers as primitive types, it is these methods that would be the reason you'd work with a number in the form of an object.

JAVA.AWT CLASSES

The java.awt package holds the classes that make up the Abstract Windowing Toolkit, or AWT. These classes enable you to create applets that include graphical user interface elements such as buttons, menus, and dialog boxes, as shown in Figure 8-16.

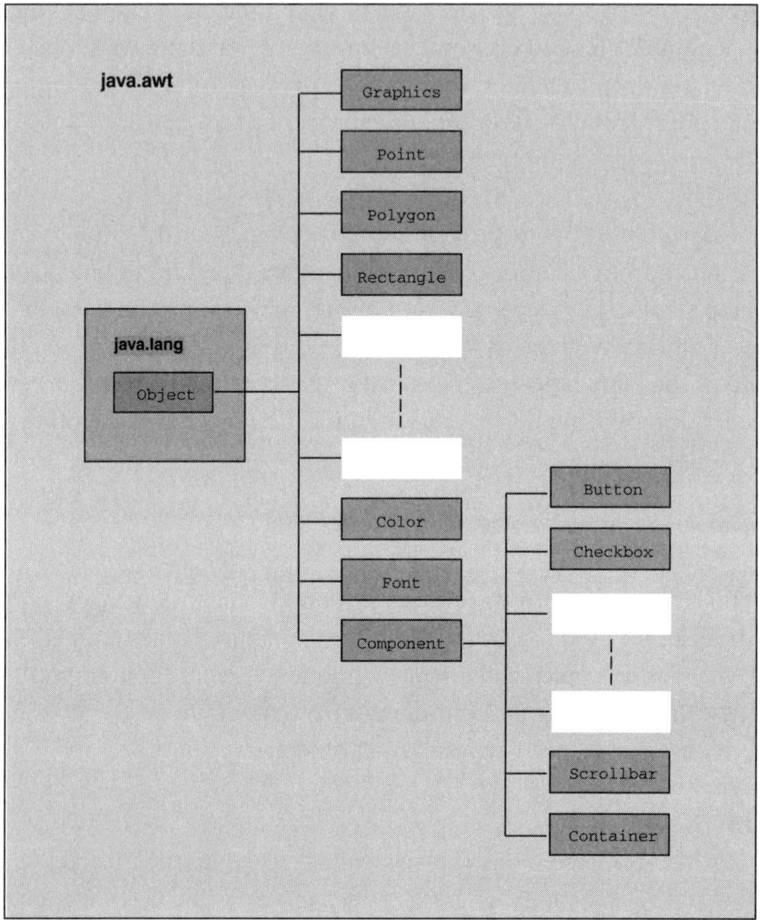

Figure 8-16
A partial class hierarchy of the java.awt package.

THE GRAPHICS CLASS

The `Graphics` class defines a device-independent interface to graphics. That is, a `Graphics` object is a drawing area that displays graphics and responds to graphics commands that are independent of the host machine.

You've already seen that Java automatically creates a `Graphics` object for your applet when a user first encounters your applet. The Java runtime then passes that object to certain methods, including the `paint()` method that redraws the applet:

```
public void paint(Graphics g) {
    g.drawString("This applet simply draws text", 10, 20);
}
```

The `Graphics` class defines a number of methods that an applet can use to draw shapes. In the preceding snippet, you can see that one such method is `drawString()`—the method your applet uses to draw text to an applet. A few other examples of `Graphics` class drawing methods are `drawLine()`, `drawOval()`, `fillPolygon()`, and `setColor()`.

THE COLOR CLASS

The `Color` class is used to create objects that each define a single color. Once defined, a color can be used in drawing by passing the `Color` object to one of several drawing methods defined by the `Graphics` class. For example, after defining a `Color` object you can have all subsequent drawing take place in that color by invoking the `setColor()` method defined in the `Graphics` class.

THE COMPONENT CLASS

The `Component` class is an abstract class; your applet won't ever create a `Component` object. Instead, your applet makes great use of some of the many classes extended from the `Component` class.

As shown in Figure 8-16, all of the graphical user interface elements that your applet might include are extended from the `Component` class. The `Container` class is another class that is extended from the `Component` class.

As an abstract class, the `Component` class exists to define a number of methods that are useful to the many classes that inherit them. For example, the `keyDown()` and `mouseDown()` methods are useful in responding to user actions that take place in the applet area. The `setBackground()` and `setFont()` methods are used to set the background color of the applet and to set the default font for text drawn to the applet.

You'll encounter `Component` methods throughout this book and throughout your applet programming endeavors. Because so many classes are extended from this class, you might not be aware of the fact that it is the `Component` class that defines these methods rather than the class with which you are working.

JAVA.APPLET CLASSES

The `java.applet` package consists of just a single class—the `Applet` class. Like all classes, the `Applet` class is extended from the `Object` class. The class hierarchy from the `Object` class to the `Applet` class, however, includes a few other classes that you'll work with later in this book. Figure 8-17 shows that the `Applet` class inherits from the `Object`, `Component`, `Container`, and `Panel` classes.

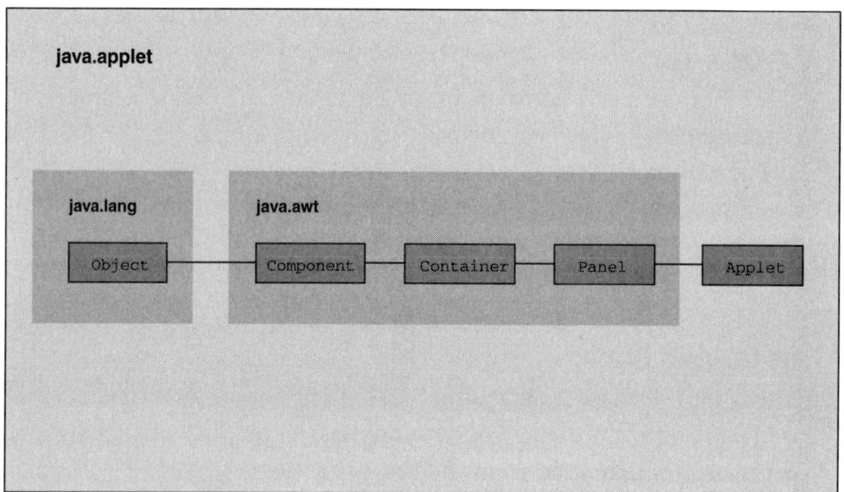

Figure 8-17
The class hierarchy of the java.applet package.

What You've Learned

A package is a means of grouping classes together for organizational purposes. A Java class is analogous to a library in C or C++. While you can create your own packages that consist of classes you've written, the most important packages are the ones defined by Sun. Together, the classes in this set of packages form the Java Application Programming Interface, or Java API.

CHAPTER 9

Graphics and Fonts

Applications that need to run on several types of machines are often heavy on text and sparse on graphics. That's because the graphics routines used by programmers aren't machine-independent: They rely on a certain operating system's being present. Java applets change all of the that. While the Java graphics routines are superficially machine-independent (you use one routine to achieve the same graphical results regardless of the machines on which your applet executes), internally they are machine-dependent (Java runtime uses the best graphical routine that is native to the machine hosting the applet). This clever technique enables you, the programmer, to create sophisticated graphics without worrying about which platforms your applet appears on.

In this chapter you'll see how to use many of the classes and methods Java defines for working with graphics. And because Java treats text as just another form of graphics, this chapter also covers the ways in which you can change the style of text your applet uses.

Drawing Fundamentals

Before discussing how to draw various graphic shapes and stylized text, let's take a brief look at *how* drawing takes place in an applet. We'll also look at how you establish *where* your applet's drawing will appear.

HOW GRAPHICS ARE DRAWN

When a Java-capable browser encounters a Web page that holds an applet, the browser automatically creates an object of the Graphics class. Recall from Chapter 8 that the Graphics class is one of several classes in the java.awt package. We'll have plenty more to say about the java.awt package and the Graphics class throughout this chapter. For now, it is sufficient to know that this Graphics object acts as a palette in which applet drawing occurs. Whenever a Web page needs to be updated, the Java interpreter that is part of the browser passes the Graphics object to the applet's paint() method. It is within the paint() method where the drawing that is particular to the applet takes place:

```
public void paint( Graphics g ) {
  // draw the applet here
}
```

As you learned in Chapter 8, the paint() method is one of many methods that is inherited by every subclass of the Applet class. All applets extend the Applet class, so all applets are subclasses of the Applet class, and, consequently, all applets include a paint() method. It is up to your applet to redefine the body of the paint() method such that it properly handles all of the drawing necessary to create your applet in the Web browser window.

An applet is always a subclass of the Applet class and thus always inherits a paint() method. When an applet needs to be updated, the Java runtime always invokes this method. This is how an applet is drawn. Now it's time to see how you specify where graphics are drawn within your applet.

WHERE GRAPHICS ARE DRAWN

If you've ever programmed applications that are designed to run in a graphical environment, you're familiar with the idea of a coordinate system. Each pixel of the monitor's screen is assigned a coordinate pair. In most systems, the pixel in the upper left corner of the monitor's screen is considered the origin and is given the coordinates of (0, 0). A pixel coordinate pair is formatted as (x, y), where *x* is the number of pixels from the origin in the horizontal direction and *y* is the number of pixels from the origin in the vertical direction. In such a system, pixels located to the right of the origin have increasingly greater *x* values, and pixels located down from the origin have increasingly greater *y* values.

Figure 9-1 shows a hypothetical monitor with dimensions of 640 × 480 pixels. This figure shows the coordinate pairings for the pixels that lie in each corner of this monitor. This figure also shows the pixel coordinate pair for the starting location of a string of text written with the following call to `drawString()`:

```
g.drawString( "Testing one, two, three.", 80, 240 );
```

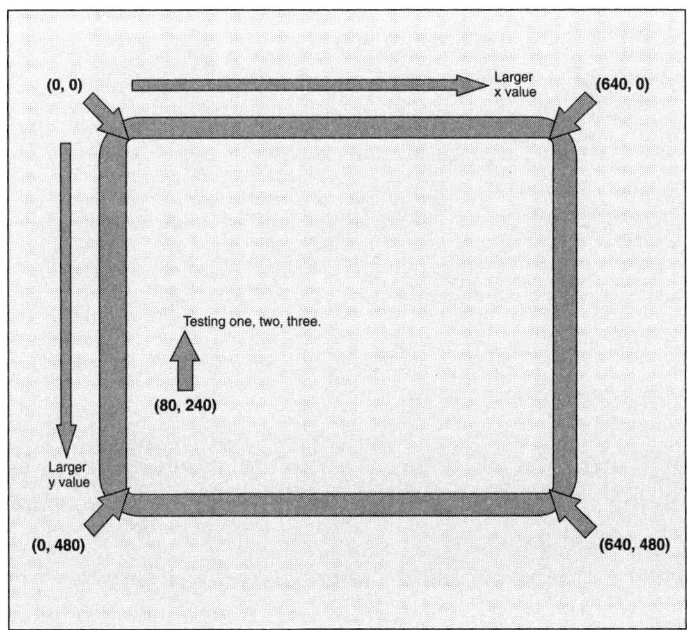

Figure 9-1
The coordinate system of a monitor

Regardless of the programming environment, drawing to a graphical user interface takes place in a window—not directly in the monitor's screen. As shown in Figure 9-2, a window has its own coordinate system with an origin independent of the monitor screen's origin. As the window moves about the screen, this private coordinate system moves with it. This enables a drawing to always appear in the same relative spot in the window.

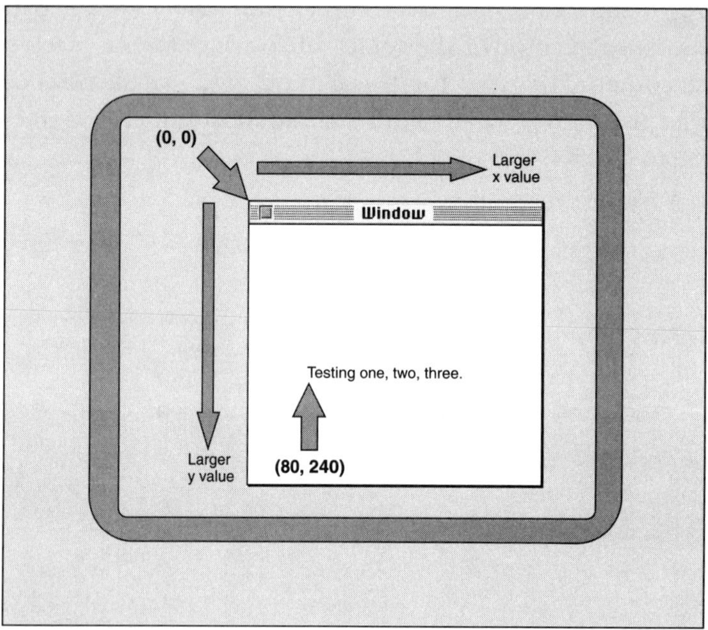

Figure 9-2
The coordinate system of a window

The line of text shown in Figure 9-1 uses the monitor screen's upper left corner as the origin. The line of text in Figure 9-2 uses the *window's* upper left corner as the origin.

Although Java applets appear in a window (the Web browser window), the upper left corner of the window is *not* the point of origin. An applet, like a window, has its own private coordinate grid—a grid system that has its origin independent of the monitor and the window in which the applet appears. The origin of an applet is always considered to be the upper left corner of the applet itself—not the upper left corner of the window in which the applet appears. Recall from Chapter 2 that the HTML `<applet>` tag (which is used on the HTML file that displays the applet) enables an applet to be placed anywhere on a Web page. Figure 9-3 shows the coordinate system of an applet that appears on a Web page.

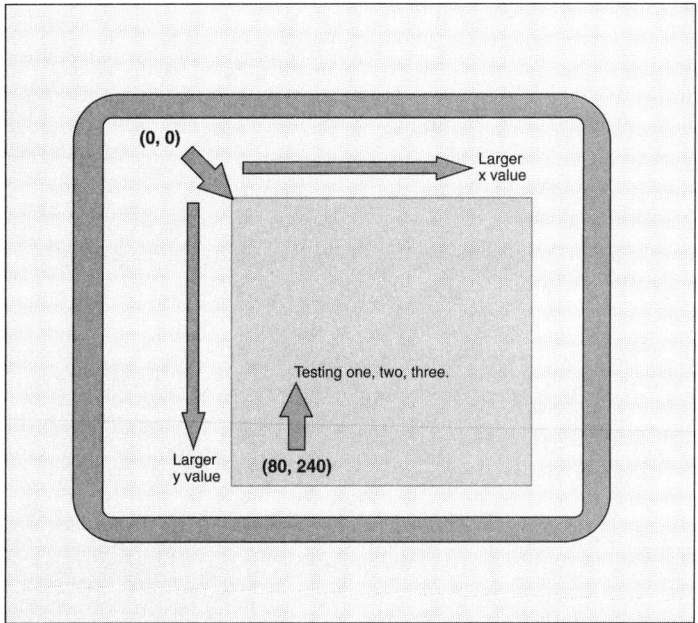

Figure 9-3
The coordinate system of an applet

The Java runtime makes sure an applet's coordinate grid always has its origin in the applet's upper left corner. That will never be a programming consideration of yours.

Graphics and the java.awt Package

In Chapter 8 you read that the "awt" in the name `java.awt` stands for Abstract Windowing Toolkit. In that chapter you also saw that the `java.awt` package holds the many classes and methods that draw graphics and handle text. Figure 9-4 shows some of the many classes in this important and powerful package.

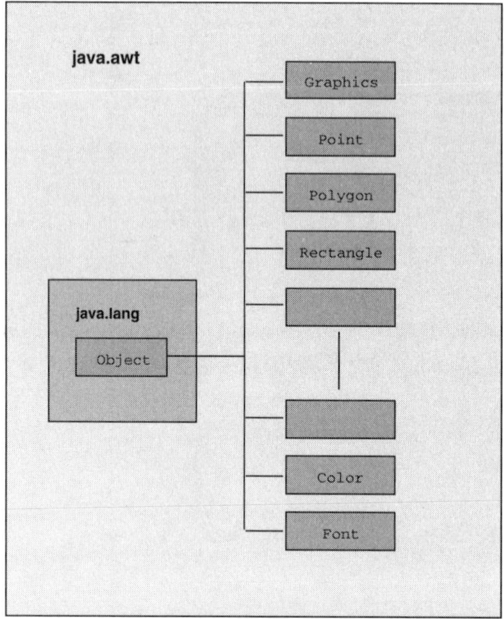

Figure 9-4
The classes of the java.awt package

This chapter exposes you to each of the classes listed in Figure 9-4. Subsequent chapters introduce you to still other classes in the `java.awt` package.

THE GRAPHICS CLASS

When your applet is loaded to a browser, the Java interpreter that is part of the browser creates an object of the `Graphics` class. This object is then passed to the applet's `paint()` method. Every time the applet needs to be refreshed, the object is passed again to the applet's `paint()` method, as shown here:

```
public void paint( Graphics g ) {
  // draw the applet here
}
```

Within the paint() method your applet uses this Graphic object, now referenced by variable g, anytime drawing takes place. You've seen this numerous times with the drawString() method:

```
g.drawString( "This is a test", 20, 50 );
```

As shown in the following Graphics class definition, the drawString() method is just one of many methods in the Graphics class.

```
public abstract class java.awt.Graphics extends java.lang.Object
{
  // constructors
  protected Graphics();

  // methods
  public abstract void clearRect(int x, int y, int width,
                                  int height);
  public abstract void clipRect(int x, int y, int width,
                                 int height);
  public abstract void copyArea(int x, int y, int width,
                                 int height, int dx, int dy);
  public abstract Graphics create();
  public Graphics create(int x, int y, int width, int height);
  public abstract void dispose();
  public void draw3DRect(int x, int y, int width, int height,
                         boolean raised);
  public abstract void drawArc(int x, int y, int width, int height,
                                int startAngle, int arcAngle);
  public void drawBytes(byte data[], int offset, int length, int x,
                        int y);
  public void drawChars(char data[], int offset, int length, int x,
                        int y);
  public abstract boolean drawImage(Image img, int x, int y,
                                    Color bgcolor,
                                    ImageObserver observer);
  public abstract boolean drawImage(Image img, int x, int y,
                                    ImageObserver observer);
  public abstract boolean drawImage(Image img, int x, int y,
                                    int width, int height,
                                    Color bgcolor,
                                    ImageObserver observer);
  public abstract boolean drawImage(Image img, int x, int y,
                                    int width, int height,
                                    ImageObserver observer);
  public abstract void drawLine(int x1, int y1, int x2, int y2);
```

```
  public abstract void drawOval(int x, int y, int width,
                                 int height);
  public abstract void drawPolygon(int xPoints[],int yPoints[],
                                    int nPoints);
  public void drawPolygon(Polygon p);
  public void drawRect(int x, int y, int width, int height);
  public abstract void drawRoundRect(int x, int y, int width,
                                       int height, int arcWidth,
                                       int arcHeight);
  public abstract void drawString(String str, int x, int y);
  public void fill3DRect(int x, int y, int width, int height,
                          boolean raised);
  public abstract void fillArc(int x, int y, int width, int height,
                                int startAngle, int arcAngle);
  public abstract void fillOval(int x, int y, int width,
                                 int height);
  public abstract void fillPolygon(int xPoints[], int yPoints[],
                                    int nPoints);
  public void fillPolygon(Polygon p);
  public abstract void fillRect(int x, int y, int width,
                                 int height);
  public abstract void fillRoundRect(int x, int y, int width,
                                       int height, int arcWidth,
                                       int arcHeight);
  public void finalize();
  public abstract Rectangle getClipRect();
  public abstract Color getColor();
  public abstract Font getFont();
  public FontMetrics getFontMetrics();
  public abstract FontMetrics getFontMetrics(Font f);
  public abstract void setColor(Color c);
  public abstract void setFont(Font font);
  public abstract void setPaintMode();
  public abstract void setXORMode(Color c1);
  public String toString();
  public abstract void translate(int x, int y);
}
```

In this chapter we'll examine several of the drawing methods found in this invaluable Java class.

SHAPE-DRAWING CLASSES AND METHODS

The `Graphics` class, which is part of the `java.awt` package, includes a number of methods that make it easy to draw shapes such as rectangles and polygons. Yet the `java.awt` package also defines separate classes for these shapes. So why aren't these shape-drawing methods defined with their particular shape class? Because often you don't need to define a shape object in order to draw the shape. For example, to draw a rectangle, you use the `drawRect()` method that is part of the `Graphics` class:

```
g.drawRect( 30, 10, 200, 60 );
```

As you'll see later in this chapter, the parameters for `drawRect()` establish the boundaries of the rectangle that is being drawn. When drawing a rectangle in this manner, no object of the `Rectangle` class need be explicitly created. To simply draw a rectangle, use this method from the `Graphics` class. If, however, you need to *work* with a rectangle or rectangles, create objects using the `Rectangle` class and then invoke one or some of the many methods that are a part of this class. As an example, if two rectangles are to be drawn and your applet needs to know if they intersect at any point, create two `Rectangle` objects. The `Graphics` method `drawRect()` can be used to draw these rectangles (as it is used to draw rectangles whose boundaries are specified only by values rather than by `Rectangle` objects). Then, to see if the rectangles intersect, use the `intersects()` method that is a part of the `Rectangle` class.

In this chapter you'll see examples of how to work with both the shape-drawing methods that are a part of the `Graphics` class and the shape-manipulating methods that are a part of the shape classes.

THE COLOR CLASS

When you draw and fill shapes, the default color is black. But Java doesn't limit you to drawing just in black and white. You can use the `Color` class to define `Color` objects. Each object defines a single color. Once your applet has defined a color, it can change the default color used for drawing shapes and for the background against which shapes are drawn.

THE FONT CLASS

The `java.awt` package includes a class that you can use to alter the way in which text appears in an applet. As you'll see in this chapter, you use a `Font` object to hold characteristics (such as font type, style, and size) for a single font. You can then use this object to affect any text that's drawn in an applet.

In Java, text is considered graphic in nature. That is, it's drawn to an applet in a manner similar to how other graphics are drawn. Mere humans categorize text quite differently than graphics, but to Java the distinction is less clear. For that reason you'll often see text (and the way the look of the text is controlled—fonts) discussed right alongside shape-drawing.

Points

The focus of this section is on the `Point` class that is part of the `java.awt` package. Unlike other shapes defined in the `Graphics` class, points are not defined by a method in the `Graphics` class.

DRAWING POINTS

Strange as it sounds, in Java you never actually draw points. Instead, you draw a line with the length of a single pixel. To do that, you use the `drawLine()` method defined in the `Graphics` class. To draw a point, draw a line that has a length of 0. That is, draw a line that has an end coordinate that is the same as its start coordinate. Because the default size of a line is a single pixel, this results in a line one pixel long—which is the same as a point. The `drawLine()` method is discussed in the Lines section later in this chapter.

THE POINT CLASS

While the `drawLine()` method of the `Graphics` class suffices for drawing a point, you should still be familiar with the `Point` class that is a part of the java.awt package; some of the methods in java.awt classes require a Point object as a parameter.

THE POINT CLASS DEFINITION

Notice in the following definition of the Point class that the class is extended from the Object class. As you know, every Java class is a subclass (or a subclass of a subclass) of the Object class. The following is the complete definition for the Point class:

```
public class java.awt.Point extends java.lang.Object
{
  // instance variables
  public int   x;
  public int   y;

  // constructors
  public Point(int x, int y);

  // methods
  public boolean equals(Object obj);
  public int hashCode();
  public void move(int x, int y);
  public String toString();
  public void translate(int dx, int dy);
}
```

If your applet declares a Point object, any of the Point class methods can be used to manipulate that point.

USING POINT OBJECTS

You create a Point object as you create any object—using new. The constructor for Point requires that you pass two parameters: the horizontal (*x*) location of the point and the vertical (*y*) location of the point. Together these two values make up the point's coordinate pair. For example, to define a point that is 70 pixels from the left edge of an applet and 100 pixels down from the top of an applet, use the pair (70, 100). These coordinates result in an *x* value of 70 and a *y* value of 100, as follows:

```
Point  thePoint;

thePoint = new Point( 70, 100 );
```

The following applet listing makes use of the `move()` method that is a part of the `Point` class. In this example two `Point` objects are created. The first object has a coordinate pair of (10, 20). The second object is initialized to the origin, or (0, 0). The applet then shows how the coordinates of one `Point` object can be assigned the coordinates of another. Next, the `move()` method is invoked on the second object to move its coordinates 40 pixels in the *x* direction and 50 pixels in the *y* directions. The result of invoking `move()` is that the second `Point` object will have a coordinate pair of (50, 70).

```
import java.applet.*;
import java.awt.*;

public class MyGraphics extends Applet {

  Point        thePt1;
  Point        thePt2;

  public void init() {

    thePt1 = new Pt( 10, 20 );
    thePt2 = new Pt( 0, 0 );

    thePt2.x = thePt1.x;
    thePt2.y = thePt1.y;
    thePt2.move( 40, 50 );
  }

  public void paint( Graphics g ) {

    g.drawString( "First I'm here...", thePt1.x, thePt1.y );
    g.drawString( "Now I'm over here...", thePt2.x, thePt2.y );
  }

}
```

In this chapter you'll see the source code for a number of short, simple applets like the one shown previously. For the sake of brevity, we'll omit the import statements. In subsequent listings, assume both the `java.applet` and `java.awt` packages are always imported.

One other note about the preceding listing. The MyGraphics applet takes care of initializations in the `init()` method that all applets inherit from the `Applet` class. In some examples we could omit this method and throw everything in the paint() method. Because the paint() method is repeated every time the applet needs updating, though, that approach would be inefficient.

Executing the preceding applet results in two strings being written to the applet. Figure 9-5 illustrates.

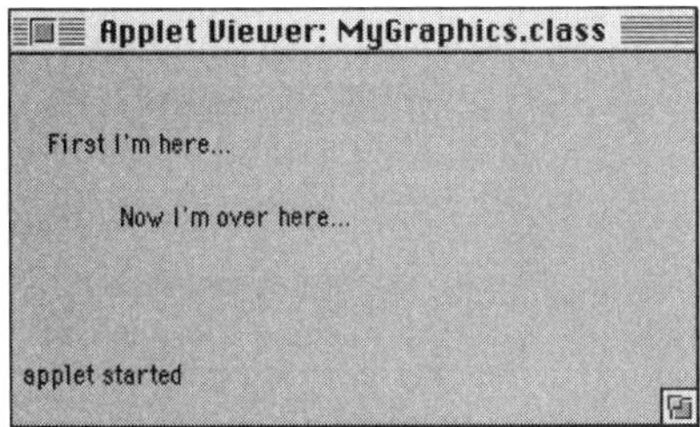

Figure 9-5
The results of running an applet that uses Point objects

In Figure 9-5 you can see that the applet's paint() method draws two lines of text. It is the coordinates of the two Point objects that determine the starting position of each of these two lines.

Lines

In contrast to the definition of points in Java, a drawing routine *does* exist for lines in the Graphics class, but *no* Line class is devoted to defining line objects.

To draw a line, invoke the drawLine() method defined in the Graphics class. This method accepts four arguments. The first two arguments define the coordinate pair for the start of the line, and the last two define the coordinate pair for the end of the line. Each argument is of type int, so the method call can be described in Java code as follows:

```
int startX;
int startY;
int endX;
int endY;

g.drawLine( startX, startY, endX, endY );
```

As an example, consider an applet that is 200 pixels in width and 300 pixels in height. To draw a line that starts at the upper left corner of the applet and extends diagonally to the lower right corner, use this call:

```
g.drawLine( 0, 0, 200, 300 );
```

The following listing is for an applet that draws two lines. The results of running this applet are shown in Figure 9-6.

```
public class MyGraphics extends Applet {

  public void paint( Graphics g ) {

    g.drawLine( 10, 20, 200, 20 );
    g.drawLine( 10, 40, 200, 150 );
  }

}
```

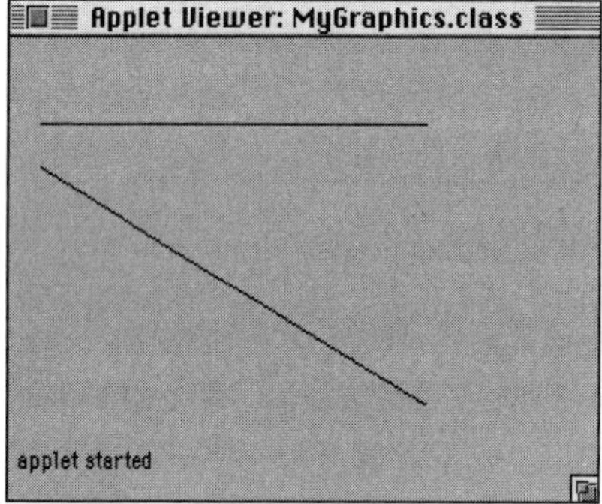

Figure 9-6
The results of running an applet that uses the drawLine() method

The horizontal line pictured in Figure 9-6 starts at point (10, 20) and extends to point (200, 20). The diagonal line starts at point (10, 40) and ends at point (200, 150).

Rectangles

The `Graphics` class provides methods for drawing both rectangles and shapes called *round rectangles*, which are rectangles with rounded corners. Round rectangles can be used to draw buttons that appear in windows and dialog boxes of a graphical user interface.

DRAWING RECTANGLES

The `Graphics` class includes a method to draw the frame (or outline) of a rectangle, and a method to draw a solid (or filled) rectangle. To frame a rectangle, invoke the `drawRect()` method. This method requires four parameters. The first two make up the coordinate point for the upper left corner of the rectangle. The third parameter holds the rectangle's width, and the fourth parameter defines the rectangle's height. Each parameter is of type `int`, as follows:

```
int topLeftX;
int topLeftY;
int width;
int height;

g.drawRect( topLeftX, topLeftY, width, height );
```

To draw the frame of a rectangle that has an upper left corner at point (30, 10) and a lower right corner of (230, 70), invoke `drawRect()` as follows:

```
g.drawRect( 30, 10, 200, 60 );
```

To draw a solid black rectangle, use the `fillRect()` method that is defined in the `Graphics` class. The four parameters of this method serve the same purpose as those used in the `drawRect()` method. In this next snippet, a solid rectangle with coordinates of (30, 100) and (230, 160) is drawn:

```
g.fillRect( 30, 100, 200, 160 );
```

The following applet draws two rectangles—one framed and the other solid. Figure 9-7 shows how the applet would appear in a window.

```
public class MyGraphics extends Applet {

  public void paint( Graphics g ) {

    g.drawRect( 30, 10, 200, 60 );
    g.fillRect( 30, 100, 200, 160 );
  }
}
```

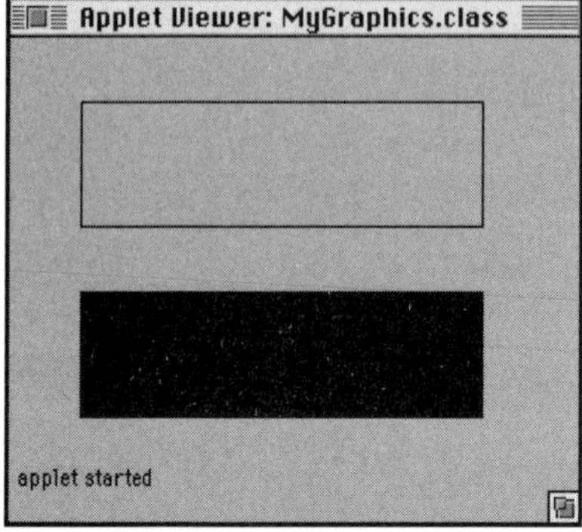

Figure 9-7
The results of running an applet that uses both the drawRect() and fillRect() methods

The bottom rectangle in Figure 9-7 appears black—not only because this is a black-and-white book but also because `fillRect()` and other shape-filling methods draw in black by default. Later in this chapter, you'll see how to change the default color in which shapes are filled.

DRAWING ROUND RECTANGLES

A round rectangle is a rectangle that has each corner rounded. To define such a shape conceptually, follow the steps shown in Figure 9-8. Begin with a normal rectangle (as shown in the upper left of the figure). Next, as pictured in the upper right of Figure 9-8, imagine another rectangle inscribed within the first. This inscribed rectangle should be buttressed up into a corner of the first rectangle. Now, draw an arc from one corner of the inscribed rectangle to the other, as pictured in the lower left of the figure.

Repeat this arc-drawing process for each of the original rectangle's corners. When you finish, remove the parts of the rectangle edge that lie outside of the arcs. Also remove the inscribed rectangles. The result—shown at the lower right of Figure 9-8—is a round rectangle.

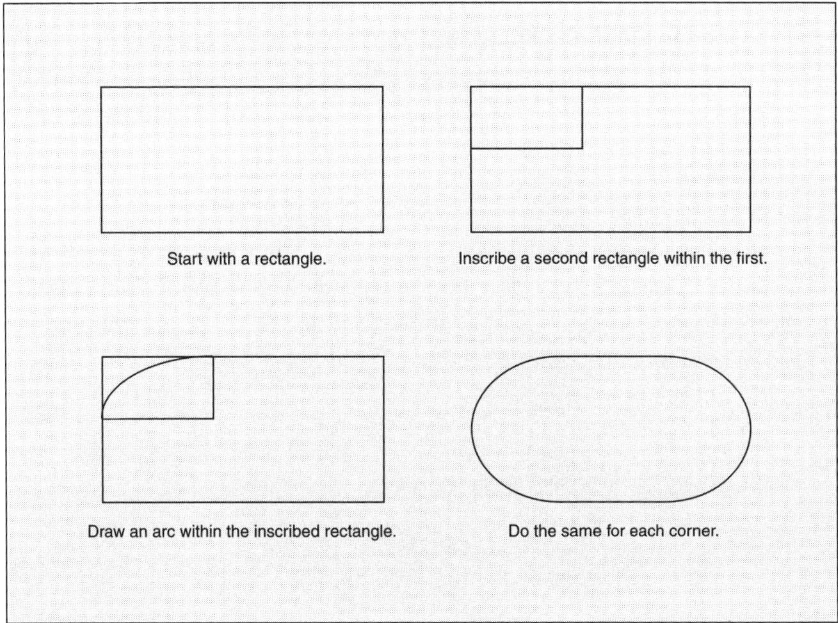
Start with a rectangle.
Inscribe a second rectangle within the first.
Draw an arc within the inscribed rectangle.
Do the same for each corner.

Figure 9-8
The conceptual steps to set up a round rectangle

To perform all of the steps shown in Figure 9-8, simply call the `drawRoundRect()` method that is a part of the `Graphics` class. The purpose of the first four of the six parameters this method accepts is the same as that used in a call to `drawRect()`: It defines the boundaries of a rectangle. The fifth and sixth parameters specify the height and width of each of the rectangles that should be inscribed within the original rectangle. The values of these last two parameters then determine the degree of arc that the corners of the round rectangle will have, as follows:

```
int topLeftX;
int topLeftY;
int width;
```

```
int height;
int arcWidth;
int arcHeight;

g.drawRoundRect( topLeftX, topLeftY, width, height,
        arcWidth, arcHeight );
```

To draw a framed round rectangle that has an upper left coordinate of (30, 10), a lower right coordinate of (230, 70), and a corner rounding that follows an arc that fits in a rectangle 30 pixels by 30 pixels, use this code:

```
g.drawRoundRect( 30, 10, 200, 60, 30, 30 );
```

Figure 9-9 shows two round rectangles. The top rectangle is drawn using a call to `drawRoundRect()`. The bottom rectangle is drawn using a different method found in the `Graphics` class—`fillRoundRect()`. The parameters of `fillRoundRect()` are identical to those used for `drawRoundRect()`.

```
public class MyGraphics extends Applet {

  public void paint( Graphics g ) {

    g.drawRoundRect( 30, 10, 200, 60, 30, 30 );
    g.fillRoundRect( 30, 100, 200, 60, 200, 60 );
  }

}
```

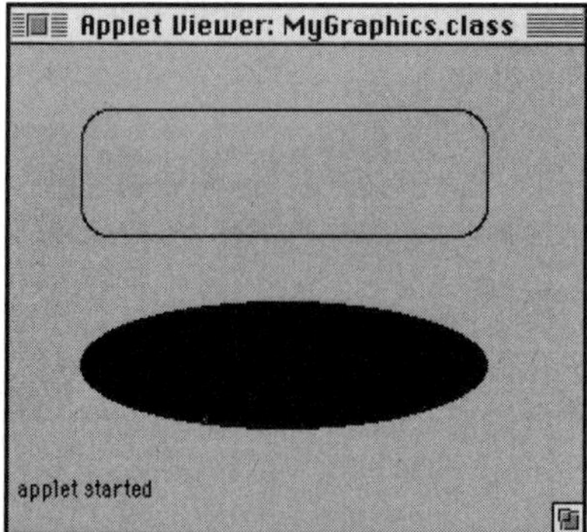

Figure 9-9
The results of running an applet that uses both the drawRoundRect() and fillRoundRect() methods

When the width and height of the rectangle used to form the rectangle's corner arcs are the same as the width and height of the rectangle (as in the `fillRoundRect()` example previously), the round rectangle becomes an oval. If the boundaries of the main rectangle happen to form a square, then the result is a circle. Thus an oval is a special case of a round rectangle, and a circle is a special case of an oval. This next applet uses the round rectangle-drawing methods to draw both a framed circle and a filled circle. The result of executing this applet is shown in Figure 9-10.

```
public class MyGraphics extends Applet {

  public void paint( Graphics g ) {

    g.drawRoundRect( 30, 20, 120, 120, 120, 120 );
    g.fillRoundRect( 90, 90, 160, 160, 160, 160 );
  }
}
```

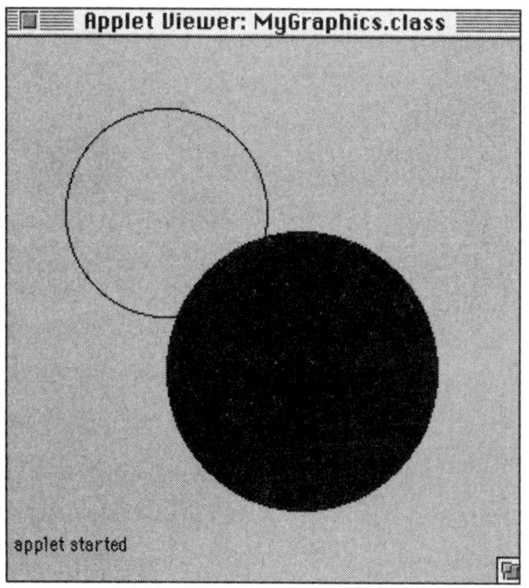

Figure 9-10

The results of running an applet that uses the drawRoundRect() and fillRoundRect() methods to draw circles

The `Graphics` class provides a couple of methods specifically meant for drawing ovals (and, thus, circles)—`drawOval()` and `fillOval()`. They're covered ahead in the Ovals section.

THE RECTANGLE CLASS

If your applet needs only to draw rectangles, the methods of the `Graphics` class suffice. If, however, your applet needs to move or resize or perform other tasks with rectangles, you should create objects of the `Rectangle` class so that you can use the methods of this class to take care of these tasks for you.

THE RECTANGLE CLASS DEFINITION

The following is the complete listing for the `Rectangle` class.

```
public class java.awt.Rectangle extends java.lang.Object
{
  // instance variables
  public int  height;
  public int  width;
  public int  x;
  public int  y;

  // constructors
  public Rectangle();
  public Rectangle(Dimension d);
  public Rectangle(int width, int height);
  public Rectangle(int x, int y, int width, int height);
  public Rectangle(Point p);
  public Rectangle(Point p, Dimension d);

  // methods
  public void add(int newx, int newy);
  public void add(Point pt);
  public void add(Rectangle r);
  public boolean equals(Object obj);
  public void grow(int h, int v);
  public int hashCode();
  public boolean inside(int x, int y);
  public Rectangle intersection(Rectangle r);
  public boolean intersects(Rectangle r);
  public boolean isEmpty();
```

```
  public void move(int x, int y);
  public void reshape(int x, int y, int width, int height);
  public void resize(int width, int height);
  public String toString();
  public void translate(int dx, int dy);
  public Rectangle union(Rectangle r);
}
```

Note from the number of constructors that you have a variety of ways to define the boundaries of a rectangle at the time the `Rectangle` object is created.

USING RECTANGLE OBJECTS

To create a `Rectangle` object, use `new`. The following example creates an object that defines a rectangle with an upper left corner at coordinate (20, 50) and a lower right corner at coordinate (100, 200):

```
Rectangle      theRect;

theRect = new Rectangle( 20, 50, 80, 150 );
```

The following applet provides an example of the use of the `intersects()` method defined in the `Rectangle` class. To see if one rectangle intersects a different rectangle, invoke `intersects()` from one object while passing the second object as a parameter. The `intersects()` method returns a value of `true` if the rectangles intersect anywhere, and a value of `false` if they don't.

```
public class MyGraphics extends Applet {

  Rectangle    theRect;
  Rectangle    anotherRect;
  boolean      doIntersect;

  public void init() {

    theRect = new Rectangle( 30, 40, 100, 100 );
    anotherRect = new Rectangle( 110, 120, 40, 80 );

    doIntersect = theRect.intersects( anotherRect );
  }
```

```
    public void paint( Graphics g ) {
      g.drawString("Intersect = " + doIntersect, 10, 20 );
      g.drawRect( theRect.x, theRect.y, theRect.width,
            theRect.height );
      g.drawRect( anotherRect.x, anotherRect.y, anotherRect.width,
            anotherRect.height );
    }

}
```

Executing the preceding applet results in `doIntersect` having a value of `true`. Figure 9-11 illustrates how this version of the MyGraphics applet would appear in a window.

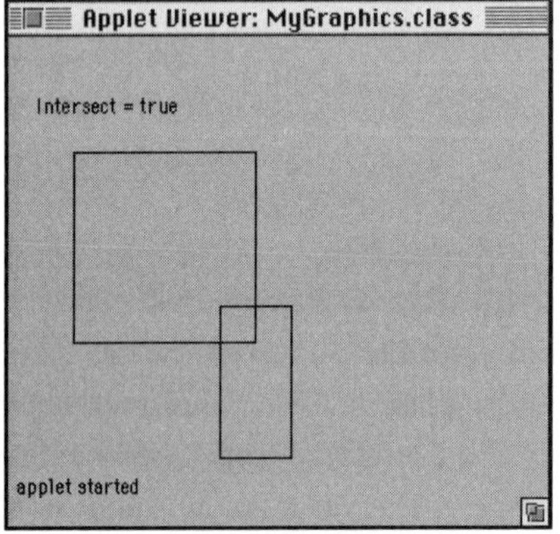

Figure 9-11
The results of running an applet that uses Rectangle objects

Ovals

The `java.awt` package does not define a class for creating oval objects. However, a couple of oval methods exist in the `Graphics` class.

To draw the frame of an oval, call `drawOval()`. The parameters of `drawOval()` are analogous to those for `drawRect()`: The first two define the upper left coordinate for the shape, while the third and fourth define the width and height of the shape:

```
int topLeftX;
int topLeftY;
int width;
int height;

g.drawOval( topLeftX, topLeftY, width, height );
```

To draw a solid oval, call the `fillOval()` method. The parameters to this method are used in the same manner as the parameters for `drawOval()`.

This next applet draws two ovals. The first oval, which appears on the left of Figure 9-12, is framed and has an upper left coordinate of (10, 20) and a lower right coordinate of (210, 130). The second oval, shown on the right of the same figure, has an upper left coordinate of (230, 20) and a lower right coordinate of (340, 130).

```
public class MyGraphics extends Applet {

  public void paint( Graphics g ) {

    g.drawOval( 10, 20, 200, 110 );
    g.fillOval( 230, 20, 110, 110 );
  }

}
```

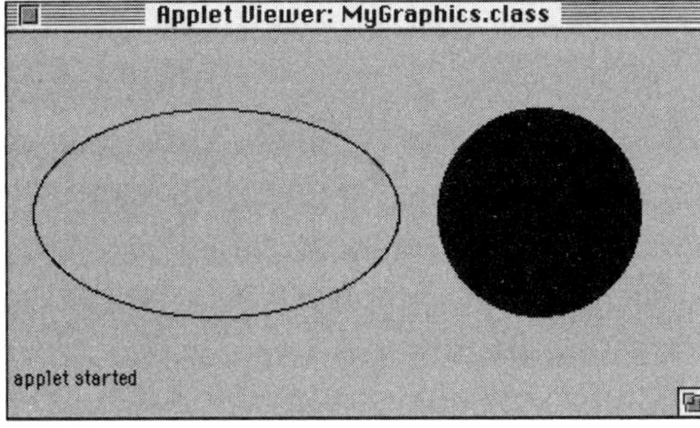

Figure 9-12
The results of running an applet that uses both the drawOval() and fillOval() methods

In Figure 9-12 you can see that the oval on the right side is a circle. To create a circle, simply use the same value for the third and fourth parameters as for the oval-drawing method.

Polygons

To define a closed shape bounded by straight lines, use either one of the polygon-drawing methods defined in the `Graphics` class or create a `Polygon` object.

DRAWING POLYGONS

To define a polygon, you list a number of coordinate pairs. Each coordinate is a point to which a line is drawn in a connect-the-dots fashion. If the ending coordinate is the same as the starting coordinate, the result is an enclosed shape—a polygon.

The `drawPoly()` method found in the `Graphics` class outlines a polygon. The first of the three parameters that `drawPoly()` accepts is the number of coordinate pairs, or points, that will be used to define the polygon. The second parameter is an array of `ints`, each of which is an *x*-coordinate. The third parameter is a similar array, with each value defining a *y*-coordinate:

```
int numPts;
int xPtsArray[];
int yPtsArray[];

g.drawPoly( numPts, xPtsArray, yPtsArray );
```

We'll rely on Figure 9-13 for our example of how to set up and draw a polygon. The polygon pictured in this figure has five sides and five labeled points. The upper left corner of the applet—the origin of the coordinate system—is also shown as a reference.

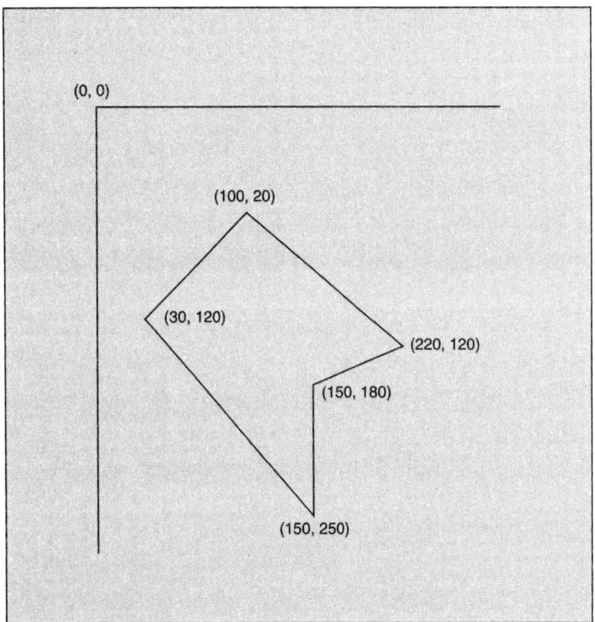

Figure 9-13
The coordinates of the points that make up a five-sided polygon

The polygon in Figure 9-13 is made up of five points, but we'll be using six: the sixth point has the same coordinates as the first. Without this final value, Java won't close up the polygon when drawing it. Because there are six points, we'll assign the `npoints` variable the value of 6, as follows:

```
npoints = 6;
```

Next, we'll allocate memory for the two integer arrays:

```
xpoints = new int[npoints];
ypoints = new int[npoints];
```

Now we'll fill the arrays. Arbitrarily selecting the uppermost point as the first point, we give it an *x*-coordinate value of 100 and a *y*-coordinate value of 20:

```
xpoints[0] = 100;
ypoints[0] = 20;
```

Moving clockwise, the second point has coordinates of 220 and 120:

```
xpoints[1] = 220;
ypoints[1] = 120;
```

The remaining array elements are assigned values in the same way up to and including the last polygon point. The assignment of the array elements that hold this last polygon point—which is the same as the first point—looks like this:

```
xpoints[5] = 100;
ypoints[5] = 20;
```

The following is an applet that defines and draws the polygon pictured in Figure 9-14.

```
public class MyGraphics extends Applet {

  int  npoints;
  int  xpoints[];
  int  ypoints[];

  public void init() {

      npoints = 6;
      xpoints = new int[npoints];
      ypoints = new int[npoints];

      xpoints[0] = 100;
      ypoints[0] = 20;
      xpoints[1] = 220;
      ypoints[1] = 120;
      xpoints[2] = 150;
      ypoints[2] = 180;
      xpoints[3] = 150;
      ypoints[3] = 250;
      xpoints[4] = 30;
      ypoints[4] = 120;
      xpoints[5] = 100;
      ypoints[5] = 20;
  }

  public void paint( Graphics g ) {
```

```
    g.drawPolygon( xpoints, ypoints, npoints );
  }

}
```

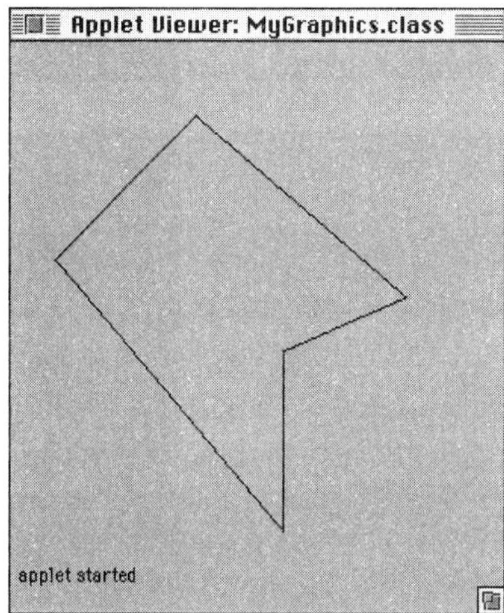

Figure 9-14
The results of running an applet that uses the drawPoly() method

To draw a polygon that is solid, use the `fillPolygon()` method in place of the `drawPolygon()` method. Figure 9-15 shows the results of running the previous applet when the `paint()` method is changed to hold a call to `fillPolygon()` rather than a call to `drawPolygon()`, as follows:

```
public void paint( Graphics g ) {

  g.fillPolygon( xpoints, ypoints, npoints );
}
```

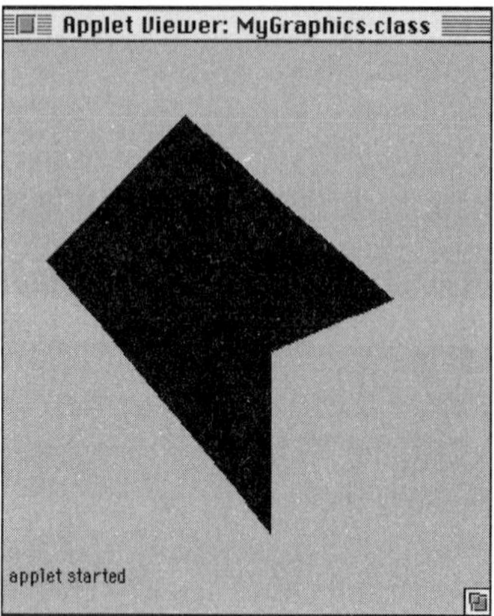

Figure 9-15
The results of running an applet that uses the fillPoly() method

THE POLYGON CLASS

To *draw* a polygon, you use the methods of the `Graphics` class; to *work* with a polygon, however, you need to create a `Polygon` object.

THE POLYGON CLASS DEFINITION

The following listing shows the definition of the `Polygon` class, as given in the `java.awt` package.

```
public class java.awt.Polygon extends java.lang.Object
{
  // instance variables
  public int  npoints;
  public int  xpoints[];
  public int  ypoints[];

  // constructors
  public Polygon();
  public Polygon(int xpoints[], int ypoints[], int npoints);

  // methods
```

```
  public void addPoint(int x, int y);
  public Rectangle getBoundingBox();
  public boolean inside(int x, int y);
}
```

USING POLYGON OBJECTS

To create a `Polygon` object, use `new`. Before doing this, set up the two arrays that hold the polygon's coordinates and assign a value to the variable that holds the number of points that will be used to define the polygon, as follows:

```
public class MyGraphics extends Applet {

  Polygon      thePoly;
  int  npoints;
  int  xpoints[];
  int  ypoints[];

  public void init() {

      npoints = 6;
      xpoints = new int[npoints];
      ypoints = new int[npoints];

      xpoints[0] = 100;
      ypoints[0] = 20;
      xpoints[1] = 220;
      ypoints[1] = 120;
      xpoints[2] = 150;
      ypoints[2] = 120;
      xpoints[3] = 150;
      ypoints[3] = 250;
      xpoints[4] = 30;
      ypoints[4] = 120;
      xpoints[5] = 100;
      ypoints[5] = 20;

      thePoly = new Polygon( xpoints, ypoints, npoints );
  }

  public void paint( Graphics g ) {

      g.drawPolygon( thePoly );
  }

}
```

Executing the preceding applet results in the same polygon pictured back in Figure 9-14.

Color

By default, an applet draws shapes in black on a background color established by the user's browser—usually gray. The Java language, however, is designed to create executables that run on today's graphical user interfaces, thus it doesn't force this color limitation upon you. In this section you'll see that the `Color` class makes it simple for you to control the colors used in the drawing of graphics.

THE RGB COLOR MODEL

Computers and computer languages use numbers to define just about everything. So it should be no surprise to you that to define a particular color to be displayed in an applet, the Java language relies on a system of numbers that each map to a color. The system used by Java is the RGB model—or Red-Green-Blue model.

The RGB model isn't unique to Java. It's a color-coding system that's been in existence for quite a while and is used by a variety of computer languages.

In the RGB color system, you select a numerical value for each of three colors: red, green, and blue. These numbers serve as a weighting factor that describe how much of each individual color exists in the final, single color—a color that is the result of combining the three individual RGB colors.

In the RGB model, the higher the number for one of the three colors, the more intense is that color's contribution to the resulting color. For instance, if red is given a large numerical value, and green and blue are given values of zero, then the resulting color will be red. If, on the other hand, both red and blue are given large values while green is given a value of zero, the resulting color will be a combination of red and blue—a shade of purple.

When all three RGB colors are at their minimum values, the resulting color is black, and when all three colors are at their maximum values, the resulting color is white. To many this may seem somewhat counterintuitive; it might seem that a lack of color would result in white, while combining each color to its fullest would result in black. This is such because the RGB model relies on the way light-produced color works: Turning on the red, green, and blue phosphors of a TV screen (or computer monitor) produces white.

In Java, the range of values that an individual red, green, or blue component can have is a minimum of 0 and a maximum of 255. A single color is expressed as the values of the three components, in the order red, green, blue. For instance, the color blue, which has a red component of 0, a green component of 0, and a blue component of 255, would be expressed as (0, 0, 255).

The Color class

In Java, you define a single color by creating an object of the `Color` class. This class, defined in the `java.awt` package, is as follows:

```
public final class java.awt.Color extends java.lang.Object
{
  // fields
  public final static Color black;
  public final static Color blue;
  public final static Color cyan;
  public final static Color darkGray;
  public final static Color gray;
  public final static Color green;
  public final static Color lightGray;
  public final static Color magenta;
  public final static Color orange;
  public final static Color pink;
  public final static Color red;
  public final static Color white;
  public final static Color yellow;

  // constructors
```

```
  public Color(float r, float g, float b);
  public Color(int rgb);
  public Color(int r, int g, int b);

  // methods
  public Color brighter();
  public Color darker();
  public boolean equals(Object obj);
  public int getBlue();
  public static Color getColor(String nm);
  public static Color getColor(String nm, Color v);
  public static Color getColor(String nm, int v);
  public int getGreen();
  public static Color getHSBColor(float h, float s, float b);
  public int getRed();
  public int getRGB();
  public int hashCode();
  public static int HSBtoRGB(float hue, float saturation,
                             float brightness);
  public static float[] RGBtoHSB(int r, int g, int b,
                                 float hsbvals[]);
  public String toString();
}
```

Of most importance to you will be the many fields of the `Color` class. To create a new color to use in drawing, you can use a `Color` constructor and specify the color yourself. Here we're creating a `Color` object that represents the color blue:

```
Color  blueColor = new Color( 0, 0, 255 );
```

Because the `Color` class defines a number of commonly used colors for you, however, it's more likely that you'll go ahead and use one of these predefined colors rather than define your own:

```
setColor( Color.blue );
```

In the preceding line the `setColor()` method (a method defined in the `Component` class) is used to set the current color to blue. The same effect could be achieved in a more roundabout way as follows:

```
Color  blueColor = new Color( 0, 0, 255 );

setColor( blueColor );
```

THE SETCOLOR() METHOD

In the preceding section, you saw an example that used the `setColor()` method. A call to this method will be your primary means of using color. A call to `setColor()` establishes the color that will be used for subsequent drawing. This color is then used until another call to `setColor()` is encountered. In this next applet the first three of four overlapping rectangles are drawn in blue, while the last one is drawn in red:

```
import java.awt.*;
import java.applet.*;

public class ColoredRectangles extends Applet {

  public void paint( Graphics g ) {

    g.setColor( Color.blue );
    g.drawRect( 20, 20, 100, 100 );       // frame a blue rect
    g.fillRect( 60, 60, 100, 100 );       // fill a blue rect
    g.fillRect( 100, 100, 100, 100 );     // fill a blue rect

    g.setColor( Color.red );
    g.fillRect( 140, 140, 100, 100 );     // fill a red rect
  }
}
```

The ColoredRectangles applet frames the first rectangle and fills in the last three rectangles with color.

Fonts

In Java, text isn't written, it's drawn. So it makes sense for text-drawing classes and methods to appear in the Abstract Windowing Toolkit, right along with the classes and methods used for drawing shapes.

THE FONT CLASS DEFINITION

You'll rely on the Font class of the java.awt package to define the look of text that's drawn in an applet. The definition of that class is as follows:

```
public class java.awt.Font extends java.lang.Object
{
  // instance variables
  protected String     name;
  protected int        size;
  protected int        style;

  // class variables
  public final static int       BOLD;
  public final static int       ITALIC;
  public final static int       PLAIN;

  // constructors
  public Font(String name, int style, int size);

  // methods
  public boolean equals(Object obj);
  public String getFamily();
  public static Font getFont(String nm);
  public static Font getFont(String nm, Font font);
  public String getName();
  public int getSize();
  public int getStyle();
  public int hashCode();
  public boolean isBold();
  public boolean isItalic();
  public boolean isPlain();
  public String toString();
}
```

FONT CHARACTERISTICS

To establish the look of the text that's drawn in an applet, you'll set three text characteristics of the font in which the text is drawn: the name, style, and size of the font.

FONT NAME

All computer systems can and do have numerous fonts available, yet it's recommended that your applet only use five of them. The machine-independent names Java gives these five preferred fonts are as follows:

- Helvetica
- TimesRoman
- Courier
- Dialog
- DialogInput

You can consider these five fonts to be standard enough to be assured that they'll each appear in the system of any user who encounters your applet. Although it's possible to use other fonts, you'll usually want to stick with these five to ensure that your applet is portable.

Note that the Java font names may not match the exact name of a font present in your system. Don't worry about that: Each Java font name is mapped to a font common to each machine to which Java has been ported. For example, when an applet is run on a Macintosh, the Java font name Helvetica causes applet writing to take place in the Helvetica font. On a machine running Windows, the name of the font is Arial. On a UNIX system, the Adobe-Helvetica font is used. All of these fonts look similar.

Information about a font is held in a `Font` object. The `Font` class is a class defined in the `java.awt` package. When your applet selects a font to use, all subsequent text drawing is affected. Each call to the `Graphics` method `drawString()` results in the drawing of text in this current font. When you create a new `Font` object, you'll set the name of the font as well as both the style and the size of the font. The creation of a new `Font` object is described in more detail after we cover font style and point size.

FONT STYLE

Today's systems that use a graphical user interface can display fonts in a variety of styles. While these systems may implement perhaps dozens of styles and combinations of styles, Java recognizes only a few. Again, as is the case for font names, this is done for reasons of portability: Your applet should set a font to a style that will most certainly exist on any machine that can run the applet.

The Font class that is a part of the java.awt package defines three class variables to serve as font style constants, as follows:

```
public final static int BOLD = 1;
public final static int ITALIC = 2;
public final static int PLAIN = 0;
```

You can use these constants with the Font class name rather than with a particular Font object. For example, to set the current text drawing style to bold, you use Font.BOLD. The style constants can also be combined by simply adding them. To set the current text drawing style to bold italic, you use Font.BOLD + Font.ITALIC. These constants are used at the time you create a Font object.

POINT SIZE

The point size of a font defines the actual size of a font. As with the font name and font style, this characteristic is set when you create a Font object.

USING FONT OBJECTS

To define the look of drawn text, create a new Font object that holds this information. Then use this object at any time to alter newly drawn text.

CREATING A FONT OBJECT

A Font object encapsulates a font type, or name, a font style, and a font size. As with other object types, use new to create the Font object. The Font constructor accepts three arguments to set the three font characteristics. The following snippet creates a Font object that can be used to draw text in a bold Courier font 48 points in size:

```
Font   theFont;

theFont = new Font( "Courier", Font.BOLD, 48 );
```

SETTING THE CURRENT FONT

Once your applet has a Font object, you can use the Graphics method setFont() to set the current writing style to the characteristics of that object. In this next snippet a Font object is created to draw text in the Courier font, with bold and italic style and a point size of 24. The snippet then draws three lines of text. The first uses the default font that Java defines for the system on which the applet is running. The second and third calls to drawString() appear after a call to setFont(), so both of the lines displayed by these calls will appear with the characteristics established in the Font object named theFont. Figure 9-16 shows the results.

```
Font   theFont;

theFont = new Font( "Courier", Font.BOLD + Font.ITALIC, 24 );

g.drawString( "This line is in default font", 10, 20 );

g.setFont( theFont );
g.drawString( "This line is in theFont font", 10, 60 );
g.drawString( "This line is also in theFont font", 10, 100 );
```

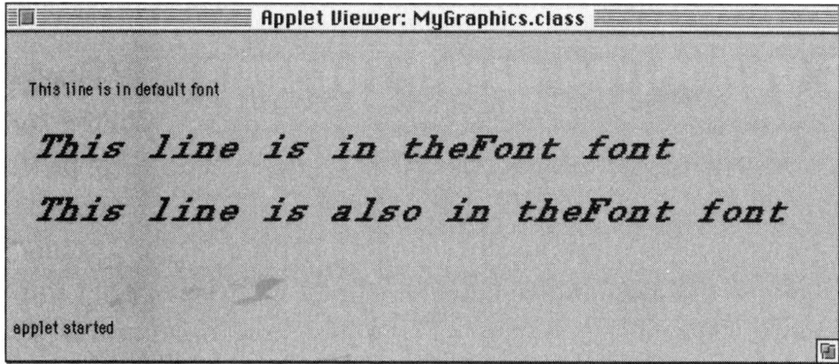

Figure 9-16
The results of running an applet that uses a Font object and the setFont() method

The setFont() method should be called anytime your applet needs to display text in a look that differs from the current one. In this next applet, four Font objects are defined. The setFont() and drawString() methods are each then called four times to generate the same text, but in four different looks. Figure 9-17 shows the results of running the applet.

```
public class MyGraphics extends Applet {
```

```
Font plainHelv;
Font italicHelv;
Font boldHelv;
Font italicBoldHelv;

public void init() {

  plainHelv = new Font( "Helvetica", Font.PLAIN, 24 );
  italicHelv = new Font( "Helvetica", Font.ITALIC, 24 );
  boldHelve = new Font( "Helvetica", Font.BOLD, 24 );
  italicBoldHelv = new Font( "Helvetica",
                          Font.BOLD + Font.ITALIC, 24 );
}

public void paint( Graphics g ) {

  g.setFont( plainHelv );
  g.drawString( "Font, style, size example", 10, 20 );

  g.setFont( italicHelv );
  g.drawString( "Font, style, size example", 10, 50 );

  g.setFont( boldHelv );
  g.drawString( "Font, style, size example", 10, 80 );

  g.setFont( italicBoldHelv );
  g.drawString( "Font, style, size example", 10, 110 );
}

}
```

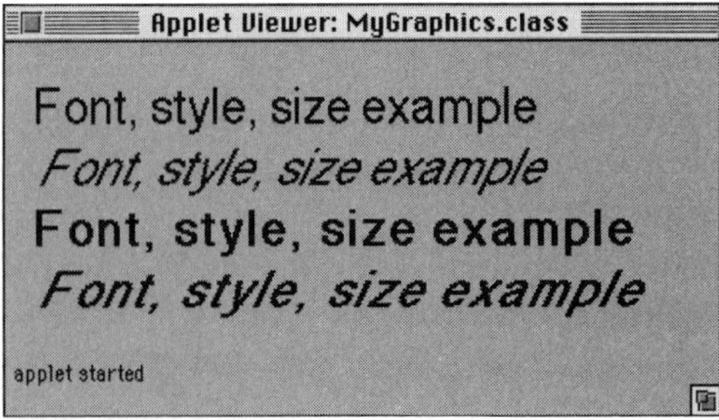

Figure 9-17
The results of running an applet that uses several Font objects and the setFont() method

What You've Learned

When you draw in an applet, you do so by specifying pixel values that determine where the drawing takes place within the applet. The pixel values you provide define points in a coordinate system. In Java programming, the upper left corner of an applet has the coordinate pair (0, 0). Starting at this origin and moving right a pixel and down a pixel places you at the coordinate pair (1, 1).

When you draw a shape to an applet, you'll generally rely on one of the many shape-drawing methods of the `Graphics` class. For example, the `fillRect()` method enables you to easily draw a solid rectangle. The location of the rectangle is specified in parameters for `fillRect()` and uses the above-mentioned coordinate pairing system.

The `Color` class makes it easy to draw color graphics. By invoking the `setColor()` method, you can change the current color used by Java. After a call to `setColor()`, all subsequent shape-drawing takes place in the new color.

In Java, text is considered another form of graphics. By defining text in this way Java makes it easy to change the characteristics of drawn text. You'll rely on methods of the `Font` class to alter the look of the text your applet draws.

CHAPTER

10 Animation

In Chapter 9 you learned about Java graphics. Adding graphics to an applet gives the applet a visual appeal that mere text cannot achieve. Bringing those graphics to life with animation takes this concept a step further. In this chapter, you'll learn how to add smooth animation to any of your applets. You'll also see how threads make it possible for your applet to perform other tasks while this animation is taking place.

Simple Animation

Animation in an applet can be performed by drawing to the applet again and again. You're familiar with using the `paint()` method to achieve your drawing results—which means you're already part of the way toward creating animated effects.

Updating an Applet

In several places throughout past chapters, you've seen how an applet is updated. When an applet needs updating (due to it being partially or fully obstructed and then brought back into view), the Java runtime that is a part of the user's Web browser automatically invokes the applet's `paint()` method. If the applet defines a `paint()` method, the defined method is executed. If the applet doesn't define such a method, the empty `paint()` method defined in the `Applet` class is simply executed.

To create animation, an applet's `paint()` method is called repeatedly. In such a scenario, however, it isn't the Java runtime that calls `paint()`. For animation to take place, your applet is responsible for making these calls.

THE START() METHOD

In Chapter 3, you had a very brief look at an automated task that the `Applet` class takes care of for an applet: updating an applet's contents by invoking a `paint()` method. Besides the `paint()` method, an applet has other methods that service other requests made on the Java runtime. These methods handle the tasks of initialization, starting, stopping, destroying, and painting. Each of these duties is implemented through methods defined in the `Applet` class. If you want to add functionality to one of these empty methods, you have your applet override that method and add the code necessary to give the method meaning. You've seen plenty of examples that override the Applet `paint()` method to give an applet the power to paint itself.

To start an applet running, the Java runtime invokes the Applet `start()` method just after it invokes its `init()` method. As defined in the `Applet` class, `start()` is an empty method: It does nothing. For an applet that performs animation, you'll want to override `start()` and use this method to start up the animation, as follows:

```
public void start() {

    while ( true ) {
        // redraw the applet
    }
}
```

The preceding version of `start()` uses the Boolean value `true` in a `while` statement intentionally to create an infinite loop. The body of the loop redraws the applet. The effect is that when the applet is initially loaded, the `start()` method executes and continuously redraws the applet for the life of the applet.

THE REPAINT() AND UPDATE() METHODS

The `paint()` method is invoked automatically when an applet needs to be redrawn. To redraw the applet "manually," call the `repaint()` method, as follows:

```
public void start() {

    while ( true ) {
        repaint();
    }
}
```

Like the `paint()` method, the `repaint()` method is defined by the `Component` class. In Chapter 8, you saw that while earlier chapters (chapters that preceded our discussions and diagrams of the Java class hierarchy) referred to the `paint()` method as a method of the `Applet` class, it is actually a method defined in the `Component` class and ***inherited*** by the `Applet` class. The same is true of the `repaint()` method.

The `repaint()` method calls yet another method of the `Component` class—the `update()` method. The `update()` method clears the applet by filling it with the background color and then invokes the `paint()` method to handle applet redrawing.

ANIMATION THROUGH REDRAWING

By repeatedly calling `repaint()` within its `start()` method, an applet continually redraws itself. If the applet's `paint()` method does different drawing tasks on different invocations, the result—voilà!—is animation. The following snippet shows one possible format for achieving this goal:

```
boolean       toggleIsOn = false;

public void paint( Graphics g ) {

    if ( toggleIsOn == false )
    {
        // do one thing
        // set toggle to on
    }
    else // toggleIsOn is true
    {
        // do another thing
        // set toggle to off
    }
}
```

The preceding version of `paint()` relies on the current value of the Boolean variable `toggleIsOn` to determine which of two blocks of code should be executed. After performing the drawing task from either the `if` or the `else` section, `toggleIsOn` is set to a state opposite to its current state. That ensures that the next time `paint()` is invoked, the opposing block of code gets executed.

A SIMPLE ANIMATION EXAMPLE

The MyAnimation applet is an example of a simple applet that uses the technique of calling `repaint()` from within a loop to achieve animation. When MyAnimation runs, two strings continuously alternate within the applet. Figure 10-1 provides two looks at the same applet.

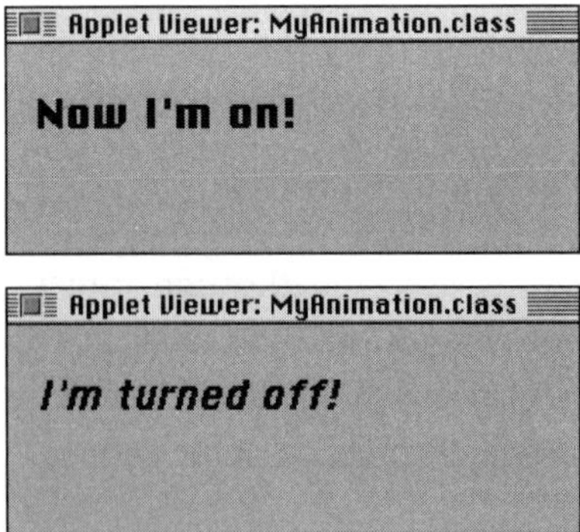

Figure 10-1
The results of running the MyAnimation applet in an applet viewer

The top of Figure 10-1 shows the applet's single window with the first string written to it while the bottom of the figure shows the applet's same window a moment later when the second string has replaced the first. The following is the source code listing for MyAnimation:

```
import java.awt.*;
import java.applet.*;

public class MyAnimation extends Applet {
```

```
    Font      italicFont;
    Font      boldFont;
    boolean   toggleIsOn;

    public void init() {

        italicFont = new Font( "TimesRoman", Font.ITALIC, 18 );
        boldFont = new Font( "TimesRoman", Font.BOLD, 18 );
        toggleIsOn = false;
    }


    public void start() {

        while ( true ) {
            repaint();
        }
    }


    public void paint( Graphics g ) {

        if ( toggleIsOn == false )
        {
            g.setFont( italicFont );
            g.drawString( "I'm turned off!", 10, 20 );
            toggleIsOn = true;
        }
        else // toggleIsOn is true
        {
            g.setFont( boldFont );
            g.drawString( "Now I'm on!", 10, 20 );
            toggleIsOn = false;
        }
    }

}
```

The MyAnimation applet begins by declaring three variables. Font variables `italicFont` and `boldFont` are used to hold the characteristics of the text that will be used to draw the strings "I'm turned off!" and "Now I'm on!" The `Font` class and `Font` objects are topics covered in Chapter 9. The third variable, `toggleIsOn`, keeps track of which string should be drawn next. These three variables all receive their values in the applet's `init()` method.

An alternate and equally acceptable approach for initializing the variables is to omit the `init()` method and perform the initializations at the time of declaration, as follows:

```
Font     italicFont = new Font( "TimesRoman", Font.ITALIC, 18 );
Font     boldFont = new Font( "TimesRoman", Font.BOLD, 18 );
boolean  toggleIsOn = false;
```

When a user moves to the Web page that includes the MyAnimation applet, the Java interpreter that is a part of the Web browser invokes the applet's `start()` method. This triggers the start of the animation. The animation continues until the user leaves the Web page.

Animation takes place in the applet's `paint()` method. This method uses a call to the `setFont()` method (described in Chapter 9) to establish the characteristics of the font that is to be used for text drawing, draws a line of text, and then toggles the `toggleIsOn` variable to its opposite state.

Two problems with MyAnimation

After you compile `MyAnimation.java`, try running the MyAnimation applet in an applet viewer. You'll notice a couple of serious problems with the applet—one related to timing and the other to resources.

The timing problem

When the viewer opens a window and displays the applet in it, you'll see that the two text strings alternate a little slowly. While your first impression may be that the applet is running slowly, the problem is in fact that the applet is running too fast!

The `while` loop in the `start()` method is executing thousands of times each second, so `repaint()` gets called thousands of times per second. The job of the `repaint()` method is to invoke the `update()` method *as soon as possible*. That means that if the `repaint()` method is called often enough and fast enough, the relatively time-consuming `update()` method won't be invoked each time `repaint()` is called. The result is that while `repaint()` is called thousands of times, `update()` (and thus `paint()`, which `update()` invokes) is only called a few times.

You can set up a simple test to verify the preceding problem by including a couple of counters in the applet's code. Begin by declaring two integer variables, as follows:

```
int countStart = 0;
int countPaint = 0;
```

Next, increment one of the variables within the loop in the `start()` method, like this:

```
public void start() {

    while ( true ) {
        repaint();
        countStart++;
    }
}
```

Increment the second variable in the `paint()` method. Make two calls to `drawString()` to write the values of the counters to the applet at each pass through `paint()`, as follows:

```
public void paint( Graphics g ) {

    if ( toggleIsOn == false )
    {
        // set font, draw string, toggle
    }
    else // toggleIsOn is true
    {
        // set font, draw string, toggle
    }

    countPaint++;

    g.drawString("countStart = " + countStart, 10, 40 );
    g.drawString("countPaint = " + countPaint, 10, 60 );
}
```

Figure 10-2 shows how the MyAnimation applet looks after running for a few seconds. Here you can see that while the loop has executed many thousands of times, the `paint()` method has only been called a few times.

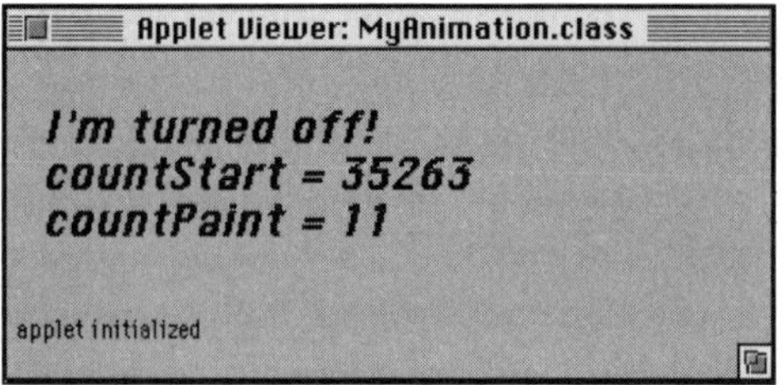

Figure 10-2
The results of running a version of MyAnimation that includes test code

The problem of MyAnimation's running too fast can be avoided by adding a short delay within the `while` loop in the `start()` method. Later in this chapter, we'll do just that.

MONOPOLIZATION OF RESOURCES

A second problem with MyAnimation is that because the animation is taking place in an infinite loop, the Java runtime is "locked out" of performing other tasks. That is, this one applet can only perform this one task. If a second applet were on the same Web page, it wouldn't run. More importantly, running the animation within this closed loop prevents the Java runtime from doing anything else—including displaying the MyAnimation applet in the first place! While MyAnimation will be displayed and will run in an applet viewer, neither will happen if you load the applet to a Web server and visit the Web page where the applet is *supposed* to appear.

The problem of having MyAnimation monopolizing Java can be solved by using the time-sharing technique known as *threads*. This topic is one that is very important to Java programming and is covered in detail next.

Better Animation Using Threads

Most computer programs—regardless of the language in which they're written or the system on which they are running—run in a single stream of execution. Things move in sequence rather than in tandem: When one task of a program is completed, another begins. In Java, this stream of execution is called a *thread of execution*, or, more simply, a *thread*. Java differs from most other languages in that the code that gets generated is capable of running in multiple threads. Having code that can allocate different tasks to different threads speeds up the execution of the code.

Multithreading in Java

As an example of how a program operates in a single-threaded environment, consider a program that must perform a complex calculation and run an animation. Here one task follows the other. Because both tasks are handled within the same thread of execution, the tasks cannot be worked on simultaneously.

Because of the great speed of today's computer processors, the delay caused by one operation may often not even be noticeable; the complex calculation just mentioned may be completed and the animation started in such a quick period of time that to the computer user it may seem like both events occurred at the same time. In a single-threaded scenario, other operations, however, may result in noticeable delays. Providing each operation with its own thread in which to run greatly reduces this delay. The Java language provides you with this ability to create multithreaded applets.

On a computer that has a single processor, multiple threads aren't actually running in parallel. Instead, the processor first devotes time to one thread, then to another. After a moment, the processor again returns control to the first thread. This alternating of control gives the illusion of parallel processing. On a machine that does have more than one processor, Java threads will in fact truly be run concurrently. The fact that Java applets are MP-hot, or multiple processor-aware, is worthy of note: Multiprocessor computers are becoming more common and will eventually be the norm.

An applet always runs in a thread—even if you don't explicitly create one. In fact, an applet is always multithreaded; the Java runtime includes a garbage collection thread that is always running in conjunction with your applet. Any threads you explicitly add to your applet run in tandem with the applet's main thread and the garbage collection thread.

THE THREAD CLASS

The `Thread` class defines the variables, constructors, and methods available to a thread. Figure 10-3 shows that the `Thread` class is part of the `java.lang` package. The `java.lang` package also includes an interface named `Runnable` that the `Thread` class uses. We discuss Interfaces in general in Chapter 8. The `Runnable` interface is described later in this chapter. Figure 10-3 also highlights the two `Thread` methods that your threaded applets will always invoke: `start()` and `stop()`.

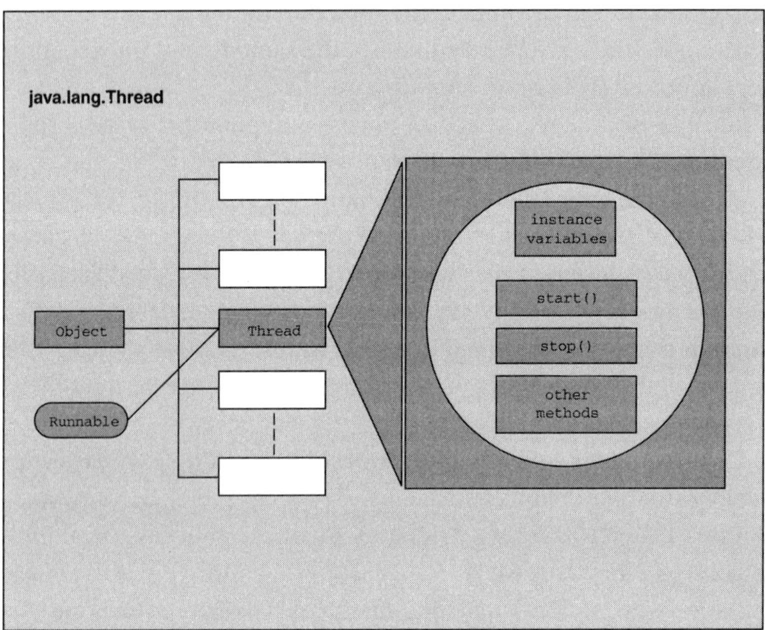

Figure 10-3
The hierarchy of the Thread class

The `Thread` class `start()` method is used to begin execution of a thread. When this method is invoked, it in turn calls a method that your applet is responsible for defining. This applet-defined method, which is always named `run()`, defines what action should be handled by the thread. After `start()` invokes this `run()` method, control is immediately returned to the applet's main thread. When the thread is finished (typically when the user leaves the Web page that holds the applet that runs the thread), the `Thread` class `stop()` method is used to end the execution of a thread.

ADDING A THREAD TO AN APPLET

Adding a thread to an applet is a straightforward process—regardless of the task that the new thread is being created to handle. This list summarizes the steps you take to add a thread to an applet:

1. **Implement the `Runnable` interface.** Define the `Applet` class so it implements the Java `Runnable` interface.
2. **Create and start the thread.** Create a new thread and start it up.
3. **Define the body of the thread.** Define a method that performs a task for the thread to handle.
4. **Stop the thread.** Stop the thread when the user exits from the Web page that holds the applet.

Over the next several pages, we'll follow the preceding four steps to modify the MyAnimation applet source code so that it runs the animation in its own thread. To differentiate this new version of the applet from the old, we'll assign it the name `MyAnimation2`.

IMPLEMENTING THE RUNNABLE INTERFACE

The first step to creating a class that can be multithreaded is to have that class implement the `Runnable` interface. You do this by using the keyword `implements` followed by the name of the interface to implement, like this:

```
public class MyAnimation2 extends Applet implements Runnable {

    // rest of applet code here
}
```

You don't need to import a package to make use of the `Runnable` interface. This interface is defined in `java.lang`—a package that is always available for your applet's use. This also applies to making use of the `Thread` class; it too is defined in `java.lang`.

In the `java.lang` package, the `Runnable` interface is defined as follows:

```
public abstract interface Runnable {

    public abstract void run();
}
```

Chapter 8 described an interface as a means of grouping together a number of method prototypes. The methods themselves aren't defined within the interface; that's left up to whatever class implements the interface. An interface is simply a convenient way to ensure that classes can access the same set of methods so that each class implements a similar set of behaviors. As shown previously, the `Runnable` interface lists only one method—`run()`. It is up to the applet to override `run()`. As you'll see, this applet-defined version of `run()` is responsible for handling the task or tasks for which the thread is being created.

CREATING AND STARTING THE THREAD

To create a thread, begin by declaring a variable of the `Thread` class, as follows:

```
Thread theThread;
```

In the previous version of MyAnimation, we used the applet's `start()` method both to start and perform the animation. In MyAnimation2, we'll use the applet's `start()` method to create the thread and then start up the animation. Instead of handling the task of performing the animation in `start()`, we'll handle it in the `run()` method that we'll be defining a little later. Here's how it looks:

```
public void start() {

     if ( theThread == null ) {
          theThread = new Thread( this );
          theThread.start();
     }
}
```

A `Thread` object is allocated using `new`. The one parameter to the `Thread` constructor is the object that defines the `run()` method that the thread will use. In the preceding code, you can see that the `Thread` constructor is being told that `this` is the object that holds the definition of `run()`. In Java, `this` is a keyword that is implicitly defined as a reference to the current object. Recall that when a Java-enabled browser encounters a page with an applet on it, the browser downloads the `Applet` class file from the Web page server, and the Java runtime then creates an object from this class. In the preceding code, the `this` keyword that is being passed to the `Thread` constructor refers to the applet object.

We'll be defining a method named run() in the Applet class. The Thread class defines its own method named run() that is used in circumstances not covered here. When we write theThread.start(), the Thread class start() method is invoked. This method invokes the run() method. But how do we let the Thread object know that we want it to use the version of run() defined in the Applet class rather than the version defined in the Thread class? Passing the Thread constructor a reference to the applet object gives the Thread object that information.

Unlike an applet's init() method, which is called only a single time, an applet's start() method may be called more than once. For example, if the portion of the Web page that holds the applet is scrolled out of view and then back into view, the applet stops and then restarts. Because start() might execute more than once, we check to make sure that the thread doesn't already exist before we go ahead and create and start it. The first time that start() runs, the variable theThread will have its default value of null (as all reference variables do). After the first execution of start(), theThread will reference a Thread object and will thus have a non-null value.

The Applet class and the Thread class both define a start() method. The Applet class start() method is automatically invoked by the Java runtime when the applet is loaded. The Thread class start() method needs to be explicitly called by a Thread object, as in theThread.start().

DEFINING THE BODY OF THE THREAD

The Runnable interface consists of a prototype for just one method—a method named run(). Bringing this interface into an applet means that the applet should define such a method. When the thread's start() method is invoked, it will in turn call this run() method. The thread expects that the run() method will perform the work for which the thread was created. Because of this expectation, the applet-defined run() method is referred to as the *body* of the thread.

For the MyAnimation2 applet, the run() method can consist of a loop that calls repaint(), as follows:

```
public void run() {

    while ( true ) {
        repaint();
    }
}
```

This is the same code that was used in the start() method defined in the previous version of the MyAnimation applet.

Stopping the Thread

When the user leaves the current Web page, the thread that's running the animation should be stopped. We can take care of that job with the stop() method. Like start(), stop() is a method defined by the Applet class. Again like start(), stop() gets executed automatically by Java runtime. When the user leaves the current Web page, the Java runtime invokes the applet's stop() method. In this method, we can call the Thread class stop() method to halt execution of the Thread object referenced by theThread. Here we'll also set theThread to null to indicate that the thread has completed its execution and that the Thread object is available for garbage collection. The code for stopping the thread is as follows:

```
public void stop() {

    if ( theThread != null ) {
        theThread.stop();
        theThread = null;
    }
}
```

The MyAnimation2 Applet

You've seen all the pieces that make up a threaded applet. Now let's put them together to form the completed MyAnimation2 applet.

In the source code for MyAnimation2, the init() and paint() methods remain unchanged from MyAnimation. The start() method has changed, and the run() and stop() methods are new. Here is the complete listing for MyAnimation2.java:

```
import java.awt.*;
import java.applet.*;


public class MyAnimation2 extends Applet implements Runnable {
```

```
Font      italicFont;
Font      boldFont;
boolean   toggleIsOn;
Thread    theThread;


public void init() {

    italicFont = new Font( "TimesRoman", Font.ITALIC, 18 );
    boldFont = new Font( "TimesRoman", Font.BOLD, 18 );
    toggleIsOn = false;
}


public void start() {

    if ( theThread == null ) {
        theThread = new Thread( this );
        theThread.start();
    }
}


public void run() {

    while ( true ) {
        repaint();
    }
}


public void stop() {

    if ( theThread != null ) {
        theThread.stop();
        theThread = null;
    }
}


public void paint( Graphics g ) {

    if ( toggleIsOn == false )
    {
```

```
                g.setFont( italicFont );
                g.drawString( "I'm turned off!", 10, 20 );
                toggleIsOn = true;
            }
            else // toggleIsOn is true
            {
                g.setFont( boldFont );
                g.drawString( "Now I'm on!", 10, 20 );
                toggleIsOn = false;
            }
        }

    }
```

METHODS USED IN MYANIMATION2

The last few pages have covered several methods—some of which have identical names. Table 10-1 summarizes how we've used a thread to create a simple animated effect. The table also explains the use of the different methods.

Table 10-1
Methods Used in MyAnimation2

Method	Explanation
`Applet` class `start()`	Inherited by the applet and overridden, it is automatically invoked when the user comes to the Web page holding the applet. As such, it is the perfect place to create the new `Thread` object.
`Thread` class `start()`	Invoked by the `Thread` object to do the work of starting up the thread.
`Applet`-defined `run()`	Used to define what the thread does. This `run()` method gets invoked by the `Thread` class `start()` method. The `Thread` class also defines a `run()` method—a method not used here.
`Applet` class `stop()`	Inherited by the applet and overridden, it is automatically invoked when the user leaves the Web page holding the applet. That makes it a good place to stop the thread from executing and to mark the thread's reference as null.

RUNNING THE MYANIMATION2 APPLET

After compiling the MyAnimation2.java file, run the resulting applet in an applet viewer. The results will appear identical to the first version of this applet; the applet runs, but it appears to update slowly. So, just what was accomplished by adding a thread? The improvement will be noticed in real-world situations. If you incorporate MyAnimation2 in a Web page, the applet will be properly displayed and will execute.

Because the animation now runs in its own thread, the Java runtime is capable of devoting resources both to the applet and to any other tasks it needs to handle. As a simple test of this, try including the applet in more than one place on your Web page. To do that, simply use the <applet> tag more than once in the HTML file that displays your Web page. Here's an example:

```
<html>
<head>
<title>My Home Page</title>
</head>
<body>
<h1>Welcome to My Web Page!</h1>
<hr>
If you have a Java-capable browser you'll be able to see three
    versions of the MyAnimation2 applet below this text.<br>
<hr>
<applet code="MyAnimation2.class" width=200 height=50>
</applet>
<hr>
<applet code="MyAnimation2.class" width=200 height=50>
</applet>
<hr>
<applet code="MyAnimation2.class" width=200 height=50>
</applet>
</body>
</html>
```

If you use the preceding code as the HTML file for your home page and have the MyAnimation2.class file in the same directory as that HTML file, your Web page would look similar to the one shown in Figure 10-4.

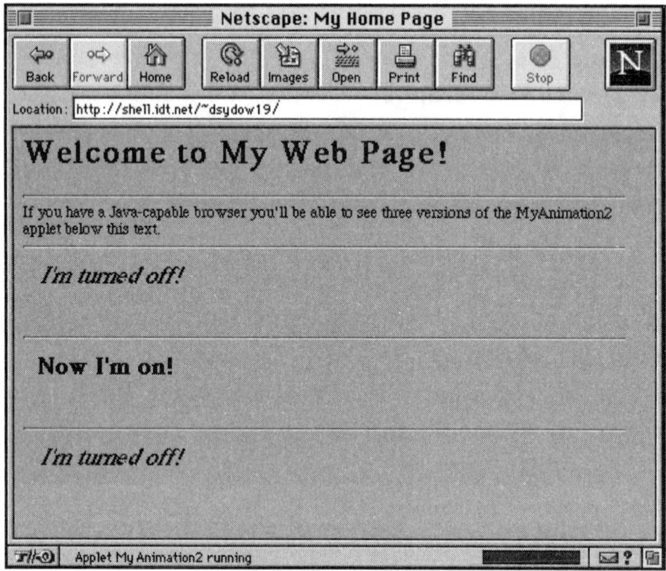

Figure 10-4
The results of running the MyAnimation2 applet in a Web browser

Having each applet perform its animation in its own thread ensures that the Java runtime sees to it that the host machine's processor alternately allots time to first one applet and then another.

The delay in execution seen in an applet viewer isn't present in the Java virtual machine that is a part of your Web browser. Here you'll see that the applet gets repainted at an impressive pace. In fact, the text string alternates so quickly that you'll want to slow things down. In the next section, we'll do that when we once again modify the animation applet.

Exceptions

In Java, an *exception* is an exceptional condition that arises during the running of an applet; it's usually something out of the ordinary requiring special attention. This condition is one that is beyond the control of the applet, but still must be dealt with in some way.

TRADITIONAL MEANS OF HANDLING EXCEPTIONS

Some operations are by nature more prone to error: They're more likely to generate an exception. The allocation of memory is one such operation; there may be an insufficient amount of free memory for the allocation. Writing to a file is another such operation; the file may already be in use. Lines of code that are used for these types of operations are the ones that have traditionally included a "safety net" of error-checking code. Your own C or C++ programs may have included code similar to the code shown in Figure 10-5.

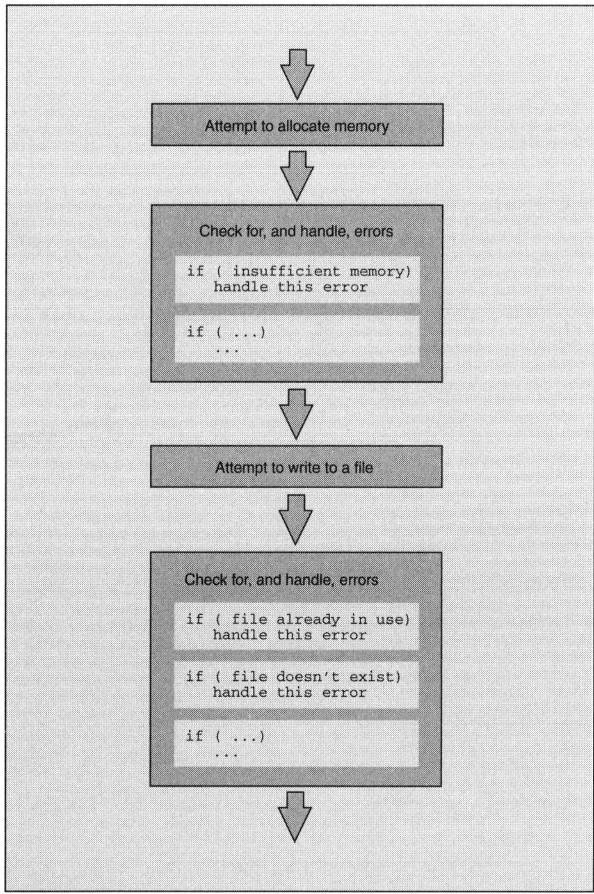

Figure 10-5
The traditional way of handling exceptions

JAVA'S MEANS OF HANDLING EXCEPTIONS

The method of error detection and error handling shown in Figure 10-5 can result in rather unwieldy code. Java reduces the amount of code required by building exception handling into the language. When your applet is about to attempt something that could produce an error, you embed that code into a `try` ***block***. Following the `try` block should be one or more `catch` ***blocks***. The `try` block tries out the code, and the `catch` block catches any errors. If the code in the `try` block generates no errors, the `catch` block is skipped. Figure 10-6 illustrates.

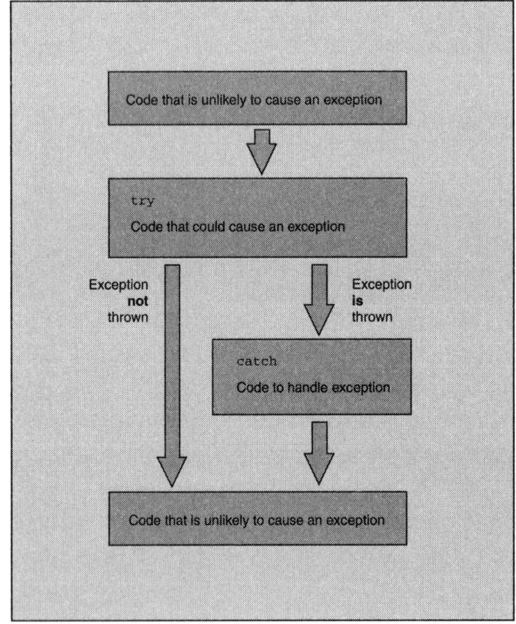

Figure 10-6

The way Java handles exceptions

EXCEPTIONS AS OBJECTS

A Java exception is an object of the class `Throwable` or one of its subclasses. Figure 10-7 shows that the `Throwable` class has two subclasses: the `Error` class and the `Exception` class. Most exception objects will be instances of one of the many subclasses of the `Exception` class.

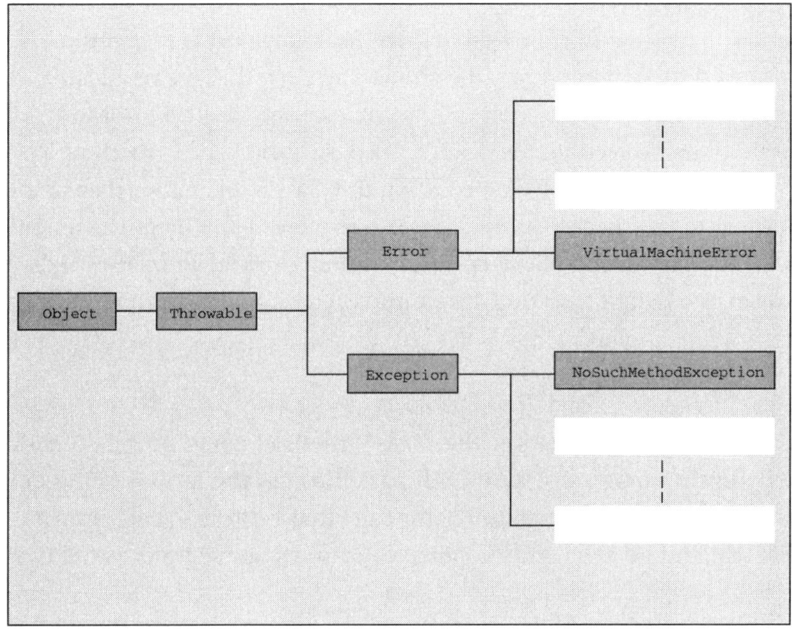

Figure 10-7
The Throwable class and some of its subclasses

To add exception-handling to your code, place the code that is to be tested within a `try` block, and place any error-handling code within a `catch` block, as follows:

```
try {
    // code that may throw an exception
}
catch ( ExceptionType e ) {
    // code to handle the exception
}
```

The `catch` keyword is followed by a pair of parentheses. Within these parentheses should be the class type of the exception that is to be caught and a name for the exception; the format is similar to the definition of a method that has a single parameter.

EXCEPTIONS AND THE ANIMATION EXAMPLE

Earlier in this chapter, we said that the MyAnimation applet could be improved by slowing down the animation. Now that we've added a thread to the animation applet, that task becomes easy. The `Thread` class defines a method that is used for just such a purpose—the `sleep()` method. This is a class method that can be called using the class name rather than an object. The `sleep()` method requires a single parameter—the length of time to delay the processing of the currently running thread, in milliseconds. To pause for a half of a second, for example, call `sleep()` like this:

```
Thread.sleep( 500 );
```

To delay the animation, the `sleep()` method could be called within the body of the `while` loop. Here each pass through the loop is being delayed by one quarter of a second. That means that `repaint()`, and in turn `update()` and `paint()`, will be called four times per second, as follows:

```
public void run() {

    while ( true ) {
        repaint();
        Thread.sleep( 250 );
    }
}
```

While the preceding call to `sleep()` is syntactically correct, compiling this code results in an error. Figure 10-8 shows that one particular Java compiler reports that an exception must be caught.

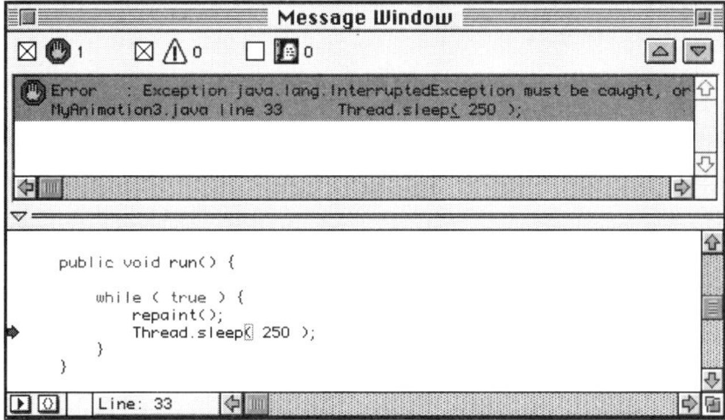

Figure 10-8

A Java compiler reporting that a method call requires a catch

The compile-time error came about because, in Java, some methods must include a catch when invoked. The `sleep()` method of the `Thread` class is such a method. How do you know which methods require a catch? As Figure 10-8 shows, omitting the catch and compiling is one sure way to determine this information!

Here's the final, correct version of the `run()` method:

```
public void run() {

    while ( true ) {
        repaint();
        try {
            Thread.sleep( 250 );
        }
        catch ( InterruptedException e ) {
        }
    }
}
```

If you replace the `run()` method defined in MyAnimation2 with this version you'll have MyAnimation3—an applet that is slowed down enough to enable the user to read the text of the two messages as they alternate.

What You've Learned

When an applet needs updating, its `paint()` method is automatically invoked by the Java runtime. If you want to tell your applet to update itself at any time, you can do so by invoking its `repaint()` method. By repeatedly doing so, you achieve animated effects. To generate smoother animation, place the animation code in its own thread. A thread of execution is a separate process that gets CPU time dedicated to it.

CHAPTER 11

Mouse- and Keyboard-Related Events

Receiving and responding to user input is one of the factors that differentiates applets from other parts of a Web page. After all, you can easily display text and graphics on a Web page without an applet.

Up to this point, all of the example applets described in this book have been passive. That is, while each of the applets displayed text or graphics, none of them interacted with the user in any way. In this chapter, however, you'll see how you can make an applet respond to user actions—such as a click of the mouse button or a press of a keyboard key.

In Java, a user action is an *event*. To give your applet the greatest flexibility in reacting to user actions, what might at first be thought of as a single event is actually considered two separate events. For example, a press of the mouse button is considered to be a `mouseDown` event. A release of the pressed button is considered a second event, a `mouseUp` event. The same applies to a press of a keyboard key (a `keyDown` event) and the release of that key (a `keyUp` event).

When an event occurs, Java runtime takes note of it and stores information about the event in an object of the `Event` class type. This process is automatic—your applet doesn't need to do anything in order for event information to be stored in such an object.

The Event Class Definition

The definition of the `Event` class, which is a part of the java.awt package, is shown as follows. The definition is particularly large and unwieldy looking, so after the definition we'll devote several pages to understanding it.

```
public  class  java.awt.Event extends  java.lang.Object {

    // instance variables
    public Object    arg;
    public int       clickCount;
    public Event     evt;
    public int       id;
    public int       key;
    public int       modifiers;
    public Object    target;
    public long      when;
    public int       x;
    public in        y;

    // class variables assigned to the id field
    public final static int  ACTION_EVENT;
    public final static int  GOT_FOCUS;
    public final static int  KEY_ACTION;
    public final static int  KEY_ACTION_RELEASE;
    public final static int  KEY_PRESS;
    public final static int  KEY_RELEASE;
    public final static int  LIST_DESELECT;
    public final static int  LIST_SELECT;
    public final static int  LOAD_FILE;
    public final static int  LOST_FOCUS;
    public final static int  MOUSE_DOWN;
    public final static int  MOUSE_DRAG;
    public final static int  MOUSE_ENTER;
    public final static int  MOUSE_EXIT;
    public final static int  MOUSE_MOVE;
    public final static int  MOUSE_UP;
    public final static int  SAVE_FILE;
    public final static int  SCROLL_ABSOLUTE;
    public final static int  SCROLL_LINE_DOWN;
    public final static int  SCROLL_LINE_UP;
    public final static int  SCROLL_PAGE_DOWN;
    public final static int  SCROLL_PAGE_UP;
    public final static int  WINDOW_DEICONIFY;
    public final static int  WINDOW_DESTROY;
    public final static int  WINDOW_EXPOSE;
    public final static int  WINDOW_ICONIFY;
    public final static int  WINDOW_MOVED;

    // class variables assigned to the key field
    public final static int  DOWN;
    public final static int  END;
    public final static int  F1;
```

```
    public final static int  F2;
    public final static int  F3;
    public final static int  F4;
    public final static int  F5;
    public final static int  F6;
    public final static int  F7;
    public final static int  F8;
    public final static int  F9;
    public final static int  F10;
    public final static int  F11;
    public final static int  F12;
    public final static int  HOME;
    public final static int  LEFT;
    public final static int  PGDN;
    public final static int  PGUP;
    public final static int  RIGHT;
    public final static int  UP;

    // class variables assigned to the modifiers field
    public final static int  ALT_MASK;
    public final static int  CTRL_MASK;
    public final static int  META_MASK;
    public final static int  SHIFT_MASK;

    // constructors
    public Event(Object target, int id, Object arg);
    public Event(Object target, long when, int id, int x, int y,
              int key, int modifiers);
    public Event(Object target, long when, int id, int x, int y,
              int key, int modifiers, Object arg);

    // methods
    public boolean controlDown();
    public boolean metaDown();
    protected String paramString();
    public boolean shiftDown();
    public String toString();
    public void translate(int dX, int dY);
}
```

Event Objects

When an event occurs, Java creates an `Event` class object and gives your applet access to it.

By now, you should be used to declaring an object variable of a class type and then using `new` to allocate memory for that object, create the object, and receive a reference to the object. When an event occurs, Java runtime creates an object of the `Event` class type. Because Java, rather than your applet, creates the object, how does the object become available to your applet? As shown in Figure 11-1, one of the instance variables defined in the `Event` class is a reference to the object itself.

```
public  class  java.awt.Event extends  java.lang.Object
{

     // instance variables
     public Object   arg;
     public int      clickCount;
     public Event    evt;   <—— Holds a reference to the Event object
     public int      id;
     public int      key;
     public int      modifiers;
     public Object   target;
     public long     when;
     public int      x;
     public int      y;

     // class variables

     // constructors

     // methods
}
```

Figure 11-1

The Event class defines an instance variable that serves as a reference to the Event object.

When you need to work with the `Event` object Java creates, you do so by overriding a method that your applet inherits. For instance, to enable your applet to respond to a keystroke, you redefine the `keyDown()` method:

```
public boolean keyDown( Event evt, int key ) {

    // handle a press of a key
}
```

As shown in the keyDown() method, methods defined to handle an event always receive a reference to the system's Event object as a parameter. It is the evt instance variable that is passed to such a method. Your applet won't be responsible for the value of evt: This field gets filled in by Java when it creates the Event object.

STORING EVENT INFORMATION

The instance variables of the Event class are used to describe a single event. Of most importance is id—a variable that holds an event's ID value. When an event occurs, Java creates an Event object and fills in the id field with a value that represents the type of the event (a mouseDown or keyUp event, for example). To determine an event's type, your applet can check the value of the id instance variable and compare this value to the constants defined in the Event class, as shown in Figure 11-2.

```
public  class  java.awt.Event extends  java.lang.Object {

     // instance variables
     public Object   arg;
     public int      clickCount;
     public Event    evt;
     public int      id;
     public int      key;
     public int      modifiers;
     public Object   target;
     public long     when;
     public int      x;
     public int      y;

     // class variables assigned to the id field
     ...
     ...
     public final static int  KEY_PRESS;
     public final static int  KEY_RELEASE;
     ...
     ...
     public final static int  MOUSE_DOWN;
     public final static int  MOUSE_DRAG;
     public final static int  MOUSE_ENTER;
     public final static int  MOUSE_EXIT;
     public final static int  MOUSE_MOVE;
     public final static int  MOUSE_UP;
     ...
     ...

     // constructors

     // methods
}
```

Figure 11-2
The Event class defines numerous constants that represent different event types.

KEYBOARD-RELATED EVENTS

If an event involves the press of a key, Java runtime fills the `Event` object's key instance variable with an integer value that represents that key. If the pressed key isn't an alphanumeric key, but rather an action key (such as an arrow key or function key), Java instead stores a constant in the `key` field. You can determine if the user pressed an action key by comparing the value in the `key` field with the class variables defined in the `Event` class, as shown in Figure 11-3.

```
public  class  java.awt.Event extends  java.lang.Object {

     // instance variables
     public Object   arg;
     public int      clickCount;
     public Event    evt;
     public int      id;
     public int      key;
     public int      modifiers;
     public Object   target;
     public long     when;
     public int      x;
     public int      y;

     // class variables assigned to the id field
     public final static int  DOWN;
     ...
     ...
     public final static int  UP;

     // constructors

     // methods
}
```

Figure 11-3

The Event class defines numerous constants that represent different keyboard key types.

In addition to examining the value held in the key instance variable, your applet will be capable of gaining more insight into the user's actions by checking to see if a modifier key was held down at the time of the event. To do this, invoke one of the `Event` methods that relates to modifiers, such as `shiftDown()`.

MOUSE-RELATED EVENTS

If an event involves the mouse, Java runtime stores in the `Event` object's `x` and `y` instance variables the location of the cursor at the time the event occurred, as shown in Figure 11-4.

```
public  class  java.awt.Event extends  java.lang.Object {

     // instance variables
     public Object   arg;
     public int      clickCount;
     public Event    evt;
     public int      id;
     public int      key;
     public int      modifiers;
     public Object   target;
     public long     when;
     public int      x;
     public int      y;

     // class variables

     // constructors

     // methods
}
```

Location of the cursor at the time the mouse button was pressed

Figure 11-4

The Event class defines two instance variables that are used to hold the coordinates of the cursor at any given moment.

EXAMPLE OF AN EVENT OBJECT

If the user clicks the button of his or her mouse, Java generates an `Event` object. Java fills the object's `evt` instance variable with a reference to the object so that methods in his or her applet will be capable of accessing the other information held in the object. Java also assigns the `id` field a value of `MOUSE_DOWN` to indicate that a `mouseDown` event occurred. If the user had the cursor, say, 130 pixels in from the left of the applet and 60 pixels down from the applet's top at the moment of the mouse click, then these are the values Java would store in the object's x and y instance variables. Figure 11-5 illustrates what the Event object would look like with the occurrence of such an event.

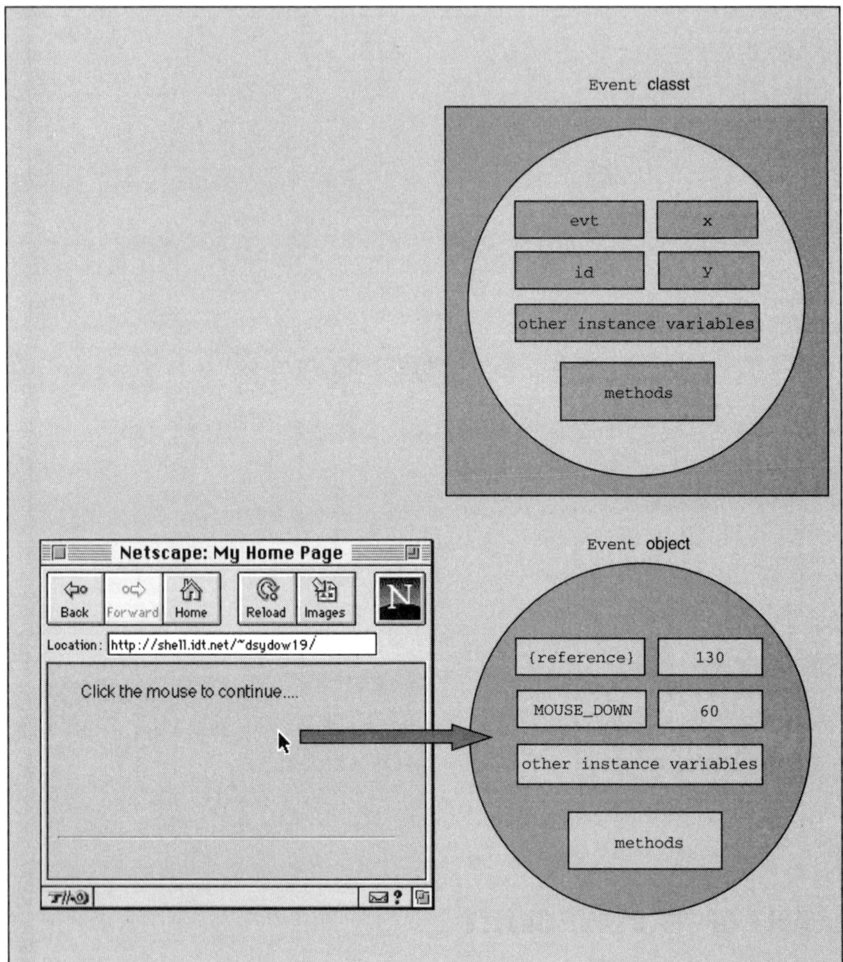

Figure 11-5

A mouse click in an applet generates an Event object and places event information in that object.

Mouse Events

If your applet interacts with the user, it will no doubt be one that responds to events involving the mouse. In particular, your applet can determine if the user pressed or released the mouse button, if the user is dragging the mouse with the button depressed, or if the user is moving the mouse without holding the button down.

THE mouseDown() METHOD

If your applet is to respond to a mouse click by the user, you'll have your applet watch for `mouseDown` events (and perhaps `mouseUp` events as well). To handle a `mouseDown` event, your applet should override the `mouseDown()` method—a method that is defined in the `Component` class. The following is the format of that method:

```
public boolean mouseDown( Event evt, int x, int y ) {

    // handle the case of the mouse button being clicked
}
```

As mentioned earlier in this chapter, Java runtime passes an event reference to a method that responds to an event. In the preceding snippet you can see this behavior. You can also see that Java passes other event information that is pertinent to the event type being handled. For a click of the mouse button, your applet may want to know where within the applet the user clicked. The `x` and `y` parameters give your applet that information.

The `mouseDown()` method returns a `boolean` value to the caller. Because Java runtime is the instigator of this method, this `boolean` value will be returned to Java. The purpose of the return value is to let Java know whether the event was completely handled by your overridden method. If it was (as will almost always be the case), the value returns `true`:

```
public boolean mouseDown( Event evt, int x, int y ) {

    // handle the case of the mouse button being clicked

    return true;
}
```

If your version of mouseDown() didn't handle the event completely, the value returns false. A returned value of false tells Java that it must further process the event.

EXAMPLE 1: USING THE MOUSEDOWN() METHOD ALONE

A typical way to handle a click of the mouse button is to use mouseDown() to supply your applet with the pixel coordinate location of the cursor at the time of the click:

```
protected int     xLocation;
protected int     yLocation;

public boolean mouseDown( Event evt, int x, int y ) {

    xLocation = x;
    yLocation = y;

    return true;
}
```

After mouseDown() executes, your applet will have the point of the mouse click stored in its xLocation and yLocation variables.

The following is an example that's intended to draw a circle at the point of the mouse click:

```
import java.awt.*;
import java.applet.*;


public class MouseTest1 extends Applet {

    protected int     xLocation;
    protected int     yLocation;

    public boolean mouseDown( Event evt, int x, int y ) {

        xLocation = x;
        yLocation = y;

        return true;
    }
```

```
    public void paint( Graphics g ) {

        g.drawOval( xLocation - 5, yLocation - 5, 10, 10 );
    }

}
```

Just before the preceding listing, we said that the *intention* of the applet is to draw a circle each time the user clicks the mouse. As written, it won't! That's because the occurrence of an event doesn't always trigger Java to invoke the `paint()` method. In the next version of this applet we'll work to overcome this shortcoming.

EXAMPLE 2: USING REPAINT() WITH MOUSEDOWN()

To force the applet to redraw itself, we can use a trick learned in Chapter 10: We can have the applet explicitly invoke the `repaint()` method. In this next applet listing, we've done just that. Running the applet causes a circle with a diameter of 10 pixels to be drawn at the point at which the user clicks the mouse, as shown in Figure 11-6.

```
public class MouseTest2 extends Applet {

    protected int     xLocation;
    protected int     yLocation;

    public boolean mouseDown( Event evt, int x, int y ) {

        xLocation = x;
        yLocation = y;

        repaint();

        return true;
    }

    public void paint( Graphics g ) {

        g.drawOval( xLocation - 5, yLocation - 5, 10, 10 );
    }

}
```

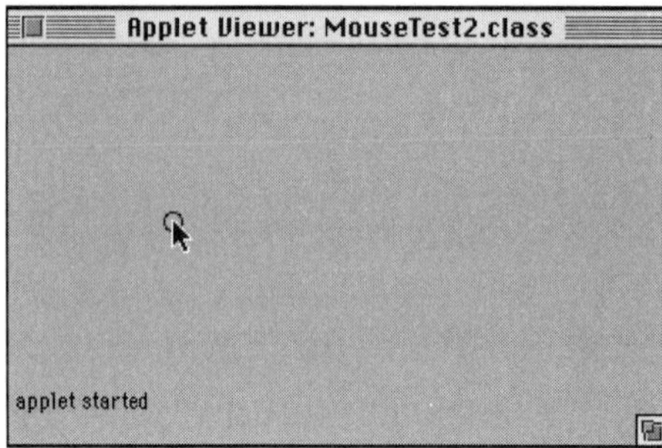

Figure 11-6
The results of running the MouseTest2 applet

EXAMPLE 3: USING GETGRAPHICS() WITH MOUSEDOWN()

Our previous listing resulted in a working applet—if our intention is to have only one circle drawn to the applet at any time. Recall that the `repaint()` method invokes the `update()` method, which clears the applet before drawing to it. That means that if an existing circle is drawn to the applet, it will be erased at the next click of the mouse button.

If we want to preserve the contents of the applet and draw a new circle at each mouse click, we can perform our drawing from within the `mouseDown()` method rather than rely on the `paint()` method. The `paint()` method is invoked automatically by Java runtime whenever an applet needs to be updated. That makes `paint()` a useful method. However, for drawing at times other than update periods, your applet doesn't need to rely on `paint()`.

Drawing methods always work on an object of the `Graphics` class. When a call is made to `paint()`, Java passes a reference to the `Graphics` object of the applet itself to `paint()`. To draw at a time of our own choosing, we'll need to get this reference ourselves. To do that, we rely on the `getGraphics()` method that's a part of the `Component` class. To use this method, declare a `Graphics` object and then call `getGraphics()`:

```
Graphics g = getGraphics();
```

After the preceding step, variable `g` can be used in any drawing operation:

```
g.drawOval( xLocation - 5, yLocation - 5, 10, 10 );
```

Here's a final version of the applet that handles a click of the mouse. After running the MouseDownEvt applet and clicking the mouse button several times, the result looks like that shown in Figure 11-7.

```
public class MouseDownEvt extends Applet {

    protected int     xLocation;
    protected int     yLocation;

    public boolean mouseDown( Event evt, int x, int y ) {

        xLocation = x;
        yLocation = y;

        Graphics g = getGraphics();
        g.drawOval( xLocation - 5, yLocation - 5, 10, 10 );

        return true;
    }
}
```

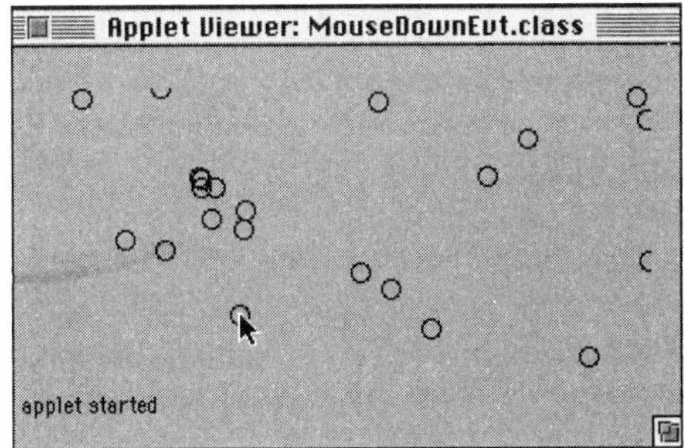

Figure 11-7
The results of running the MouseDownEvt applet

THE MOUSEUP() METHOD

In addition to the `mouseDown()` method, the `Component` class defines a `mouseUp()` method. If your applet needs to know if the user released the mouse button after pressing it, this method should be overridden. The format of `mouseUp()` is the same as `mouseDown()`:

```
public boolean mouseUp( Event evt, int x, int y ) {

     // handle the case of the mouse button being released
}
```

If we choose to, we can achieve results identical to those of the MouseDownEvt applet by having our applet watch for and respond to `mouseUp` events rather than `mouseDown` events.

The MouseDownUpEvt applet, whose listing is shown next, works with both `mouseDown` and `mouseUp` events. When the user clicks the mouse button, Java invokes `mouseDown` to draw a circle at the point of the mouse click. When the user releases the mouse button, Java invokes `mouseUp` to draw a square at the point of release. If the user clicks the mouse button and releases it at the same point, the circle and square will appear together. If the user clicks the mouse button, then drags the mouse before releasing the button, the circle and square will be drawn at different locations. Figure 11-8 shows the applet after several mouse clicks.

```
public class MouseDownUpEvt extends Applet {

     protected int     xLocation;
     protected int     yLocation;

     public boolean mouseDown( Event evt, int x, int y ) {

          xLocation = x;
          yLocation = y;

          Graphics g = getGraphics();
          g.drawOval( xLocation - 5, yLocation - 5, 10, 10 );

          return true;
     }
```

```
    public boolean mouseUp( Event evt, int x, int y ) {

        xLocation = x;
        yLocation = y;

        Graphics g = getGraphics();
        g.drawRect( xLocation - 5, yLocation - 5, 10, 10 );

        return true;
    }
}
```

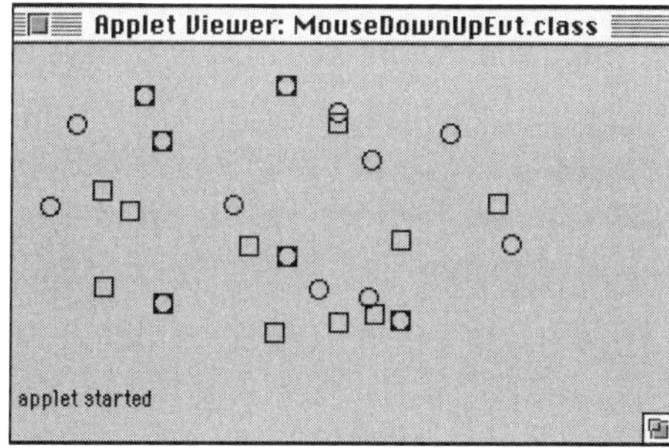

Figure 11-8
The results of running the MouseDownUpEvt applet

THE MOUSEDRAG() AND MOUSEMOVE() METHODS

Your applet can respond to the user's moving the mouse as well as to the user's clicking its button. When the user presses the mouse button and moves the mouse, Java responds by issuing a `mouseDrag` event. If your applet is to handle this event type it should override the `mouseDrag()` method:

```
public boolean mouseDrag( Event evt, int x, int y ) {

    // handle the case of the mouse being dragged

    return true;
}
```

To follow the mouse as it's moved without the button being pressed, override the `mouseMove()` method:

```
public boolean mouseMove( Event evt, int x, int y ) {

    // handle the case of the mouse being moved

    return true;
}
```

USING THE MOUSEDRAG() METHOD

When the user clicks or releases the mouse button, Java invokes `mouseDown()` or `mouseUp()` a single time. The `mouseDrag()` method differs in its operation from these two methods in that it is *continually* invoked by Java as the mouse is dragged. As long as the mouse button is held down and the user is moving the mouse, the Java runtime will keep calling `mouseDrag()`, passing new *x* and *y* coordinates each time. These *x* and *y* values thus reflect the location of the cursor at any given moment in its trip about the applet.

In the following example, `mouseDrag()` is used to draw lines. Here a call to `drawLine()` is made to draw a line of zero length (the starting point of the line and the end point of the line are specified as one in the same). Because a line has a default width of one pixel, such a line will be one pixel in length. Because `mouseDrag()` is continually being called, the one-pixel line will be drawn over and over, following the user's movements of the mouse. Figure 11-9 illustrates drawing using the `mouseDrag()` method (as well as the author's keen artistic talents).

```
public class MouseDragEvt extends Applet {

    protected int     xLocation;
    protected int     yLocation;


    public boolean mouseDrag( Event evt, int x, int y ) {

        Graphics g = getGraphics();
        g.drawLine( x, y, x, y );

        return true;
    }
}
```

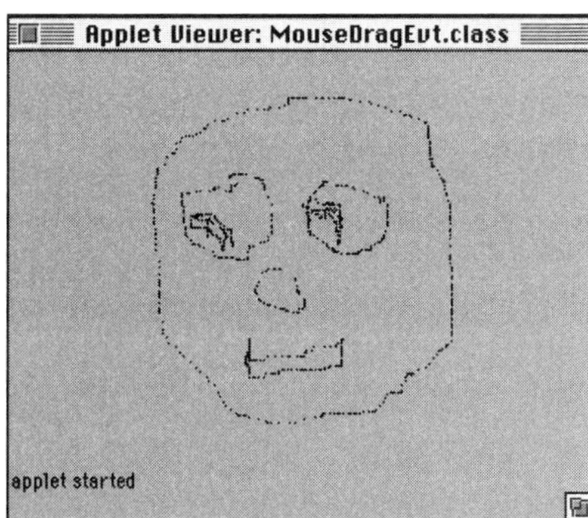

Figure 11-9
The results of running the MouseDragEvt applet

STORING COORDINATES PASSED TO MOUSEDRAG()

In the previous example, you surely noticed that the lines drawn by the applet are not smooth. In fact, if the mouse is moved rapidly, the lines will be broken up quite a bit. This happens because the mouse is being dragged at a speed faster than Java can invoke `mouseDrag()`.

We can improve upon the previous example by storing the coordinates passed to `mouseDrag()`. Preserving these values between calls to `mouseDrag()` enables us to draw a line that always starts at the end point of the previous line. This means there will be no gaps in each line no matter how fast the user drags the mouse.

Storing the coordinates that define the location of the mouse at the time the user clicks the mouse button is an easy task. We'll declare two integer variables and assign them the coordinates that Java passes to `mouseDown()`. When the user drags the mouse, we'll make use of these saved values: They'll become the starting point of the line that is drawn. As the user drags the mouse, we'll again make use of these same two variables. When the mouse is dragged, `mouseDrag()` is repeatedly called. Each time `mouseDrag()` executes, the saved coordinates will be used as the start of a line, while the coordinates Java passes to `mouseDrag()` will be used as the end point of the line.

This new applet sets the start of the line to the point at which the user clicks the mouse. Because we're using the `xLocation` and `yLocation` variables as the starting point of the line, we need to provide these variables with initial values:

```
public class DrawIt extends Applet {

    protected int    xLocation;
    protected int    yLocation;

    public boolean mouseDown( Event evt, int x, int y ) {

        xLocation = x;
        yLocation = y;

        return true;
    }

    public boolean mouseDrag( Event evt, int x, int y ) {

        Graphics g = getGraphics();
        g.drawLine( xLocation, yLocation, x, y );

        xLocation = x;
        yLocation = y;

        return true;
    }
}
```

Figure 11-10 shows the result of drawing with our improved drawing applet.

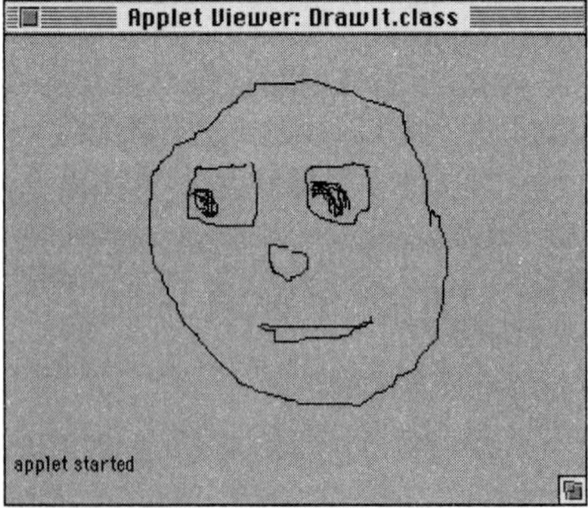

Figure 11-10
The results of running the DrawIt applet

USING THE MOUSEMOVE() METHOD

The mouse button doesn't have to be pressed in order for the applet to be aware that the user is moving the mouse. This next example is identical to the first `mouseDrag()` applet listing—with the exception that the name of the applet's one method has been changed from `mouseDrag()` to `mouseMove()`. When you run the MouseMoveEvt applet, you'll notice that drawing takes place anytime you pass the cursor over the applet—even if the mouse button isn't pressed:

```
public class MouseMoveEvt extends Applet {

    protected int    xLocation;
    protected int    yLocation;

    public boolean mouseMove( Event evt, int x, int y ) {

        Graphics g = getGraphics();
        g.drawLine( xLocation, yLocation, x, y );

        xLocation = x;
        yLocation = y;

        return true;
    }
}
```

Keyboard Events

You've just seen an applet that recognizes mouse movements. Of equal importance are applets that can respond to keystrokes.

KEYDOWN EVENTS

Just as your applet can tell when the user presses the mouse button, it can also tell when the user presses a keyboard key. If your applet overrides the `keyDown()` method, it can respond in any way to a keystroke. The following is the format of the `keyDown()` method:

```
public boolean keyDown( Event evt, int key ) {

    // handle the case of the a key being pressed

    return true;
}
```

When the user types a key, Java invokes `keyDown()`. In doing that, Java passes along a reference to the `Event` object that holds information about the `keyDown` event as well as the value of `key`. Recall that this `Event` instance variable holds an integer value representing the pressed key.

To make use of `keyDown()`, use the method to examine the value in the passed parameter key. Because this value is an integer rather than a character, you'll need to cast it to type `char` if you're going to echo its alphanumeric value back to the screen. The following example does just that in order to write out the character to the applet:

```
import java.awt.*;
import java.applet.*;

public class KeyDownEvt extends Applet {

    public boolean keyDown( Event evt, int key ) {

        Graphics g = getGraphics();
        g.drawString( "You typed a: " + (char)key, 10, 20 );

        return true;
    }
}
```

Figure 11-11 shows the results of typing an uppercase letter S.

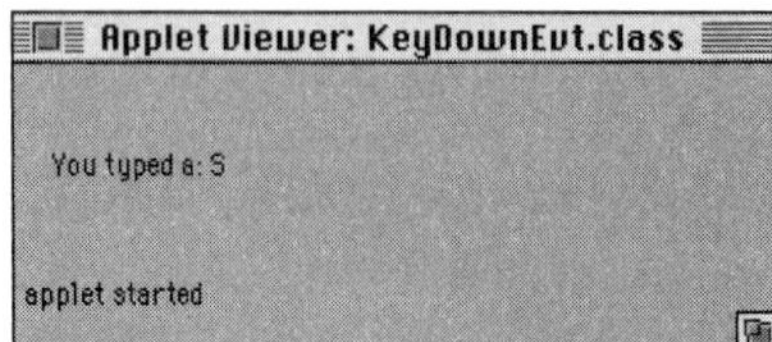

Figure 11-11
The results of running the KeyDownEvt applet

ACTION KEYS

In Java, a keyboard key that exists to perform some action rather than to input a character is called an *action key*. Examples of action keys are the arrow keys as well as all of the function keys on the keyboard. Your applet can test whether an action key has been pressed by comparing the value of key with the key-related class variables that make up some of the many constants defined in the `Event` class:

```
public boolean keyDown( Event evt, int key ) {

    switch ( key ) {

        case Event.DOWN:
            // do some action related to the Down arrow key
            break;

        case Event.UP:
            // do some action related to the Up arrow key
            break;

        // other action key constants here
    }

    return true;
}
```

This next example applet checks for the occurrence of keystrokes that involve any of the four arrow keys. If the user presses one of these keys, `keyDown()` offsets the value of one of the two variables used to keep track of an oval that's been painted onto the screen. The `repaint()` method is then called to redraw the circle in its new, moved position. If you run the ActionKeys applet, you'll see that the effect is that of a circle moving all about the applet—with you in complete control of its direction.

```
public class ActionKeys extends Applet {

    protected int    xLocation = 10;
    protected int    yLocation = 10;

    public boolean keyDown( Event evt, int key ) {

        switch ( key ) {
```

```
            case Event.DOWN:
                yLocation += 2;
                break;

            case Event.UP:
                yLocation -= 2;
                break;

            case Event.RIGHT:
                xLocation += 2;
                break;

            case Event.LEFT:
                xLocation -= 2;
                break;
        }

        repaint();

        return true;
    }


    public void paint( Graphics g ) {

        g.fillOval( xLocation, yLocation, 15, 15 );
    }
    }
```

Figure 11-12 illustrates what you'll see at any given moment when you run the ActionKeys applet.

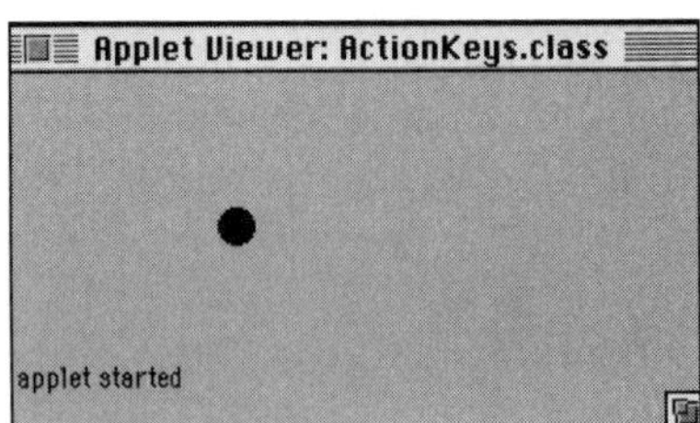

Figure 11-12
The results of running the ActionKeys applet

MODIFIER KEYS

In Java, a keyboard key that exists to be used in conjunction with other keys is called a *modifier key*. The Shift key and Control keys are the primary examples of modifier keys. Your applet can test to see if the user is holding down a modifier key (either alone or with some other key) by invoking one of the `Event` methods.

To see if the Shift key is pressed, call `shiftDown()`. To see if the Control key is pressed, call `controlDown()`. Methods are invoked through objects, so you know that you'll need to use the dot and an object. The object is the event itself, a reference to which is passed in the `evt` parameter. The following illustrates how one of these methods is typically used:

```
public boolean keyDown( Event evt, int key ) {

    if ( evt.shiftDown() == true )
        // perform some action
    else
        // perform some other action

    return true;
}
```

The last example applet in this chapter checks to see if the Shift key is pressed at the same time an arrow key is pressed. If Shift is down, the applet will move a drawn oval 20 pixels in the direction of the pressed arrow key rather than the 2 pixels the applet normally moves it.

```
public class ModifierKeys extends Applet {

    protected int    xLocation = 10;
    protected int    yLocation = 10;
    protected int    multiplier;

    public boolean keyDown( Event evt, int key ) {

        if ( evt.shiftDown() == true )
            multiplier = 10;
        else
            multiplier = 1;

        switch ( key ) {
```

```
            case Event.DOWN:
                yLocation += ( 2 * multiplier );
                break;

            case Event.UP:
                yLocation -= ( 2 * multiplier );
                break;

            case Event.RIGHT:
                xLocation += ( 2 * multiplier );
                break;

            case Event.LEFT:
                xLocation -= ( 2 * multiplier );
                break;
        }

        repaint();

        return true;
    }


    public void paint( Graphics g ) {

        g.fillOval( xLocation, yLocation, 15, 15 );
    }
}
```

The ModifierKeys applet works in the same manner as the ActionKeys applet in the previous example. The only difference between the two applets is that ModifierKeys performs a check to see if the Shift key is down at the time an arrow key is pressed.

What You've Learned

An event is an action of which an applet is aware and to which the applet can optionally respond. An event can be initiated by the user (as when the mouse button is clicked) or by Java itself (as when the applet needs refreshing, or redrawing). Two of the most important events are `mouseDown` and `keyDown`. If you enable your applet to respond to these events, your applet will be active rather than passive: The user will be able to interact with your applet.

When an event occurs, Java creates an `Event` object that holds information about the event and then passes this object to a number of methods that your applet can override. If your applet does override one of these methods, your version of the method will make use of the `Event` object information in order to handle the event appropriately.

CHAPTER

12

Adding a GUI to Your Applets

The many example applets that we've presented so far have all been very simple in nature. Typically, each performed a single task, such as writing a line of text or displaying an image. While these examples each served the admirable purpose of demonstrating some Java programming technique; they did little to show off the power of Java: None of them pushed the envelope. The Java language and the Java runtime (the Java virtual machine) were designed to work in the graphical user interface (GUI) environments of today's computers. In this chapter you'll see how to develop applets that meet the expectations of sophisticated, Web-savvy computer users—applets that contain GUI elements such as buttons, checkboxes, text fields, and pop-up menus.

The Abstract Windowing Toolkit (AWT)

The preceding chapters have shown you that Java applets can show text in a variety of fonts and styles, display simple graphic shapes and complex, colorful graphic images, run animation, and play sounds. While all of these capabilities help you create exciting and dynamic applets, Java's real right to fame is its capability of including graphical user interface elements within an applet. The Java *Abstract Windowing Toolkit* (or AWT) is what enables you to do this. The Abstract Windowing Toolkit is an abstract toolkit of code that enables programmers to include the GUI elements of window-based operating systems.

CROSS-PLATFORM APPLET INTERFACE ELEMENTS

Operating systems that use a graphical user interface include a collection, or library, of routines that make it easier for programmers to include GUI elements in their own applications. For example, Macintosh programmers have access to thousands of Apple-written routines collectively referred to as the Toolbox, while Windows programmers use the many Microsoft-written functions of the Windows application programming interface (API). Regardless of the language you use—C, C++, Pascal, or some other language—to program for one of these systems, your development environment enables you to include calls to functions in these libraries.

Java is designed for the development of applets and applications that run on operating systems with graphical user interfaces. Consequently, you might expect that Java would enable programmers to access the GUI functions provided by the various operating systems on which Java applets and applications can execute. And it does. Yet to program in Java, a person needs no knowledge of any of the specific functions that make up the GUI libraries of operating systems such as Windows 95 or the Mac OS. Java's Abstract Windowing Toolkit resolves this seemingly contradictory situation by providing an abstract layer that enables Java programmers to *indirectly* make use of the GUI libraries of various operating systems.

When you include a GUI element, or component, in your applet, it takes on a different appearance, depending upon which operating system is executing the applet. For example, if your applet includes two buttons it will look different when the Web page on which it appears is viewed in, say, the Windows version of Netscape Navigator and the Macintosh version of this same browser. Figure 12-1 illustrates this difference.

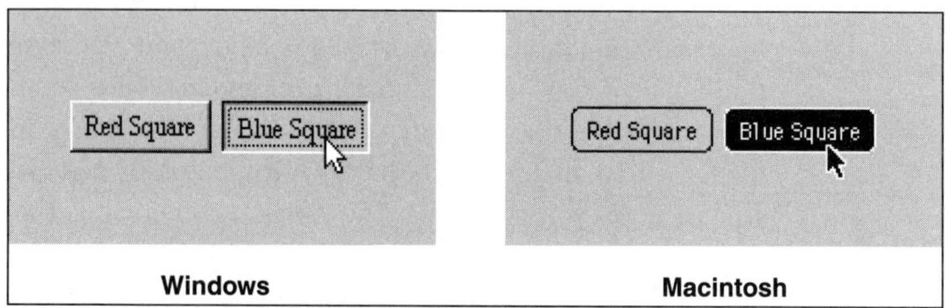

Figure 12-1

Java user interface components look different under different operating systems.

The details of how to include buttons in an applet appear later in this chapter. Here, without explanation, we'll present the Java code that would create the two buttons shown in Figure 12-1:

```
protected Button      redButton;
protected Button      blueButton;

redButton = new Button( "Red Square" );
blueButton = new Button( "Blue Square" );

add( redButton );
add( blueButton );
```

The specifics of how the preceding code works are not important here. What is important is the fact that this one set of Java applet code can invoke both Windows *and* Macintosh GUI functions to produce the two results shown in Figure 12-1. Of greater significance still is the fact that the Java programmer doesn't need to have any familiarity with the Windows-specific or Macintosh-specific code used to display the buttons. It's up to the Java runtime present in the user's Java-enabled browser to map the preceding applet code to the OS-specific code for the operating system on which the applet is currently running.

Because of their popularity, we've focused on Windows and Macintosh systems in this discussion. But as of this writing, a Java development environment exists for Solaris, and Java applets run on Java-enabled browsers that run on machines that use Sun's Solaris operating system. In the near future, Java will be ported to other operating systems as well.

AWT CLASSES

The Java Abstract Windowing Toolkit, or AWT, consists of the classes found in the `java.awt` package. While all of the Java packages are important, the fact that Sun gave the `java.awt` package its own acronym provides a hint that this package is especially significant. The fact that *every* example in this book has imported the `java.awt` package emphasizes this significance. Figure 12-2 shows the hierarchy of several of the classes discussed in this chapter.

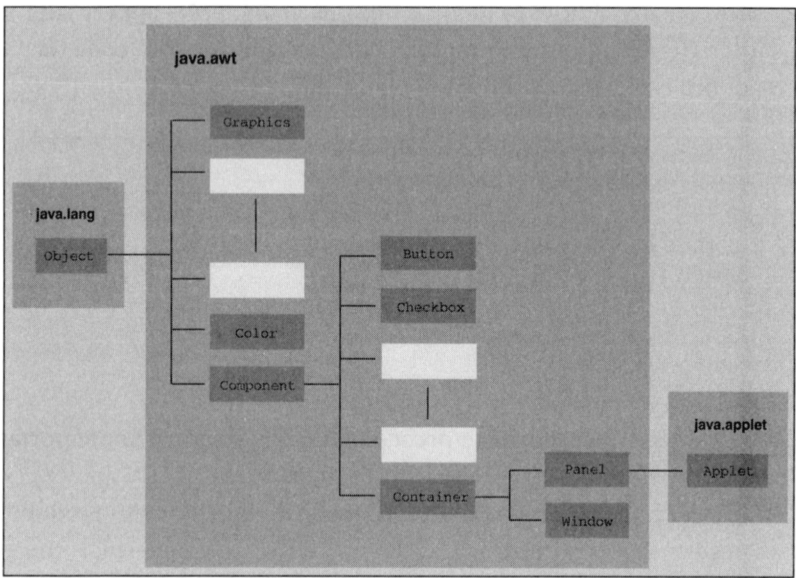

Figure 12-2
The java.awt package hierarchy of classes

THE COMPONENT CLASS

Throughout this book, many of the classes of the `java.awt` package have been highlighted. In this chapter, the focus is on the `Component` class and its many subclasses.

The `Component` class is an abstract class: It exists not as a class from which you create objects, but instead as a class that provides a common set of methods that are inherited by all of its many subclasses. As an abstract class, your applets won't define variables of the `Component` class, but will instead define variables of its subclasses. The classes used to define user interface components are such classes. Some of these classes, such as `Button` and `Checkbox`, appeared in Figure 12-2. In this chapter, you'll see examples that declare variables of type `Button` and type `Checkbox`, but you won't find any examples that declare variables of type `Component`.

THE CONTAINER CLASS

As shown in Figure 12-2, the `Container` class is one of the many subclasses of the `Component` class. Like its `Component` superclass, the `Container` class is an abstract class. Its purpose is to add its own methods to the large body of methods that it inherits from the `Component` class, and then pass all of these methods on to its own two subclasses: the `Panel` class and the `Window` class.

A container, which is itself a component, is used to hold other components—typically user interface components (also known as *UI components*), such as buttons, checkboxes, and text fields. In this chapter, you'll see examples that create `Panel` objects.

THE PANEL CLASS

If your applet contains UI components, you'll want to arrange them within the applet in a way that is visually appealing to the user. `Panel` objects help facilitate this task. A panel has properties that make it easy to specify the arrangement and spacing of UI components. We cover the `Panel` class in great detail in this chapter.

THE APPLET CLASS

By now you're quite familiar with the `Applet` class; every applet is a class that is extended from this class. The `Applet` class is a subclass of the `Panel` class, meaning that its main purpose is to hold other things. In past examples, you've seen that these "things" can be strings of text, graphical shapes, or graphic images. In this chapter, you'll see that UI components are also included in this list.

User Interface Components

Java user interface components, usually referred to as *UI components*, are objects that represent the items or elements found in most graphical user interface environments: buttons, checkboxes, text fields, pop-up menus, and so forth.

ADDING A UI COMPONENT TO AN APPLET

A UI component is always an object of one of the subclasses of the `Component` class: a button is an object of the `Button` class, a checkbox is an object of the `Checkbox` class, and so forth. To create a UI component, you create an object of one of these classes. To add the UI component to an applet, follow these three steps:

1. Declare a variable of the appropriate subclass of the `Component` class.
2. Create an instance of the UI component by using `new`.
3. Add the UI component to the applet using the `add()` method.

Here's a specific example that follows the preceding steps to add a button with the label "Done" to an applet:

```
protected Button      doneButton;

redButton = new Button( "Done" );
add( doneButton );
```

After being created, a UI component must always be added to a container. As Figure 12-2 showed, the `Applet` class is a subclass of the `Panel` class, which is a subclass of the `Container` class, which is a subclass of the `Component` class. In the `java.awt` class hierarchy, it may be an indirect path from the `Applet` class back to the `Container` class, but that is irrelevant to the fact that an applet is a type of container. Because an applet is a container, you can add any UI component to it.

Because a UI component can be added to a container other than the applet, Java doesn't automatically add a newly created UI component to the applet. You need to invoke the `add()` method defined in the `Container` class to handle that task. Invoking `add()` adds the UI component named in the parameter to the current class. That is, the preceding call to add could be rewritten as:

```
this.add( doneButton );
```

UI components are often organized within panels (objects of the `Panel` class), and then these panels are placed in an applet. In such an instance the `add()` method is used to add a UI component to the panel (which, again, is itself a container). The `add()` method is also then used to add the panel to the applet. This type of nesting of components within components is described in detail later in this chapter.

Primary UI components

On the next several pages, we'll look at how to add buttons, checkboxes, checkbox groups (also referred to as radio buttons), text fields, choice menus (also referred to as pop-up menus), and labels to an applet. Each of the many simple example applets will display one or more of these primary UI components.

When you click on one of the components in any of the example applets, the component responds by providing some indication that it has been selected. For example, clicking on a checkbox either adds a check to that box (if it was unchecked prior to the click) or clears the box (if it was already checked). Such a response is inherent to the UI component: You don't write any code to generate this reaction. Giving a component a purpose, however, does require coding effort on your part. For instance, if you click on a button labeled "Display Image," the button highlighting will change to indicate that the button is being selected, but no image will be displayed automatically. You'll need to write the Java code that does that. Later in this chapter, we'll examine how your applet becomes aware of which UI component has been selected and how it should respond.

The following discussions and examples are accompanied by figures that show UI components in a Web browser running on a Windows 95 system. As mentioned near the start of this chapter, the exact look of user interface components is determined by the OS of the machine that displays the applet. While the *look* of a UI component is dependent on the operating system, the *placement* of the same UI component in an applet (or any other container) isn't. Instead, UI component positioning is established through the use of *layout managers* in your Java code. We cover layout managers later in this chapter.

BUTTONS

A *button* is a UI component intended to bring about some immediate action when clicked.

A button is an instance of the `Button` class. To create a button, use `new` along with the `Button` class constructor that accepts a single argument—a string that becomes the title that is displayed in the button. After creating the button, call the `add()` method to add the button to the applet.

The following snippet creates and displays a button titled "Calculate Now"—a button that would presumably be used in an applet that performed some mathematical operation on some user-entered values:

```
protected Button      calculateButton;

calculateButton = new Button( "Calculate Now" );
add( calculateButton );
```

If your applet fails to display a button—or any other UI component—the reason may be that you forgot to include a call to `add()`. If you fail to add a component to an applet, the component won't be displayed.

The Buttons example that appears next is an applet that displays two buttons—one named "Red Square" and the other named "Blue Square." Including the code that creates and displays the UI components in an applet's `init()` method is a common practice—and one we'll use throughout this chapter.

```
import java.awt.*;
import java.applet.*;

public class Buttons extends Applet {

    protected Button  redButton;
    protected Button  blueButton;


    public void init() {

        redButton = new Button( "Red Square" );
        blueButton = new Button( "Blue Square" );

        add( redButton );
        add( blueButton );
    }
}
```

Figure 12-3 shows how the preceding applet looks when executed on a machine running Windows 95.

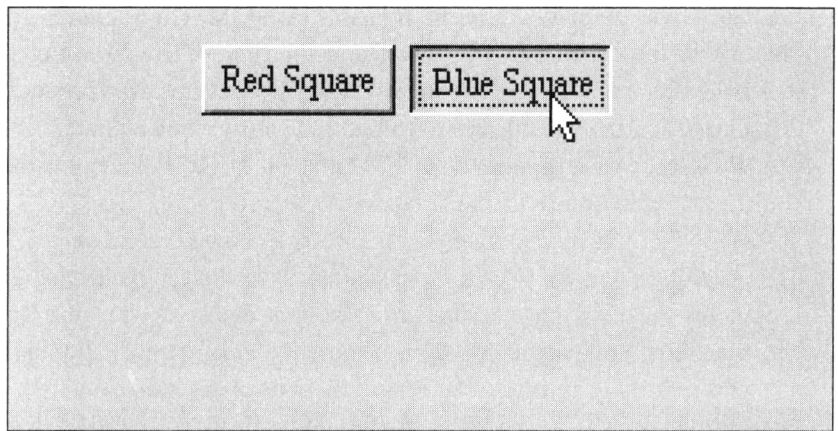

Figure 12-3
An applet that displays two buttons

Later in this chapter, we'll modify the Buttons applet so that clicking on either of the buttons actually does something! A click on the Red Square button will draw a red square in the lower part of the applet, while a click on the Blue Square button will, of course, draw a blue square.

Earlier we mentioned that UI component placement is governed by something called a layout manager. The default layout manager used by an applet places UI components in a row, starting from the left side of the applet and moving to the right. The row appears near the very top of the area of the applet. The ordering of components within this row is determined by the ordering of the calls to the `add()` method. After all UI components have been added, the layout manager centers this row within the area of the applet. This is shown for the two buttons in Figure 12-3. If the space occupied by the UI components exceeds the width of the applet, one or more of the components will be bumped to a new row. The layout manager will then center both rows within the applet.

CHECKBOXES

A *checkbox* is a UI component that is used to turn an option on or off. Each time a checkbox is clicked, it toggles to its opposite state. If the checkbox was unchecked before the user clicks on it, it becomes checked. If the checkbox was checked at the time of the mouse click on it, it becomes unchecked. Clicking on a checkbox typically produces no immediate action. Instead, it is not until a click on a button (such as a button labeled something such as "OK," "Done," or "Do It") that the value of the checkbox becomes of importance to the applet.

A checkbox is an instance of the `Checkbox` class. To create a checkbox, use `new` along with the `Checkbox` class constructor that expects a single argument—a string that becomes the title that is displayed to the right of the checkbox. Follow the creation of the checkbox with a call to `add()`.

This following snippet creates and displays a checkbox labeled "Round off result"—a checkbox that could be used in an applet to give the user the option of displaying some calculated result as either an integer or a floating-point value:

```
protected Checkbox    roundResultCheck;

roundResultCheck = new Checkbox( "Round off result" );
add( roundResultCheck );
```

Creating a checkbox in the preceding fashion results in a checkbox that appears in the applet initially unchecked. To create a checkbox that is checked, use a different `Checkbox` constructor, as follows:

```
roundOffCheck = new Checkbox( "Round off result", null, true );
```

The second parameter (`null`) is the name of a *checkbox group*. A checkbox group is set of related checkboxes (or radio buttons)—a topic described next. If the checkbox isn't a part of a group, then pass `null` as this parameter. The third parameter is a Boolean value that indicates whether the checkbox should appear checked (`true`), or unchecked (`false`).

The Checkboxes applet is an example that displays two checkboxes. In this example, the first checkbox appears unchecked, while the second appears checked. Here we've used checkboxes to let the user determine whether a red square or a blue square should be drawn in the applet.

```
import java.awt.*;
import java.applet.*;

public class Checkboxes extends Applet {

    protected Checkbox       redCheck;
    protected Checkbox       blueCheck;


    public void init() {

        redCheck = new Checkbox( "Red Square" );
        blueCheck = new Checkbox( "Blue Square", null, true );

        add( redCheck );
        add( blueCheck );
    }
}
```

Figure 12-4 demonstrates how the preceding Checkboxes applet appears in a browser.

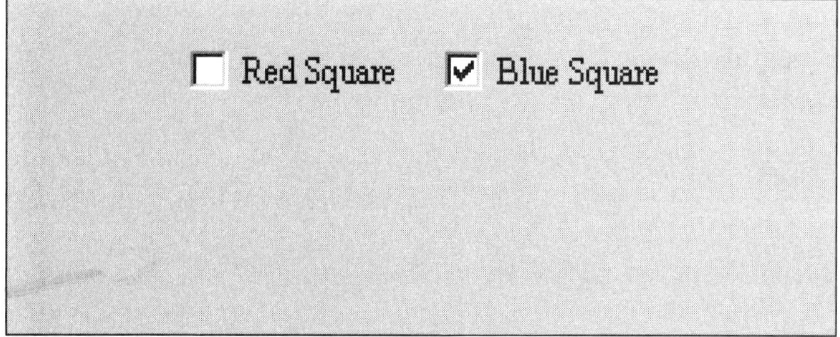

Figure 12-4
An applet that displays two checkboxes

RADIO BUTTONS

When more than one checkbox appears in an applet, often no relationship exists between them. That is, each represents a means of setting an option unrelated to the options of the other checkboxes: Clicking on one checkbox has no effect on the other checkboxes. There's a second way to implement checkboxes, and that's to group them together into a cluster where each *is* related to the others. Such a grouping of checkboxes is called a set of *radio buttons,* or a checkbox group. When the user clicks on one checkbox in a group, that checkbox always become checked—regardless of its setting prior to the mouse click. If the clicked-on checkbox was unchecked prior to the mouse click, whatever checkbox *was* on now becomes unchecked.

A group of checkboxes, or set of radio buttons, is an instance of the `CheckboxGroup` class. A `CheckboxGroup` object groups together any number of objects of the `Checkbox` class. To create a set of radio buttons, create a checkbox group using `new` along with the `X` constructor that needs no arguments. Then, create any number of checkboxes. Each checkbox that is to become a part of the checkbox group should name that checkbox group in the second parameter in the code that creates the checkbox.

The CheckGroup applet modifies and improves the prior example (the Checkboxes applet). Recall that the two checkboxes in the Checkboxes applet were unrelated to one another: Both could be checked or unchecked in any combination at the same time. Assuming the checkboxes are to be used to select a color for a single rectangle, it makes more sense to group these two checkboxes together as a pair of radio buttons. Doing so prevents both checkboxes from being on at the same time. Here's the CheckGroup applet:

```
import java.awt.*;
import java.applet.*;

public class CheckGroup extends Applet {

    protected CheckboxGroup  colorGroup;
    protected Checkbox       redCheck;
    protected Checkbox       blueCheck;


    public void init() {

        colorGroup = new CheckboxGroup();

        redCheck = new Checkbox( "Red Square", colorGroup, false );
        blueCheck = new Checkbox( "Blue Square", colorGroup, true
```

```
        );

            add( redCheck );
            add( blueCheck );
        }
    }
```

Figure 12-5 shows how the CheckGroup applet appears on a Windows 95 machine. Note that under some operating systems, when checkboxes are grouped together, the checkboxes have a look that is different from checkboxes that aren't grouped into a set of radio buttons. You can confirm this by comparing Figure 12-5 with Figure 12-4.

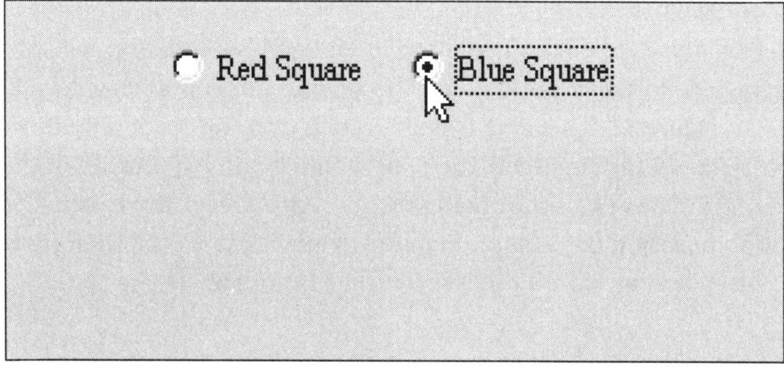

Figure 12-5
An applet that displays two radio buttons

TEXT FIELDS

A ***text field*** is a UI component that enables the user to enter a string of any length. Your applet can then retrieve this string for its own use.

A text field is an instance of the `TextField` class. To create a text field, use `new` with the `TextField` constructor that requires two arguments. The first argument is a string of text that appears in the text field when the user's browser displays the applet. The second argument is an integer value that specifies the width of the text field. This second parameter is the number of characters that will be *visible* on screen; it isn't a number that restricts the number of characters in which the user can type. As an example, consider the following snippet:

```
protected TextField   titleText;

titleText = new TextField( "Enter a title", 25 );
add( titleText );
```

This code creates a text field that can display 25 characters. If the user types in a longer string, the displayed text will scroll horizontally in the text field. When the applet reads in the text (demonstrated later in this chapter), the entire string is read—regardless of the number of characters in the string.

The TwoTextFields example that follows results in an applet that displays two text fields: They're shown in Figure 12-6. The first field appears with the string "Enter a title" in it. The second field appears with no string. In Figure 12-6, a string is being typed into the second field. To type a new string in the first field, the user would begin by clicking in the field and, with the mouse button held down, dragging over the existing text and then releasing the mouse. Typing any new text would then replace the existing string. Here's the TwoTextFields applet:

```
import java.awt.*;
import java.applet.*;

public class TwoTextFields extends Applet {

    protected TextField      titleText;
    protected TextField      artistText;


    public void init() {

        titleText = new TextField( "Enter a title", 25 );
        artistText = new TextField( 15 );

        add( titleText );
        add( artistText );
    }
}
```

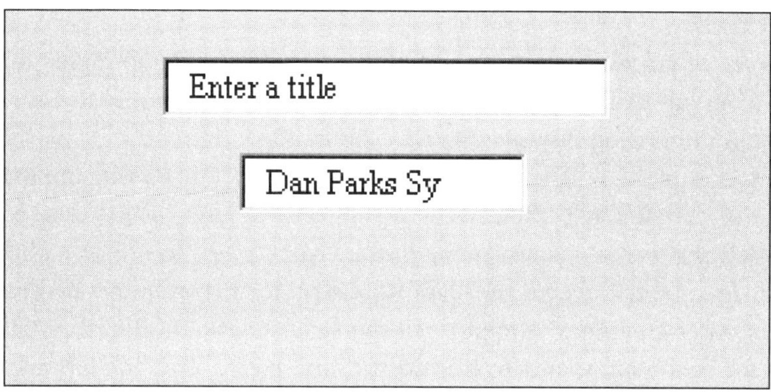

Figure 12-6
An applet that displays two text fields

Text fields are one type of control that can really benefit from *labels*—a type of component we mentioned briefly near the start of this chapter, but one we haven't covered in detail yet. Figure 12-7 shows how the TwoTextFields applet would look if we associated a label with each of the text fields. We'll modify the TwoTextFields applet a little later in this chapter so that it matches the one pictured in this figure.

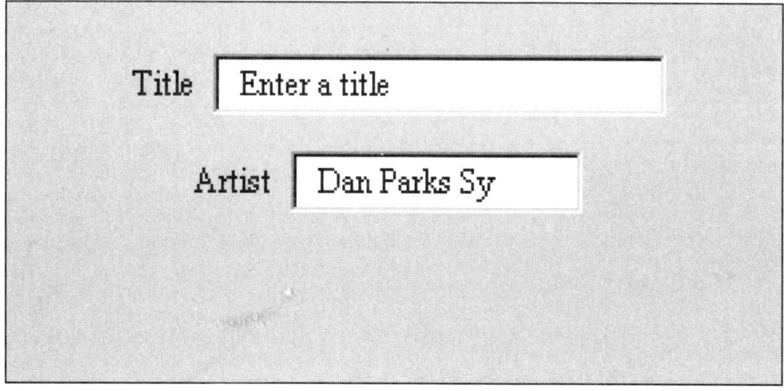

Figure 12-7
An applet that displays two text fields with two labels

CHOICE MENUS

A *choice menu* is a UI component also known as a pop-up menu. A choice menu contains any number of menu items, with only the currently selected item being displayed in the applet. Clicking on the displayed item presents the entire menu (the menu "pops up" from the applet) from which any item may be selected.

A choice menu is an instance of the `Choice` class. To create a choice menu, use `new` along with the `Choice` constructor that requires no arguments. After creating the menu, call the `addItem()` method of the `Choice` class for each item that is to be added to the menu. The one argument to the `addItem()` method is a string that represents the item to add to the menu. After all items have been added, make the usual call to the `add()` method of the `Container` class to add the entire menu to the applet.

The TwoChoiceMenus applet creates and displays two choice menus, as shown in the following code. Figure 12-8 shows the two menus that result, with the first popped up. Note that calls to `addItem()` in the applet code are prefaced with the name of the `Choice` object to which the items are being added. The `add()` method doesn't need to be prefaced in such a way because here, as in previous examples, it is adding the UI component named in its parameter to the current applet.

```
import java.awt.*;
import java.applet.*;

public class TwoChoiceMenus extends Applet {

    protected Choice  colorMenu;
    protected Choice  titleMenu;


    public void init() {

        colorMenu = new Choice();
        titleMenu = new Choice( );

        colorMenu.addItem( "Red" );
        colorMenu.addItem( "Blue" );

        titleMenu.addItem( "The Red Square" );
        titleMenu.addItem( "The Blue Square" );
```

```
            titleMenu.addItem( "My Colorful Square" );
            titleMenu.addItem( "In Need of Art Lessons!" );

            add( colorMenu );
            add( titleMenu );
        }
    }
```

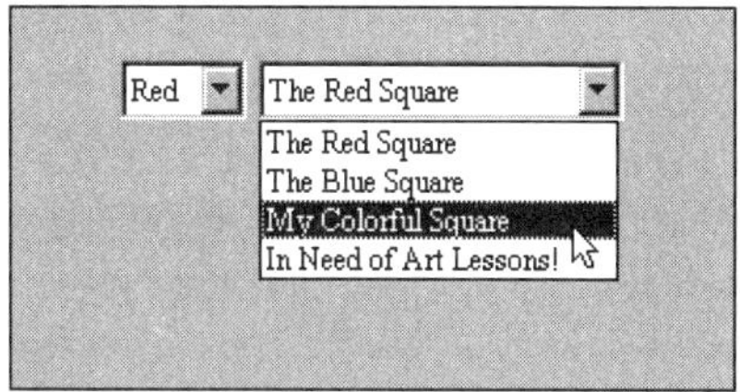

Figure 12-8
An applet that displays two pop-up, or choice, menus

LABELS

A *label* is a UI component that is string of text used to label another UI component. A label is an instance of the `Label` class. To create a label, use `new` with the `Label` class constructor that expects a single argument—a string that is to be used as the label. After creating the label, invoke `add()` to add the label to the applet.

This next snippet creates and displays a label titled "Enter a value":

```
protected Label       valueLabel;

valueLabel = new Label( "Enter a value" );
add( valueLabel );
```

A label isn't "attached" to any one component, but instead can be associated with a particular component by adding the label to the applet just before the component to be labeled is added. In the following snippet, a label is added just before a text field is added. The result is an applet that displays the string "Enter a value" to the left of a text field.

```
protected Label       valueLabel;
protected TextField   valueText;

valueLabel = new Label( "Enter a value" );
add( valueLabel );
valueText = new TextField( 8 );
add( valueText );
```

The TwoLabels applet that follows is a modification of this chapter's TwoTextFields applet. In TwoLabels, a label has been created and added prior to the addition of each text field. Figure 12-9 illustrates the results of executing TwoLabels.

```
import java.awt.*;
import java.applet.*;

public class TwoLabels extends Applet {

    protected TextField      titleText;
    protected TextField      artistText;
    protected Label          titleLabel;
    protected Label          artistLabel;


    public void init() {

        titleText = new TextField( "Enter a title", 25 );
        artistText = new TextField( 15 );

        titleLabel = new Label( "Title" );
        artistLabel = new Label( "Artist" );

        add( titleLabel );
        add( titleText );
        add( artistLabel );
        add( artistText );
    }
}
```

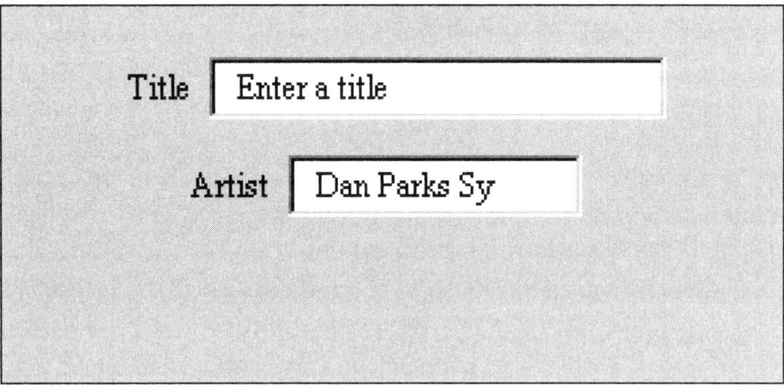

Figure 12-9
An applet that displays two text fields and two labels

Note that if the order of the calls to `add()` is changed, the labels won't appear in the desired places within the applet. For example, if the two text fields are added to the applet before the labels are added, the result would be as pictured in Figure 12-10.

```
add( titleText );
add( artistText );
add( titleLabel );
add( artistLabel );
```

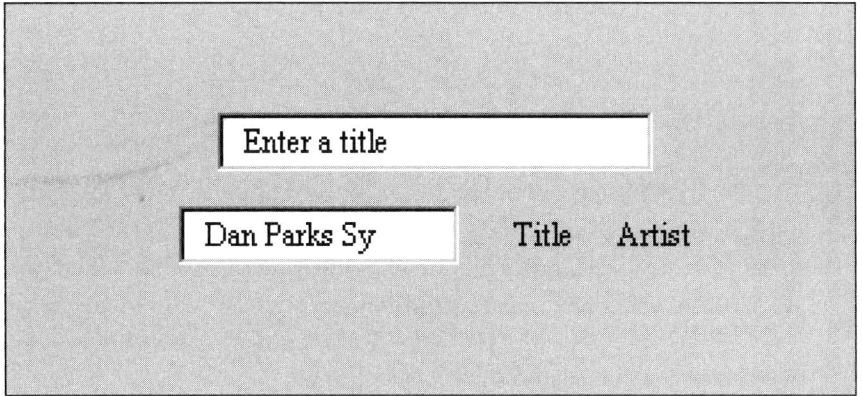

Figure 12-10
An applet that displays its text fields and labels in an incorrect order

Organizing Components

User interface components are always added to a container. As mentioned, an applet is itself a container, so it's acceptable to add UI components directly to an applet—as we've done in the examples up to this point.

When you add components to an applet, the only control you have of the placement of the components lies in the order in which you add the components using the `add()` method. While having this input into component ordering is of some help, this limited control over component organization is usually unacceptable. Adding components to an applet in this manner places all of the components in a row. (If the space occupied by the components exceeds the width of the applet area, the components may line up on additional rows.)

Typically, when you create an applet, you'll have a more logical arrangement of components in mind: A set of radio buttons may be displayed vertically along an edge of the applet; all of the buttons that perform certain actions may be located horizontally near the bottom of the applet, and so forth. Through the use of panels and layout managers, you can gain the control of component placement necessary to implement these kinds of displays.

As in the preceding examples, clicking on a UI component in one of the examples in this section won't make it perform any particular action. The purpose of the discussions that follow is to demonstrate how to organize the components about which you learned in the preceding section. Giving components real purpose is discussed later in this chapter.

PANELS

To organize UI components into groups, your applet should make use of *panels*—objects of the `Panel` class. By creating panels and then nesting these panels in the larger applet panel (an applet is itself a panel), you create separate areas where you can designate that UI components be placed.

ADDING MULTIPLE UI COMPONENTS WITHOUT PANELS

Before creating panels and adding them to an applet, we'll take a look at an applet that doesn't use any panels other than the applet itself. The

ButtonCheckbox applet includes more than one type of UI component per applet. This example applet provides a reference base from which we'll implement panels in subsequent examples.

Consider an applet consisting of five UI components. Two of the UI components are buttons named "Previous" and "Next," while the remaining three UI components are radio buttons with the names "Slow," "Medium," and "Fast." While our example applet won't actually provide functionality for these components, we'll assume that the buttons can be used to "flip" through a series of images. We'll further assume that a click of one of the buttons displays an image for a short time and that the image then fades until it disappears. In such an applet the three radio buttons could enable the user to control the speed of image-fading.

Here is the code for ButtonCheckbox:

```
import java.awt.*;
import java.applet.*;

public class ButtonCheckbox extends Applet {

    protected Button          previousButton;
    protected Button          nextButton;
    protected CheckboxGroup   speedGroup;
    protected Checkbox        slowCheck;
    protected Checkbox        mediumCheck;
    protected Checkbox        fastCheck;


    public void init() {

        previousButton = new Button( "Previous" );
        nextButton = new Button( "Next" );
        add( previousButton );
        add( nextButton );

        speedGroup = new CheckboxGroup();
        slowCheck = new Checkbox( "Slow", speedGroup, false );
        mediumCheck = new Checkbox( "Medium", speedGroup, true );
        fastCheck = new Checkbox( "Fast", speedGroup, false );
        add( slowCheck );
        add( mediumCheck );
        add( fastCheck );
    }
}
```

If these five components are added in the order shown in the ButtonCheckbox listing, the resulting applet looks like the one pictured in Figure 12-11.

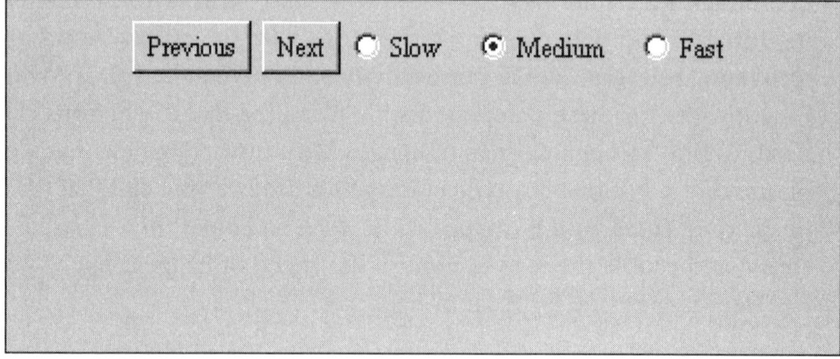

Figure 12-11
An applet that displays five user interface components

ARRANGING COMPONENTS BY CHANGING APPLET SIZE

Next, consider that we'd like to have the five UI components in the ButtonCheckbox applet displayed in two rows—as shown in Figure 12-12.

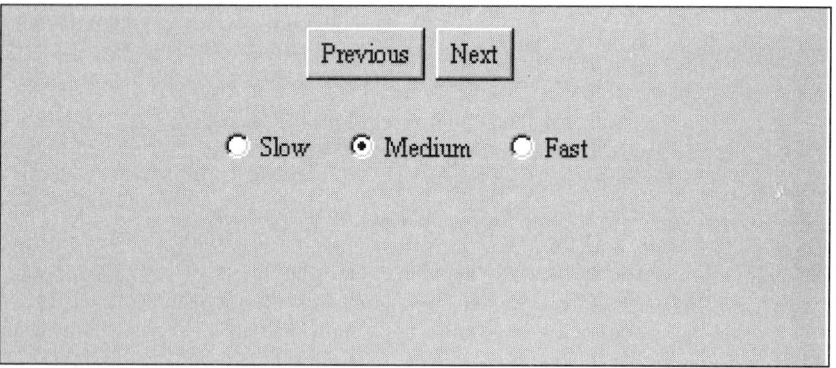

Figure 12-12
An applet that displays its user interface components in two rows

If we want to try to force the components into two rows, we can change the size of the applet as specified in the `<applet>` tag of the HTML file used to display the applet. By decreasing the applet's size, we can force one or more components to wrap to a second row—as shown in Figure 12-13.

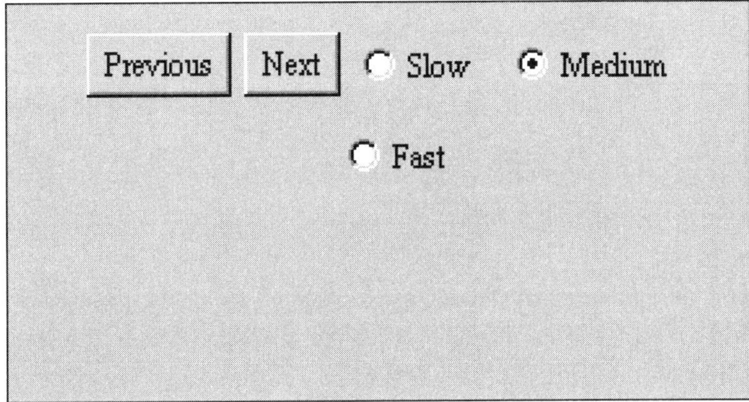

Figure 12-13
An applet that has one of its user interface components wrapped to a second line

In this particular example, we can't get the two buttons to stay on top and have the three radio buttons wrap; if we make the applet small enough to force all three radio buttons to a new row, the applet becomes so small that a new, third row is created. Figure 12-14 illustrates.

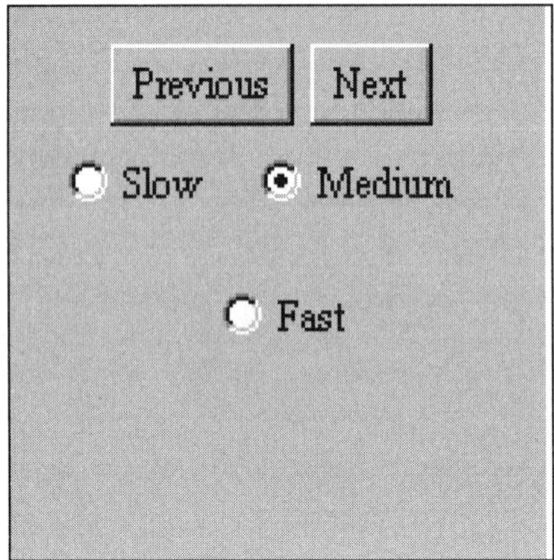

Figure 12-14
An applet that has one of its user interface components wrapped to a third line

ARRANGING COMPONENTS USING PANELS

The solution to our dilemma is to create two panels and nest them within the applet panel. Panels have no outline or shading that makes them visible. Instead, they're invisible areas that serve as boundaries for the Java runtime to use in the placement of components. For our particular example, we'd like two panels: one to hold the buttons, another to hold the radio buttons. Figure 12-15 uses an empty applet and lines to make it very apparent where we'd like the panels to appear. This figure includes a border around the entire applet. While we'll be concentrating on the two panels represented by `Panel` objects, the applet includes a third panel—the applet itself.

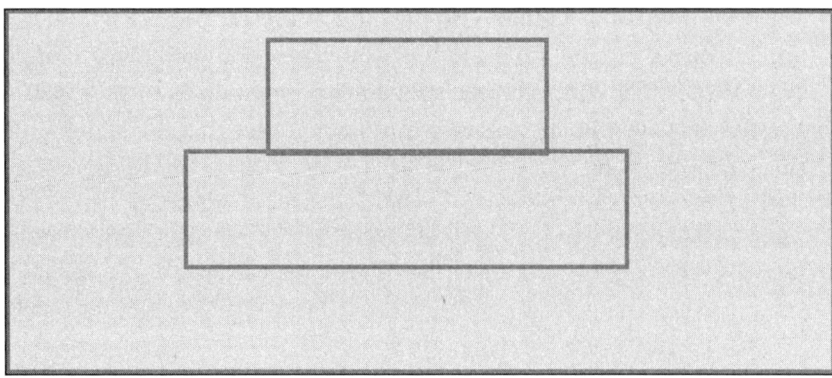

Figure 12-15
Panels define invisible areas that each serve to hold components.

After creating the two panels, we'll add the five UI components to the applet. As we add the components, we'll specify the panel to which each should be added. The resulting applet should look like the one pictured in Figure 12-16.

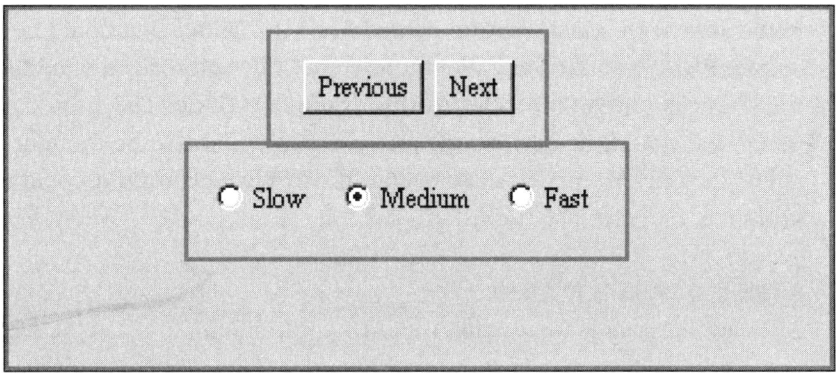

Figure 12-16
The use of panels helps better organize the user interface components of an applet.

CREATING A PANEL AND ADDING IT TO AN APPLET

To create a panel, declare a variable of the `Panel` class. Then use `new` along with the `Panel` constructor, which requires no parameters. To associate the panel with the applet (that is, to nest the new panel object within the applet panel), use the add() method as you've done with other component types. In the following snippet, we add two new panels to an applet—one panel that holds the applet's two buttons, another that holds the applet's three radio buttons.

```
protected Panel       buttonPanel;
protected Panel       checkboxPanel;

buttonPanel = new Panel();
checkboxPanel = new Panel();
add( buttonPanel );
add( checkboxPanel );
```

Here we state that an applet is a panel. Earlier we said that an applet is a type of container. We also said an applet was a type of component. Can applets really be all of these things? Refer to Figure 12-2 to see where the Applet class fits into the java.awt hierarchy, and you'll see that an applet can in fact be all of these things. If this sounds a bit confusing, keep in mind that all sorts of things can be organized so that they fall into several categories. For instance, consider the organization of vehicles. We could start with a major group named Vehicles. Under that could be two subgroups—Motorized and Nonmotorized. Under Motorized would fall Cars, Trucks, and Motorcycles. In this example, a Harley-Davidson could be considered in the Motorcycle group. But it could also be thought of as falling into the Motorized class or into the Vehicle class. Or it could be considered all of these things.

ADDING UI COMPONENTS TO A PANEL

After adding panels to an applet, add UI components to the panels. In the past, we used the add() method without specifying a panel, which told Java to add the component to the applet panel. Here's how we would have added the Previous button:

```
protected Button      previousButton;

previousButton = new Button( "Previous" );
add( previousButton );
```

To instead add this button to a specific panel, invoke the add() method using one of the panel objects. The preceding code would then be rewritten as follows:

```
protected Button      previousButton;

previousButton = new Button( "Previous" );
buttonPanel.add( previousButton );
```

The MutliplePanels applet that follows uses the code from the previous applet example—ButtonCheckbox—and modifies it to place the two buttons in one panel and the three radio buttons in a second panel. The results appear in Figure 12-17. To provide emphasis as to where the panels are located in the applet, we've added a paint() method to the applet. This method does nothing more than change the background color of the applet. Doing so affects the applet, but it doesn't affect the background of either of the Panel objects.

```
import java.awt.*;
import java.applet.*;

public class MultiplePanels extends Applet {

    protected Button          previousButton;
    protected Button          nextButton;
    protected CheckboxGroup   speedGroup;
    protected Checkbox        slowCheck;
    protected Checkbox        mediumCheck;
    protected Checkbox        fastCheck;
    protected Panel           buttonPanel;
    protected Panel           checkboxPanel;

    public void init() {

        buttonPanel = new Panel();
        checkboxPanel = new Panel();
        add( buttonPanel );
        add( checkboxPanel );

        previousButton = new Button( "Previous" );
        nextButton = new Button( "Next" );
        buttonPanel.add( previousButton );
        buttonPanel.add( nextButton );
```

```
        speedGroup = new CheckboxGroup();
        slowCheck = new Checkbox( "Slow", speedGroup, false );
        mediumCheck = new Checkbox( "Medium", speedGroup, true );
        fastCheck = new Checkbox( "Fast", speedGroup, false );
        checkboxPanel.add( slowCheck );
        checkboxPanel.add( mediumCheck );
        checkboxPanel.add( fastCheck );
    }


    public void paint( Graphics g ) {

        setBackground( Color.red );
    }

}
```

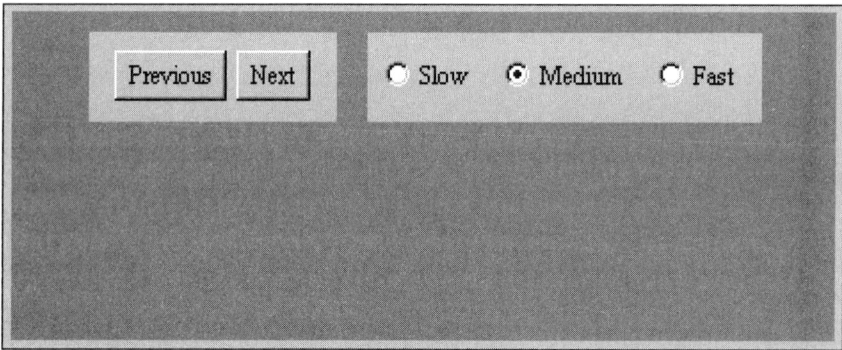

Figure 12-17
The results of running the MultiplePanels applet

From Figure 12-17, it would appear that our use of panels was a failure: While the UI components have been placed in two panels, they still all appear in a single row in the applet. However, if we make the applet smaller using the `<applet>` tag, we get the results shown in Figure 12-18. When the applet is made small enough that the Fast radio button needs to wrap, all three of the radio buttons wrap together. This is because the entire panel is wrapping.

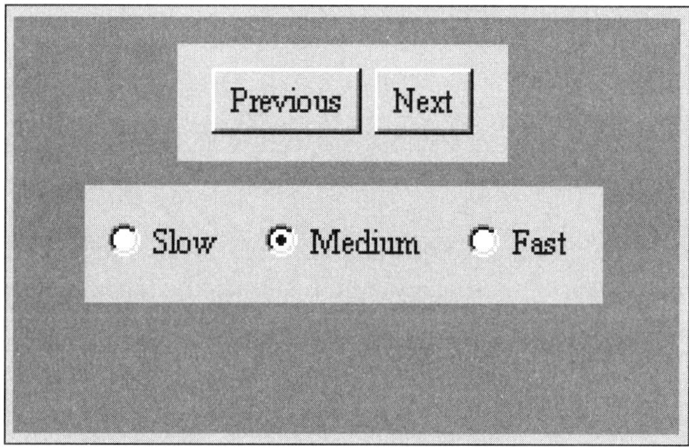

Figure 12-18

The results of running the MultiplePanels applet in a smaller applet area

Later in this chapter, you'll see how to further refine component arrangements by using layout managers to control the placement of UI components within a panel.

As is the case when adding other component types (such as the buttons or radio buttons), it is the order in which the panels are added to the applet that determines the order in which the panels appear in the applet. We first added the panel that is to hold the buttons, so any UI components added to that panel will appear first.

INSETS

You normally place panels adjacent to one another, as shown in Figure 12-18, with only a small gap between them. If the components in one panel end up too close to components in a different panel, you'll want to use *insets* to separate the panels from one another.

DEFINING THE INSETS OF A COMPONENT

The `Insets` class is a `java.awt` class that defines the top, left, bottom, and right margins to be applied to an object of a class extended from the `Container` class. The `Container` class defines an `insets()` method that your applet can override. The purpose of `insets()` is to create an `Insets` object that gets returned to the Java runtime, as follows:

```
public Insets insets() {

    // create a new Insets object and return it to Java
}
```

The following is an example definition of the `insets()` method. This version of `insets()` establishes insets of 20 pixels on the top and bottom of the object and insets of 30 pixels on the left and right of the object. We've added a comment to the single line that makes up the body of `insets()` to point out the order of the parameters in the `Insets` constructor.

```
public Insets insets() {

    return new Insets( 20, 30, 20, 30 );  // T, L, B, R
}
```

Because the `insets()` method is defined in the `Container` class, any class that is extended from the `Container` class can override the `insets()` method. Figure 12-19 is a trimmed-down version of the `java.awt` hierarchy presented back in Figure 12-2, and serves as a reminder that any class that extends either the `Panel` or the `Applet` classes has access to the methods (such as `insets()`) defined in the `Container` class.

Repositioning UI components with insets

The ButtonCheckbox example earlier in this chapter created an applet that displayed two buttons and three radio buttons. It used no panels other than the applet itself. The resulting applet displayed its five UI components in a row centered along the top of the area defined by the `<applet>` tag in the HTML file used to display the applet. If the applet area is made larger (as defined in the `<applet>` tag), the five components remain centered horizontally and still appear right near the top of the applet area. Figure 12-20 illustrates.

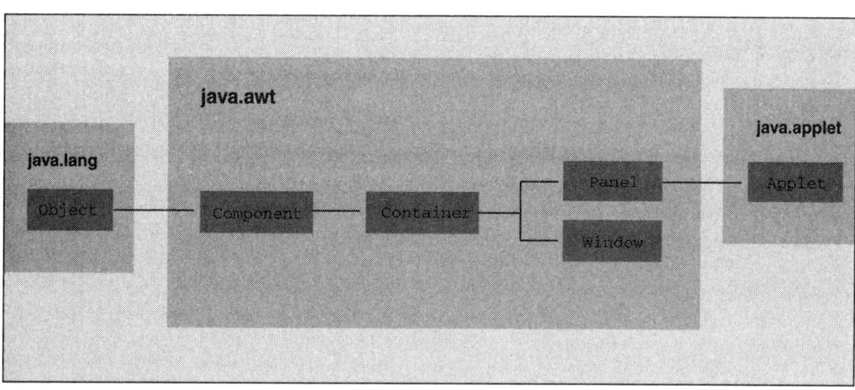

Figure 12-19
The Panel and Applet classes inherit the methods of the Container class.

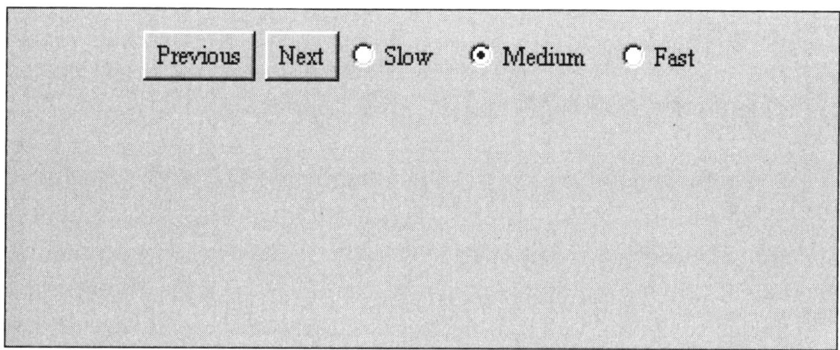

Figure 12-20
The ButtonCheckbox applet displays five UI components in the top-center of the applet's area.

If an `insets()` method is added to the same code used in the ButtonCheckbox applet, the five UI components can be repositioned within the applet area. For example, the following `insets()` method provides a 70-pixel inset along the top of the applet area and a 100-pixel inset along the left of the applet area. Figure 12-21 shows the look of the applet when it defines this `insets()` method.

```
public Insets insets() {

    return new Insets( 70, 100, 0, 0 );  // T, L, B, R
}
```

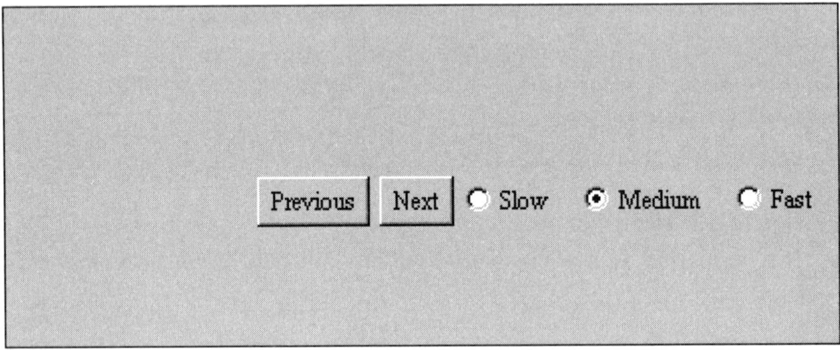

Figure 12-21
Insets applied to the ButtonCheckbox applet result in the five UI components being displayed in a different part of the applet's area.

Normally, Java centers the UI components of an applet horizontally within the area of the applet. This still holds true with insets, but only *after* the insets have been applied. In the preceding example, the UI components are moved 70 pixels down from the top of the applet and 100 pixels over from the left of the applet, and *then* the components are centered in the remaining area of the applet.

Like the `init()` method, if an `insets()` method is present in an applet's class definition, then the Java runtime automatically executes the method when the applet is executed. The following example defines both an `init()` and `insets()` method:

```
import java.awt.*;
import java.applet.*;

public class AppletInsets extends Applet {

    protected Button         previousButton;
    protected Button         nextButton;
    protected CheckboxGroup  speedGroup;
    protected Checkbox       slowCheck;
```

```
        protected Checkbox        mediumCheck;
        protected Checkbox        fastCheck;


        public void init() {

            previousButton = new Button( "Previous" );
            nextButton = new Button( "Next" );
            add( previousButton );
            add( nextButton );

            speedGroup = new CheckboxGroup();
            slowCheck = new Checkbox( "Slow", speedGroup, false );
            mediumCheck = new Checkbox( "Medium", speedGroup, true );
            fastCheck = new Checkbox( "Fast", speedGroup, false );
            add( slowCheck );
            add( mediumCheck );
            add( fastCheck );
        }


        public Insets insets() {

            return new Insets( 70, 100, 0, 0 );  // T, L, B, R
        }
    }
```

The preceding listing is identical to this chapter's ButtonCheckbox listing—except for the addition of the `insets()` method.

Using Insets with Panels

The preceding example demonstrated how you can use insets to vary the location of UI components in an applet. A more practical use of insets is to organize UI components within individual panels, with these panels then placed within an applet. We'll do that in this section's PanelClasses example applet.

When the PanelClasses applet executes, your browser (or applet viewer) displays an applet like the one pictured in Figure 12-22. As you can infer from the shading in the figure, the PanelClasses applet uses a different background color for each of the applet's two panels and for the applet itself. In the figure, you see that the UI components appear farther down from the top of the applet than they did in the MultiplePanels example (see Figure 12-17). You should also notice that the distance between the buttons and the radio buttons has increased compared to the MultiplePanels example. Insets are the reason for both of these changes in UI component spacing.

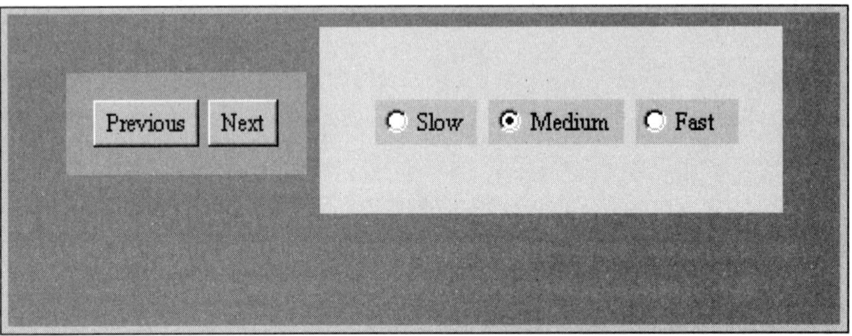

Figure 12-22
The results of running the PanelClasses applet

If the values in the `<applet>` tag are adjusted to reduce the applet's size, the panel holding the radio buttons will wrap. This wrapping is shown in Figure 12-23. Again, because of insets, the spacing between components is greater than it was in the similar applet that didn't use insets (compare Figure 12-23 with Figure 12-18).

All of the example applets in this book make use of several Java classes such as the `Applet` class, the `Graphics` class, and so forth. All of the examples to this point, however, have only *defined* a single class—the class that becomes the applet itself (and is a class extended from the `Applet` class). The example described next is this book's first applet that defines more than a single class.

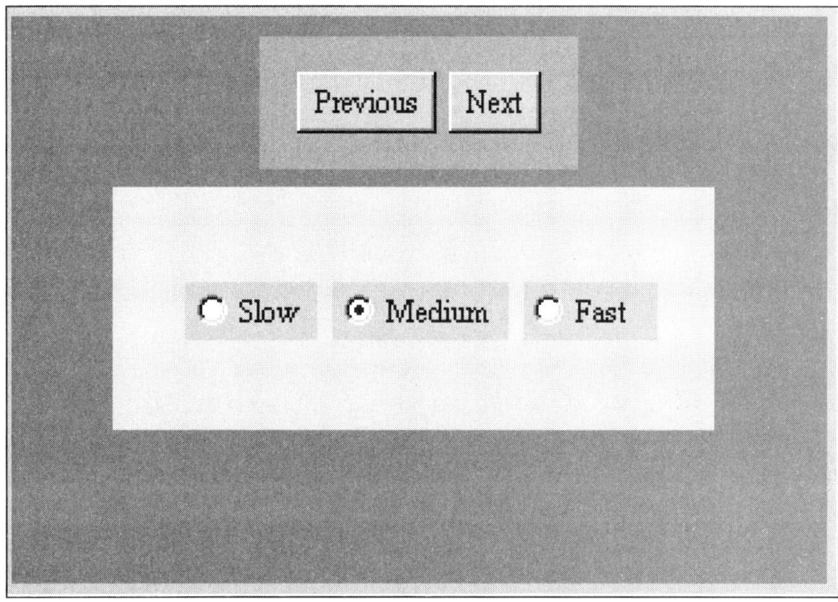

Figure 12-23
The results of running the PanelClasses applet in a smaller applet area

A TEMPLATE FOR DEFINING PANEL CLASSES

The `insets()` method creates an `Insets` object that holds four inset values. The Java runtime applies these inset values to one object—the object whose class defines the `insets()` method. In the AppletInsets example, it was the `Applet` class that included an `insets()` method, so the insets were applied to the applet itself. To create insets for individual panels, you'll make each panel its own class. If your panel classes each extend the `Panel` class, then each of your panel classes inherits the `insets()` method (which the `Panel` class inherits from the `Container` class).

The following snippet can be considered a template for writing an applet that defines classes that are used to create panels that will be nested within an applet. After this listing, we'll examine a specific example that makes use of this template.

```
public class TheApplet extends Applet {

    // declare an instance variable for each panel
```

```
    // define an init() method to create the new panels
    // by using new, as in:
    //     aPanel = new OneTypeOfPanel();

    // add the newly created  panel here
}


public class OneTypeOfPanel extends Panel {

    // define an instance variable for each UI component
    // that will be included in this type of panel

    // define a constructor that creates each UI component
    // and adds each to a panel

    // define an insets() method to define insets for this panel
}


public class AnotherTypeOfPanel extends Panel {

    // define an instance variable for each UI component
    // that will be included in this type of panel

    // define a constructor that creates each UI component
    // and adds each to a panel

    // define an insets() method to define insets for this panel
}
```

When you create a class other than the `Applet` class, strive to make it generic: Doing so makes such classes easy to reuse in other applets that you write. For this example, we'll create a panel class that holds the Previous and Next buttons. This class won't define any specific actions for the buttons to take; it will simply define a panel that holds the buttons. That makes this class potentially useful in other applets as well. For example, one applet might use this class to add two buttons that enable a user to flip through a number of images to be displayed in one area of the applet, while another applet could use the same class to add two buttons that enable a user to cycle through a number of sounds.

THE SOURCE CODE LISTING FOR THE PANELCLASSES APPLET

The PanelClasses applet follows the previously mentioned template for writing an applet that defines classes that are to be used to include panels in an applet. The complete source code listing for the PanelClasses applet is as follows:

```
import java.awt.*;
import java.applet.*;

public class PanelClasses extends Applet {

    protected PageTurnPanel   buttonPanel;
    protected SpeedPanel      checkboxPanel;

    public void init() {

        buttonPanel = new PageTurnPanel();
        checkboxPanel = new SpeedPanel();
        add( checkboxPanel );
        add( buttonPanel );
    }

    public void paint( Graphics g ) {

        setBackground( Color.red );
        buttonPanel.setBackground( Color.blue );
        checkboxPanel.setBackground( Color.green );
    }
}


public class PageTurnPanel extends Panel {

    protected Button  previousButton;
    protected Button  nextButton;

    PageTurnPanel() {

        previousButton = new Button( "Previous" );
        nextButton = new Button( "Next" );
        add( previousButton );
        add( nextButton );
    }

    public Insets insets() {
```

```
            return new Insets( 10, 10, 10, 10 );  // T, L, B, R
        }
    }


    public class SpeedPanel extends Panel {

        protected CheckboxGroup  speedGroup;
        protected Checkbox       slowCheck;
        protected Checkbox       mediumCheck;
        protected Checkbox       fastCheck;

        SpeedPanel() {

            speedGroup = new CheckboxGroup();
            slowCheck = new Checkbox( "Slow", speedGroup, false );
            mediumCheck = new Checkbox( "Medium", speedGroup, true );
            fastCheck = new Checkbox( "Fast", speedGroup, false );
            add( slowCheck );
            add( mediumCheck );
            add( fastCheck );
        }

        public Insets insets() {

            return new Insets( 30, 30, 30, 30 );  // T, L, B, R
        }
    }
```

After compiling a Java source code file that defines multiple classes (as the `PanelClasses` example does), you'll find a `.class` file for each class defined in the source file. In the preceding example, you'll find files named `PanelClasses.class`, `PageTurnPanel.class`, and `SpeedPanel.class` on your hard drive. The `.class` file that has the name of the `Applet` class (such as `PanelClasses.class` in our example) is the bytecode file for the applet file. As always, you'll upload this file to the server that holds your Web page files. Additionally, however, you'll need to upload the other `.class` files to the same directory on your Web server.

Next, we'll take a look at the workings of this listing.

A WALK-THROUGH OF THE PANELCLASSES SOURCE CODE

The `PanelClasses` class of the PanelClasses applet declares two instance variables—one for each panel that is placed in the applet, as follows:

```
protected PageTurnPanel      buttonPanel;
protected SpeedPanel         checkboxPanel;
```

This same class defines two methods: `init()` and `paint()`. The ~~init()~~ method creates two panels. To do this, use `new` along with the constructor appropriate for the type of panel being created, as follows:

```
public void init() {

    buttonPanel = new PageTurnPanel();
    checkboxPanel = new SpeedPanel();
    add( checkboxPanel );
    add( buttonPanel );
}
```

As we've done in previous examples in this chapter, the `paint()` method is used here simply for the purpose of highlighting the area occupied by a panel or applet. By setting the background color of each panel (including the applet) to a different color, the area that each panel occupies becomes obvious when you execute the applet. Note that when `setBackground()` is called without naming a panel, the current panel is the `target`. In the following snippet, the `setBackground()` call that doesn't name a panel is made from within the PanelClasses applet, so the applet is the `target`. The other two calls to `setBackground()` are prefaced with a panel variable and the dot, so the changes to the background colors that these calls make will apply to these particular panels rather than to the applet, as follows:

```
public void paint( Graphics g ) {

    setBackground( Color.red );
    buttonPanel.setBackground( Color.blue );
    checkboxPanel.setBackground( Color.green );
}
```

This applet is our first that makes use of a class of our own creation. The `PageTurnPanel` class is used as a template for creating panel objects that each contain two buttons—one labeled "Previous," the other labeled "Next." Assuming the two buttons in the panel object that results from this class will be used to "turn" pages (to use the same area alternately to display one image and then another), *PageTurnPanel* seems an appropriate name for our new class. The class begins by declaring two instance variables—one for each of the two buttons the panel holds, as follows:

```
protected Button      previousButton;
protected Button      nextButton;
```

While it's unlikely that any one applet would create more than one panel of this class type, the class is still reusable in the sense that *other* applets might find the class of use. A different applet could be given access to `PageTurnPanel` in either of two ways. First, we could copy the class definition and paste it into the `.java` file of the applet that was to create a `PageTurnPanel` object. Alternately, we could create a package (as described in Chapter 8) that included the `PageTurnPanel` class and then have an applet import that package.

Next, the class defines a constructor method that creates the two buttons and adds them to a panel, as follows:

```
PageTurnPanel() {

    previousButton = new Button( "Previous" );
    nextButton = new Button( "Next" );
    add( previousButton );
    add( nextButton );
}
```

The preceding is the method that gets executed when the PanelClasses applet creates a new `PageTurnPanel` panel. The following line of code is from the `init()` method of the `PanelClasses` class:

```
buttonPanel = new PageTurnPanel();
```

The PageTurnPanel class ends by defining an insets() method, as follows:

```
    public Insets insets() {

        return new Insets( 10, 10, 10, 10 );  // T, L, B, R
    }
}
```

Recall that panels are a type of container. The applet is a type of panel (the Applet class extends the Panel class), so the applet (specifically, the PanelClasses class) is also a container. The insets() method is defined in the Container class, so both the PanelClasses class and the PageTurnPanel class inherit this method. This means that each of these two classes can (and do) define their own version of the insets() method.

The class that defines the second type of panel—the SpeedPanel class—follows an approach similar to the one used to define the PageTurnPanel class: An instance variable is declared for each UI component, a constructor method is defined that creates and adds the UI components to the panel, and an insets() method is defined that establishes the empty space surrounding the panel. Here's the code for the SpeedPanel class:

```
public class SpeedPanel extends Panel {

    protected CheckboxGroup   speedGroup;
    protected Checkbox        slowCheck;
    protected Checkbox        mediumCheck;
    protected Checkbox        fastCheck;

    SpeedPanel() {

        speedGroup = new CheckboxGroup();
        slowCheck = new Checkbox( "Slow", speedGroup, false );
        mediumCheck = new Checkbox( "Medium", speedGroup, true );
        fastCheck = new Checkbox( "Fast", speedGroup, false );
        add( slowCheck );
        add( mediumCheck );
        add( fastCheck );
    }

    public Insets insets() {

        return new Insets( 30, 30, 30, 30 );  // T, L, B, R
    }
}
```

MAKING PANEL CLASSES MORE GENERIC

Earlier we stated that it is advantageous to make your class definitions as generic as possible to increase the potential for reuse in other applets. The PanelClasses applet didn't do an adequate job of defining generic classes. This was intentional: We wanted to make it very obvious just what the classes of the `PanelClasses` example were to accomplish. Now that you've had some exposure to applet-defined classes, we can clean things up a little by redesigning the PanelClasses applet.

The purpose of the `PageTurnPanel` class is to add two buttons and insets to a panel. In the `PanelClasses` example, we hard-coded the names of the two buttons within the `PageTurnPanel` class. There's really no need to do this. We can instead pass the names of the buttons to the class via the class constructor method. To break from the idea that the class can only be used to create buttons that have the purpose of flipping pages, we'll also rename the class and its two instance variables. Here's the new version of the `PageTurnPanel` class, now given the more generic name `TwoButtonPanel`:

```
class TwoButtonPanel extends Panel {

    protected Button  firstButton;
    protected Button  secondButton;

    TwoButtonPanel( String name1, String name2 ) {

        firstButton = new Button( name1 );
        secondButton = new Button( name2 );
        add( firstButton );
        add( secondButton );
    }

    public Insets insets() {

        return new Insets( 10, 10, 10, 10 );  // T, L, B, R
    }
}
```

Figure 12-24 shows the old `PageTurnPanel` class and the new `TwoButtonPanel` class side by side so you can compare them. Figure 12-24 also shows how an object of each class type would be created.

Old version

```
class PageTurnPanel extends Panel {

   protected Button   previousButton;
   protected Button   nextButton;

   PageTurnPanel() {

      previousButton = new Button("Previous");
      nextButton = new Button("Next");
      add( previousButton );
      add( nextButton );
   }

   public Insets insets() {

      return new Insets( 10, 10, 10, 10 );
   }
}
```

```
protected PageTurnPanel  buttonPanel;

buttonPanel = new PageTurnPanel();
```

New version

```
class TwoButtonPanel extends Panel {

   protected Button   firstButton;
   protected Button   secondButton;

   TwoButtonPanel( String name1, String name2 ) {

      firstButton = new Button( name1 );
      secondButton = new Button( name2 );
      add( firstButton );
      add( secondButton );
   }

   public Insets insets() {

      return new Insets( 10, 10, 10, 10 );
   }
}
```

```
protected TwoButtonPanel   buttonPanel;

buttonPanel = new TwoButtonPanel("Previous", "Next");
```

Figure 12-24

A comparison of the PageTurnPanel class and a modified version of this class—the TwoButtonPanel class

The same technique used to alter the `PageTurnPanel` class can be used to modify the `SpeedPanel` class. The following listing is the redesigned PanelClasses applet, which is now named BetterPanelClasses.

```
import java.awt.*;
import java.applet.*;

public class BetterPanelClasses extends Applet {

    protected TwoButtonPanel  buttonPanel;
    protected ThreeRadioPanel checkboxPanel;

    public void init() {

        buttonPanel = new TwoButtonPanel( "Previous", "Next" );
        checkboxPanel = new ThreeRadioPanel( "Slow", "Medium",
    "Fast");
        add( buttonPanel );
        add( checkboxPanel );
    }


    public void paint( Graphics g ) {
```

```
        setBackground( Color.red );
        buttonPanel.setBackground( Color.blue );
        checkboxPanel.setBackground( Color.green );
    }
}


class TwoButtonPanel extends Panel {

    protected Button  firstButton;
    protected Button  secondButton;

    TwoButtonPanel( String name1, String name2 ) {

        firstButton = new Button( name1 );
        secondButton = new Button( name2 );
        add( firstButton );
        add( secondButton );
    }


    public Insets insets() {

        return new Insets( 10, 10, 10, 10 );  // T, L, B, R
    }
}


class ThreeRadioPanel extends Panel {

    protected CheckboxGroup   theGroup;
    protected Checkbox        firstCheck;
    protected Checkbox        secondCheck;
    protected Checkbox        thirdCheck;

    ThreeRadioPanel( String name1, String name2, String name3 ) {

        theGroup = new CheckboxGroup();
        firstCheck = new Checkbox( name1, theGroup, false );
        secondCheck = new Checkbox( name2, theGroup, true );
        thirdCheck = new Checkbox( name3, theGroup, false );
        add( firstCheck );
        add( secondCheck );
        add( thirdCheck );
    }
```

```
    public Insets insets() {

        return new Insets( 30, 30, 30, 30 );  // T, L, B, R
    }
}
```

A close look at the preceding BetterPanelClasses applet listing should confirm that keeping the applet-defined classes as generic as possible greatly increases the potential for reuse in other applets.

LAYOUT MANAGERS

Through the use of panels, your applet can assemble selected UI components together; the MultiplePanels applet is an example of this. By applying insets to panels, you can add a buffer, or margin, that adjusts the spacing between panels and thus between groups of UI components. The PanelClasses applet demonstrated this technique. By applying *layout managers* to panels, you can alter the positioning of UI components within each panel. A layout manager is an object that specifies component placement within a panel.

When you add components to a panel, the components appear one after another in a row, as you know. If you'd like the components to be laid out in a different fashion *within* a single panel, you can instruct the Java runtime to do so by specifying a layout manager for the panel.

Consider the examples we've been using—the applets that include five UI components. In its most recent version, this applet has two buttons in one panel and three radio buttons in another panel. Because no layout manager has been specified, each of these components appears in a horizontal row within its panel. If we'd like to have the three radio buttons appear in a column instead of a row, we can do so by specifying that the panel that holds the checkboxes include a layout manager. We can further specify how many areas, or *cells*, into which this layout manager should divide the panel. In this example we'd want three cells arranged in a column—one cell for each of the three radio buttons. Figure 12-25 illustrates.

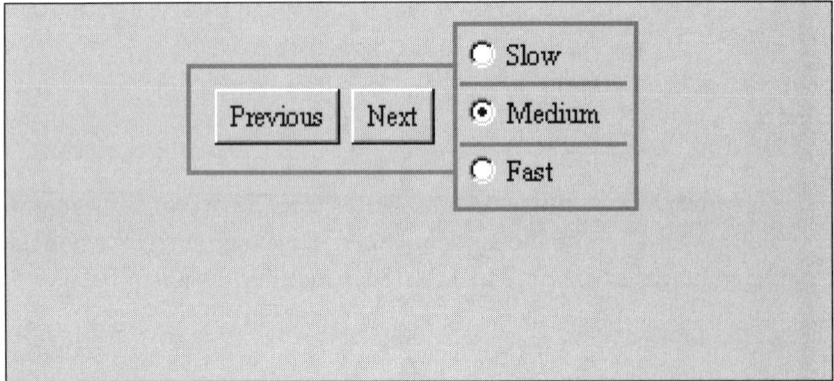

Figure 12-25
A panel can be subdivided into cells, each of which holds a single UI component.

As is the case for panels themselves, cells within a panel exist only to provide Java with guidance in laying out components; they aren't entities visible to the user. Contrary to this fact, Figure 12-25 uses lines to give you a clear indication of how cells help position components within a panel.

Component placement as shown in Figure 12-25 can be achieved using a `GridLayout` layout manager. We'll use this layout manager later to place an applet's radio buttons in a vertical column. First, though, we'll look at the `FlowLayout` layout manager—the default layout manager that Java uses for a panel when an applet doesn't specify a particular manager.

The FlowLayout manager

An applet can optionally invoke the `Container` method `setLayout()` to specify a layout manager for the applet. Typically this is done within the applet's `init()` method, as follows:

```
public void init() {

    setLayout( new FlowLayout() );

    // code to create and add components
}
```

The setLayout() method requires a single argument—an object of one of the layout manager classes. In the preceding example, a new object of the FlowLayout class is created to serve this purpose. The FlowLayout class is defined in the java.awt package.

Once a layout manager is associated with an applet, the placement of all UI components added to the applet conforms to the spacing guidelines of that particular layout manager. The FlowLayout manager specifies that components, as they are added, should appear in a single row near the top of the applet. After all the components are added, this row should be horizontally centered in the area that the applet occupies. If the components occupy an area greater than the width of the applet, another row is started. Each row is then centered horizontally.

If we applied the FlowLayout manager to one of this chapter's example applets that displays two buttons and three radio buttons, there would be no visible change in the look of the applet. That's because the FlowLayout manager is the layout manager that all applets use by default. The FlowLayout manager is of greater worth when it is implemented using its constructor that accepts a parameter—as is being done in the following line of code:

```
setLayout( new FlowLayout( FlowLayout.LEFT ) );
```

The FlowLayout class defines three constants, or class variables, that can be used to alter the centering of components in an applet that uses the FlowLayout manager. The LEFT constant forces the components to start at the left edge of the applet. The RIGHT constant forces the components to be right-justified within the applet. Finally, the CENTER constant centers the components. Because these are class variables, they need not be invoked by a particular object. Instead, preface the constant with the class name and the dot—as done previously. Figure 12-26 shows the result of using the FlowLayout manager with the LEFT constant.

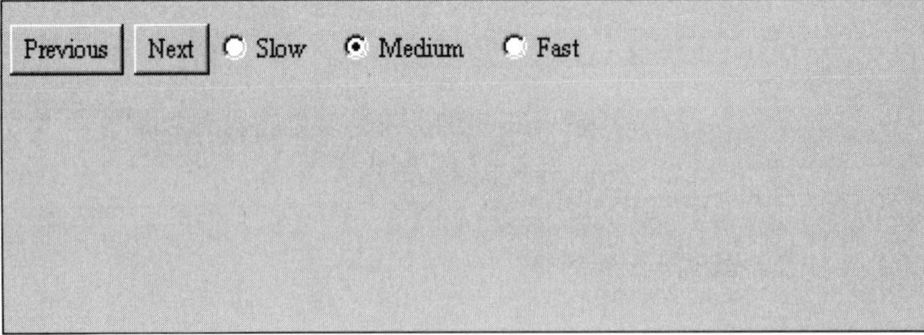

Figure 12-26
An applet with a FlowLayout manager applied to it with a LEFT constant

To change the distance between components in a panel governed by the `FlowLayout` manager, use the third `FlowLayout` constructor. In this constructor, you specify the component centering as before, but you also use the second parameter to specify the horizontal pixel distance between components and the third parameter to specify the vertical pixel distance between components (should any of the components wrap), as follows:

```
setLayout( new FlowLayout( FlowLayout.CENTER, 30, 30 ) );
```

The preceding call to `setLayout()` results in components that are horizontally centered in the applet, with a 30 pixel space placed between each. Figure 12-27 shows the results.

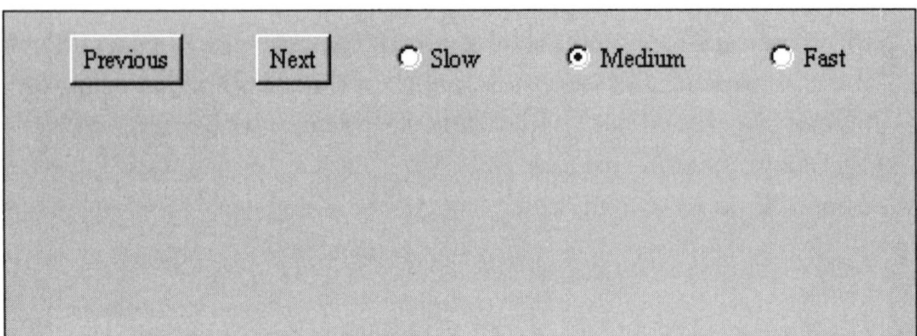

Figure 12-27
An applet with a FlowLayout manager with cell spacing applied to it

THE GRIDLAYOUT MANAGER

A second, and perhaps more useful, layout manager is the `GridLayout` manager. This manager divides an applet into a number of areas, or cells—each of which can hold a single component. When creating a `GridLayout` object, pass two values to the `GridLayout` constructor. The first value serves as the number of rows of cells; the second value serves as the number of columns of cells. For example, the following call to `setLayout()` results in an applet that is divided into two rows of four cells—for a total of eight cells:

```
setLayout( new GridLayout( 2, 4 ) );
```

As components are added to an applet that uses a `GridLayout` manager, Java runtime places each component in its own cell—starting from the upper left cell and moving to the right. After the manager fills the first row, the component that it adds next appears in the leftmost cell of the next row.

A layout manager doesn't have to be applied to an applet; it can be applied to any container. This means that an applet that defines panel classes can specify a different layout manager for each panel class. Consider the `ThreeRadioPanel` class defined in the BetterPanelClasses applet example that we introduced several pages back. Recall that this class placed three radio buttons in a panel and set a 30-pixel inset on each side of the panel. In a new version of the constructor method of this class, we'll add a single line of code—a call to `setLayout()`—as follows:

```
setLayout( new GridLayout( 3, 1 ) );
```

Here we've specified that a `GridLayout` manager be used for the panel created by this class. We've further specified that this layout manager divide the panel into three rows of one cell each. The effect of doing this is that when the three radio button components are added to the panel, they'll be placed in the panel vertically (one component per cell). The new version of the `ThreeRadioPanel` class appears as follows. Figure 12-28 shows how the BetterPanelClasses applet appears when we make this single addition to the code in its `ThreeRadioPanel` class.

```
class ThreeRadioPanel extends Panel {

    protected CheckboxGroup  theGroup;
    protected Checkbox       firstCheck;
    protected Checkbox       secondCheck;
    protected Checkbox       thirdCheck;

    ThreeRadioPanel( String name1, String name2, String name3 ) {

        setLayout( new GridLayout( 3, 1 ) );   // ** NEW CODE **

        theGroup = new CheckboxGroup();
        firstCheck = new Checkbox( name1, theGroup, false );
        secondCheck = new Checkbox( name2, theGroup, true );
        thirdCheck = new Checkbox( name3, theGroup, false );
        add( firstCheck );
        add( secondCheck );
        add( thirdCheck );
    }


    public Insets insets() {

        return new Insets( 30, 30, 30, 30 );  // T, L, B, R
    }
}
```

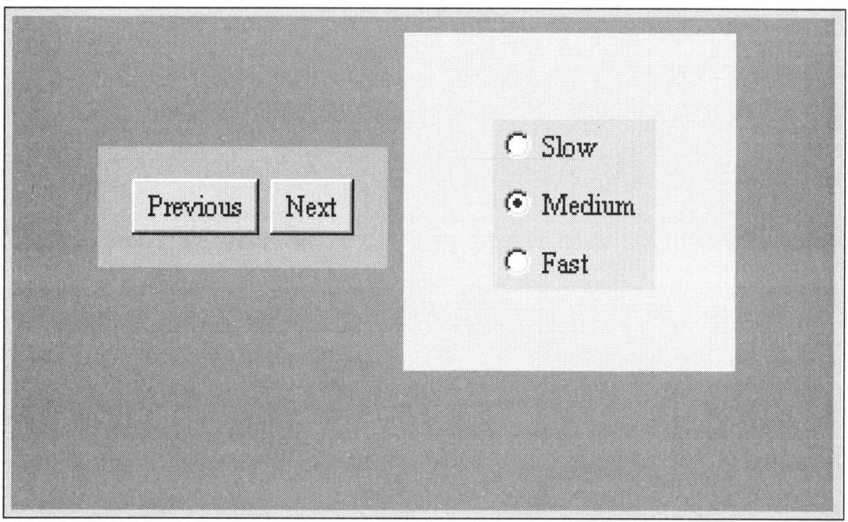

Figure 12-28
Applying a GridLayout manager to the ThreeRadioPanel class of the BetterPanelClasses applet results in radio buttons that are displayed vertically.

Once again assume that the example applet discussed here includes `setBackground()` calls that are used to give each of the two panels and the applet a different colored background. This is done simply to make it easier to see the area covered by each panel.

A `GridLayout` manager can optionally specify pixel values that serve to add horizontal and vertical gaps between components. To create these gaps, include the pixel values as the third and fourth parameters to the `GridLayout` constructor, as follows:

```
setLayout( new GridLayout( 3, 1, 0, 25 ) );
```

The preceding code specifies a `GridLayout` manager creating three rows of one column per row. It also specifies a spacing of 25 pixels between the vertical cells. Because only one component will appear in any row, the value of the horizontal gap (the space between components that appear in the same row) is unimportant and has been set to 0. Figure 12-29 shows the result of using the new `GridLayout` manager. To see the difference that the spacing parameters make, compare the spacing between radio buttons shown in Figure 12-29 with the spacing shown in Figure 12-28.

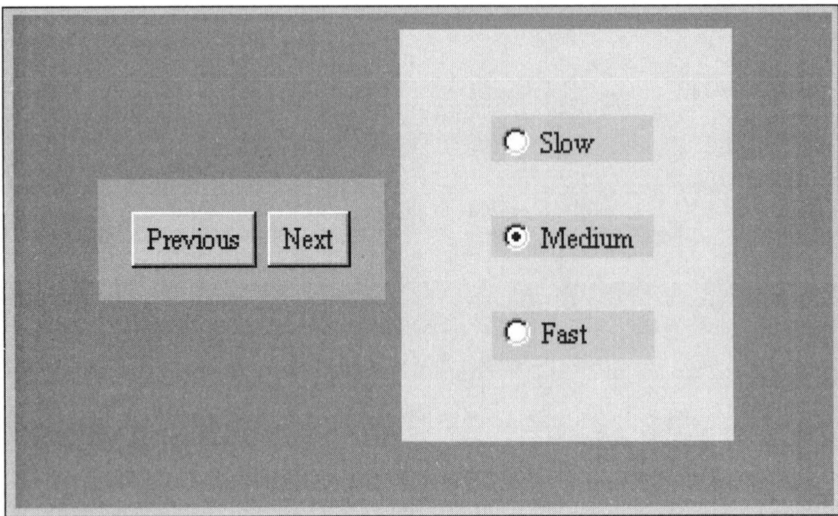

Figure 12-29
Applying a GridLayout manager with gaps to the ThreeRadioPanel class of the BetterPanelClasses applet results in radio buttons that include vertical spacing between them.

The two buttons in the applet's other panel could be spaced farther apart by using a `GridLayout` manager in the class that creates these buttons. Specifying a single row with two columns keeps the two buttons positioned horizontally. Including a pixel value greater than 0 as the third parameter to the `GridLayout` constructor separates the two buttons horizontally. Figure 12-30 shows the results of running the applet with the following call to `setLayout()` included in the `TwoButtonPanel` class:

```
setLayout( new GridLayout( 1, 2, 30, 0 ) );
```

A single layout manager is responsible for adjusting the spacing between *components* within a single panel. To adjust the spacing between *panels*, use insets in one or both of the classes that define the panels—as we've been doing. Figure 12-30 shows an applet that includes `insets()` methods in each of its two panel classes. Figure 12-31, on the other hand, shows how the same applet looks when we remove the `insets()` methods.

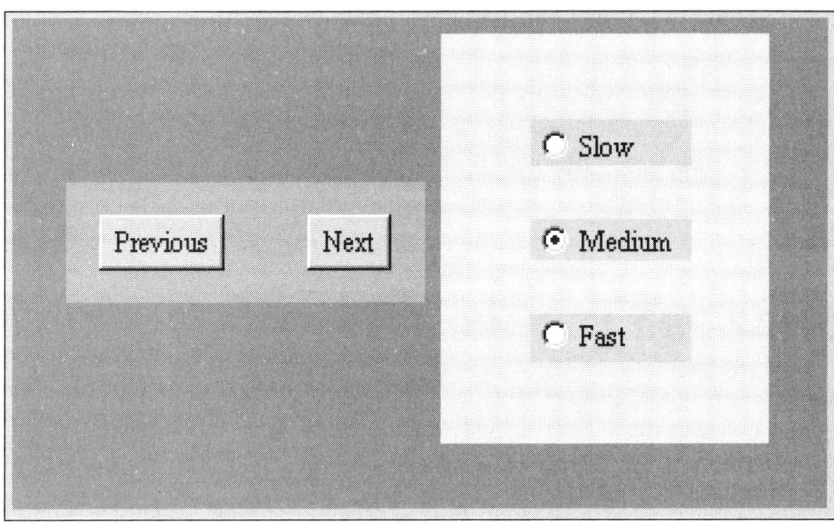

Figure 12-30
Applying a GridLayout manager with gaps to the TwoButtonPanel class of the BetterPanelClasses applet results in buttons that include horizontal spacing between them.

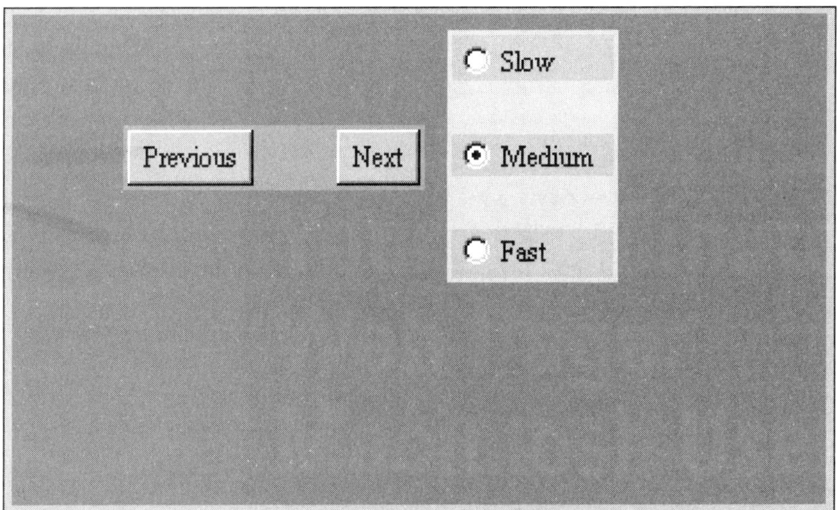

Figure 12-31
When insets are removed from the BetterPanelClasses applet, the panels move closer together.

By combining panels and layout managers with an applet, you'll be able to lay out the UI components in just about any way you see fit. And because this method of component layout doesn't involve any hardcoded pixel coordinate values, the likelihood of your layout looking good on the variety of systems that will be hosting your applet is greatly improved.

Component Functionality

At this point, you know that user interface elements such as buttons and checkboxes are objects of classes extended from the `Component` class. You also now know that components can be arranged within the confines of a panel and that, because the `Applet` class is extended from the `Panel` class, an applet itself is a panel. We still haven't covered one important aspect of user interface components, though: how to work with them! In this section, you'll see how to get your applet to actually do something when a user clicks on a button or checkbox, or types in a text field.

EVENTS AND USER INTERFACE COMPONENTS

When a user interacts with a UI component, the Java runtime generates an event. Fortunately, from Chapter 11 you know quite a bit about events.

EVENTS AND THE ACTION() METHOD

The `Component` class from which all UI components are extended defines an `action()` method. Like the `paint()` method defined by `Component` class, if your applet chooses to implement `action()`, then Java invokes the applet version of this method whenever appropriate. Here's an overview of what `action()` looks like:

```
public boolean action( Event evt, Object arg ) {

    // determine which UI component was interacted with,
    // then handle the action accordingly

    return true;
}
```

Java passes your applet two pieces of information when a UI component-related event occurs, and it does so in the form of the two parameters in `action()`. The first is the `Event` object itself; this is the same object you learned about in Chapter 11. The second parameter is a generic `Object` that can hold different types of information. Depending on the type of action that occurs, Java passes different information in this second parameter.

Your applet should implement its `action()` method so that the method first determines which UI component received the action, then responds to that action. The `action()` method should end by returning a value of `true` if the action is considered handled—as will most always be the case.

To determine which component receives an event, examine the `target` field of the `Event` object that Java passes to the `action()` method. In general, this is accomplished as follows:

```
if ( evt.target == component1 ) {
    // code to handle an event
    // directed at one component
}
else if ( evt.target == component2 ) {
    // code to handle an event
    // directed at a second component
}
else if ( ... )
```

AN APPLET WITH FUNCTIONAL UI COMPONENTS

Earlier in this chapter, you saw an example of an applet that displayed two buttons in an applet—one labeled "Red," the other labeled "Blue." Here's the source code listing for that applet, called Buttons:

```
public class Buttons extends Applet {

    protected Button  redButton;
    protected Button  blueButton;


    public void init() {

        redButton = new Button( "Red Square" );
        blueButton = new Button( "Blue Square" );
```

```
        add( redButton );
        add( blueButton );
    }
}
```

The Buttons applet has one very large drawback: It doesn't do anything when a user clicks on a button. To remedy that, we'll add an `action()` method to its source code. We'll also rename the improved applet Action, as follows:

```
import java.awt.*;
import java.applet.*;

public class Action extends Applet {

    protected Button  redButton;
    protected Button  blueButton;


    public void init() {

        redButton = new Button( "Red Square" );
        blueButton = new Button( "Blue Square" );
        add( redButton );
        add( blueButton );
    }


    public boolean action( Event evt, Object arg ) {

        Graphics g = getGraphics();

        if ( evt.target == redButton ) {
            g.setColor( Color.red );
            g.fillRect( 100, 60, 100, 100 );
        }
        else if ( evt.target == blueButton ) {
            g.setColor( Color.blue );
            g.fillRect( 100, 60, 100, 100 );
        }

        return true;
    }
}
```

The `action()` method begins by declaring a `Graphics` variable named `g` and then calling the `Component` method `getGraphics()` to get a reference to the current graphics object. Java always has a reference to this object; in fact, it passes this reference to some methods, such as `paint()`. However, our applet doesn't innately have this reference; it needs to request it from the Java runtime. Once the applet has the reference, it can use any of the methods of the `Graphics` class to draw graphics in the applet as follows:

```
Graphics g = getGraphics();

// now go ahead a draw using Graphics methods, as in:
g.fillRect( 100, 60, 100, 1000 );
```

Next, the `action()` method determines which of the two buttons received the action (that is, which of the two buttons was clicked on), and then draws a square of the proper color. To do this, an `if-else` statement compares the `target` field of the `Event` object `evt` to the variable names of the UI components. The body of the `if` handles a click on one button; the body of the `else` handles a click on the other button. In both cases, the `Graphics` method `setColor()`sets the color that is used in subsequent calls to other `Graphics` methods. Figure 12-32 shows the results of clicking on the Blue Square button.

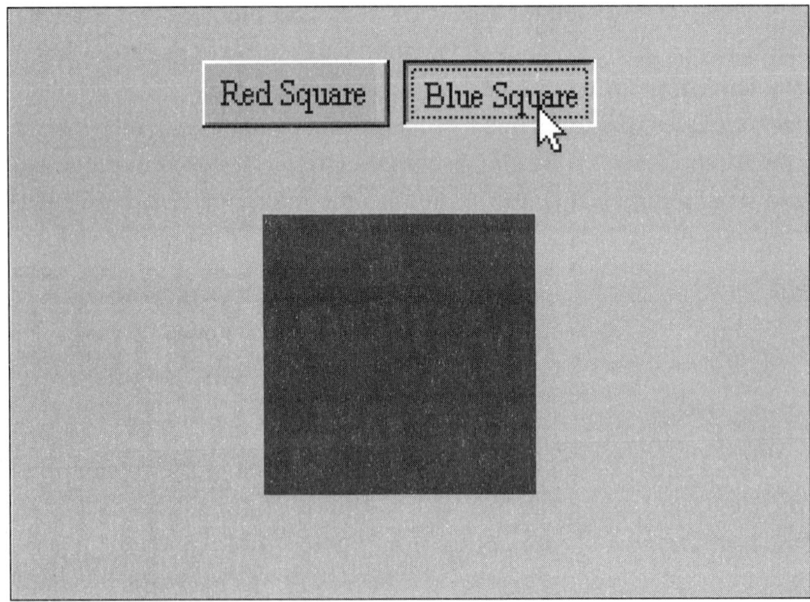

Figure 12-32
The result of running the Action applet

This book isn't printed in color, so you'll have to take our word for it that the box pictured in Figure 12-32 is blue!

ACTION HANDLING AND UI COMPONENT TYPES

Now that you know how to handle an action that involves a button, the process of handling actions involving other component types will seem straightforward.

MODIFYING THE ACTION() METHOD

If your applet holds several UI components of several different component types, the cascading `if-else` statement at the heart of your applet's `action()` method may become quite large. To make matters easier for anyone reading your Java code (and, possibly, to make coding easier on yourself if you ever change your code after a considerable lapse of time), you can use the if-else section of the action() method as a sort of branching-off point rather than as the place where all action's are handled, as follows:

```
if ( evt.target instanceof Button )
    // invoke applet-defined method that handles an
    // action involving a button
else if ( evt.target instanceof Checkbox )
    // invoke applet-defined method that handles an
    // action involving a checkbox
```

You can use the Java keyword instanceof to obtain a Boolean value that answers the question of whether one particular object is an instance of a particular class. In the preceding snippet, we first use instanceof to compare the object named in the target field of the Event object evt to the Button class. If the object in the target field is in fact an instance of the Button class, the if statement is valid, or true, and an applet-defined routine is called to handle the action. A similar technique is used to test the target to see if it was a checkbox object.

AN APPLET WITH THE NEW ACTION() METHOD

The Action applet listed a couple of pages back was the first example applet that used an action() routine. Before going on to a comprehensive example, let's modify that simple applet to take advantage of our new style of action() method, as follows, in what we'll now call the RevisedAction applet:

```
import java.awt.*;
import java.applet.*;

public class RevisedAction extends Applet {

    protected Button  redButton;
    protected Button  blueButton;


    public void init() {

        redButton = new Button( "Red Square" );
        blueButton = new Button( "Blue Square" );
        add( redButton );
        add( blueButton );
    }
```

```
    public boolean action( Event evt, Object arg ) {

        if ( evt.target instanceof Button )
            handleButton( arg );

        return true;
    }


    public void handleButton( Object arg ) {

        Graphics g = getGraphics();

        if ( (String)arg == "Red Square" ) {
            g.setColor( Color.red );
            g.fillRect( 100, 60, 100, 100 );
        }
        else if ( (String)arg == "Blue Square" ) {
            g.setColor( Color.blue );
            g.fillRect( 100, 60, 100, 100 );
        }
    }
}
```

The preceding RevisedAction applet displays the same two buttons that the Action applet displays. In fact, the RevisedAction applet behaves exactly the same as the Action applet. We've rewritten the applet merely to provide a short and simple example of using the `instanceof` keyword and of calling an applet-defined method.

In RevisedAction, the `action()` method begins by comparing the `target` to the `Button` class. If the UI component receiving the action is in fact an object of the `Button` class, the `handleButton()` method is invoked. Because the RevisedAction applet has no other types of components, `action()` doesn't have to include any further tests.

The `handleButton()` method holds code similar to the code included within the `action()` method of the Action applet. Here we've relocated the code to its own method for clarity.

One point of note in the `handleButton()` method is the use of the lone parameter that is passed to the method. When `action()` invokes `handleButton()`, it passes along the `Object` held in `arg`—a parameter that the `action()` method received from the Java runtime. As mentioned, this parameter holds different information depending on the type of UI component that is involved in the event that triggers the call to `action()`. If the UI component is a button, then Java passes the name of the button in this parameter. Because Java passes this name as a generic `Object` rather than as a `String`, `arg` is typecast to a `String` for the `if-else` comparison that is made in `handleButton()`.

AN APPLET WITH BUTTONS AND RADIO BUTTONS

Our new format for the `action()` method works with any number of types of components. In the MoreAction applet that follows next, we try it out on an applet that holds two radio buttons and two buttons. Recall that checkboxes organized into a checkbox group are considered radio buttons.

```
import java.awt.*;
import java.applet.*;

public class MoreAction extends Applet {

    protected Button         redButton;
    protected Button         blueButton;
    protected CheckboxGroup  sizeGroup;
    protected Checkbox       smallCheck;
    protected Checkbox       bigCheck;
    protected boolean        drawSmall = true;


    public void init() {

        sizeGroup = new CheckboxGroup();
        smallCheck = new Checkbox( "Small", sizeGroup, true );
        bigCheck = new Checkbox( "Large", sizeGroup, false );
        add( smallCheck );
        add( bigCheck );

        redButton = new Button( "Red Square" );
        blueButton = new Button( "Blue Square" );
        add( redButton );
        add( blueButton );

    }


    public boolean action( Event evt, Object arg ) {

        if ( evt.target instanceof Button )
```

```
            handleButton( arg );
        else if ( evt.target instanceof Checkbox )
            handleCheckbox( evt.target );

        return true;
    }


    public void handleCheckbox( Object check ) {

        if ( (Checkbox)check == smallCheck )
            drawSmall = true;
        else
            drawSmall = false;
    }


    public void handleButton( Object arg ) {

        Graphics g = getGraphics();

        if ( (String)arg == "Red Square" )
            g.setColor( Color.red );
        else if ( (String)arg == "Blue Square" )
            g.setColor( Color.blue );

        g.clearRect( 100, 60, 100, 100 );

        if ( drawSmall == true )
            g.fillRect( 100, 60, 50, 50 );
        else
            g.fillRect( 100, 60, 100, 100 );

    }
}
```

The `action()` method of the preceding MoreAction applet uses `instanceof` to determine the UI component type. If the component is a button, then `handleButton()` is called. If the component is a checkbox, then a new applet-defined method is invoked—`handleCheckbox()`—as follows:

```
if ( evt.target instanceof Button )
    handleButton( arg );
else if ( evt.target instanceof Checkbox )
    handleCheckbox( evt.target );
```

The `handleButton()` method used the preceding snippet is similar to the version used in the previous applet. Here, however, a call is made to clear the area where rectangles are drawn before the new rectangle is drawn. In the RevisedAction applet, this wasn't necessary: Either button drew the same size rectangle, so one rectangle could simply overwrite the other. The MoreAction applet, however, includes radio buttons that enable the user to specify the size of the rectangle to draw. If a large rectangle is drawn followed by a small one, without erasing the first rectangle, the result is a smaller rectangle drawn over the larger one.

The `handleCheckbox()` method receives the `target` in its one parameter. Because the `target` field of the `Event` object is defined as a generic `Object`, this parameter must be typecast to a `Checkbox` in order to be used in a comparison with the checkbox variable names. Once it is determined which checkbox was involved in the action, a Boolean variable is set in order to specify whether a small or big square should be drawn.

Figure 12-33 shows the result of running the applet if the Small checkbox is clicked on and then the Blue Square button is clicked.

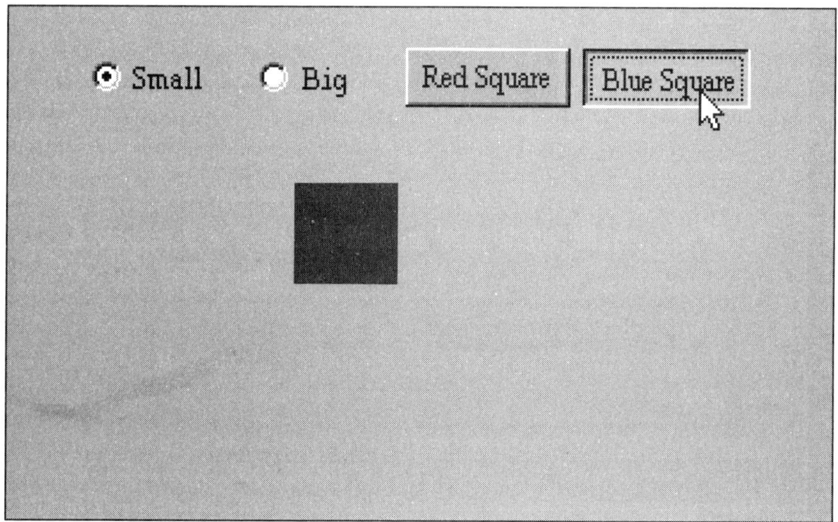

Figure 12-33
The result of running the MoreAction applet

What You've Learned

The Abstract Windowing Toolkit is the name given to the classes of the `java.awt` package. This important package provides all the resources you need to give your applet a graphical user interface. You achieve a GUI by including user interface components, or UI components, in your applet. Such components include buttons, checkboxes, radio buttons, text fields, menus, and labels. Your applet can make use of layout managers to organize these components in panels—areas within an applet.

To add functionality to the UI components of an applet, you override the `Component` class `action()` method. In this method, you determine which type of component receives the action (such as a button receiving a mouse click) and then respond to that action in a way appropriate for your particular applet.

CHAPTER

13 Getting Started with Java Applications

Although this book has focused on the development of Java applets, we will end by giving you a taste of the development process for the other type of bytecode file that a Java compiler can create—a platform-independent Java application.

This chapter walks you through the process of creating a Java source code file, compiling it, and then running the resulting Java application with a Java interpreter.

Using the JDK to Develop Applications

In Chapter 2, you read about the Java Development Kit, or JDK. There you saw how this development tool helps you create Java applications. Sun Microsystems has released several versions of the JDK. To make sure that you have the most recent version of the JDK for your machine, visit Sun's Java Web page at `http://www.javasoft.com`. There you'll always find the latest version of the JDK.

Other Java programming environments exist, including products by Symantec and Metrowerks. You can, of course, use any of these more fully integrated environments (they include built-in editing and debugging support) to do your Java application programming.

Source Code for a Sample Java Application

This chapter examines the development of a very simple Java application. The entire source code listing for the Java application we've named MyFirstApplication appears here:

```
public class MyFirstApplication {

    public static void main( String arg[] ) {
        System.out.println("This application simply draws text" );
    }
}
```

Java source code is platform-independent. Consequently, you can use this listing exactly as it appears here—regardless of the system you use for programming. When you run MyFirstApplication on your own computer, you'll see the words "This applet simply draws text" on your screen.

A Java application doesn't require an HTML file to execute, as an applet does. The java binary code serves as the Java interpreter, and the application uses this binary code to run instead of using a Java interpreter built into a Web browser.

Type in the source code and compile it to create your first Java application. If you're running Windows 95, read the following section. If you're developing on a Macintosh, skip ahead to Creating a Sample Application—Macintosh Developers.

Creating the Sample Application—Windows 95 Developers

If you program using Windows 95, you can develop your application with the Windows JDK that's included on this book's CD-ROM.

USING THE SUN JDK FOR WINDOWS 95

You should be able to find the Windows 95 version of the JDK on this book's CD-ROM in a folder named `java`. If you find the JDK in a different folder—or if you've renamed the folder—you should change the name of the folder to `java` so you can more easily follow along with this walk-through of the applet development process. If you worked through the Chapter 2 creation of an example applet, you should be familiar with the JDK and its folder hierarchy.

The `java` folder contains some files and several other folders. For creating a Java application, the most important folders are `bin` and `demo`. The `bin` folder holds the executables of the tools you use when you develop an applet. The tool named javac is the Java Compiler, which you use to compile your Java source code. This is the same compiler that's used to compile source code files that become Java applets. The program named java is a Java interpreter. Recall that while a Java applet or application is machine-independent, the host machine must be equipped with a Java interpreter for the applet or application to run.

The `demo` folder is a good place to house your own Java applications—each in its own subfolder. If you look in the `MyFirstApplication` folder, you'll find two files: `MyFirstApplication.java` and `MyFirstApplication.class`. The file with the `.java` extension is the Java source code file; the same extension used for Java applet source code is used for source code that will become a Java application. After compiling a `.java` file, a `.class` file is generated. This `.class` file holds the Java application—the bytecode executable file.

WRITING THE SOURCE CODE

You can start in on your own Java application by first creating a new folder to hold the `.java` source code file you'll be writing. In this walk-through, we'll call this new folder `MyFirstApplication` and place it in the existing `demo` folder.

You create Java source code in a text file. Because the JDK doesn't come with its own text editor, you'll need to use your own editor or word processor. Here we'll select the MS-DOS Prompt item from the Windows 95 Start menu to open a DOS window so we can use the DOS editor.

First, move to the `MyFirstApplication` directory. Then type `edit` followed by the name of the new text file. As was the case for applets, a Java source code file always has the same name as the applet itself followed by the `.java` extension. Figure 13-1 shows what you should type if you have created the `MyFirstApplication` folder in the `demo` folder.

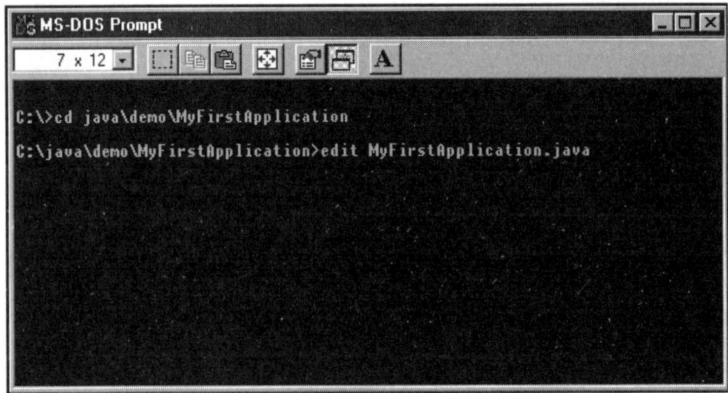

Figure 13-1
Use the DOS editor to create a new, empty Java source code file.

Now, in the blank text file, type in the following code.

```
public class MyFirstApplication {

    public static void main( String arg[] ) {
        System.out.println("This application simply draws text" );
    }
}
```

If you're using the DOS editor, your editor window should look similar to the one shown in Figure 13-2.

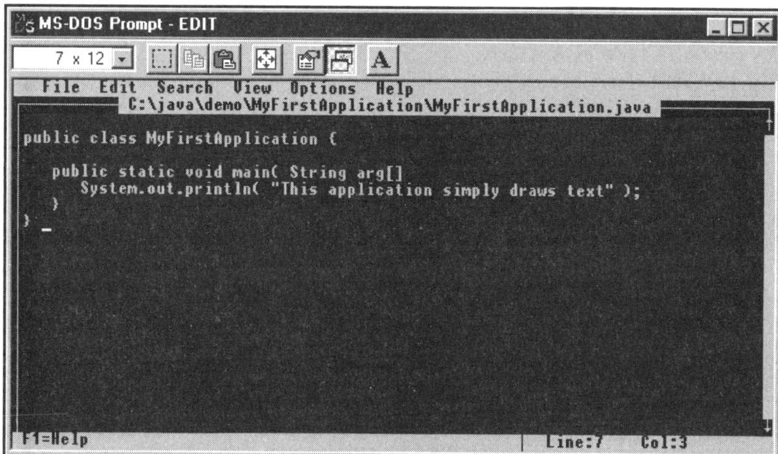

Figure 13-2
Your source code for MyFirstApplication.java should look like this.

Finally, save the file and quit the text editor or word processor. Now you're ready to compile the source code.

COMPILING THE SOURCE CODE

To compile a Java source code file, use the Java Compiler that's a part of the JDK—just as you did in Chapter 2 when you created an applet. If you're not at the DOS prompt, go there now. From the directory that holds the source code file, type `javac` (the name of the Java Compiler), followed by the name of the source code file—in this example, `MyFirstApplication.java`. Figure 13-3 shows what the screen should look like.

After a few moments, the javac program finishes compiling. When the DOS prompt reappears, compilation is complete. Your `MyFirstApplication` folder should now have two MyFirstApplication files in it—the `MyFirstApplication.java` source code file and the `MyFirstApplication.class` file, which contains the Java application.

If the compilation fails, you'll see an error message in the DOS window. If that happens, look over the code in your `MyFirstApplication.java` source code file and verify that it matches the code in Figure 13-2 exactly. If it does match, you might want to try using a couple of commands that eliminate compile-time errors. Move to the C: drive, and then from the DOS prompt, type the following:

```
C:\>set homedrive=c:
```

Press Enter and then at the next DOS prompt, type the following:

```
C:\>set homepath=\
```

After you have entered these two commands, try running the javac compiler again. The compilation should be successful.

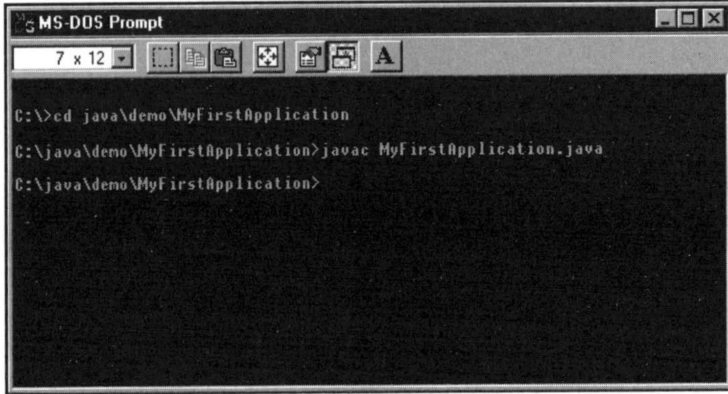

Figure 13-3
At the DOS prompt, compile the MyFirstApplication.java source code file.

RUNNING THE APPLICATION

After you have successfully compiled the `MyFirstApplicaton.java` source code file, you'll have a `MyFirstApplication.class` file in your `MyFirstApplication` folder. This new file is the bytecode that represents the MyFirstApplication Java application.

To run a Java application, you need to run the Java interpreter. On a Windows 95 machine, this interpreter is named java and is located in the `bin` directory of the JDK.

You can run appletviewer from the DOS prompt by first moving into the folder that holds your Java application. Then, type `java MyFirstApplication` (the name of the Java interpreter executable file followed by the name of the `.class` file). Note that you should omit the `.class` extension when typing in the name of the Java application to run. Figure 13-4 shows how the window should appear.

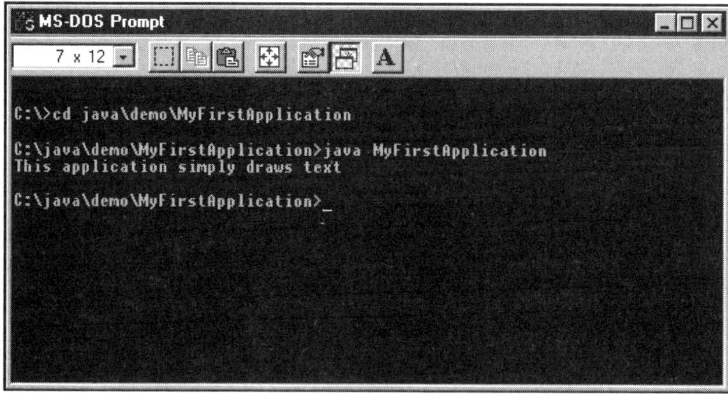

Figure 13-4
The results of running your first application!

Creating the Sample Application—Macintosh Developers

If you program on a Macintosh and you have any version of System 7.5, you can develop your first applet using the Macintosh JDK that's included on this book's CD-ROM.

The Sun Java Development Kit (JDK) originally could be used only to create Java applets—not Java applications. To create Java applications using the JDK, you'll need to have version 1.0.2 or later of the Macintosh JDK. You can download it from Sun's Java World Wide Web page (`http://www.javasoft.com`).

USING THE SUN JDK FOR MACINTOSH

If you worked through the Chapter 2 creation of an example applet, you should be familiar with the JDK and its folder hierarchy. When you open the JDK folder, you should find a few other folders and several files. Of the files, the ones named Java Compiler and Java Runner are the most important for our purposes. You use Java Compiler to compile your Java source code into a Java application. This is the same compiler that's used to compile source code files that become Java applets. The program named Java Runner is a Java interpreter. Recall that while a Java applet or application is machine-independent, the host machine must be equipped with a Java interpreter for the applet or application to run

The Sample Applications folder holds several more folders—each containing an example application. If you look in the MyFirstApplication folder, you'll find two files: `MyFirstApplication.java` and `MyFirstApplication.class`. The file with the `.java` extension is the Java source code file: The same extension used for Java applet source code is used for source code that will become a Java application. After compiling a `.java` file, a `.class` file is generated. This `.class` file holds the Java application—the bytecode executable file.

A Java application doesn't require an HTML file to execute, as an applet does. The java binary code serves as the Java interpreter, and the application uses this binary code to run instead of using a Java interpreter built into a Web browser.

WRITING THE SOURCE CODE

You can start in on your own Java application by first creating a new folder to hold the `.java` source code file you'll be writing. In this walk-through, we'll call this new folder `MyFirstApplication` and place it in the existing Sample Applications folder.

You create Java source code in a text file. Because the JDK doesn't come with its own text editor, use your own favorite text editor or a word processor capable of saving files in a text-only format.

Regardless of the editor or word processor you use, open a new, empty file and type in the following code:

```
public class MyFirstApplication {

    public static void main( String arg[] ) {
        System.out.println("This application simply draws text" );
    }
}
```

If you use a text editor such as SimpleText, your editor window should look similar to the one shown in Figure 13-5.

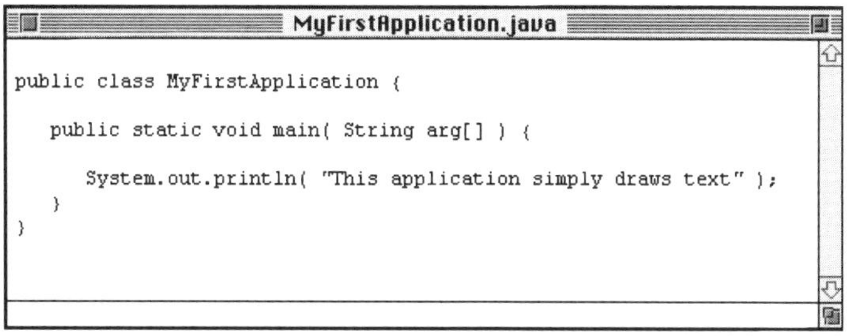

```
MyFirstApplication.java

public class MyFirstApplication {

   public static void main( String arg[] ) {

      System.out.println( "This application simply draws text" );
   }
}
```

Figure 13-5
The source code file for MyFirstApplication.java looks like this in the Macintosh SimpleText editor.

Before quitting the editor, save the file as `MyFirstApplication.java`. As mentioned, a Java source code file always has the same name as its corresponding applet followed by the `.java` extension.

COMPILING THE SOURCE CODE

To compile your Java source code, use the Java Compiler program that comes with the Sun JDK. From Chapter 2 you know that the JDK takes advantage of the drag-and-drop capabilities of a Macintosh running System 7.5. To compile the Java source code file, drag the file and drop it on the Java Compiler icon.

When you drop a file with a `.java` extension on the Java Compiler icon, the compiler launches and compiles the file. The compiler window indicates that the compiler is idle when compilation is complete. At that time your MyFirstApplication folder should have two MyFirstApplication files in it: the source code file (`MyFirstApplication.java`) and the Java application (`MyFirstApplication.class`).

If the compilation isn't successful, you'll see an error message in a separate window. If this happens, look over the code in your `MyFirstApplication.java` source code file and verify that it is identical to the sample code shown earlier in Figure 13-5.

RUNNING THE APPLICATION

After you compile the `MyFirstApplication.java` source code file, you have a `MyFirstApplication.class` file in your MyFirstApplication folder. This new file is the bytecode that represents the MyFirstApplication Java application.

To run a Java application, you need to run the Java interpreter. On a Macintosh, this interpreter is named Java Runner and is located in the JDK.

You can run your Java application simply by dragging its `.class` file to the Java Runner and dropping it on the Applet Runner's icon. When you do that, you'll see the dialog box pictured in Figure 13-6. A Java application can be written so that, upon running, the application accepts arguments. The MyFirstApplication application doesn't make use of arguments, so simply click on the OK button.

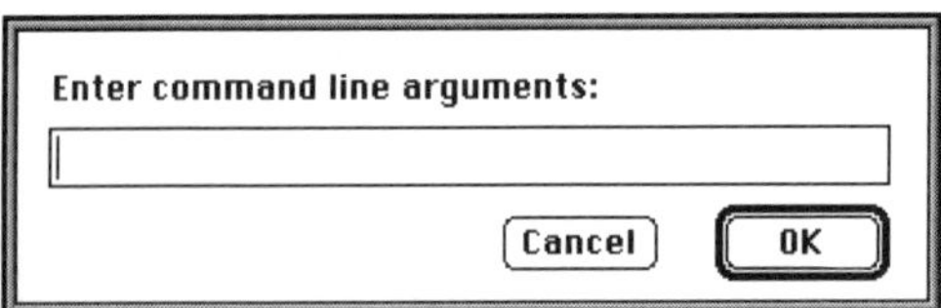

Figure 13-6
The Macintosh Java interpreter prompts you to enter any arguments the Java application needs.

On the Macintosh, the Java interpreter automatically opens a standard output window in which text is displayed. Figure 13-7 shows this window as it appears when MyFirstApplication executes.

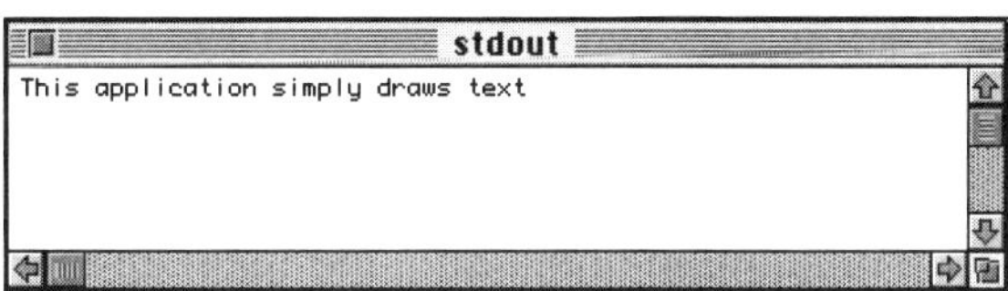

Figure 13-7
Use Java Runner to run the MyFirstApplication Java application.

What You've Learned

A Java application, like a Java applet, starts as a `.java` source code file. Again, like an applet, this source code file gets compiled into a bytecode file with a `.class` extension. Both a Java applet and a Java application require a Java interpreter in order to run. Because a Java application doesn't require a Web browser (or an applet viewer) in order to execute, the Java application doesn't need to be included in an HTML file (as an applet does). While an applet is generally small in size, a Java application may be large. A Java applet doesn't have to be small, but the fact that it gets downloaded to the user's machine when encountered on a Web page makes its size a factor. Because a Java application will be resident on the user's hard drive (like any other type of application), maintaining a small size is of far less importance.

APPENDIX

HTML: A Bare-Bones Primer

A thorough tutorial or reference of HTML (HyperText Markup Language) is beyond the scope of this book. A complete study of this language requires a text of its own; for example, you can pick up a copy of Alan Simpson's *HTML Publishing Bible, Windows 95 Edition* (IDG Books Worldwide, 1996) if you're interested in learning more about HTML. If you'd like to start with a quick overview of HTML, then this appendix is for you.

An HTML Document

An HTML document is a text file that holds the *tags*, or commands, that specify how a Web page should be laid out. These tags denote such things as where text should appear on a page and how that text should look—specifically, whether the text should be in a plain style or bold and whether the text should appear in a normal font size or in a larger font used for headings. Tags also specify where graphics should appear on a page,and in what external file the graphic images are held in. A Web browser that opens such a page is then responsible for loading the images that appear in the graphic image files.

As a reference, this appendix uses the `index.html` file that is also used in Appendixes B and C. The following is the complete listing for `index.html`:

```
<html>
<head>
<title>My Home Page</title>
</head>
<body>
<h1>Welcome to My Home Page</h1>
<hr>
If you have a Java-capable browser you'll
be able to see, and play, the Tic-Tac-Toe
applet that appears below this text.<br>
<br>
<applet code="TicTacToe.class" width=120 height=120>
</applet>
<br>
</body>
</html>
```

You can create your own `index.html` file by launching any text editor and creating a new file. The platform you use (Macintosh, Windows, or whatever) doesn't matter: HTML files are portable from one platform to another. The editor you use is also unimportant—provided you save the file as an unformatted text file. That is, if you use a word processor such as Microsoft Word, save the file using the text file option rather than as a Word file.

Basics of HTML

An HTML tag, or command, designates where different elements start and end on a Web page.

Format of an HTML tag

A tag is always enclosed by the `<` and `>` characters. The following are all examples of HTML tags: `<title>`, `<hr>`, and `<body>`.

Some page elements are defined by both a start-tag and an end-tag. As its name implies, a *start-tag* signals the start of an element. The *end-tag* designates the end of that same element and is always the same as its corresponding start-tag—except that it is preceded by a slash character (/). Here's an example that uses the `<title>` start-tag and `</title>` end-tag to define the title of a Web page:

```
<title>Dan's Home Page</title>
```

Other elements require only a single tag. An example is a line break. To signal the end of a paragraph of text, you use the `<br>` tag. There is no complementary `</br>` tag.

The examples in this book use lowercase for HTML tags. HTML isn't case-sensitive, so it's up to you whether your HTML appears in uppercase or lowercase. To a Web browser reading an HTML file, it's all the same. For example, both `<TITLE>` and `<title>` are valid tags.

FORMAT OF AN HTML PAGE

A document that is to be considered an HTML document begins with the `<html>` start-tag and finishes with the `</html>` end-tag. An HTML document consists of a head and a body. The head contains the title of the page. The tags `<head>` and `</head>` mark the start and end of the head. The body contains the content of the Web page. The tags `<body>` and `</body>` mark the start and end of the body. Figure A-1 uses the `index.html` file to highlight the tags just discussed.

BASIC HTML TAGS

HTML consists of quite a number of tags, but if you know about a dozen, that's is enough to get you started in HTML programming. You already know a few of the most common commands: The previous section described the `<html>`, `</html>`, `<head>`, `</head>`, `<body>`, and `</body>` tags.

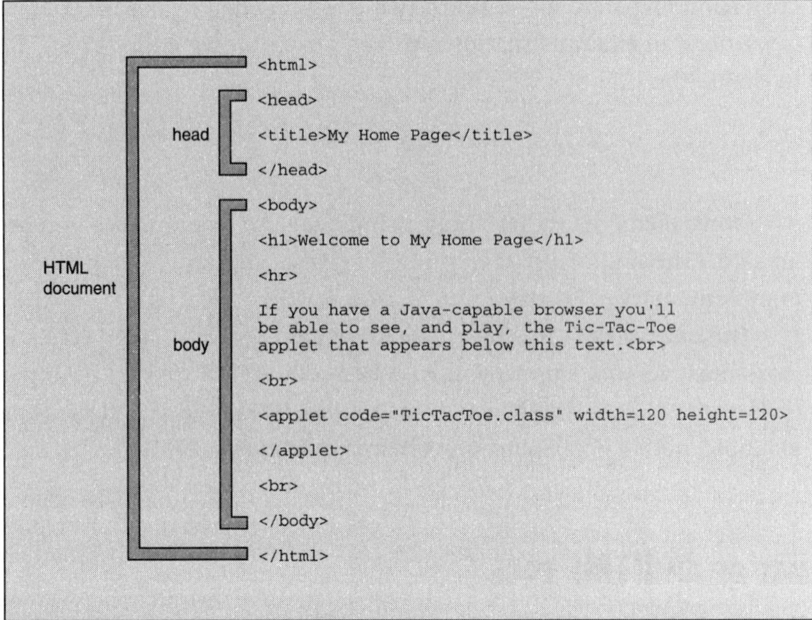

Figure A-1
An HTML file with some primary tags identified

The Web page head contains the page's title. Web browsers such as Netscape Navigator display this title in the title bar of the window that holds the page. Use the <title> and </title> tags to mark the start and end of the page's title; the text that appears between these two tags is the page title. You've already seen this example of the use of the title tags:

```
<title>Dan's Home Page</title>
```

To designate text to be used for headings, you can use any of six <hx> tags. Replace the *x* in <hx> with a value in the range of 1 through 6. The tag <h1> indicates a first level heading (the heading that uses the largest font); the tag <h6> is used for a sixth level heading (the heading that uses the smallest font). Each <hx> start-tag needs to be balanced with a </hx> end-tag. The following example writes out a heading in the font size and style used for each of the six different heading levels. For comparison, the snippet ends with a line of nonheading text. Figure A-2 shows the results of these tags as they'd appear in a Web browser.

```
<h1>This is a 1st level heading</h1>
<h2>This is a 2nd level heading</h2>
<h3>This is a 3rd level heading</h3>
<h4>This is a 4th level heading</h4>
<h5>This is a 5th level heading</h5>
<h6>This is a 6th level heading</h6>
This is "normal" text (text that isn't marked to be a heading).
```

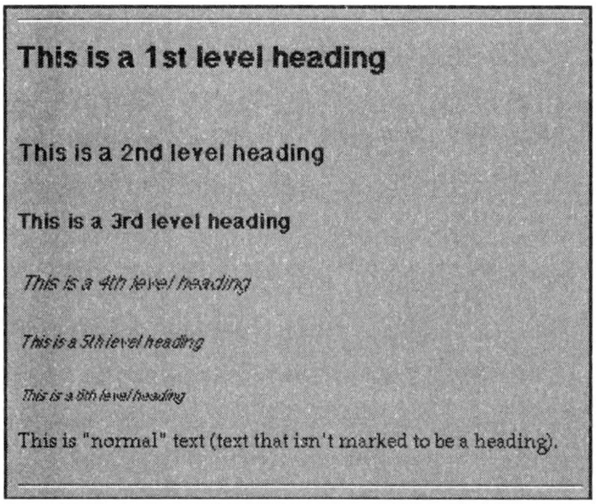

Figure A-2

An example of different levels of headings, as displayed in a Web browser

A section of text that word-wraps in the text editor you use to create the HTML file also word-wraps when viewed in a Web browser. To explicitly end a line of text, use the `<br>` tag (the ***br*** indicates a line ***break***). The `<br>` tag specifies a line break between words. To illustrate the use of the `<br>` tag, Figure A-3 shows a simple HTML file as viewed in both a text editor and a Web browser. Note that the `<br>` tag needs no end-tag.

Use the `<hr>` tag to insert a divider between sections of a Web page. Like the `<br>` tag, the ***horizontal rule*** command has no end-tag. Figure A-4 uses the code from the `index.html` example to illustrate the tags that have just been described.

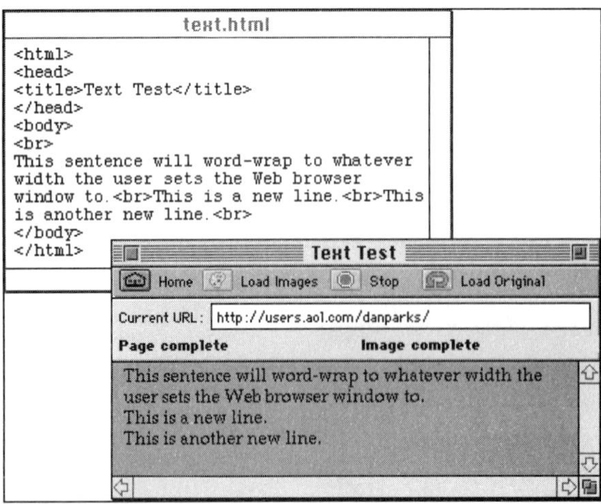

Figure A-3
The effect of <br> tags on a Web page

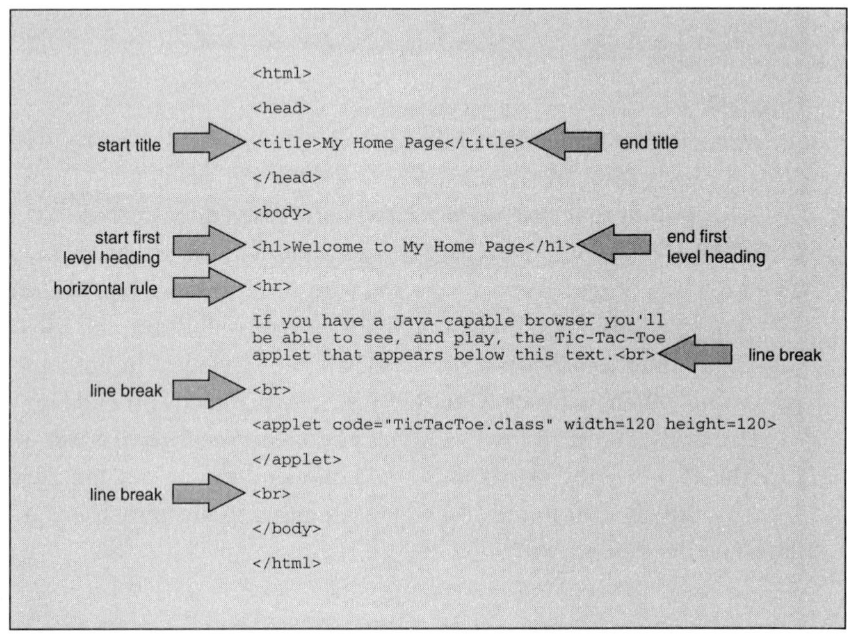

Figure A-4
An HTML file with some commonly used tags identified

THE <APPLET> HTML TAG

To include an applet in your Web page, use the `<applet>` start-tag and the `</applet>` end-tag—as shown in this example:

```
<applet code="MyFirstApplet.class" width=200 height=100></applet>
```

The `code` ***attribute*** is used to specify the name of the applet `.class` file from which the applet should be loaded. To display an applet on a page, only the applet's code (which is housed in the `.class` file) is needed; the Java source isn't important here. The `<applet>` tag tells the browser to look only in the directory, or folder, that holds the page's HTML file, so make sure you store the applet `.class` file there.

The `width` and `height` attributes tell the Web browser how much page space should be given to the applet. You'll adjust these attributes according to the amount of room your applet requires. Note that the `width` and `height` attributes determine the space devoted to the applet; they don't determine where on the page the applet appears. The applet's placement on a page is determined by whatever precedes the `<applet>` tag in the HTML file. For instance, in the `index.html` file used in this appendix, the Tic-Tac-Toe applet appears in a 120 × 120-pixel area after the heading, a horizontal rule, and some descriptive text:

```
<h1>Welcome to My Home Page</h1>
<hr>
If you have a Java-capable browser you'll
be able to see, and play, the Tic-Tac-Toe
applet that appears below this text.<br>
<br>
<applet code="TicTacToe.class" width=120 height=120>
```

Depending on how an applet is written, increasing the area it occupies either may increase the size of the applet's graphics or may simply add more blank page space around the applet's graphics. The Tic-Tac-Toe applet is an example of the former. Doubling the `width` and `height` attributes—as is done in the following snippet—doubles the size of the Tic-Tac-Toe board. Figure A-5 illustrates. On the left of Figure A-5, you see part of a Web page that uses `width` and `height` values of 240. On the right, you see part of the same page with `width` and `height` attributes set to 120.

Note that though the attribute values differ in the two examples, the starting point for the applet (the distance down from the top of the Web page) remains the same.

```
<applet code="TicTacToe.class" width=240 height=240>
```

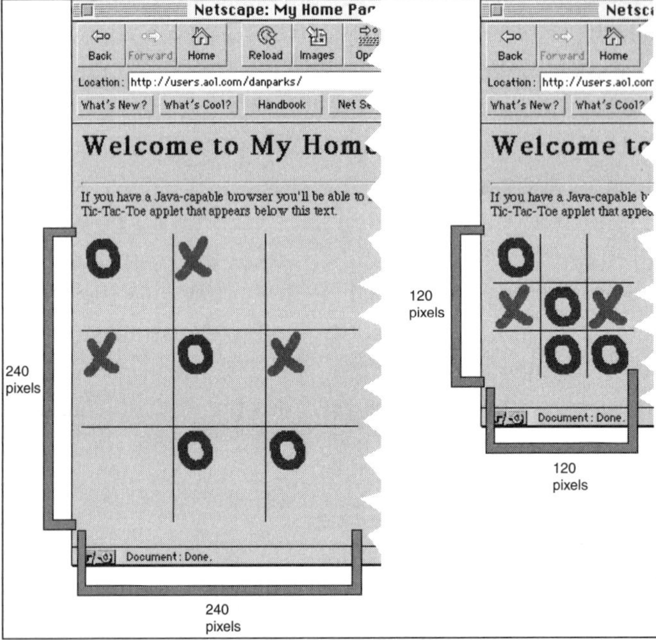

Figure A-5
An example of the impact of changing the width and height attributes of the <applet> tag

The `<applet>` start-tag must be accompanied by the `</applet>` end-tag. You can optionally place text between the two tags. If you do that and your Web page is encountered by a user surfing the Web with a browser that isn't Java-capable, the text will appear on the page in place of the applet. If the user is using a Java-capable browser, the text won't appear. The following snippet provides an example of a practical use for this text:

```
<applet code="TicTacToe.class" width=240 height=240>
Next time you visit this page, use a Java-capable browser
to view the applet that is located right here!
</applet>
```

A Web Page with an Applet

By now you've seen the Java listing for the same `index.html` file several times. If you use a Java-capable browser such as Netscape Navigator to view the Web page that gets generated from this file, you'll see a page like the one shown in Figure A-6.

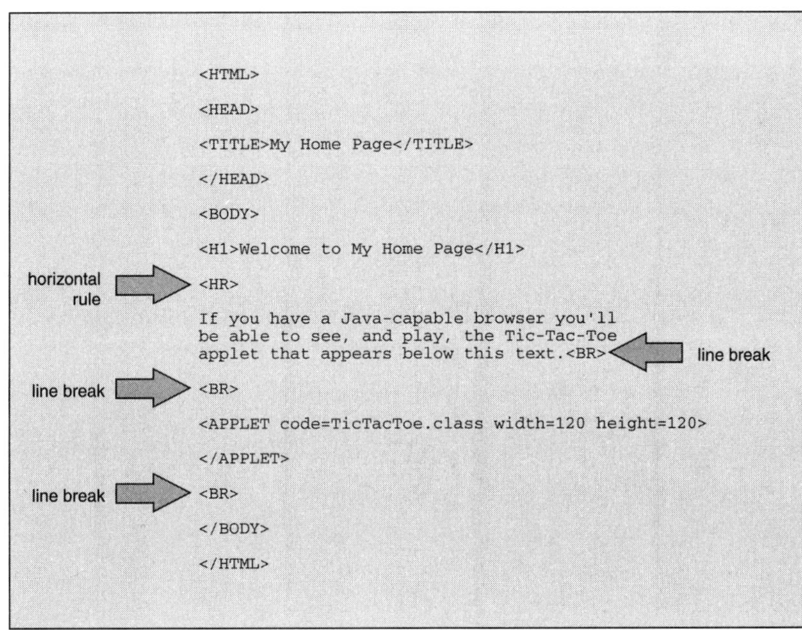

Figure A-6

The Web page that results from the example index.html file

APPENDIX

B Your 15-Minute Web Page: Windows Users

This appendix describes how Windows users can quickly set up a World Wide Web page. If you're a Macintosh user, skip this appendix. Instead, refer to Appendix C, "Your 15-Minute Web Page: Macintosh Users." It holds similar information.

AOL, Windows, and Your Web Page

If you're one of the nearly six million computer users who has an America Online (AOL) account, you can set up your own Web page in just a few minutes. You don't need any special lines, connections, or software. All you need is an AOL account and the standard America Online access software supplied to all AOL users. Best of all, aside from the time you spend online, there's no cost to create or maintain your Web page!

America Online has a `users.aol.com` FTP/WWW site that is a server. Any AOL member can use this site to easily set up a home directory. Once set up, your home page is accessible to everyone browsing the Web—regardless of how they're connected to the Internet. What's more, someone surfing the Net does not need to be an AOL user to access your Web page. As with visiting any Web site, all a person needs to know is the URL of your Web page.

Because all AOL users have their Web pages on the `users.aol.com` server, you know that your URL will include this server name. The file or files that make up your individual page will be kept on this server in a directory with the same name as your *screen name*—also referred to as your *user name*. If your screen name includes any spaces, omit the spaces when typing in your URL. The format of the URL of your Web page is thus as follows:

```
http://users.aol.com/ScreenName
```

As an example, if your screen name happens to be `DanParks`, your Web page has the following URL:

```
http://users.aol.com/DanParks
```

Your URL isn't case-sensitive. Thus a user could enter, say, the URL `http://users.AOL.com/danparks` into a Web browser and still make it to the same Web page.

What else would be true if your screen name were `DanParks`? You'd be in big trouble—that's the author's AOL screen name! To visit a Web page that holds a Java applet, feel free to use your Java-capable browser to stop in at `http://users.aol.com/DanParks`. While you're there, you can use your browser to look at the HTML source that makes up the page. If you use Netscape Navigator as your browser, use the Document Source menu item from the View menu. Note that, as of this writing, you can use your AOL account to set up a Web page, but, ironically, the AOL Web browser *doesn't* display applets that are present on Web pages.

Your HTML File

Any Web home page requires an HTML file (also referred to as an HTML *document*). This file holds the *tags*, or commands, that specify text and graphics placement on the Web page. The file may also hold hypertext links to other Web pages and now may even make use of the `<applet>` tag to specify that a Java applet be included on the Web page. While you might want to develop a fairly complex Web page, for this test run you should keep things simple. For your first attempt at creating a Web page, create a new, empty text file using any text editor. A Web page HTML file is often named index.html. America Online *requires* that you give your file this name. So that's what we'll do. Save the file as index.html, then type in the following HTML code:

```
<html>
<head>
<title>My Home Page</title>
</head>
<body>
<h1>Welcome to My Home Page</h1>
<hr>
If you have a Java-capable browser you'll
be able to see, and play, the Tic-Tac-Toe
applet that appears below this text.<br>
<br>
<applet code="TicTacToe.class" width=120 height=120>
</applet>
<br>
</body>
</html>
```

That's it! The preceding is all the HTML code you'll need for a very simple Web page. Take a good look at the listing, as it serves as the example used in the remainder of this appendix. If you aren't familiar with HTML, refer to Appendix A for a look at the very basics of this language of the Web. To keep you on familiar ground, the examples in Appendix A use this same HTML listing.

Uploading a File to AOL

The information that defines your Web page is kept in a file or files stored on an America Online server. When someone surfing the Web enters the URL of your Web page into their browser, that browser locates your files on the AOL server and loads them.

MOVING TO MYPLACE

America Online makes it easy to get your Web-related file or files from your hard drive to the AOL server. America Online has set up an online area named MyPlace that is used exclusively for working with such files. If you aren't logged on to AOL, dial up the online service now. Then follow these steps to get to the MyPlace area:

1. Choose Keyword from the Go To menu. The Keyword window appears.
2. Type `MyPlace`.
3. Click on the Go button. The MyPlace window appears.
4. Click on the Go to My Place icon. Your own workspace window appears.

After the fourth step, you'll find yourself in a directory on an AOL server. Each AOL member is allotted a 2MB storage area; this is the area where you are now. Figure B-1 shows the window you'll see. This directory is your own file storage area; no other AOL members can access it.

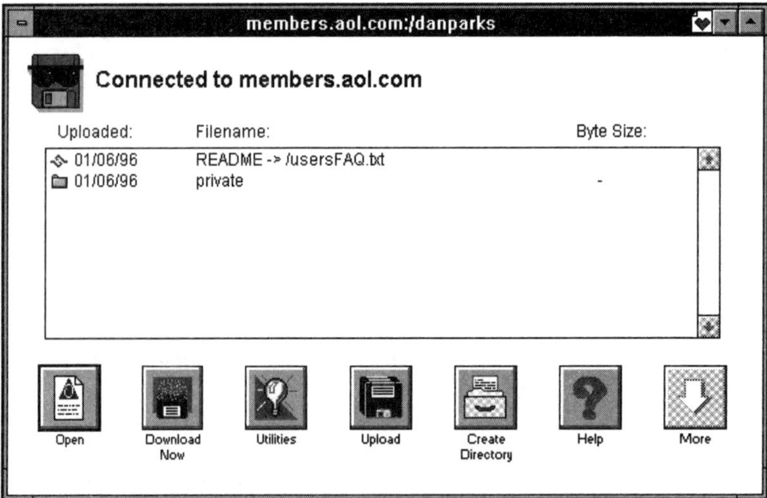

Figure B-1
The window that displays the root directory of your AOL Web workspace

When you first enter your workspace, you'll see a `README` file that provides information about MyPlace; you can double-click on the filename to read it online or download it. You'll also find a folder named `private` in your workspace. This folder holds data used by AOL and should be left untouched.

Uploading a file to MyPlace

Your AOL Web page relies on HTML code found in a file named `index.html`. Earlier in this appendix, you created such a file. Now it's time to upload it to MyPlace. To do that, follow these steps. Start at the workspace window shown in Figure B-1 previously.

1. Click on the Upload icon. The file upload window shown in Figure B-2 appears.

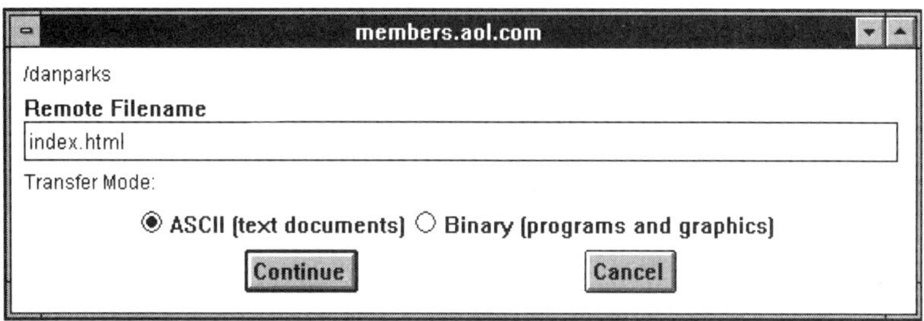

Figure B-2
The window used to specify information about a file to upload to your workspace

2. Type the name of the file that is about to be uploaded. In this example, you're uploading the `index.html` file, so type `index.html`.
3. Click on the Transfer Mode radio button that best matches the file type of the file that is to be uploaded. In this example, you're uploading the HTML file, which is a text file, so click on the ASCII (text documents) radio button. (Later in this appendix, you'll see an example of uploading a binary file.)
4. Click on the Continue button. The Select File window appears.
5. Click on the Select File icon. The Attach File window appears—as shown in Figure B-3.

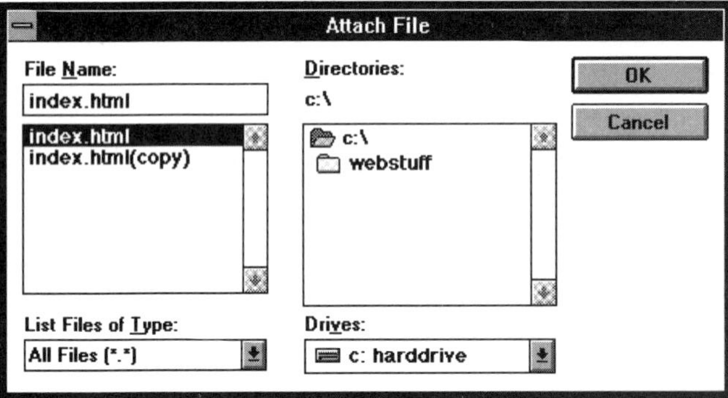

Figure B-3

The window used to select a file to upload to your workspace

6. Use the Drives pop-up menu in the lower right of the window to select the drive that holds the file to upload.
7. If the file to upload is in a subdirectory, double-click on that directory in the list on the right of the window.
8. Click on the file to upload in the list on the left of the window. The selected file will then be listed in the File Name box at the top left of the window. In this example, the `index.html` file was added from a folder named `webstuff`. The `webstuff` folder also holds a backup copy of the HTML file.
9. Click on the OK button. The Attach File window will be dismissed, and the Select File window will again be visible.
10. Click on the Send icon to upload the selected file. A file transfer window appears to show you the progress of the upload. When the upload is complete, the File Transfer Complete window appears.
11. Click on the OK button. You'll find yourself back at the window that enables you to type in the name and type of the file to upload.
12. Click on the Cancel button. Here you're "canceling" the window, not the file transfer you just performed; the file has been successfully transferred.

After performing the preceding steps, your workspace will now hold a copy of the `index.html` file—as shown in Figure B-4.

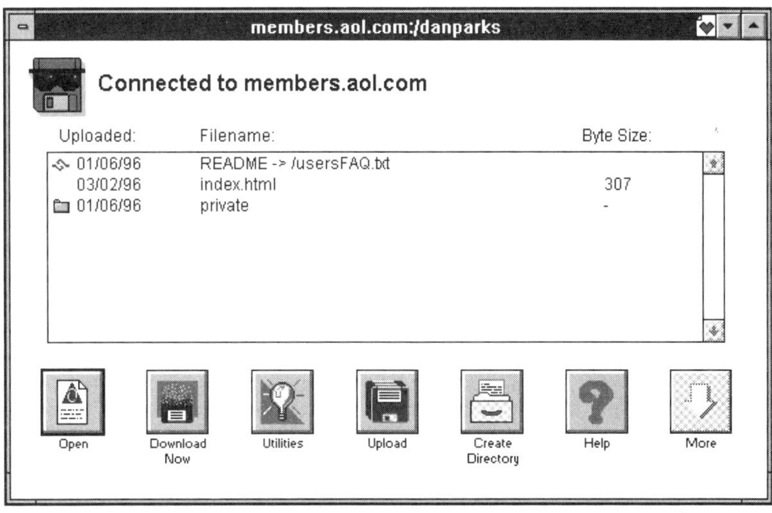

Figure B-4
The root directory of an AOL Web workspace after a file has been uploaded to it

A QUICK TEST OF YOUR NEW WEB PAGE

For a simple Web page that doesn't display any graphics, the HTML file is all you need. In this example, additional files will be necessary to create the finished Web page. Still, even with only the `index.html` file uploaded, you can run a quick test to verify that you now have a presence on the World Wide Web.

To run your test, use whichever Web browser you're accustomed to using. If you're still logged on to America Online and you have the AOL Web Browser, you can launch that software now. Type in the URL for your Web page and press the Enter key. Recall that the URL for your page will be `http://users.aol.com/` followed by your AOL screen name (less any spaces that appear in the screen name) and a slash. Thus the URL for an AOL member with a screen name of Jo Jo 3 would be as follows:

```
http://users.aol.com/JoJo3/
```

Your Web browser then moves to your Web page. Because you haven't loaded the Tic-Tac-Toe applet to your AOL workspace, the attempt by the browser to load the applet will fail, so don't be alarmed if your browser displays an error message like the one shown at the bottom of the Netscape Navigator window pictured in Figure B-5. For this quick test, that's okay. You can still consider the test a success: You now know that you're on the Web! Figure B-5 shows the current content of your Web page. This figure shows what *any* Netter who has your URL and Netscape Navigator will see. Other Web browsers will yield similar results.

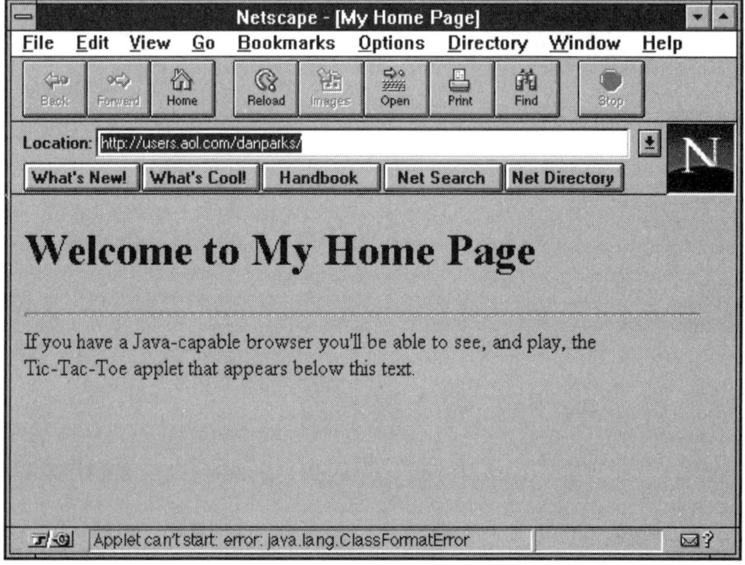

Figure B-5
A Web page that references an applet, but doesn't have that applet in its workspace

Adding an Applet to Your AOL Workspace

The `<applet>` tag in your HTML file lists the code for the Tic-Tac-Toe applet as one of its three attributes (the other two attributes being the pixel width and pixel height that should be devoted to the applet graphics), as follows:

```
<applet code="TicTacToe.class" width=120 height=120>
```

When a Web browser reaches your Web page, it attempts to load the Java code from a file named `TicTacToe.class`. To include the applet on your page, you need to make sure that this file exists in your workspace in the same directory as your `index.html` file. And because the Tic-Tac-Toe applet makes use of graphics files it expects to find in a folder named `images`, your workspace will also need to include such a folder and image files. After creating a new folder and uploading the applet and graphics files, your workspace should look similar to the one pictured in Figure B-6.

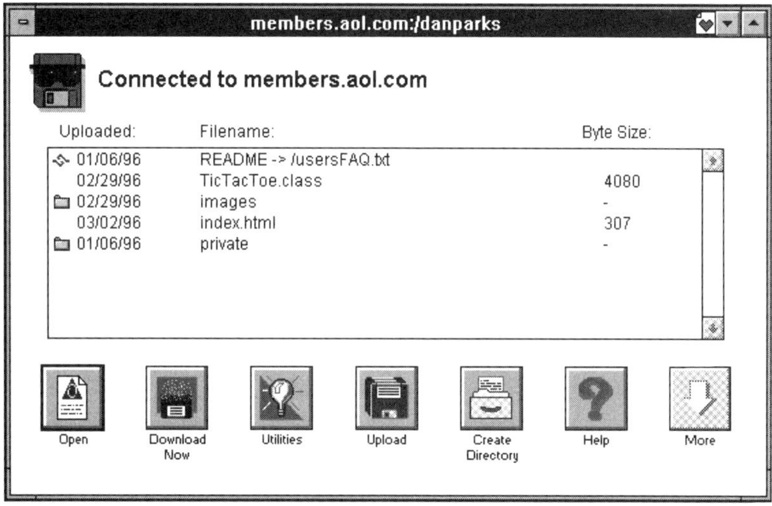

Figure B-6

The root directory of an AOL Web workspace after a folder has been added

UPLOADING THE APPLET

Uploading an applet to your workspace is as easy as uploading the `index.html` text file. To summarize, here are the steps for uploading an applet:

1. Move to your AOL Web workspace (your MyPlace area).
2. Click on the Upload icon to begin the upload process.
3. Type the name of the applet file to upload. In this example that would be `TicTacToe.class`. Note that you are uploading the Java

compiled code—the applet itself—rather than the Java source code found in the `TicTacToe.java` file.

4. Click on the Binary (programs and graphics) radio button rather than the ASCII (text documents) button.
5. Continue on to the file selection window. Locate the applet file and click on it. In this example, you'll most likely find the `TicTacToe.class` file in the folder of the programming development environment you used to create the applet.
6. Click on the OK button.
7. Click on the Send icon.

CREATING A NEW DIRECTORY

If your applet uses external files, you'll need to upload those files to your workspace as well. The Tic-Tac-Toe applet uses graphics files and sound files. For simplicity, here we'll just add the graphics files; the sound files aren't necessary to play the Tic-Tac-Toe game. The applet source code specifies that the two GIF graphics files will be in a directory named `images`. Before uploading the graphics files, you need to create this new directory in your workspace, as follows:

1. Move to your AOL Web workspace (your MyPlace area).
2. Click on the Create Directory icon. The Remote Directory Name window appears.
3. Type the name of the directory (folder) to create. In this example you type `images`—as shown in Figure B-7.

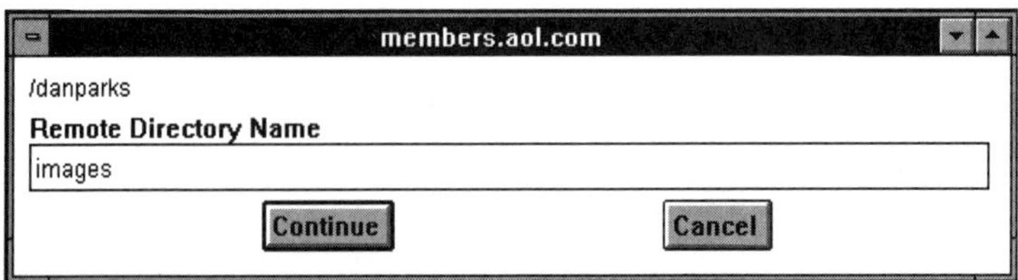

Figure B-7
The window used to create a new directory in the AOL Web workspace

4. Click on the Continue button. A window appears confirming that the folder has been created.
5. Click on the OK button. You'll find yourself back at the Remote Directory Name window.
6. Click on the Cancel button to again display your workspace window.

After performing the preceding steps, your workspace will now hold a new, empty folder named `images`. Now you can upload the two GIF files to this folder.

UPLOADING THE GIF GRAPHICS FILES

The process of uploading a GIF file to your workspace is the same as uploading an applet. The Tic-Tac-Toe applet expects to find GIF files named `cross.gif` and `not.gif` in a directory named `images`. You've just created that directory in your AOL Web workspace. Now upload these two graphics files. To add the files, follow these steps:

1. Move to your AOL Web workspace (your MyPlace area).
2. Double-click on the `images` folder icon to move to that folder. Any upload you now perform will result in a file ending up in this subdirectory.
3. Click on the Upload icon to begin the upload process.
4. Type the name of one of the files to upload, such as `cross.gif`.
5. Click on the Binary (programs and graphics) radio button.
6. Continue on to the file selection window. Locate the GIF file and click on its name. In this example, you'll find the GIF files in the folder named `images` in a folder within your Java programming development environment directory.
7. Click on the OK button.
8. Click on the Send icon to upload the file.
9. Repeat steps 4 through 8 to add the second GIF file, `not.gif`.

Testing Your Web Page

With the Tic-Tac-Toe applet and the two GIF files added to your AOL workspace, it's time to test out your Web page. To view an applet on a Web page, you need to visit that page with a Java-capable browser—a browser that has a built-in Java interpreter. As of this writing, the America Online browser *isn't* Java-capable. That means that while the AOL browser will take you to a Web page that holds a Java applet, it won't display that applet. Sun's HotJava and Netscape's Navigator are two examples of browsers that *are* Java-capable. Figure B-8 shows what a Web page looks like if it is based on the `index.html` file presented in this appendix and is viewed with the Windows version of Netscape Navigator 2.0.

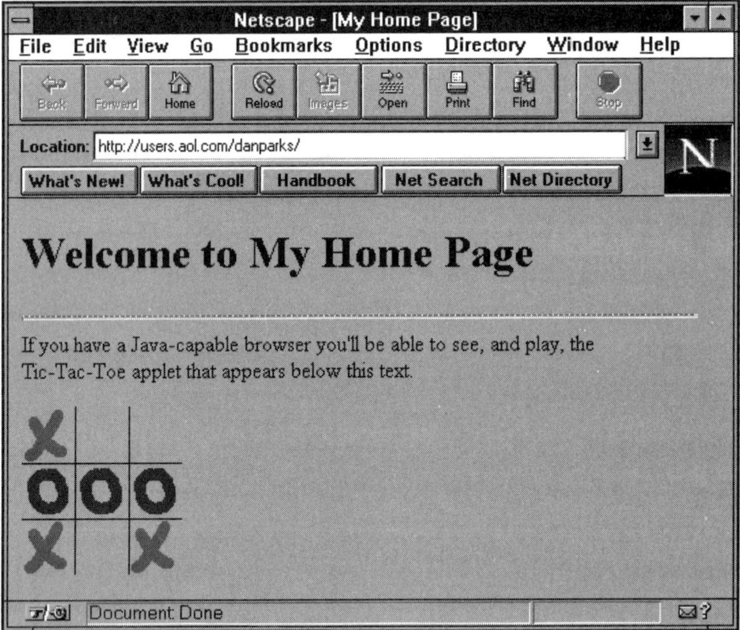

Figure B-8
A Web page that references an applet

As an exercise, create an `audio` directory as you did the `images` directory. Then add the sound files used by the Tic-Tac-Toe applet—just as you added the two graphics files. Before uploading the sound files, double-click on the `audio` folder in your workspace to make sure the sound files end up in that folder.

A Better Web Page

After experimenting with this simple example, you'll want to create a more sophisticated Web page. To do so, edit the `index.html` file that is on your hard drive (uploading the `index.html` file to AOL of course leaves the original file on your hard drive). Then go to your My Place workspace on AOL. Delete the `index.html` file that's currently there and replace it with your new version of this file.

To delete a file in your workspace, first click once on the file's name. Then click on the Utilities icon. In the dialog box that opens, click on the Delete icon.

To replace the `index.html` file, upload the new version. To do that, just follow this appendix's steps for uploading a file.

APPENDIX C

Your 15-Minute Web Page: Macintosh Users

This appendix describes how Macintosh users can quickly set up a World Wide Web page. If you're a Windows user, skip this appendix. Instead, jump back to "Appendix B: Your 15-Minute Web Page: Windows Users"; it holds similar information.

AOL, the Macintosh, and Your Web Page

If you're one of the nearly six million or so computer users who has an account with America Online (AOL), you can set up your own Web page in just a few minutes. You don't need any special lines or connections; you'll do everything through your AOL account. Best of all, aside from the time you spend online, there's no cost to create or maintain your Web page!

America Online has a `users.aol.com` FTP/WWW site that is a server. Any AOL member can use this site to easily set up a home directory. Once set up, your home page is accessible to everyone browsing the Web—regardless of how they're connected to the Internet. What's more, someone surfing the Net doesn't need to be an AOL user to access your Web page. As with visiting any Web site, all a person needs to know is the URL of your Web page.

Because all AOL users have their Web pages on the `users.aol.com` server, you know that your URL will include this server name. The file or files that make up your individual page will be kept on this server in a directory with the same name as your *screen name*—also referred to as your *user name*. If your screen name includes any spaces, omit the spaces when typing in your URL. The format of the URL of your Web page is thus as follows:

```
http://users.aol.com/ScreenName
```

As an example, if your screen name happens to be `DanParks`, your Web page has the following URL:

```
http://users.aol.com/DanParks
```

Your URL isn't case-sensitive. Thus a user could enter, say, the URL `http://users.AOL.com/danparks` into a Web browser and still make it to the same Web page.

What else would be true if your screen name were `DanParks`? You'd be in big trouble—that's the author's AOL screen name! To visit a Web page that holds a Java applet, feel free to use your Java-capable browser to stop in at `http://users.aol.com/DanParks`. While you're there, you can use your browser to look at the HTML source that makes up the page. If you use Netscape Navigator as your browser, use the Document Source menu item from the View menu. Note that, as of this writing, you can use your AOL account to set up a Web page, but, ironically, the AOL Web browser *doesn't* display applets that are present on Web pages.

Your HTML File

Any Web home page requires an HTML file (also referred to as an HTML *document*). This file holds the *tags*, or commands, that specify text and graphics placement on the Web page. The file may also hold hypertext links to other Web pages and now may even make use of the `<applet>` tag to specify that a Java applet be included on the Web page. While you might want to develop a fairly complex Web page, for this test run you should keep things simple. For your first attempt at creating a Web page, create a new, empty text file using any text editor (such as SimpleText or TeachText). A Web page HTML file is often named `index.html`. America

Online *requires* that you give your file this name. So that's what we'll do. Save the file as `index.html`, then type in the following HTML code:

```
<html>
<head>
<title>My Home Page</title>
</head>
<BbodyODY>
<h1>Welcome to My Home Page</Hh11>
<hr>
If you have a Java-capable browser you'll
be able to see, and play, the Tic-Tac-Toe
applet that appears below this text.<br>
<br>
<applet code="TicTacToe.class" width=120 height=120>
</applet>
<br>
</body>
</html>
```

That's it! The preceding is all the HTML code you'll need for a very simple Web page. Take a good look at the listing, as it serves as the example used in the remainder of this appendix. If you aren't familiar with HTML, refer to Appendix A for a look at the very basics of this language of the Web. To keep you on familiar ground, the examples in Appendix A use this same HTML listing.

Uploading a File to AOL

The information that defines your Web page is kept in a file or files stored on an America Online server. When someone surfing the Web enters the URL of your Web page into their browser, that browser locates your files on the AOL server and loads them.

Moving to MyPlace

America Online makes it easy to get your Web-related file or files from your hard drive to the AOL server. America Online has set up an online area named MyPlace that is used exclusively for working with such files. If you aren't logged on to AOL, dial up the online service now. Then follow these steps to get to the MyPlace area:

1. Choose Keyword from the Go To menu. The Keyword window appears.
2. Type `MyPlace`.
3. Click on the Go button. The MyPlace window appears.
4. Click on the Go to My Place icon. Your own workspace window appears.

After the fourth step, you'll find yourself in a directory on an AOL server. Each AOL member is allotted a 2MB storage area; this is the area where you are now. Figure C-1 shows the window you'll see. This directory is your own file storage area; no other AOL members can access it.

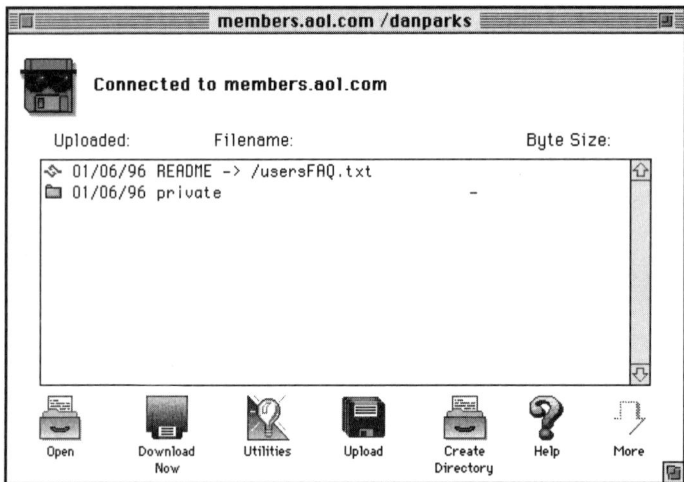

Figure C-1
The window that displays the root directory of your AOL Web workspace

When you first enter your workspace, you'll see a `README` file that provides information about MyPlace; you can double-click on the filename to read it online or download it. You'll also find a folder named `private` in your workspace. This folder holds data used by AOL and should be left untouched.

Uploading a file to MyPlace

Your AOL Web page relies on HTML code found in a file named `index.html`. Earlier in this appendix, you created such a file. Now it's time to upload it to MyPlace. To do that, follow these steps. Start at the workspace window shown in Figure C-1 previously.

1. Click on the Upload icon. The file upload window shown in Figure C-2 appears.

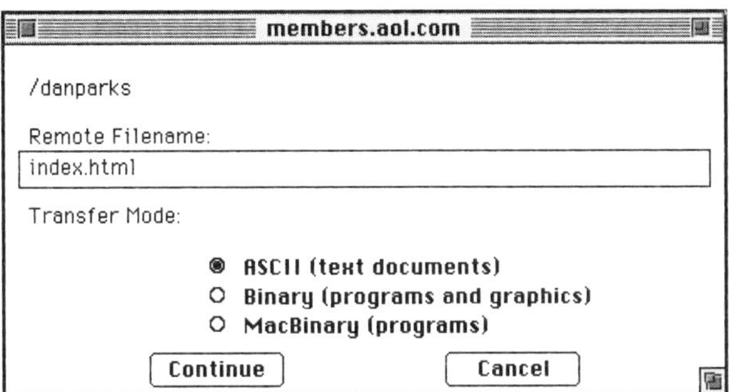

Figure C-2
The window used to specify information about a file to upload to your workspace

2. Type the name of the file that is about to be uploaded. In this example, you're uploading the `index.html` file, so type `index.html`.
3. Click on the Transfer Mode radio button that best matches the file type of the file that is to be uploaded. In this example, you're uploading the HTML file, which is a text file, so click on the ASCII (text documents) radio button. (Later in this appendix, you'll see an example of uploading a binary file.)
4. Click on the Continue button. The File Selection window appears.
5. Click on the OK button. The window shown in Figure C-3 appears.

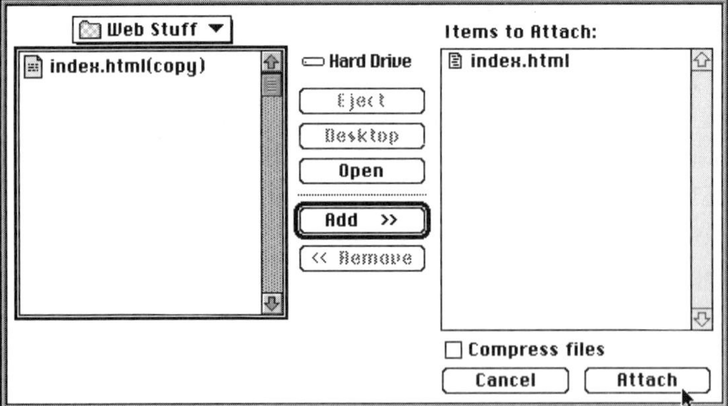

Figure C-3

The window used to select a file to upload to your workspace

6. Use the pop-up menu that appears above the list of files on the left side of the window to move to the folder that holds the file to upload.
7. Find the file to upload in the list on the left side of the window and click once on its name.
8. Click on the Add >> button. The selected file will move to the list on the right side of the window. In this example, the `index.html` file was added from a folder named `Web Stuff`. The `Web Stuff` folder also holds a backup copy of the HTML file.

Select only one file to add to your workspace. As you'll see in just a bit, you can add more than one file to your MyPlace work area, but you must add files one at a time rather than in a group.

9. Click on the Attach button. A file transfer window appears to show you the progress of the upload. When the upload is complete, the File Transfer Complete window appears.
10. Click on the OK button. You'll find yourself back at the window that enables you to type in the name and type of the file to upload.
11. Click on the Cancel button. Here you're "canceling" the window, not the file transfer you just performed; the file has been successfully transferred.

After performing the preceding steps, your workspace will now hold a copy of the `index.html` file—as shown in Figure C-4.

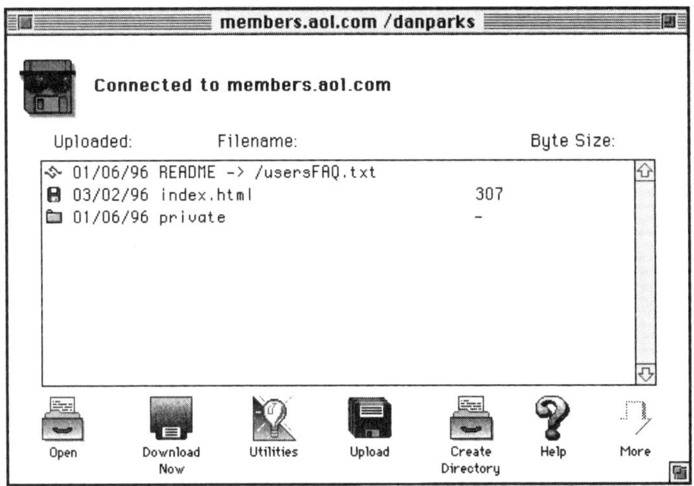

Figure C-4
The root directory of an AOL Web workspace after a file has been uploaded to it

A QUICK TEST OF YOUR NEW WEB PAGE

For a simple Web page that doesn't display any graphics, the HTML file is all you need. In this example, additional files will be necessary in your workspace to create the finished Web page. Still, even with only the `index.html` file uploaded, you can run a quick test to verify that you now have a presence on the World Wide Web.

To run your test, use whichever Web browser you're accustomed to using. If you're still logged on to America Online and you have the AOL Web Browser, you can launch that software now. Type in the URL for your Web page and press the Return key. Recall that the URL for your page will be `http://users.aol.com/` followed by your AOL screen name (less any spaces that appear in the screen name) and a slash. Thus the URL for an AOL member with a screen name of Jo Jo 3 would be as follows:

```
http://users.aol.com/JoJo3/
```

Your Web browser then moves to your Web page. Because you haven't loaded the Tic-Tac-Toe applet to your AOL workspace, the attempt by the browser to load the applet will fail, so don't be alarmed if your browser displays an error message like the one shown at the bottom of the Netscape Navigator window pictured in Figure C-5. For this quick test, that's okay. You can still consider the test a success: You now know that you're on the Web! Figure C-5 shows the current content of your Web page. This figure shows what *any* Netter who has your URL and Netscape Navigator will see. Other Web browsers will yield similar results.

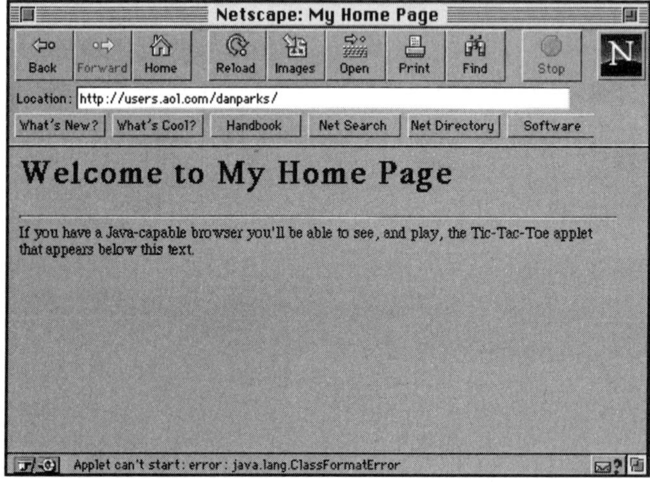

Figure C-5

A Web page that references an applet, but doesn't have that applet in its workspace

Adding an Applet to Your AOL Workspace

The `<applet>` tag in your HTML file lists the code for the Tic-Tac-Toe applet as one of its three attributes (the other two attributes being the pixel width and pixel height that should be devoted to the applet graphics), as follows:

```
<applet code="TicTacToe.class" width=120 height=120>
```

When a Web browser reaches your Web page, it attempts to load the Java code from a file named `TicTacToe.class`. To include the applet on your page, you need to make sure that this file exists in your workspace in the same directory as your `index.html` file. And because the Tic-Tac-Toe applet makes use of graphics files it expects to find in a folder named `images`, your workspace will also need to include such a folder and image files. After creating a new folder and uploading the applet and graphics files, your workspace should look similar to the one pictured in Figure C-6.

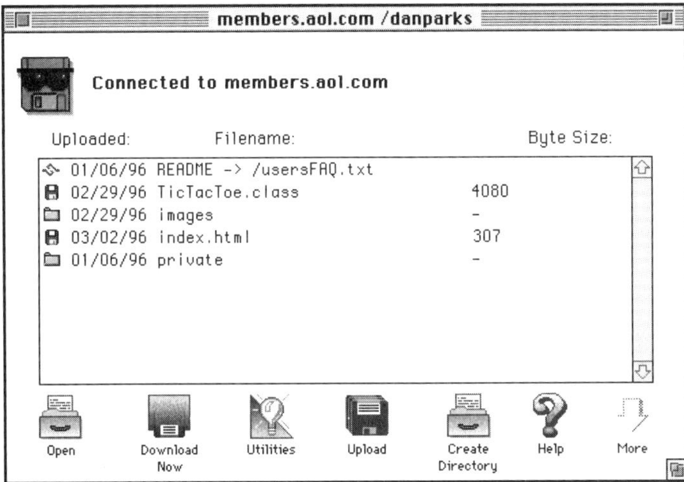

Figure C-6
The root directory of an AOL Web workspace after a folder has been added

UPLOADING THE APPLET

Uploading an applet to your workspace is as easy as uploading the `index.html` text file. To summarize, here are the steps for uploading an applet:

1. Move to your AOL Web workspace (your MyPlace area).
2. Click on the Upload icon to begin the upload process.
3. Type the name of the applet file to upload. In this example that would be `TicTacToe.class`. Note that you are uploading the Java com-

piled code—the applet itself—rather than the Java source code found in the `TicTacToe.java` file.

4. Click on the Binary (programs and graphics) radio button rather than the ASCII (text documents) or MacBinary (programs) buttons.
5. Continue on to the file selection window. Locate the applet file and add it to the Items to Attach list. In this example, you'll most likely find the `TicTacToe.class` file in the folder of the programming development environment you used to create the applet.
6. Attach the file.

CREATING A NEW DIRECTORY

If your applet uses external files, you'll need to upload those files to your workspace as well. The Tic-Tac-Toe applet uses graphics files and sound files. For simplicity, here we'll just add the graphics files; the sound files aren't necessary to play the Tic-Tac-Toe game. The applet source code specifies that the two GIF graphics files will be in a directory named `images`. Before uploading the graphics files, you need to create this new directory in your workspace, as follows:

1. Move to your AOL Web workspace (your MyPlace area).
2. Click on the Create Directory icon. The Remote Directory Name window appears.
3. Type the name of the directory (folder) to create. In this example you type `images`—as shown in Figure C-7.

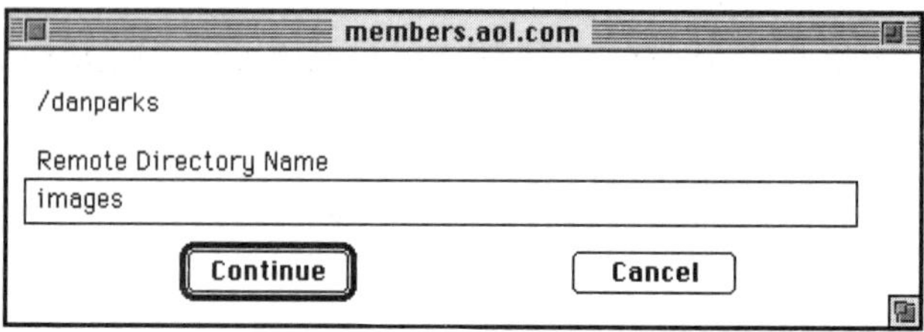

Figure C-7
The window used to create a new directory in the AOL Web workspace

4. Click on the Continue button. A window appears confirming that the folder has been created.
5. Click on the OK button. You'll find yourself back at the Remote Directory Name window.
6. Click on the Cancel button to again display your workspace window.

After performing the preceding steps, your workspace will now hold a new, empty folder named `images`. Now you can upload the two GIF files to this folder.

UPLOADING THE GIF GRAPHICS FILES

The process of uploading a GIF file to your workspace is the same as uploading an applet. The Tic-Tac-Toe applet expects to find GIF files named `cross.gif` and `not.gif` in a directory named `images`. You've just created that directory in your AOL Web workspace. Now upload these two graphics files. To add the files, follow these steps:

1. Move to your AOL Web workspace (your MyPlace area).
2. Double-click on the `images` folder icon to move to that folder. Any upload you now perform will result in a file ending up in this subdirectory.
3. Click on the Upload icon to begin the upload process.
4. Type the name of one of the files to upload, such as `cross.gif`.
5. Click on the Binary (programs and graphics) radio button.
6. Continue on to the file selection window. Locate the GIF file and add it to the Items to Attach list. In this example, you'll find the GIF files in the folder named `images` in a folder within your Java programming development environment directory.
7. Attach the file.
8. Repeat steps 4 through 7 to add the second GIF file, `not.gif`.

Testing Your Web Page

With the Tic-Tac-Toe applet and the two GIF files added to your AOL workspace, it's time to test out your Web page. To view an applet on a Web page you need to visit that page with a Java-capable browser—a browser that has a built-in Java interpreter. As of this writing, the America Online browser *isn't* Java-capable. That means that while the AOL browser will take you to a Web page that holds a Java applet, it won't display that applet. Sun's HotJava and Netscape's Navigator are two examples of browsers that *are* Java-capable. Figure C-8 shows what a Web page looks like if it is based on the `index.html` file presented in this appendix and is viewed with the Macintosh version of Netscape Navigator 2.0.

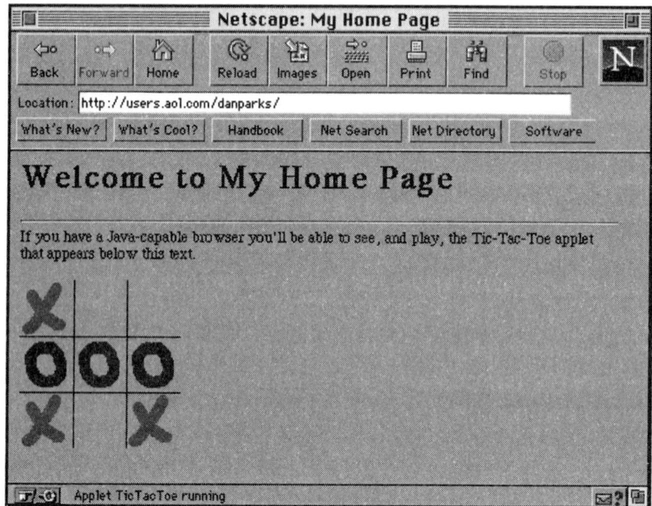

Figure C-8
A Web page that references an applet

As an exercise, create an audio directory as you did the `images` directory. Then add the sound files used by the Tic-Tac-Toe applet—just as you added the two graphics files. Before uploading the sound files, double-click on the `audio` folder in your workspace to make sure the sound files end up in that folder.

A Better Web Page

After experimenting with this simple example, you'll want to create a more sophisticated Web page. To do so, edit the `index.html` file that is on your hard drive (uploading the `index.html` file to AOL of course leaves the original file on your hard drive). Then go to your My Place workspace on AOL. Delete the `index.html` file that's currently there and replace it with your new version of this file.

To delete a file in your workspace, first click once on the file's name. Then click on the Utilities icon. In the dialog box that opens, click on the Delete icon.

To replace the `index.html` file, upload the new version. To do that, just follow this appendix's steps for uploading a file.

Index

• Symbols •

• A •

• B •

• C •

• D •

• E •

• F •

• G •

(continued)

(continued)

• N •

• O •

(continued)

• S •

(continued)

• X •

• Y •

IDG BOOKS WORLDWIDE, INC. END-USER LICENSE AGREEMENT

Read This. You should carefully read these terms and conditions before opening the software packet(s) included with this book ("Book"). This is a license agreement ("Agreement") between you and IDG Books Worldwide, Inc. ("IDGB"). By opening the accompanying software packet(s), you acknowledge that you have read and accept the following terms and conditions. If you do not agree and do not want to be bound by such terms and conditions, promptly return the Book and the unopened software packet(s) to the place you obtained them for a full refund.

1. **License Grant.** IDGB grants to you (either an individual or entity) a nonexclusive license to use one copy of the enclosed software program(s) (collectively, the "Software") solely for your own personal or business purposes on a single computer (whether a standard computer or a workstation component of a multiuser network).The Software is in use on a computer when it is loaded into temporary memory (i.e., RAM) or installed into permanent memory (e.g., hard disk, CD-ROM, or other storage device). IDGB reserves all rights not expressly granted herein.
2. **Ownership.** IDGB is the owner of all right, title, and interest, including copyright, in and to the compilation of the Software recorded on the disk(s)/CD-ROM. Copyright to the individual programs on the disk(s)/CD-ROM is owned by the author or other authorized copyright owner of each program. Ownership of the Software and all proprietary rights relating thereto remain with IDGB and its licensors.
3. **Restrictions on Use and Transfer.**

   (a) You may only (i) make one copy of the Software for backup or archival purposes, or (ii) transfer the Software to a single hard disk, provided that you keep the original for backup or archival purposes. You may not (i) rent or lease the Software, (ii) copy or reproduce the Software through a LAN or other network system or through any computer subscriber system or bulletin-board system, or (iii) modify, adapt, or create derivative works based on the Software.

   (b) You may not reverse engineer, decompile, or disassemble the Software. You may transfer the Software and user documentation on a permanent basis, provided that the transferee agrees to accept the terms and conditions of this Agreement and you retain no copies. If the Software is an update or has been updated, any transfer must include the most recent update and all prior versions.

4. **Restrictions on Use of Individual Programs.** You must follow the individual requirements and restrictions detailed for each individual program in "The Companion CD-ROM" section of this Book. These limitations are contained in the individual license agreements recorded on the disk(s)/CD-ROM. These restrictions may include a requirement that after using the program for the period of time specified in its text, the user must pay a registration fee or discontinue use. By opening the Software packet(s), you will be agreeing to abide by the licenses and restrictions for these individual programs. None of the material on this disk(s) or listed in this Book may ever be distributed, in original or modified form, for commercial purposes.

5. **Limited Warranty.**

   (a) IDGB warrants that the Software and disk(s)/CD-ROM are free from defects in materials and workmanship under normal use for a period of sixty (60) days from the date of purchase of this Book. If IDGB receives notification within the warranty period of defects in materials or workmanship, IDGB will replace the defective disk(s)/CD-ROM.

   (b) IDGB AND THE AUTHOR OF THE BOOK DISCLAIM ALL OTHER WARRANTIES, EXPRESS OR IMPLIED, INCLUDING WITHOUT LIMITATION IMPLIED WARRANTIES OF MERCHANTABILITY AND FITNESS FOR A PARTICULAR PURPOSE, WITH RESPECT TO THE SOFTWARE, THE PROGRAMS, THE SOURCE CODE CONTAINED THEREIN, AND/OR THE TECHNIQUES DESCRIBED IN THIS BOOK. IDGB DOES NOT WARRANT THAT THE FUNCTIONS CONTAINED IN THE SOFTWARE WILL MEET YOUR REQUIREMENTS OR THAT THE OPERATION OF THE SOFTWARE WILL BE ERROR FREE.

   (c) This limited warranty gives you specific legal rights, and you may have other rights which vary from jurisdiction to jurisdiction.

6. **Remedies.**

   (a) IDGB's entire liability and your exclusive remedy for defects in materials and workmanship shall be limited to replacement of the Software, which may be returned to IDGB with a copy of your receipt at the following address: Disk Fulfillment Department, Attn: Jumping to Java, IDG Books Worldwide, Inc., 7260 Shadeland Station, Ste. 100, Indianapolis, IN 46256, or call 1-800-762-2974. Please allow 3-4 weeks for delivery. This Limited Warranty is void if failure of the Software has resulted from accident, abuse, or misapplication. Any replacement Software will be warranted for the remainder of the original warranty period or thirty (30) days, whichever is longer.

(b) In no event shall IDGB or the author be liable for any damages whatsoever (including without limitation damages for loss of business profits, business interruption, loss of business information, or any other pecuniary loss) arising from the use of or inability to use the Book or the Software, even if IDGB has been advised of the possibility of such damages.

(c) Because some jurisdictions do not allow the exclusion or limitation of liability for consequential or incidental damages, the above limitation or exclusion may not apply to you.

7. **U.S. Government Restricted Rights.** Use, duplication, or disclosure of the Software by the U.S. Government is subject to restrictions stated in paragraph (c) (1) (ii) of the Rights in Technical Data and Computer Software clause of DFARS 252.227-7013, and in subparagraphs (a) through (d) of the Commercial Computer—Restricted Rights clause at FAR 52.227-19, and in similar clauses in the NASA FAR supplement, when applicable.

8. **General.** This Agreement constitutes the entire understanding of the parties and revokes and supersedes all prior agreements, oral or written, between them and may not be modified or amended except in a writing signed by both parties hereto which specifically refers to this Agreement. This Agreement shall take precedence over any other documents that may be in conflict herewith. If any one or more provisions contained in this Agreement are held by any court or tribunal to be invalid, illegal, or otherwise unenforceable, each and every other provision shall remain in full force and effect.

CD-ROM Installation Instructions

On the CD-ROM included with this book, you'll find the Java source code for the book's examples, the Java Development Kit (JDK) from Sun Microsystems, Inc., a host of award-winning applets, and an evaluation copy of the Microline Component Toolkit 3.0 (Lite Version).

The Java Development Kit can be used to compile any of this book's examples. Make sure to read Chapter 2 of this book to get a description of the JDK as well as a walk-through of the process of writing and compiling a simple applet.

A collection of ready-to-run applets can be found in the **javacup** folder on this CD-ROM. Copy the entire folder to your CD-ROM, and then decompress the tar.gz format file from that folder.

The Microline Component Toolkit can be found in the folder called **microline.**

Windows 95/Windows NT Installation

If you're a Windows 95 or Windows NT programmer, copy the entire **windows95** folder to your hard drive. Within the **windows95** folder is a **jdk** folder that holds the Windows 95 version of the Java Development Kit and a **book** folder which itself holds numerous folders. Each of these folders contains the Java source code and compiled applets for one of the examples listed in this book.

Macintosh Installation

If you're a Macintosh programmer, copy the entire **macintosh** folder to your hard drive. In this **macintosh** folder is a **jdk** folder that holds the Mac version of the Java Development Kit and a **book** folder. In the **book** folder you'll find several more folders-each contains the Java source code and compiled applets for one of the examples listed in this book.

Sun Workstation Installation

If you're an owner of a Sun Workstation computer, copy the **Solaris2.x** folder to your hard drive. In that folder you'll find a **jdk** folder that holds the Java Development Kit for versions 2.x or greater of the Solaris operating system.